Productivity, Technology, and Capital

Productivity, Technology, and Capital

Economic Analysis, Managerial Strategies, and Government Policies

Bela Gold
Case Western Reserve University

LexingtonBooks
D.C. Heath and Company
Lexington, Massachusetts
Toronto

Library of Congress Cataloging in Publication Data

Gold, Bela.
Productivity, technology, and capital.

Includes bibliographies and index.
1. Industrial productivity. 2. Technological innovations. I. Title.
HD56.G64 658.5 79-4749
ISBN 0-669-02957-2

Published simultaneously in Canada.

Printed in the United States of America.

International Standard Book Number: 0-669-02957-2

Library of Congress Catalog Card Number: 79-4749

Contents

List of Tables and Figures

Tables

Figures

Preface

There are very good reasons for the growing concern in recent years about the decreasing rate of advances in the productivity and technological capabilities of wide sectors of industry. But these do not seem to be widely understood as yet. It is not surprising, therefore, that simplistic and erroneous diagnoses have encouraged support for ineffectual and even counterproductive policies.

The following analyses are based on extensive research on industrial productivity and technology in a variety of industries in the United States and overseas over a period of more than 25 years. Statistical studies at the level of individual industries have been supplemented with detailed examinations of operations at the level of single plants and even component departments in efforts to identify the factors shaping adjustments in performance. Additional field studies have focused on managerial values, expectations, evaluative criteria, and decision-making processes.

Key findings in respect to productivity changes will be found to emphasize (1) that they have been conceived too narrowly and have not been adequately measured, (2) that the relative importance of the factors affecting them has undergone important changes in recent decades, (3) that such primary determinants differ substantially among industries, (4) and that the effects of productivity increases are often widely at variance with expectations. Misconceptions are also widespread concerning the risks and rewards of seeking to develop major technological advances and the rapidity with which successful innovations replace prior technologies. Even more important, however, is the basic conclusion which emerges: diminishing rates of progress in the productivity and technological capabilities of major sectors of industry are attributable in greatest measure not to complacency, indifference, sloth, or ignorance, but to the absence of incentives attractive enough to offset the active deterrents to undertaking such improvement efforts.

Part I concentrates on needed revisions in the basic concepts, methodologies, and measures to be employed if actual and prospective innovations are to be evaluated more realistically. Part II then presents a variety of empirical studies—differing in the kinds of innovations covered, the levels of aggregation at which evaluations are made, and the national context of the operations covered—as the basis for indicating the relevance of the reorientations suggested in Part I and also introducing the need for still further broadening of those perspectives. Finally, Part III examines alternative managerial and governmental strategies for accelerating advances in industrial productivity and technological capabilities.

Earlier forms of much of the material in the following chapters have appeared in the following publications: Chapters 2 and 16 in *The Quarterly Review of Economics and Business,* Spring 1977 and Winter 1978, respectively; Chapter 3 in *Omega: The International Journal of Management Science* (London), February 1973, and in *Rivista Internazionale di Scienze Economiche E Commerciali* (Padua), February 1977; Chapter 4 in J. DeBandt (ed.), *Le Capital Dans La Fonction de Production* (Paris: Centre National de la Recherche Scientifique 1978); Chapter 5 in *Productivity Analysis in Industry: Report to the Social Science Research Council of Great Britain* (London: Imperial College of Science and Technology, 1973); Chapter 6 in J. DeBandt (ed.), *L'Information Économique et L'Industrie* (Paris: Édition Cujas, 1973); Chapters 7 and 10 in *Journal of Industrial Economics* (London), September 1974 and September 1976, respectively; Chapter 8 in *Revue d'Économie Industrielle* (Paris), Spring 1978; Chapter 9 in S. Eilon, B. Gold, and J. Soesan, *Applied Productivity Analysis for Industry* (Oxford: Pergamon, 1976); Chapter 11 in *Iron and Steel Engineer,* April 1978; Chapter 12 in *Iron and Steelmaker,* December 1978; Chapter 13 is in M. Baker (ed.) *Industrial Innovation* (London: Macmillan, 1979); Chapter 14 in *Research Management,* July 1975; and Chapter 15 in P.C.A. Malotaux et al. (eds.), *Organizatie Wetanschap en Praktijk* (Rotterdam: Stenfert Kroese, 1976). Deep appreciation is expressed to the editors and publishers for permission to reprint these papers. The present volume, however, represents the first appearance of the entire analytical framework.

I also wish to express my deep appreciation for research support over the years from the Ford Foundation, the National Science Foundation, the Social Science Research Council (United States), the American Council of Learned Societies, the Social Science Research Council (Great Britain), Resources for the Future, and above all, to the Timken Foundation, whose endowment has provided continuing support for my chair in industrial economics and for the Research Program in Industrial Economics of which I am the director.

1 Objectives, Expectations, and Analytical Difficulties

Recent decades have been characterized by increasing acceptance of the belief that advances in productivity and technology constitute the most promising source of long-term gains in economic welfare. Such advances certainly could help to increase economic growth, raise standards of living, offset natural resource stringencies, ease inflationary pressures, and even increase leisure, but not without accompanying costs and seldom without extended delays. Moreover, underlying such eventual global potentials, one must recognize an array of more specific and immediate effects, some of which tend to be less universally welcome. Hence efforts to achieve fuller understanding of variations in the rate of advances in productivity and technology must begin by recognizing that such gains are subject to resistances as well as stimuli.

Developing sounder bases for programs to reinvigorate the rate of advances in productivity and technology also requires displacing an array of simplistic generalizations about their sources and benefits which have gained widespread acceptance in the course of increasing public discussion of this problem. And even the contributions of much scholarly research need to be reexamined carefully because they frequently rely on assumptions, concepts, and methodologies which fall short of focusing realistically on the complexities of the actual processes and interrelationships involved.

Convergent and Divergent Interests

Improvements in productivity and technological capabilities are primarily the result of decisions by particular groups. Moreover, these decisions obviously tend to give much heavier weight to the specific criteria representing the group's own interests and responsibilities than to the amorphous aspirations of society at large. Accordingly, one set of useful insights into the causes of variations in the rate of productivity increases and technological advances may be provided by considering differences in the evaluative profiles of the key groups influencing such decisions.

Actual changes in industrial productivity and technological capabilities take place in individual plants, and they are initiated by management decisions. In the private firms of the Unites States, the basic objective of such decisions is neither to increase productivity nor to improve technology, but rather to increase profitability. Profitability may be increased, however, through a variety of means, including improvements in product design, marketing, pricing, financing, and procurement. Hence managements are likely to commit resources to programs for improving productivity or technology only up to whatever level seems to offer greater returns than these other alternatives relative to the costs, risks, and time delays involved. In short, managements are prepared to leave productivity levels unchanged, or even to reduce them, if that should appear to be more profitable—and this is not infrequently the case, as will be discussed later.

The next groups affected by managerial decisions involving changes in productivity and technology—and whose responses may have some effect on managerial evaluations—are the suppliers of the inputs involved, with labor usually the foremost. Their primary objectives tend to center around increasing wage rates, maintaining employment, improving fringe benefits, and reducing job hazards and discomforts. Because such goals may be promoted by some improvements in productivity and technology but undermined by others, members of the work forces affected and their trade unions may be much more favorable to some of these improvements than to others. And their responses to such innovations, in the form of demands for accompanying adjustments in wage rates, employment levels, working conditions, and fringe benefits, may significantly alter managerial evaluations of the prospective benefits of seeking to develop or to adopt particular improvements. Such decisions may also be influenced, of course, by the availability and prices of other inputs affected by particular innovations, especially capital. Even prospective adjustments in the availability and prices of particular materials and forms of energy may affect managerial evaluations of technological options when such inputs are unusually scarce or under tight control by suppliers.

Consumers also may react more favorably to some improvements in productivity and technology than to others. They tend to applaud those yielding more durable, service-free, safer, and lower-priced products. But often they are less favorable to those which reduce variety in products responsive to wide differences in needs or tastes. In such product categories, managements cannot help comparing the cost benefits of prospective innovations with possibly offsetting market penalties.

The most important of the remaining possible sources of influence on managerial decisions concerning potential improvements in productivity and technology is the government. Over the long run, the government seeks to promote a wide array of objectives, including reasonable economic growth, rising standards of living, the development and effective utilization of natural resources, minimization of involuntary unemployment, maintenance of a strongly competitive position in international trade, and, of course, the safeguarding of the nation's military security. It is recognized that improvements in industrial productivity and technological capabilities may offer major contributions toward achieving such objectives. But it is also apparent that such improvements may entail negative effects on some of these objectives, at least in the short run and in some geographical areas and industrial sectors.

For example, some improvements in productivity may increase unemployment at their points of application. Some advances in technology may undermine the competitive position of older plants and older industrial areas as well as that of smaller firms. Other technological innovations may increase demands for scarce resources or involve undesirable health, safety, and environmental effects. Thus, depending on their direct responsibilities, government agencies may differ widely in their enthusiasm for increasing productivity levels in various industrial settings and for accelerating the development and diffusion of particular types of technolgocial advances.

But managerial decisions about innovations that may improve productivity levels and technological capabilities are likely to be affected even more directly by government policies concerning the prospective profitability of such undertakings. Among the most influential of these may be tax policies, regulatory restrictions, and in some industries, the prevention of unfair competition from foreign producers. It is important to consider, therefore, whether such policies, and especially recent modifications in them, have tended to encourage or discourage greater managerial commitments to programs seeking to increase industrial productivity and technological capabilities.

Even this brief review would seem to demonstrate the existence of significant differences and even of some conflicts among the objectives of various groups capable of influencing the managerial decision which largely determine the pace of productivity and technological changes in U.S. industries. Hence any efforts to encourage acceleration of such advances would have to take account of the fact that this objective is not universally accepted, and therefore, that policies to promote it effectively must seek to minimize opposition while also increasing the incentives for prospective contributors to such gains.

Widespread Beliefs and Analytical Expectations

Simplistic generalizations about the sources and benefits of advances in productivity and technology seem to have gained widespread acceptance because of the general yearning for easily comprehensible explanations of the complexities surrounding us and because of our ready reliance on intuition, logic, casual reading, and fragmentary personal experience in the absence of patently authoritative knowledge. Nor are technical specialists, industrial executives, government officials, and economists immune to the acceptance of such beliefs. The simple fact is that inquiries by scientists and engineers have usually been concentrated solely on the technological aspects of selected process and equipment developments. Managers have almost invariably restricted their analyses to the operational effectiveness and costs of individual projects. And government officials and academic economists have, with few exceptions, attempted to appraise productivity and technological improvements at such highly aggregative levels as to ignore both the nature of the specific innovations underlying observed results and the network of linkages by means of which such innovations eventually influence economic relationships. Accordingly, even these specialists have tended to supplement their respective cores of hard knowledge with successive layers of untested assumptions in seeking to assess the broader effects of past and prospective innovations and related policies.

Perhaps the most general of the commonly accepted sets of interconnected beliefs in this area may be summarized as follows:[1]

1. Technological innovations are inherently attractive, especially in terms of economic rewards, which are overriding considerations in business.
2. Most major technological innovations are generated by increasingly costly research and development programs, with yields roughly proportioned to the resources applied.
3. The major effect of resulting technological advances, aside from yielding new products, is to increase productivity and thereby reduce unit costs.
4. Lower unit costs and new products generate increasing profitability and growth.
5. Increasing profitability and growth foster more research and development as well as faster diffusion of innovations—thus retriggering this entire cycle.
6. Attendant broader economic benefits include the availability of a wider array of more desirable products and a tendency for manufactured goods prices to decline as a result of decreasing unit production costs.

Such beliefs gained renewed encouragement from the spectacular achievements in military and space undertakings and more direct reinforcement from some outstanding successes in industry. Further reassurance was provided by the broadly disseminated results of a small but expanding array of theoretical and empirical studies concerned with the economic effects of technological innovations. In this favorable atmosphere, industrial and government allocations for research and development (R&D) and for the diffusion of technological innovations expanded rapidly from the early 1950s until the early 1970s.

The growing momentum of acceptance led in turn to increasing criticism of those deemed to be insufficiently committed. Some firms and industries were chided for allocating only 1 or 2 percent of sales to R&D instead of 7 or 8 percent. Others were attacked for not adopting known process innovations fast enough. And such criticisms frequently were coupled with urgent recommendations for intensifying technological improvement efforts and introducing stronger governmental incentives and support for such programs. Accompanying arguments seemed to imply that the firms and industries which were their targets were either unaware of the attractive rewards available to them or preferred avoiding change, even at the cost of foregoing substantial benefits. There are, of course, bound to be some instances of one or another of these shortcomings at all times and perhaps in all economic sectors. But it would take considerable evidence to justify claims that managerial inadequacies of such gross proportions were pervasive throughout most of American industry, or even large sectors of it, for extended periods.

Accordingly, there is good reason to analyze in considerable detail all phases of the arguments and evidence underlying such critical judgments and the ameliorative policies proposed. Indeed, the desirability of doing so has been sharply accentuated in recent years, both by the reduced growth in R&D reported by government statistics (which also are presumed to reflect comparably lessened responsiveness to innovational improvements in general) and by the renewed pressures for reversing such trends.

Although the following analysis will offer a partial test of the preceding general beliefs, it is obvious that actual decisions concerning specific innovations rested on more directly relevant expectations. Among the more important of these is that increases in scale, advances in technology, and improvements in management controls would yield such benefits as the following:[2]

1. Reductions in materials and energy requirements through better technical specifications and inspection in procurement, through decreased waste and fewer rejects in processing operations, and through more effective recovery of by-products.
2. Reductions in labor requirements per unit of output through mechanization, automation, and computerization.
3. Reductions in investment requirements per unit of productive capacity through improvements in the design and efficiency of capital facilities and equipment and through improvements in the efficiency of constructing them.
4. In turn, such reductions in unit input requirements would yield roughly proportionate decreases in unit material and unit wage costs, but reductions in average capital charges per unit of output would tend to be somewhat more limited because decreases in unit material and unit labor costs caused by improved and larger-scale capital facilities and equipment would be partially offset by increased investment requirements.
5. In addition, because each major innovation is expected to engender its own distinctive effects on the components of total costs, and because major innovations are likely to be introduced at irregular periods, the adjustment patterns of various unit costs would tend to differ widely, thus causing substantial variations in cost proportions over time.

Working assumptions such as these have had an influential bearing on managerial reactions to innovative opportunities as well as on broader economic attitudes and expectations. Hence the possibility that they may often prove misleading has obviously serious implications.

But the extent of promised benefits to surrounding sectors of the economy obviously depends on the rate at which the innovations offering improvements in productivity levels and technological capabilities are adopted by prospective users. Hence optimistic expectations concerning the benefits of such innovations also reflect some widespread beliefs about technological diffusion processes. Among these beliefs, the following seem to be among the more important ones suggested by the literature:[3]

1. There tends to be substantial agreement among competitors concerning the relative importance of prospective technological advances and, hence, considerable overlapping of their efforts to achieve such advances.
2. Claimed successes tend to be quickly and expertly assessed.
3. Demonstrations of technological success and of apparent economic benefits tend to engender rapid diffusion, unless inhibited by patent or licensing restrictions.
4. The competitive benefits of adopting such innovations tend to decline as they become progressively more widely diffused, thus encouraging early adoption.
5. Diffusion rates tend to be most rapid during periods of expanding markets because of the need for additional capacity as well as the availability of increasing income.
6. Recent decades have been characterized by rising diffusion rates because of speedier information flows, higher levels of technological expertise and capabilities in industry, greater access to needed financial resources among leading producers, and heightened competitiveness in domestic and international markets.

Resulting expectations have provided the bases for both evaluating the adequacy of actual diffusion rates and formulating governmental programs concerned with encouraging the more rapid development and diffusion of industrial innovations. It is obviously desirable, therefore, that the range of applicability of such assumptions be more fully examined and that efforts be made to identify the factors responsible for any observed variations.

Needed Revisions of Research Objectives

Many empirical studies have been published seeking to determine *the* economic effects of major innovations affecting productivity and technological capabilities.[4] Extensive field experience suggests, however, that this objective is not only unattainable, but that it is analytically meaningless. Instead, such idealized purposes often have to be modified in several ways if they are to be practical targets of empirical research.

One such modification involves giving up the objective of determining *the* definitive economic effects of industrial innovations. Most such innovations do not produce clearly identifiable, fixed, and measurable shifts in a set of economic relationships. On the contrary, they commonly trigger a continuing process of changes within an intricately integrated system of physical resource flows and associated economic valuations. It is through the ensuing complex of interactions that the innovation is "digested" by means of progressively more far-reaching adaptations and its effects thereby diffused through the system and over time. As a result of such a dispersion of successive impacts and the offsetting reactions which they engender, the distinctive effects of the given innovation become increasingly indistinguishable. Hence the objective of determining *the* effects of major innovations usually has to be reformulated in favor of seeking to trace the time path of the successive changes by means of which major technological innovations are gradually absorbed into the network of economic relationships.

A second major shift in objectives often requires giving up the effort to trace the distinctive effects of individual major innovations. Three developments tend to render such determinations impractical. First, most major innovations undergo substantial changes in form, efficiency, scale, and adaptability to specialized needs and conditions, thus posing problems concerning which stage of the evolving innovation should be the focus of such efforts. Second, most major innovations seem to be characterized by "broken edges"—that is, they seem to necessitate the development of associated trains of technological innovations as well as adjustments in products and inputs while becoming effectively utilized, thereby engendering uncertainties concerning the distinctive boundaries of the innovation whose effects are to be assessed. Third, it is difficult to disentangle the effects of a given technological innovation from the simultaneous consequences engendered by other frequent changes in operations normally introduced by managerial efforts to improve performance and to adjust to shifting market pressures. Such changes may involve significant adjustments in product design, product mix, output levels, production techniques in various sectors of operations, quality standards, and maintenance provisions. Indeed, in technologically active sectors, this often results in having several technological innovations in various stages of absorption during any extended period of analysis.

Consequently, it may be necessary frequently to shift empirical research objectives from an attempt to determine the economic effects of each major technological innovation to an analysis, instead, of the combined effects of the changing mix of innovations actually experienced in a plant, firm, or industry while continuing to make intensive efforts to identify the core characteristics of each innovation, to determine its direct impacts, and to estimate its diffusion rate.

Formulating realistic empirical research objectives also requires adjustments based on recognition of the difficulties of separating the effects of technological innovations from simultaneous external pressures on factor and product markets.

Resulting interactions affecting the demand, supply, and prices of relevant inputs and outputs may be traced to three sources: externally induced pressures on product and factor markets that affect the attractiveness and eventual acceptance of available technological advances, the effects of such adoptions by an increasing proportion of producers on relationships in the product and factor markets, and the additional effects on such markets of competitive pressures unrelated to the innovations being studied as well as of broader economic forces.

Crude expedients have often been used, of course, to separate the effects of external market developments. Most of these expedients commonly involve deflating prices, by changes either in the general price level or in average market prices for particular inputs and products. But such price-deflating measures suffer from shortcomings that are particularly critical to measurement of the effects of technological innovations. In addition to shortcomings that center around the effects of innovations on the qualities and mix as well as quantities of inputs and outputs, attention must also be given to the all-too-frequent practice of analyzing factor- and product-market adjustments only after introduction of the innovations under study. But this fails to consider already prevailing trends in such markets, which may have affected diffusion of the innovation and which would represent the appropriate levels from which differential post-innovation adjustments should be measured. For example, changes in wage rates after the innovation should be related to pre-innovation trends rather than to the actual pre-innovation level alone.

In short, the effects of technological innovations tend to emerge only gradually. Moreover, these effects are overlaid by the effects of developmental improvements in the innovation itself as well as by the effects of both associated and independent technological and managerial innovations. In addition, the effects of technological innovations also interact with various external pressures on the demand, supply, and prices of relevant inputs and products. Accordingly, serious consideration must be given in formulating empirical research objectives to choosing whether to determine what the effects of given innovations would have been under various unrealistic (and often irrelevant) conditions, what actual results emerged over time under whatever conditions did prevail, or some intermediate alternative of significance for clearly specified purposes.

Some Additional Research Needs

Economists and other analysts seeking to develop broad generalizations about the interactions of technological innovations and the surrounding economic and social environment are faced with additional sources of discouragement. First, considerable time and study are usually required to accumulate the highly specialized knowledge needed to comprehend the rich texture of technological changes in the major sectors of industry, and this is necessary for exploring the network of immediate and transmitted effects. Moreover, technologies differ widely from one another, and the traditional drive of economists for maximum generality of results may also be undermined as changing technologies curtail the time span within which valid evaluative comparisons can be made.

Second, because of its belated recognition as an important focus of economic analysis, extant economic theory offers only narrowly restricted and relatively uninteresting perspectives for encompassing the evident intricacy and multidimensional ramifications of technological advances. Efforts to build a more effective bridge between economics and technology have faced equally frustrating difficulties in the opposite direction—when trying to transmit empirical findings about technology through the highly selective filters of current economic theory—for example, limiting admissible effects solely to their impacts on the magnitude of established input-output measures or on analytical tools such as production functions and essentially static short-term and long-term cost functions.[5]

These inadequacies of technical insights, analytical concepts and tools—which are reviewed in greater detail in the following chapters—obviously serve to reinforce one another. Analytical explorations of new problem areas tend to become useful only as successive probings transform initially naive speculations into progressively more sharply delineated variables, relationships, processes, and criteria. Such progress may well have been retarded in this area because of excessive reliance on the traditional ritual of the scientific method—moving smoothly from hypothesis formulation to data collection to analysis to conclusions.[6] But this approach seems to be less helpful in exploring new territory than in eventually choosing among alternative explanations of whatever phenomena have already been identified and probed in considerable detail. Surely the endless strictures to adhere to this idealized procedure should more frequently be coupled with warnings about the aridity of hypotheses crystallized without even reasonable immersion in the complex activities and environments whose characteristics are to be diagnosed and explained.[7]

Economists were free to avoid the burdens of digging more deeply into highly specialized spheres of knowledge and experience so long as they continued to concentrate on essentially academic issues. However, their sharply increased involvement in recent decades with major problems of public and private policy is not consistent with a continued primary emphasis on producing mountains of untested, and even untestable, hypotheses. Indeed, more effective guides for such policies and decisions requires a more thorough knowledge of the forces, institutions, and pragmatic criteria encountered at successive levels of aggregation and in different sectors of the economy. As a result, analytical models are likely to become more complex and more numerous. In addition, economists—like chemists, biologists, engineers, and doctors—may have to develop, and even admit to, narrower areas of expertise than accord with the current self-image of the general economist.[8]

Plan of This Book

The chapters comprising Part I will provide a critique of the prevailing methodologies and analytical concepts used in determining the effects of changes in productivity and technological capabilities along with suggested revisions. Part II will present an array of new empirical findings concerning such effects along with their implications for broadening the analytical frameworks and expectations in Part I. Part III concentrates on managerial and governmental influences on responses to alternative technological and other opportunities.

Notes

1. For a more detailed discussion of such beliefs and related publications, see Gold [8].
2. For further discussion, see Gold [9, pp. 95-96].
3. For related discussion and empirical findings, see Gold et al. [12].
4. For a recent summary of such studies, see Boylan [3].
5. For a detailed discussion of the limitations of production functions and input-output analysis, see Baird [2] and Erdilek [7]. The shortcomings of short-run cost functions are discussed in Gold [9, pp. 121–151], and the inadequacies of the long-run cost function are discussed in chapter 7.
6. For indications of the need for more pluralistic conceptions of scientific method, see Kaplan [13, pp. 27–31] and Piore [18, p. 19] as well as the wider-ranging perspectives opened by Kuhn [15].
7. On the general aspects of this problem, see Bridgman [4, pp. 18, 26]; for common shortcomings of analytical models developed in this way, see Kaplan [13, pp. 275–288], Littauer [17, p. B27], and Bross [5, p. 1,330]. For an illustration of concern about such models in economics, see Carter and Williams [6, pp. 5, 29, 59–62, and 151–152]. For illustrative constructs, see Kennedy [14, pp. 541–547] and the critiques of Hicks and Keynes by Carter and Williams [6, pp. 160–163] and Leontief [16, pp. 66–71].
8. For further discussion, see Gold [9, chapter 1].

References

[1] K. Baier and N. Rescher (eds.), *Values and the Future* (New York: Free Press, 1969, 1971).

[2] R.N. Baird, "Production Functions, Productivity and Technological Change," in Gold et al. [11].

[3] M.G. Boylan, "Reported Effects of Technological Changes," in Gold et al. [11].

[4] P.W. Bridgman, *Reflections of a Physicist* (New York: Philosophical Library, 1950).
[5] I.D.J. Bross, "Algebra and Illusion," *Science,* June 3, 1966.
[6] C.F. Carter and B.A. Williams, *Industry and Technical Progress* (London: Oxford Univ. Press, 1957).
[7] A. Erdilek, "Productivity, Technological Change and Input-Output Analysis," in Gold et al. [11].
[8] B. Gold, "The Framework of Decisions for Major Technological Innovations," in Baier and Rescher [1]. Reprinted in Gold [9].
[9] B. Gold, *Explorations in Managerial Economics: Productivity, Costs, Technology and Growth* (New York: Basic Books, 1971; London: Macmillan, 1971).
[10] B. Gold, (ed.), *Technological Change: Economics, Management and Environment* (Oxford, Pergamon, 1975, 1979).
[11] B. Gold, (ed.), *Research, Technological Change and Economic Analysis* (Lexington, Mass.: Lexington Books, D.C. Heath, 1977).
[12] B. Gold, W.S. Peirce, and G. Rosegger, "Diffusion of Major Technological Innovations in U.S. Iron and Steel Manufacturing," *Journal of Industrial Economics,* July 1970. Reprinted in Gold [10].
[13] A. Kaplan, *The Conduct of Inquiry* (San Francisco: Chandler, 1964).
[14] C. Kennedy, "Induced Bias in Innovation and the Theory of Distribution," *Economic Journal,* September 1964.
[15] T.S. Kuhn, *The Structure of Scientific Revolutions* (Chicago: Univ. of Chicago Press, 1962).
[16] W. Leontief, *Essays in Economics* (New York: Oxford Univ. Press, 1966).
[17] S.B. Littauer, "Conceptualization and Formalization–The Impossible and the Obvious," *Management Science,* October 1965.
[18] E. Piore, "Is System Science a Discipline?" in *System Theory* (New York: Polytechnic, 1965).

Part I
Needed Revisions of Prevailing Analytical Approaches

2 Analyzing Technological Effects

Increasing reliance on economic analysis in the shaping of national and industrial policies has undoubtedly had a salutary effect. But it has also exposed economists to the temptation of seeking to enhance their influence by exaggerating the thoroughness of their knowledge in many problem areas. Issues concerning technological advances, perhaps the most important source of long-term gains in productivity and economic welfare, offer a paramount example.

There has been a rapidly growing volume of theoretical and empirical studies of the sources and economic effects of technological innovations, as well as of the factors tending to accelerate or to retard their development and utilization. Unfortunately, however, few of these studies have proved pertinent to the needs of industrial executives who must choose among alternative innovational possibilities or to those government officials who grope for policies that encourage technological progress in directions likely to maximize resulting economic and social benefits. Why?

To help answer this question, the literature of the past 20 years has been analyzed from the standpoint of its applicability to an assessment of the actual effects of innovations rather than the estimated effects of hypothetical or undifferentiated groups of innovations under artificial conditions. This entails analyzing what kinds of technological changes have been dealt with, what kinds of effects have been measured, and how resulting findings have been interpreted. Digging somewhat deeper into past studies, it becomes necessary to examine the restrictiveness of the assumptions made, the limitations of the methodologies employed, and the validity of the attempted generalizations.

Among the analytical approaches most widely used are production functions and such variants as total factor productivity,[1] input-output analysis and such partial relatives as process analysis,[2] and the less sophisticated but far more popular techniques centering around labor-productivity measures and, more recently, its "value-added productivity" variant. Each of these has proved useful for some purposes. For example, production functions have yielded useful perspectives on the factors associated with the growth of the economy as a whole; input-output analysis has provided the most valuable tool available for mapping interindustry resource flows; and labor-productivity studies have helped to clarify unemployment trends. Although the absence of effective alternatives has led to widespread use of these approaches in evaluating the economic effects of major technological innovations, there seems to have been no systematic effort as yet to explore their respective strengths and limitations for this distinctive purpose.

Relevance of Purposes of Published Studies

A comprehensive review of the literature in this field emphasizes the haphazardness of the analytical focuses dealt with and the underlying vagueness of the purposes to be served by most published studies. These characteristics seem to be rooted in the implicit, though rarely expressed, fundamental assumption that the important economic effects of all technological innovations and productivity gains are essentially similar and already well-known, except with respect to their specific magnitudes in given situations. It would follow logically, therefore, that all empirical studies represent samples from the same barrel, that resulting findings should converge into widely applicable generalizations, and that these would confirm (perhaps also amplifying somewhat) the structure of concepts and theories employed in designing such empirical studies.

As a matter of fact, however, such posited homogeneities have not emerged up to the present. And there seem to be good reasons for doubting that they are likely to emerge soon—or indeed ever. Such doubts derive, in part, from the extremely wide array of developments and environments encompassed by a generalized concern with the economic effects of technological innovations. Such doubts are also reinforced by the broad range of purposes which may be pursued, even within any of the foregoing areas of substantive concern.

Most of the studies examined have concentrated on measuring the changes in labor, or in labor and capital, inputs relative to total physical output in economic sectors that have introduced technological innovations of some kind. Some have then merely reported the observed changes in average relationships among these variables. Others have supplemented such descriptive findings with inferences concerning their causes and economic benefits. Even more ambitious undertakings have sought to generalize such inferences as indicative of probable technological effects (1) in larger sectors of the economy during the period studied, (2) over future periods within the sector studied, or (3) likely to result from policy changes designed to accentuate or minimize certain past outcomes.

Systematic coverage of these purposes could be expected to strengthen the bases for improved policy formulation and decision making in industry and government with respect to the rate and direction of technological innovations. But this would require more thorough penetration into the processes that transform technological impacts into adjustments in resource flows and eventually into changes in economic relationships than is provided by the analytical approaches that have been dominant so far.

This need may be illustrated by examining the potentials and limitations of production functions, the most widely used approach, in efforts to determine the economic effects of technological innovations. Production functions are used to infer the relative contributions to changes in physical output of changes in the physical inputs of labor and capital entering into that output on the basis of measures of changes in all three variables. Application of this approach raises three questions: Who wants to know? What in particular do they need to know? To what extent do production-function findings fulfill these requirements.

Oddly enough, most economists fail to realize that managers have no need for production functions at plant or firm levels in the case of single-product operations and regard them as meaningless in the case of multiproduct operations. Such managers have no need to await ex post facto economic analyses to learn the direct effects of changes in labor or capital inputs on product-output levels. On the contrary, they know that such relationships are predetermined for each product on the basis of engineering and production decisions relating to such factors as product design, material input specifications, the mix of labor skills and manning patterns, equipment characteristics, production schedules, quality standards, and maintenance arrangements. Moreover, any deviations from such planned relationships become apparent immediately through attendant adjustments in resource flows. But such operating arrangements also reflect awareness of the loci and extent of differences among products with respect to the numerous determinants of the gross input-output relationships covered by production functions. Accordingly, such average findings for changing product mixes are of no practical value for managerial purposes.

Of course, gross input-output relationships are not predetermined at the level of groups of firms or industries, and they may not be known at all in the absence of special economic studies. But such ignorance is due in part to the absence of any centralized management decision-making responsibility at this synthetic level of aggregation.[3] In addition, it is due also to the associated difficulties of interpreting findings that cover operations whose heterogeneity reflects the effects not only of the interproduct differences noted earlier, but also of interplant and interfirm differences. These latter might include the scale of operations, modernity of facilities, capacity-utilization rates, factor prices, financial structure, primary markets, trade-union relationships, and other characteristics.

What use could be made of findings covering such heterogeneous operations? By whom? Suppose physical output rises faster than total man-hours and total capital inputs, what conclusions could be drawn that would be of analytical significance? Certainly, such findings provide no indication of which of the numerous intraproduct, interproduct, interplant, or interfirm factors listed earlier were responsible, and to what extent. Nor does it follow necessarily even that increases in physical output per unit of physical input are a "good thing," that is, are economically desirable. To make such determinations would require price, cost, and other economic evaluations and might possibly involve certain welfare considerations as well. For example, innovations offering increases in output per man-hour are frequently associated with increases in capital investment and often engender increases in wage rates, thus necessitating further analysis to determine their attractiveness to management.

In short, such production functions do not reveal the causes of observed changes and hence do not indicate either the means by which these changes might be extended (or reversed) or the benefits, if any, resulting from them. Yet these represent two of the important purposes of such studies to prospective users of the findings. Of course, after production-function parameters have been determined for some composite statistical grouping, vague explanations are often tossed in, attributing reported adjustments to "technological progress," "human capital," or other amorphous factors. Moreover, these superficial explanations are frequently associated with proposals for maintaining or accentuating the trends which have been uncovered, implying the desirability of their effects, although these have not been explored carefully in most cases.

Aside from these highly vulnerable interpretations of production-function findings, the remaining common application is to build such results into econometric models to be used for forecasting future trends in the industry studied or in larger sectors of the economy. Where these models involve essentially statistical extrapolations, their vulnerability is adequately specified by the implicit caveat associated with all such extrapolations, that the expected results depend on the continuation of average adjustment patterns of the past. But how can one estimate the likelihood of such continuing patterns with respect to production functions in the absence of analytical insights into the factors responsible for the past relationships? Moreover, these limitations of production functions at the level of industries tend to grow even more severe at still higher levels of aggregation, such as industry groups, all manufacturing, or the national economy as a whole.

It should be emphasized that there are important decisions to be made at each level of aggregation. At plant, firm, industry, and national levels, choices must be made among alternative resource commitments. Some choices must be made by industrial managements, some by financial institutions, some by trade unions and trade associations, and still others by officials of a variety of local and national government agencies. Unfortunately, production-function studies have provided few, if any, significant contributions to meeting the specialized needs of these various groups, for the reasons just given as well as for additional reasons relating to measurements which will be discussed later.

Essentially similar problems limit the applicability of input-output analysis in appraising the effects of technological innovations. Within a single product plant, changes in the technical (physical) coefficients are predetermined by the same technological and production management decisions that were listed earlier. Hence their specific causes can be identified, whereas the ex post facto changes recorded by input-output measurements do not permit such specific identification in most cases. With respect to multiproduct plants, however, changes in technical coefficients are even less likely to be identifiable through input-output analyses in the common situation involving changes in product mix, whereas these, too, are both predictable and controlled by plant management.

Although most applications of input-output analysis have involved relatively broad economic sectors, it is obvious that every increase in the level of aggregation beyond the single plant entails progressively greater difficulties in analyzing the reasons for whatever results are found. This follows from the fact that cells in an input-output matrix present the gross aggregate value of all materials, labor, and capital inputs as well as of all product outputs for all plants, firms, and industries encompassed by a defined sector. Hence, as in the case of production functions at comparable levels of aggregation, underlying interproduct, interplant, interfirm, and interindustry heterogeneities prevent determination of the sources of any changes in cell coefficients from one period to another and also prevent identification of the nature and extent of such heterogeneities within any period.

The basic concepts underlying input-output matrices are enormously instructive, or course, for economists seeking to comprehend and map resource flows on some intersectoral basis. Moreover, they provide valuable perspectives on the relative magnitudes of component sectors of the economy at given periods. Beyond such descriptive purposes, however, they are much too aggregative to permit effective evaluation of the economic effects of technological innovations except at the level of single-product plants. Nor have these matrices as yet served any purpose beyond providing unnecessary ex post facto summaries of the effects of specifically identified and managerially approved innovations.

It should also be noted that the preliminary applications of process analysis which have thus far been published seem to suffer from similar limitations. Treating an industry as if it were one integrated plant certainly yields results different from those commonly developed for managerial decision making and performance evaluations in individual plants and firms with distinctive characteristics. But it is not easy to specify how such average findings covering heterogeneous operations can be interpreted to yield effective determinations of the actual economic results of technological innovations in specific operating environments–whether relating to the input, cost, revenue, and investment effects of concern to industrial managers or to the employment, market competition, or other effects of concern to government officials.

Alternative Analytical Focuses

Alternative analytical focuses may be mapped in at least six different dimensions.[4] One of these dimensions relates to the kinds and number of innovations to be covered. Very little experience is required to recognize the enormous variety of technological innovations, even if consideration is restricted to those taking the form of hard goods, that is, facilities, equipment, instrumentation, and products. These cover a wide range of functions, operating principles, and degrees of specialization, and they also differ widely in output capabilities, input requirements, and operating efficiency. Such a crude lumping together of grossly dissimilar developments is akin to aggregating all diseases to determine their average effects. It is conceivable, of course, that this vast multiplicity of specific forms may be classified into some smaller number of categories having relevance for purposes of economic analysis. But very little has been developed along these lines to date, although this would seem to offer more constructive contributions to the uncovering of subsections of uniformity in effects than dealing with the entire jumble of technological innovations.

In addition to deciding which of the innumerable innovations is to be studied, either empirically or speculatively, the analyst faces the problem of deciding whether to concentrate on single innovations, on clusters of closely related innovations, or on the unspecified combination of all innovations introduced or operating within a given period. And even in instances where a single innovation is specified as the target of analysis, a critical choice must still be made among the frequently numerous models and their successively improved designs which usually emerge before a few types eventually establish dominance. Nor can one easily apply the seemingly simple concept of "best practice"[5] as a guide to choosing, for what is considered best by an array of prospective users differs widely with their specific operating characteristics and with the current relative urgencies of their various technological, labor, marketing, and financial pressures.[6] Thus there would seem to be no basis for expecting that the results of empirical studies will converge, regardless of which innovations are studied or how many, unless it is assumed that all innovations tend to have the same effects, or unless all effects are ignored except those hypothesized on the basis of assumed homogeneities.

A second dimension of alternative analytical focuses concerns the economic effects to be encompassed. These may be so broad as to consider resulting effects only on total unit costs or even on profitability; they may concentrate on changes in selected major categories of unit costs; or they may focus solely on the changes in input requirements per unit of output which underlie changes within one category of unit costs. However, important alternatives and associated problems remain. Technological innovations commonly affect not only the quantity of each input category per unit of output, but also the qualitative characteristics of such inputs and the nature of their productive contributions. Moreover, technological innovations often involve substitutions among major input categories, along with changes in the design and service characteristics of individual products, in the mix of products and in the level of aggregate output. The spattering of choices among this wide range of alternatives reflected by published studies, theoretical as well as empirical, thus provides another obstacle to fitting their results together, and another basis for doubting the expectation that all innovations will prove to have essentially similar effects.

A third dimension of alternative analytical focuses concerns the levels of aggregation of the operating systems to be studied. Some studies have dealt with the effects of innovations in single operating departments, while others have embraced integrated production lines or complete plants. At higher levels of aggregation, studies have covered changes in firms and even in entire industries. Beyond that, a variety of studies have sought to assess the effects of technological innovations for major sectors of the economy and the economy as a whole. It is apparent, however, that higher levels of aggregation encompass increasing analytical difficulties. Even at the plant level, the effects of an innovation in any subsector are blended with continuing relationships in all other operations, thereby tending to yield different results, depending on the nature and importance of the given innovation within the given plant. In multiplant firms and in whole industries, even greater variations may be expected, depending on the extent of diffusion of the given innovation, on possible variations in management policies, and on the extent to which other innovations are also being introduced, not to mention the effects of the earlier mentioned differences among products, plants, and firms. Indeed, interindustry comparisons and analyses at the level of national aggregates would seem to defy even identification of the innovation whose effects are being assessed, to say nothing of efforts to devise persuasive measures of such distinctive innovational effects.

A fourth dimension of alternative analytical focuses concerns the choice made among alternative industrial environments. For example, this might involve concentrating on capital goods or consumer goods industries or on industries characterized by large-scale or small-scale plants. Other significant alternatives might relate to industries that differ in the extent of competition existing in their product or factor markets, or in the rapidity of technological changes experienced in recent years. Moreover, a somewhat different perspective would be provided by differentiating among industries according to the relative importance of governmental versus market pressures in determining responsiveness to innovational opportunities.

A fifth dimension of alternative analytical focuses concerns the length of time over which results are to be appraised. It is apparent that the effects of innovations change over time. Short-term changes include modifications in the innovation, improvements in applying it efficiently, adjustments in surrounding operations to reestablish effectively integrated production, and frequently, changes in wage rates under trade-union pressure. Over somewhat longer periods, other input-factor prices are likely to change in accordance with modifications in specifications and changes in the quantities purchased as the innovation is more widely diffused. Product prices and output levels may also be changed, initially because of the qualitative changes in the product and later because of the cost adjustments shared by an increasing array of competitors. Moreover, the rates at which such changes are likely to take place clearly differ with such factors as the nature of the innovation, the time taken to effectuate the changeover, and buyer responsiveness to changes in product quality and price. Thus the duration of the period over which technological effects are studied has a major effect on the kinds of influences and outcomes likely to be covered.

A sixth dimension of alternative analytical focuses concerns the specific years covered by the studies made. There is common recognition, of course, of dissimilarities among time periods with respect to changes in general economic conditions such as output levels, prices, employment, capital availability, governmental regulations, and expenditure policies. It is also apparent that industries and individual firms may undergo substantial changes from one period to another in their growth, utilization rates, trade-union problems, and competitive pressures. Despite enormous and sometimes ingenious efforts, no generally persuasive methods have been developed to exclude the influence of such factors from determinations of the distinctive effects of innovations. Hence the effects associated with given technological innovations in one period may differ materially from the effects experienced in another period of equal duration.

In short, six major dimensions of alternative analytical focuses have been outlined for assessing the economic effects of technological innovations, and numerous further possibilities have been identified within each of these dimensions. This broad perspective has several implications. It helps to explain the continuing absence of convergence among published empirical studies. It demonstrates the need to develop a far more complex structure of theoretical expectations along with more penetrating concepts that have guided the formulation of past studies. It also raises doubts about the widespread belief that even the major economic effects of technological innovations are likely to take the form of generalizations which are both widely applicable and directly relevant to cricial evaluative or decision-making issues.

Relevance of the Concepts and Measures Used

Two of the most important components of scientific research involve the progressive reformulation of basic concepts so as to accord more fully with the unfolding characteristics of the phenomena being studied and the development of measures which are increasingly relevant to such concepts. The dominant approaches to determining the economic effects of technological innovations reflected by the published literature leave much to be desired in both of these respects.

Effects of Technological Innovations

In the case of production functions, the basic concepts have a number of significant analytical shortcomings. Perhaps the most important of these is the attempt to assess the effects of technological changes in purely physical terms. Economics differs from engineering partly in that physical resource flows and relationships must be integrated with their relative prices in order to permit economic evaluations. Indeed there can be no economic basis for choosing among alternative technological combinations of inputs and outputs so long as factor and product prices are omitted. The production-function approach commonly seeks to overcome this obvious difficulty by resorting to even more untenable assumptions, for example, that technological innovations change the quantitative magnitudes of inputs and outputs but leave essentially unchanged both their qualitative characteristics and their respective prices. However, such assumptions eliminate important and often dominant effects of most technological innovations.

The emphasis on an essentially physical conception of the relations encompassed by the production function also necessitates resort to dubious measurement expedients. For example, labor inputs are almost invariably measured in man-hours, a concept which reflects an essentially physical concept only so long as changes in the skill mix of such inputs and in the nature of their contributions to the production process are ignored. But changes in labor skills and in the nature of their contributions represent important effects of technological innovations, the former affecting the quality, factor prices, and costs associated with the physical volume of man-hours, and the latter affecting the variability of labor inputs with changes in output levels, for example, the ratio of maintenance and other indirect labor to production labor. Of course, the measurement of changes in output in purely physical terms could be even more misleading. To take economic account of changes in the size and service characteristics of different models of products within even one product line, to say nothing of aggregating such changes in many product lines, obviously necessitates resort to some form of weighting by their relative prices. Efforts to introduce a physical concept of capital inputs are still more dubious because of the extreme heterogeneity of capital goods, because of the role of capital goods as a prime target of technological innovations, and because of the resultant absence of effective price comparisons or indexes of average changes in capital goods prices.

Accordingly, the basic conceptualization of production functions as relationships between changes in physical inputs of labor and capital and changes in physical outputs cannot be effectuated at the level of actual measurements even for most plants and firms, to say nothing of industries and even larger economic sectors. Instead, efforts are made to approximate this physical concept by deflating the value of output by the change in each product's price in order to yield the implicit change in total product quantity, and by deflating capital investment (usually after depreciation) by some index of changes in capital goods prices. Such expedients are especially vulnerable, however, when the objective is to determine the economic effects of technological innovations. In part, this is due to the assumption that the individual products have remained unchanged, and hence, that any attendant changes in their prices were not influenced by the technological innovations under study. In the case of capital goods, attendant problems include the inapplicability of any broad index of capital goods prices (the vulnerability of which has already been noted) to a particular sector affected by unique technological innovations, and the absence of meaningful price comparisons between new capital goods embodying such innovations and preinnovation models. In the case of labor inputs, the inadequacy of man-hours alone is not overcome by the alternative of deflating the change in total wage payments by the change in average wage rates. This is true because the latter also omits the possible changes in labor skills and elasticity attributable to the innovation.[7] In short, the simplifying assumptions that technological advances leave both the qualitative characteristics and the prices of inputs and outputs unchanged tend to eliminate important and often dominant effects of such innovations.

Two additional difficulties associated with effectuating the concept of physical output in measuring the production of multiproduct operations should be noted. When such total output is measured by weighting the quantity of each product by its relative price, technological *advances* which lead to lower unit costs and prices for given products also engender *reductions* in the (price) weights given to such product units in computing total output, whereas *declining* productive efficiency leading to higher costs and prices would tend to *increase* the weights given to such product units in computing total output (see Gold [24, pp. 203–206]). The use of such "economically oriented" or price-weighted measures of physical output also introduces the frequently overlooked problem of differentiating changes in total output from changes in total inputs. Do changes in product value (that is in total costs plus profits) at fixed product prices measure changes in total outputs or in total inputs? If the former is true, as suggested by Fabricant [21], how are changes in total inputs to be measured? Application of the same approach would suggest measuring them in terms of changes in total costs at fixed factor prices, although differing conceptions of profits might suggest their inclusion or exclusion. But what would changes in such total-output to total-input ratios signify? Changes in efficiency levels, as implied by terms like *total factor productivity* (Kendrick [35]) and *aggregative efficiency index* (Schmookler [56]), or changes in the ratio of (deflated?) total costs to (deflated?) total revenues, that is, some form of (deflated?) profit margins, or changes in the ratio of product-price to factor-price indexes?

To answer the preceding questions precisely, it is necessary to recall that changes in these ratios may be due to variations in the price or in the quantity of each specific input per unit of unchanged product, to shifts in input-factor proportions, to changes in the product mix of output, and to differential changes between factor and product prices. The resulting amalgam of interacting effects reaches far beyond the implications of any of the simple interpretations suggested earlier. Nor can it lend itself to any other interpretation, simple or complex, until an analytical framework is developed which is focused on the relationships among such aggregates within an evaluative system that has clearly specified objectives.[8]

Still another shortcoming of concept and of measurement arises from the widely prevailing practice of applying the total-factor productivity approach as well as the production-function approach to measuring output in terms of value added rather than value of product and thereby omitting purchased materials from consideration. This ignores the fact that much of the technological improvement effort within many industries is concerned with changing the kinds and quality levels of materials purchased and altering the level of fabrication at which they are acquired. This is necessary to improve products, to shift to more readily available or cheaper materials, and to eliminate costly or difficult tasks by purchasing inputs already embodying such operations. Thus the quantity of material inputs per unit of output and their quality are as much subject to managerial improvement efforts as inputs of labor and capital—and they are just as subject to technological innovations. Moreover, material inputs frequently account for more than 50 percent of total costs in manufacturing industries, and thus also affect working-capital requirements.[9]

Finally, it should be noted in this same connection that value-added data cannot properly be adjusted by changes in the price of actual final products to calculate physical output, inasmuch as material prices and costs need not always parallel those of other inputs or products. Moreover, there are no data covering the price only of the value-added components of the final product. Of course, the inclusion of material inputs in production functions would again pose the problem of deflating material costs, not by some general index of material prices, but rather by deflating each component of material costs by an index of prices related to the particular kinds and quality grades of materials directly involved.

These shortcomings are also rooted partially in another fundamental conceptual inadequacy: regarding changes in physical input-output relationships as separate from, rather than *interactive* with, changes in factor and product prices. This accounts for the prevailing tendency to emphasize changes in such physical productivity ratios as measures of the "real" effects of technological innovations. In reality, of course, changes in the quality and mix of inputs and outputs tend to engender price reactions by increasing the demand for some specific types of inputs at the expense of others, and by offering products with altered service characteristics. Moreover, such interactions continue to develop over time as adaptive adjustments to such innovation-induced pressures are made by competitors, by factor markets, and by buyers. This basically untenable separation of the physical relationships from associated economic relationships also encourages the widespread failure to round out such studies by examining the extent to which technological innovations are a response to shifts in factor and product prices rather than a phenomenon arising from extraeconomic space and then exerting only a unidirectional impact on resources flows and prices.[10]

From the standpoint of measurement, attempts to encompass such interactions necessitates shifts in the following: the variables covered, the duration of the time periods deemed necessary to prevent truncated explorations of effects, and the form to be taken by reported findings. With respect to the variables covered, requirements would be expanded beyond physical inputs of labor and capital (and materials, where these are included, as in input-output analysis) to cover the factor prices of the specific material and labor skill and capital goods categories displaced as well as those replacing them. Moreover, it would be necessary to measure the rate of diffusion of the innovation under study as well as changes in the level of product output to appraise resulting changes in demand pressures on input factor markets. And attention would also have to be given to changes in the prices of the products affected by the innovation. With respect to the time periods to be covered, it is evident that the effects attributable to any innovation will unfold more slowly than the diffusion of the innovation itself as a result of the frictions involved in spreading information, in resolving conflicting pressures in markets, and in effectuating needed shifts in resource allocations. Hence the effects of innovations which take 10 to 15 years to account for even one-half of relevant output—as has been common in the steel and related industries (Gold [25, pp. 130–133])—are unlikely to be determined by studies covering less than 20 or 30 years.

With regard to the form of expected findings, it follows from the foregoing emphasis on interactions over a wide sector of factor and product markets and over an extended period of time, that the common tendency to report "the effects" in the form of net changes in specific variables between some starting date and some evaluation date, is likely to be misleading. What is needed, instead, are results delineating the *pattern of changes* over extended periods of time in physical input-output ratios, factor prices, unit costs, and other evaluative criteria deemed relevant by the industrial managers, government officials, or scholars whose questions are to be answered by such studies.

The latter consideration suggests another basic conceptual weakness underlying studies of the economic effects of technological innovations: the pervasive assumption that the dominant effect of technological innovations is to reduce average total unit costs. Of course, this is frequently a primary objective of innovations, but such an objective is too generalized as well as too limited to guide penetrating analyses. Such undertakings need rather to identify the more specific and immediate objectives of the decision makers in order to apply relevant evaluative criteria. For example, their direct objectives might include shifting to more abundant or cheaper materials, or to reduce energy and material waste, or to decrease the rejection rate of products because of quality defects, or to reduce the idle time of facilities, equipment, etc. But technological innovations may also be adopted for a variety of purposes which may involve increasing rather than decreasing unit costs. The most common among these relates to innovations yielding new or improved products, which are expected to generate income gains in excess of attendant cost increases. Other instances might involve the adoption of innovations permitting the needed expansion of output through the processing of lower-quality inputs or those required to meet governmental health, safety, and pollution standards.[11]

To take account of such broader objectives, it would seem necessary to extend measurements even beyond the structure of physical productivities, factor prices, and unit costs already discussed. In addition, the framework should reach out to include the resulting effects on profitability, if it is to accord with a dominant motivation in the case of industrial adoptions of innovations. And even broader considerations might have to be included to encompass innovations whose adoptions involve governmental incentives, support, or resistance.

The basic point of all this, of course, is that both the concepts and the measures which have been commonly employed in deriving production functions have ignored or offset various significant effects of common technological innovations, thus contributing less to the understanding of such effects than to minimizing them.

Several of these same shortcomings are found in most input-output analyses. Inputs and outputs are measured in terms of aggregate values, ignoring changes in quality and mix. Although the value of material inputs is subdivided according to the totals derived by "an industry" from each of its supplying "industries," labor and capital inputs are usually presented only as aggregates. In addition, all differences among the products, plants, and firms encompassed by a given industry are ignored, including even the extent to which they are utilizing the given innovation or simultaneously applying other technological, managerial, or marketing innovations as well. Hence this approach also prevents determination of most of the specific effects attributable to given technological innovations. Moreover, when comparisons are made between input-output matrices for two periods in order to appraise intervening changes, the same problems of comparability of coverage and of meaningful deflation which were discussed earlier are confronted with respect to all factor and product prices.

Effects of Research and Development Programs

Some attention may also be given to the conceptual and measurement problems involved in studies of the "productivity" and benefits of research and development (R&D) activities, which are generally regarded as the source of technological innovations.[12] Perhaps the most fundamental weakness of such undertakings is the implicit assumption that the various activities subsumed under the broad heading of R&D are sufficiently similar among a wide array of firms and industries to warrant analyzing them as if they represented essentially homogeneous operations. Resulting findings of average input-output relationships, average time lags between inputs and benefits, and average rates of profitability seem quite devoid of significance, however, when compared with the extraordinary diversity of the actual undertakings camouflaged by the simple aggregative input and output measures used.

Even simple classifications of all R&D activities into three or four stages fail to convey the far-reaching differences among firms and industries within each such stage with respect to those aspects which are of primary significance for the evaluations being attempted, the specific kinds of achievement being sought, the magnitudes of the resources committed, the levels of risk involved, the time perspectives within which final results are expected, and so on. Product-improvement targets may range from minor adjustments to meet particular customer needs to the provision of successive small increments in the attractiveness, operational efficiency, or service attributes of one or more products, or even to creating new products. Process-improvement targets cover a comparable range and often involve greater difficulties and commitments, as well as longer time perspectives, than product-improvement efforts. In addition, R&D may also include undertakings to facilitate shifts to lower-quality or cheaper material inputs, to mechanize labor tasks, to improve machine efficiency, to meet health, safety, noise, and pollution requirements, and sometimes, even to service the routine testing of purchased supplies for conformance to specifications.[13]

There is certainly no basis whatever for assuming homogeneity, even among firms in the same industry, with respect to the variety or relative emphasis among such multiple facets of R&D operations. Resulting aggregate measures and average relationships are likely to be no more meaningful than averaging the speeds of a random mix of sprinters, milers, and marathon runners or determining the average characteristics of a random collection of chemical compounds. To avoid such vulnerabilities, it would seem necessary both to develop hypotheses reflecting a more thorough exploration of the dissimilarities encompassed by the R&D label and to test each by means of samples which are more homogeneous with respect to the specified selection criteria.

A second conceptual problem underlying most efforts to assess the returns to R&D efforts derives from the simplistic assumption that changes in the level of payoffs are attributable solely to changes in the levels of R&D inputs. In reality, gains in cost saving, sales, or profits are obviously affected by changes in the effectiveness of all integral components of a firm's operations, including procurement, production, and marketing. Moreover, there is no warrant for assuming either that the contributions of these operations to improvements in the overall performance of a firm are necessarily much smaller and less consistent than those of R&D programs, or that all firms and industries tend to be equally effective in all operations except R&D, leaving the magnitude or efficiency of the latter as the primary source of differences in overall performance. R&D may be a necessary source of contributions, of course, at least from time to time. But emphasizing its role to the neglect of all other operations does not provide a persuasive conception of the complex of internal operations which management must integrate in seeking to improve results.

In this connection, it is also worth noting that calculating the profitability of allocations to R&D by comparing them with net returns at some later date is bound to yield exaggerated results to the extent that this omits all additional investments and costs in other operations, including production and marketing, which were necessary to convert research findings into new or modified products at costs low enough, and sold in quantities and at prices large enough, to yield the eventual profits. For these reasons, few experienced executives are likely to regard the results of statistical studies of the relationship of changes in R&D inputs to changes in sales or profitability as offering sound guides for the allocation of their resources.

There are a number of additional shortcomings in the simplistic conception that changes in a firm's profitability are determined by changes in its R&D inputs. For example, this view ignores the wide range of external factors affecting profitability: changes in general economic conditions, in the intensity of market competition (as affected by capacity utilization rates, the impacts of imports, the attractiveness of substitute products, etc.) and in the availability and price of needed inputs. It also ignores variations among firms and industries in the extent to which technological innovations may come, not from internal R&D, but from licensing innovations developed by others or through the purchase of equipment and facilities which embody process improvements generated elsewhere. Moreover, the concept of unidirectional causation from R&D inputs to profits hardly accords with the widespread tendency to allocate a specified percentage of sales revenues to R&D, or with the confirmatory complaints by industrial research directors about sharp budget cutbacks during periods of declining sales and profits.

A third conceptual problem confronting efforts to assess the benefits of R&D involves the assumption that the contributions of R&D can be measured in the form of reduced costs or increased revenues and profits. But this ignores the fact that such efforts seek to achieve a competitive advantage concurrently with similar efforts by competitors. Accordingly, it seems necessary to consider several alternative possibilities. If all competitors made equal commitments to R&D, had the same targets, and were equally successful on average, sometimes one and sometimes another would reach the goal first. On average, however, there might well be no consistent competitive advantage to any firm, even if all competitors kept increasing the level of R&D inputs. Under less restrictive assumptions, it is still reasonable to argue that a substantial part of any firm's R&D would have to be defensive, in the sense of trying to minimize either the advantages currently achieved by the R&D efforts of one competitor or another or the disadvantages resulting from differentially unfavorable adjustments in its own input-factor prices or supplies. In either of these cases, even successful R&D efforts would have the effect merely of reducing comparative cost, sales, and profit disadvantages instead of yielding positive gains in these areas.[14]

More generally, it is puzzling to find regression results being presented and interpreted without accompanying efforts to present a persuasive line of reasoning which presumably underlies the hypothesis being tested. For example, studies of whether R&D intensity increases with the size of the firm, the degree of concentration, or the extent of diversification frequently fail to offer supporting arguments which could not be reversed without much loss of cogency. Such analytical underpinnings might be strengthened by considering how specified differences among firms might impinge on each of the intermediate stages linking R&D inputs with payoffs. For example, the very concept of industrial research implies seeking to advance sufficiently beyond the current knowledge and practices of competitors to yield commercial benefits. Such efforts are obviously attended by risks, whose magnitudes tend to grow rapidly as targets become progressively more ambitious. Hence differences in this first stage, involving the ambitiousness of R&D objectives, may be the major source of differences in failure rates and in the time lags between R&D inputs and payoffs—and these differences may be a more important source of differences among industries, and perhaps between large and small firms, than later stages in the development of R&D efforts into sales and profits.

In the next stage, involving the conversion of R&D outputs into commercial levels of production, one might suppose that efforts to develop product improvements would engender smaller risks and shorter delays as well as more limited additional investments than major process innovations. This would identify another source of differences in R&D profitability which, however, might well cut across the firm and industry categories most closely associated with observed differences in the first stage. And in the third stage of this rough classification, the effectiveness with which new processes or products are marketed surely represents another important source of differences in R&D profitability—perhaps more closely associated with the size and financial resources of firms than with various other characteristics. Similarly, if one were concerned with the effects of the relative diversification of firms on the profitability of their R&D efforts, it would seem helpful to clarify both the expected advantages and disadvantages of diversification in this connection. The latter might include the necessity of dispersing R&D resources, as well as production and marketing improvement efforts, over a wider array of products and processes, and advantages might include the availability of a wider range of processes and products to harness the often diverse outputs of R&D efforts.

Effects of Diffusion

Most of the research concerned with the diffusion of technological innovations in industry has been focused on measuring the rates of diffusion for particular innovations and on seeking to identify the factors associated with observed differences in such rates. With respect to both of these, the key conceptual problems center around seeking to define *the innovation* and its practical range of applications meaningfully, and they derive from the very dynamics of technological improvement processes.

As has been widely explored by others (for example, Merton [43]), major technological advances frequently appear in several forms. They then tend to grow in numbers as increasing efforts are devoted to improving their effectiveness and modifying them to fit the specialized needs of major groups of prospective users. In the case of facilities and equipment innovations, resulting changes are likely to affect operating efficiency and reliability, scale of throughput, input specifications, product quality and product range, as well as labor skills and safety. Contrary to the suppositions of outsiders, such developments are often difficult, costly, and time consuming. And yet, diffusion rates may depend on the realization of improvements of these kinds.

As a result, if these stages of metamorphosis are ignored on the basis of hindsight, one may well wonder why innovations which eventually became dominant took so long to gain wide acceptance. On the other hand, recognition of the fact that each stage of development had only limited diffusion potentials would require more detailed field studies than have yet been made of the advantages and limitations of each significant improvement as well as of the resulting new application opportunities. One need hardly add that such undertakings would have to be far more penetrating than those which have yet been published and would probably alter most, if not all, published findings to date.

Similar conceptual limitations have characterized analyses of the factors affecting the diffusion rates that have been measured. The overwhelming emphasis has been on expected cost savings and profitability, although ex post facto analysis has generally failed to demonstrate that such expectations were fulfilled, much less that these were in fact determining motivations for adoption of the innovations studied. Of course, adoption decisions must have been made because of expected benefits. But it does not follow that these would have to take the form of demonstrable decreases in costs or increases in profits. Other powerful benefits, which were mentioned earlier, might have included mitigating expected increases in input-factor prices or decreases in the availability of needed materials, responding to buyer demands for higher-quality products, or acceding to governmental pressures relating to labor or community health, safety, and pollution standards. Nor can it be assumed that the expected benefits of given innovations are so clear that all competitors would assess them similarly, or even that all competitors give serious consideration to the same innovations in any given period. But these doubts suggest that the criteria applied to the evaluation of available innovations may differ widely among firms, reflecting differences in their internal urgencies, resource availabilities, and specialized expertise rather than deriving solely from the demonstrable benefits of the innovation itself. Hence the focuses of efforts to explain differences in diffusion rates may have to be expanded to include consideration of a variety of firm characteristics (Gold [25, pp. 142-146]).

Curiously enough, little serious research has been done on the advantages and disadvantages of slower versus faster rates of diffusion, or even on the nature, patterns, and effects of the diffusion of industrial technologies. It has been commonplace for economists to complain about the slowness with which various major innovations have been utilized.[16] But such criticisms have invariably been based on hindsight judgments with little detailed consideration of the options, pressures, and uncertainties confronting prospective adopters during successively earlier stages in evaluating the available forms of the innovation.[17] Instead of assuming ignorance, sloth, bias, or stupidity as the causes of such restrained rates of diffusion, it would be more helpful to make field studies of the actual considerations and evaluations responsible for the decisions made.

Also worth emphasizing in this connection is that maximizing diffusion rates might prove undesirable for economic as well as social reasons, because many innovations prove technically or economically unfeasible except under specialized conditions, and because many others become attractive only after extensive technical improvements or changes in economic conditions. Hence overeagerness in adopting innovations can involve extended periods of high-cost operations, customer dissatisfaction, and even heavy capital losses. Indeed, although there are a number of well-known cases of pioneering adoptions which have yielded large rewards—usually relating to products rather than processes—there is still no consistent evidence favoring early adoption of all innovations or indicating how to separate those which are still subject to serious risks of obsolescence or unprofitability from those already warranting adoption. Surely the development of deeper insights into the time patterns of risk and rewards associated with successively earlier and later adoptions of actual technological innovations would represent more constructive contributions than continued criticisms on the basis of only superficial analysis combined with hindsight.

Both understanding and evaluation of technological diffusion requires fuller exploration of resulting adoption patterns and their effects. The usual focus of diffusion studies is limited to competitors in the given industry. The diffusion of technological innovations, however, may also have important effects on the factor markets supplying the industry, including materials, labor, capital goods producers, and even suppliers of investment funds. In another direction, such diffusion is likely to have repercussions on the markets of the products directly affected as well as of competitive substitutes. Additional effects may concern government agencies, including effects on competition, on natural resource requirements, on employment and labor relations, on foreign trade, and on the environment. Only in this larger context can the effects of different diffusion rates be adequately evaluated as a basis for clarifying the possible advantages and disadvantages of seeking to alter them.

Vulnerability of Interpretations of Past Findings

Serious studies of the economic effects of technological innovations must begin by recognizing that such innovations engender readjustments in economic relationships: (1) through a variety of intermediate linkages, (2) within a network of interacting pressures, (3) covering an expanding horizon of operations, (4) over extended periods of time, and (5) accompanied by a variety of independent but concurrent developments. But production functions, total-factor productivity determinations, and input-output matrices do not provide such detailed mappings of the means through which technological innovations bring about eventual economic changes. Their reliance, instead, on inferring causal factors from changes in the gross relationships between inputs and outputs is not only a superficial expedient, but lends itself to serious misinterpretations.

For example, as was noted earlier, the exponential values of labor and capital inputs in production functions commonly are interpreted as indicating the extent to which an increase of 1 percent in man-hours, or of 1 percent in capital inputs, would increase total physical output.[18] This interpretation rests, however, on the assumption that each factor is paid the value of its marginal product, although the theoretical conditions which are necessary to fulfill this assumption are seldom satisfied in reality. Indeed, closer analysis of the means whereby these variables are measured—usually involving attempts to deflate value added, wages, and some measure of capital charges by more or less relevant price indexes—offers at least comparable support for a quite different interpretation of these exponential values. Specifically, they might be interpreted as representing merely the average proportions in which value added has been divided between labor and capital payments. And such income (or cost) shares need not imply any comparable proportioning, either of their respective actual contributions to increasing output or of their relative physical productivities.

Misinterpretations of results are also frequent in studies of the effects of increases in mechanization. These usually report increases in output relative to labor inputs and decreases (or smaller increases) in output relative to capital inputs, leading to interpretations that the innovation has increased labor productivity and decreased capital productivity (or increased it less than labor productivity). In fact, closer analysis suggests that, in most such instances, parts of labor's productive tasks have been shifted to machinery, thus reducing labor's contribution to output along with the reduction in the volume of labor inputs—leaving indeterminate whether labor's productive contributions per man-hour have risen, remained unchanged, or declined. But trade unions are often able to secure increases in wage rates in proportion to increases in output per man-hour, even when these are achieved via mechanization (as is commonly the case). Hence, deducing changes in labor's contributions from changes in its wage rates through the application of purely theoretical assumptions and in the absence of more penetrating analysis of the means whereby the technological innovations effectuated the observed economic changes, encourages serious misinterpretations. On the other hand, closer analysis of the actual technologies involved, and of the processes whereby innovations bring about changes in resource qualities and flows, permits more perceptive identification of changes in the relative contributions of various input factors, as well as in other characteristics of the operations affected. As will be shown in chapter 5, clarification of the constraints on factor substitutions in various technologies facilitates more effective solutions to the classical problem of determining the relative contributions of different inputs to joint products.

Another illustration of the vulnerability of speculative interpretations of changes in the gross levels of relationships provided by production functions relates to the effects over time of a cost-saving innovation affecting one or several of a plant's products. During the period of early adoptions, the total cost of producing the same level of physical output of the affected products would decline, thus yielding the expected decrease in average unit costs for the plant. But suppose that progressive diffusion combined with competition among adopters of the innovation leads to price reductions for these products based on attempts to take advantage of producers still relying on the costlier processes. Because changes in total physical output are claculated by weighting the quantity of each product by its average price over the periods being compared (if the Edgeworth formula is used), the reduction in the affected products' relative prices has the effect, as was noted earlier, of reducing their contributions to the total plant's physical output as reflected by price-weighted measures of product quantities. Hence, if total costs remain the same in this second period, but the accompanying measure of the plant's physical output declines (not because of the number of product units, but because of the price decreases effected by the innovations), then total costs relative to physical output rise. In short, factor savings which lead to cost savings and then to price reductions are accompanied by initial reductions in unit costs which then tend to erode. Accordingly, evaluations over periods long enough for competition to have forced such a pass-through of production cost savings to consumers would tend to minimize the unit-cost changes that had taken place—even though the cost and price per physical unit of output had actually declined and remained lower.

Shortcomings with respect to interpreting the results of studies of the economic effects of technological innovations are not attributable solely to ignorance of the complex interactions connecting the initiating physical resource impacts with various adjustments in economic relationships. No less disappointing, from the standpoint of the decision-making and policy-formulating concerns of industry and government officials, is the pervasive failure to improve our understanding of the sequential linkages in transmitting the various impacts of different kinds of innovations, the sources of frictions and even of offsetting pressures in these successive stages, and the timing and duration of the major stages. Insights of this kind would strengthen the bases for adoption or rejection decisions by permitting consideration of probable long-term as well as short-term outcomes. They would also facilitate setting realistic performance goals during the period of integrating the innovation into the larger complex of operations. And attention would be drawn to the need for detecting and trying to overcome possible developments which could undermine expected benefits. So long as reliance continues to be placed on the gross aggregative relationships which have been the focuses of most production-function, total-factor productivity, and input-output studies, there is reasonable basis for questioning whether the reported economic effects of technological innovations are even largely, much less wholly, attributable to the innovations from which they supposedly derive.

Such reported results are also subject to still another source of misinterpretation. This stems from the widespread failure to recognize the gross unrepresentativeness of the experiences covered by most of the published literature. Perhaps the single most important reflection of sampling bias relates to the overwhelming concentration on those innovations which hindsight reveals to have been substantial successes. It is quite conceivable, however, that these account for only a small proportion of R&D and other innovational undertakings and expenditures—as is suggested by the meager number of such triumphs reported by Mueller for one of the leading industrial research groups in the United States over a 30-year period marked by heavily increasing outlays for research [44]. In view of this possibility, much more discriminating studies would seem to be called for in order to provide more realistic perspectives on the proportion of all innovational undertakings or expenditures which result in commercially attractive outcomes. And such studies would be even more valuable to industry and government if they were to disaggregate findings according to various categories of innovational efforts.

Other aspects of unrepresentativeness in the reports which have been summarized include overconcentration on a few industries (especially pharmaceuticals, chemicals, petroleum refining, and steel) and on relatively large firms with reputations for being unusually progressive. It should be emphasized that there is nothing objectionable to exploring new fields of analysis by taking advantage of the most readily available points of entry. Difficulties develop only when such fragmentary probings are used as the basis for unjustifiably broad generalizations with policy implications.

Some critical attention might also be given to the data employed in these studies. As Kuznets pointed out long ago [37], governmental statistical data tend to be biased in accordance with the purposes for which they are collected. Hence in an environment where R&D expenditures are regarded as evidence of progressive management, and where low ratios of such outlays are regularly criticized, it would not be surprising to find statistics on R&D expenditures tending to be inflated by widespread resort to broad conceptions of the varieties of activities to be covered. Along somewhat similar lines, experience with mailed questionnaires has demonstrated that those with favorable experiences to report are more likely to reply than those with unfavorable experiences. Even in an interview situation, respondents are more likely to provide answers which reflect favorably on themselves and their organizations than the opposite, and respondents tend to be reluctant about admitting ignorance concerning matters about which they might reasonably be expected to know. Research must, of course, be carried on despite such common difficulties. But awareness of such potential biases emphasizes the need for extending probings, cross-checks, and critical evaulations before essaying generalizations with far-reaching implications.

Conclusions and Implications

It is understandable, of course, that new problems in every field are attacked at first with the concepts and tools already in hand, even though these concepts and tools were developed to deal with problems that emerged in the past. Only increasing evidence of the inadequacies of such available weapons, combined with increasing pressures for more effective progress, is likely to overcome the reluctance to abandon familiar approaches in favor of groping along unaccustomed paths and bearing the greater probabilities of frustration. Producduction functions, total-factor productivity, and input-output techniques have provided useful initial perspectives on some of the economic effects of new technologies. But there is an obvious need to strike out in new directions if economists are to contribute more effectively to the decision-making and policy-development needs of business executives and government officials.

Very little substantial help is derived from studies which are overgeneralized in their coverage of technological changes, or which involve analyses at levels of aggregation far removed from their direct impacts. Thus studies of the purported economic effects of all technological changes lumped together are of little value because technological changes obviously differ widely in the magnitudes, patterns, and duration of effects, as well as in their sources, nature, gestation periods, and diffusion rates. Similar limitations affect the applicability of studies focused on broad industry groupings whose component firms differ widely with respect to specific technologies, product mixes, input requirements, scales of operation, and competitive pressures. Nor are practical decision-making needs helped significantly by studies which correlate R&D and other innovational investments with growth or profits several or many years later, without effectively differentiating the effects either of concurrent nontechnological company and market developments or of the other efforts and costs usually involved in overcoming intervening production and marketing (and sometimes procurement and labor) problems.

The applicability of such studies is also limited by the extent to which findings have been shaped by assumptions and methodologies that insulate them from decision-making environments and evaluative criteria. For example, businessmen are not likely to exhibit great interest in determinations of what the results of technological innovation "would have been" if neither the qualities nor the prices of input factors and products had changed since the innovations were introduced. Decision makers find it difficult to interpret the significance of production functions which compare changes in *price-weighted* quantities of products with *physical* measures of man-hours, *net investment* measures of capital, and, at times, *cost* measures of material inputs. Nor is it easy for them to accept the assumption that input factors are paid in proportion to their marginal productivities, even in this imperfectly competitive world. And, as has been noted, there is ample basis for uneasiness about the seemingly incidental manipulations involved in deflating revenues, costs, and investments to estimate changes in physical inputs and outputs.

Reported results are also difficult to interpret because of wide differences among them and because of the patent unrepresentativeness of the samples on which they are based. Hence, although there is widespread agreement that successful technological advances are desirable, little is known about their frequency, their net returns to developers and pioneering adopters relative to attendant costs and burdens, or their patterns and duration in terms of broader economic and social effects. In short, prevailing findings reflect the inevitable superficiality of analyses conducted at long range, which use concepts that substitute imagination and logic for close-up and detailed exploration of the phenomena to be understood, and which rely on crude tools, weak measures, and dubious interpretations.

Accordingly, most of the generalizations about the effects of technological innovations, or of increasing allocations to R&D programs, which have gained widespread acceptance are based on shaky foundations. Because major issues of resource allocations and related policy development are involved, it seems unduly hazardous to be guided by comforting, but essentially untested and highly vulnerable generalizations. The resulting need for deeper probing of the chains of successive effects produced by technological innovations carries with it several important implications. First, the simple and fragmentary analytical approaches which have been reviewed need to be replaced by a more comprehensive framework providing systematic coverage of the network of variables involved in the processes of interaction between technological and economic factors.[19] Second, the application of such a complex framework to a wide variety of technological innovations in different industrial settings and under disparate economic conditions is likely to narrow the range of direct applicability of the resulting findings. Moreover, the economist's traditional drive for maximum generality of results is also likely to be undermined as changing technologies curtail the time span within which valid evaluative comparisons can be made. Third, and perhaps most serious, such a more comprehensive approach requires the acquisition of a great deal of highly specialized knowledge about the industrial sectors studied in order to gain an understanding of the rich texture of technological changes involved and in order to trace their successive interactions with physical input and product characteristics, and with the factor and product markets as well as with the price, cost, investment, and other economic aspects of the operations affected.[20]

Economists have been free to avoid such burdens as long as they have been willing to concentrate on general scholarly issues. But increasing efforts to provide more effective guides for public and industrial policies require more thorough knowledge of the forces, processes, and pragmatic criteria encountered at the levels of aggregation and in the particular sectors of the economy where decisions are made and where their effects are lived with. As a result, analytical models are likely to become more complex and more numerous, and economists may have to develop, and even admit to, narrower areas of expertise than accord with the current self-image of the "general economist".

Notes

1. Production functions purport to specify the relative contributions to changes in physical output of changes in the physical inputs of labor and capital entering into that output. Its most common form when used to measure productivity or the effects of technological change is the Cobb-Douglas function: $Q = AK^aL^b$, where a and b represent the relative contributions of capital and labor, and A is an index of technology in time-series studies. Total-factor productivity analysis seeks instead to determine the effects on physical output (specifically its value-added component) of changes in a combined measure of labor and capital inputs, again including a parameter representing the technology index. Major contributions among the more than 50 studies covered include those of Douglas and his associates [9, 15], Robinson [50], Solow [58, 59], Arrow et al. [3], Walters [61], and Jorgenson and Griliches [33], in addition to the survey by Kennedy and Thirlwall [36] and the work on total-factor productivity by Schmookler [56], Kendrick [35], Domar [17], and Nadiri [46]. For a detailed critique, see Baird [5].

2. Input-output analysis is based on a matrix of columns and rows representing, respectively, the value of purchased inputs received by each industry from each of the others and the value of the outputs of each industry entering into each of the others. Resulting input-output ratios in each cell are termed *technical coefficients,* and changes in these from one period to another are regarded as measures of technical changes broadly defined. In process analysis, detailed quantitative measurements are made of inputs and outputs in successive stages of production, thus yielding interstage instead of interindustry relationships. Highlights of the more than 50 papers and books covered, beyond Leontief's pioneering work [38, 39], include contributions in volumes issued by the Netherlands Economic Institute [49] and by the National Bureau of Economic Research [47] as well as books by Chenery and Clark [14] and Carter [10], including the proceedings of an international conference edited by her [11]. Useful insights are also provided by the surveys of Kennedy and Thirlwall [36], and of Kamien and Schwartz [34], as well as the volume in process analysis by Manne and Markowitz [40]. For a detailed critique, see Erdilek [20].

Traditional labor-productivity studies rely, of course, solely on changes in physical output per man-hour to measure the effects of technological and other innovations, and output is replaced by the value added (that is, product value minus the cost of purchased materials and supplies) in its "value-added productivity" variant.

3. For a discussion of important changes in the foci of decision making at different levels of aggregation and in attendant evaluative criteria, see Gold [24, pp. 44–48].

4. Among the more than 100 studies of the sources and effects of technological innovations which were reviewed, the following seemed to be the most significant for this analysis: Carter and Williams [12, 13], Griliches [27], and Solow [58] prior to 1960; and during the 1960s, Ames [2], Blaug [6], Enos [19], Hamberg [29], Hollander [30], Jewkes et al. [32], Mansfield [41, 42], Nelson [48], Salter [53], Scherer [55], and Schmookler [57]. More recent contributions of special interest include those of Freeman [22], Rosenberg [52], Nabseth and Ray [45], and Williams [62], in addition to the previously cited surveys by Kennedy and Thirlwall [36] and by Kamien and Schwartz [34].

5. As an illustration of the theoretical emphasis on "best practice" which then proves inapplicable in the following empirical sections of his analysis, see Salter [53].

6. For a more detailed review of such pressures, see Gold [25, pp. 142–144].

7. For an extended discussion of these problems, see Gold [23, pp. 15–45].

8. For further discussion, see Gold [24, pp. 56–58].

9. The costs of purchased materials and supplies have averaged about 50 percent of total value of products for "all manufacturing" in the United States for more than 75 years, according to the Census of Manufactures. For examples, see Gold [24, p. 137] and 25, p. 12].

10. For a detailed analysis along these lines, see Gold [24, pp. 193–197].

11. For a more detailed discussion, see Gold [25, pp. 142–144].

12. For a critical review of the literature, see Boylan [7] and [8].

13. For a more detailed discussion, see Gold [24, pp. 222–236].

14. For a more detailed discussion, see chapter 14.

15. See Nabseth's summary of diffusion studies [45, pp. 301–302].

16. For example, see Adams and Dirlam [1] and Ault [4].

17. For example, see Dilley and McBride [16] and Huettner [31].

18. For example, see Samuelson [54, p. 538].

19. Such a framework is presented in chapter 3. For examples of its empirical application, see Eilon et al. [18].

20. A widely accepted contrasting view is expressed by Solow [60]: "The economist really need not know at all what it feels like to be inside a steel plant—he quantifies technological change by making measurements of output per hour, or output per unit of this, or input per unit of that." For a detailed discussion, see Gold [24, pp. 32–59].

References

[1] W. Adams and J.B. Dirlam, "Big Steel, Invention and Innovation," *Quarterly Journal of Economics,* May 1966.

[2] E. Ames, "Research, Invention, Development and Innovation," *American Economic Review,* June 1961.

[3] K. Arrow, H. Chenery, B. Minhas, and R. Solow, "Capital-Labor Substitution and Economic Efficiency," *Review of Economics and Statistics,* August 1961.

[4] D. Ault, "The Continued Deterioration of the Competitive Ability of the U.S. Steel Industry: The Development of Continuous Casting," *Western Economic Journal,* March 1973.

[5] R.N. Baird, "Production Functions, Productivity and Technological Change," in Gold [26].

[6] M. Blaug, "A Survey of the Theory of Process Innovations," *Economica,* February 1963.

[7] M. Boylan, "The Sources of Technological Innovations," in Gold [26].

[8] M. Boylan, "The Economic Effects of Technological Innovations," in Gold [26].

[9] M. Bronfenbremer and P.H. Douglas, "Cross-Section Studies in the Cobb-Douglas Function," *Journal of Political Economy,* December 1939.

[10] A.P. Carter, *Structural Change in the American Economy* (Cambridge, Mass.: Harvard Univ. Press, 1970).

[11] A.P. Carter (ed.), *Proceedings of the Fourth International Conference on Input-Output Techniques–1969,* Vols. 1 and 2 (New York: American Elsevier, 1970).

[12] C.F. Carter and B.R. Williams, *Industry and Technical Progress* (London: Oxford Univ. Press, 1957).

[13] C.F. Carter and B.R. Williams, *Investment in Innovation* (London: Oxford Univ. Press, 1958).

[14] H.B. Chenery and P.G. Clark, *Interindustry Economics* (New York: Wiley, 1959).

[15] C.W. Cobb and P.H. Douglas, "A Theory of Production," *American Economic Review, Supplement,* March 1928.

[16] D.R. Dilley and D.L. McBride, "Oxygen Steelmaking–Fact vs. Folklore," *Iron and Steel Engineer,* October 1967.

[17] E.D. Domar, "On Total Productivity and All That," *Journal of Political Economy,* December 1962.

[18] S. Eilon, B. Gold, and J. Soesan, *Applied Productivity Analysis for Industry* (Oxford: Pergamon, 1976).

[19] J. Enos, *Petroelum Progress and Profits* (Cambridge, Mass.: M.I.T. Press, 1962).

[20] A. Erdilek, "The Concept and Measurement of Productivity and Technological Change in Input-Output Analysis," in Gold [26].

[21] S. Fabricant, *The Output of Manufacturing Industries, 1899–1937* (New York: National Bureau of Economic Research, 1939).

[22] C. Freeman, *The Economics of Industrial Innovation* (Baltimore: Penguin Books, 1974).

[23] B. Gold, *Foundations of Productivity Analysis* (Pittsburgh: Univ. of Pittsburgh Press, 1955).

[24] B. Gold, *Explorations in Managerial Economics: Productivity, Costs, Technology and Growth* (London: Macmillan; New York: Basic Books, 1971).

[25] B. Gold (ed.), *Technological Change: Economics, Management and Environment* (Oxford: Pergamon, 1975, 1979).

[26] B. Gold (ed.), *Research, Technological Change and Economic Analysis* (Lexington, Mass.: Lexington Books, D.C. Heath, 1977).

[27] Z. Griliches, "Research Costs and Social Returns: Hybrid Corn and Related Innovations," *Journal of Political Economy,* October 1958.

[28] Z. Griliches, "Hybrid Corn: An Exploration in the Economics of Technical Change," *Econometrica,* October 1957.

[29] D. Hamberg, *R&D: Essays on the Economics of Research and Development* (New York: Random House, 1966).

[30] S. Hollander, *The Sources of Increased Efficiency: A Study of DuPont Rayon Plants* (Cambridge, Mass.: M.I.T. Press, 1965).

[31] D.A. Heuttner, "The Development of Continuous Casting in the U.S. Steel Industry: Comment," *Economic Enquiry,* June 1974.

[32] J. Jewkes, D. Sawers, and R. Stillerman, *The Sources of Invention,* 2d. ed. (New York: Norton, 1969).

[33] D. Jorgenson and Z. Griliches, "Sources of Measured Productivity Change: Capital Input," *American Economic Review,* May 1966.

[34] M.I. Kamien and N.L. Schwartz, "Market Structure and Innovation," *Journal of Economic Literature,* March 1975.

[35] J. Kendrick, *Productivity Trends in the United States* (Princeton: Princeton Univ. Press, 1961).

[36] C. Kennedy and A. Thirlwall, "Surveys in Applied Economics: Technical Progress," *Economic Journal,* March 1972.

[37] S.S. Kuznets, "Conditions of Statistical Research," *Journal of the American Statistical Association,* March 1950.

[38] W. Leontief, *The Structure of the American Economy 1919–1939–An Empirical Application of Equilibrium Analysis* (New York: Oxford Univ. Press 1957).

[39] W. Leontief (ed.), *Studies in the Structure of the American Economy–Theoretical and Empirical Explorations in Input-Output Analysis* (New York: Oxford Univ. Press, 1953).

[40] A.S. Manne and H.M. Markowitz (eds.), *Studies in Process Analysis* (New York: Wiley, 1963).

[41] E. Mansfield, *The Economics of Technological Change* (New York: Norton, 1968).

[42] E. Mansfield, *Industrial Research and Technological Innovation* (New York: Norton, 1968).

[43] R.K. Merton, *The Sociology of Science: Theoretical and Empirical Investigation* (Chicago: Univ. of Chicago Press, 1973).

[44] W.F. Mueller, "The Origins of the Basic Inventions Underlying DuPont's Major Product and Process Innovations, 1920–1950," in R.R. Nelson (ed.), *The Rate and Direction of Inventive Activity: Economic and Social Factors* (Princeton: Princeton Univ. Press, 1962).

[45] L. Nabseth and G.F. Ray, *The Diffusion of New Industrial Processes* (Cambridge, Eng.: Cambridge Univ. Press, 1974).

[46] M.I. Nadiri, "Some Approaches to the Theory and Measurement of Factor Productivity: A Survey," *Journal of Economic Literature,* December 1970.

[47] National Bureau of Economic Research, *Input-Output Analysis: An Appraisal* (Princeton: Princeton Univ. Press, 1955).

[48] R.R. Nelson (ed.), *The Rate and Direction of Inventive Activity: Economic and Social Factors* (Princeton: Princeton Univ. Press, 1962).

[49] Netherlands Economic Institute (ed.), *Input-Output Relations* (Leiden: Stenfort Kroese, 1953).

[50] J. Robinson, "The Production Function and the Theory of Capital," *Review of Economic Studies,* 1953–1954.

[51] G. Rosegger, "Diffusion of Technology in Industry," in Gold [26].

[52] N. Rosenberg, "Factors Affecting the Diffusion of Technology," *Explorations in Economic History,* Fall 1972.

[53] W.E.G. Salter, *Productivity and Technical Change* (Cambridge, Eng.: Cambridge Univ. Press, 1960).

[54] P.A. Samuelson, *Economics,* 8th ed. (New York: McGraw-Hill, 1970).

[55] F.M. Scherer, "Firm Size, Market Structure, Opportunity and the Output of Patented Inventions," *American Economic Review,* December 1965.

[56] J. Schmookler, "The Changing Efficiency of the American Economy, 1869–1938," *Review of Economics and Statistics,* August 1952.

[57] J. Schmookler, *Invention and Economic Growth* (Cambridge, Mass.: Harvard Univ. Press, 1966).

[58] R.M. Solow, "Technical Change and the Aggregate Production Function," *Review of Economics and Statistics,* August 1957.

[59] R.M. Solow, "Investment and Technical Change," in K. Arrow et al. (eds.), *Mathematical Models in the Social Sciences* (Stanford: Stanford Univ. Press, 1960).

[60] R.M. Solow, "Education and Economic Productivity," in S. Harris and A.

Levensohn (eds.), *Education and Public Policy* (Berkeley: McCutcheon, 1965).

[61] A.A. Walters, "Production and Cost Functions: An Econometric Survey," *Econometrica*, January 1963.

[62] B.R. Williams (ed.), *Science and Technology in Economic Growth* (London: Halstead, 1973).

3 Analyzing Productivity Changes

Changes in productivity levels are recognized as a major influence on a wide range of managerial problems, including wage levels, cost-price relationships, capital investment requirements, labor utilization, and even competitive standing. The very importance of these problems, however, emphasizes the seriousness of continued widespread misunderstanding of the nature and effects of productivity adjustments.

Some Widespread Misconceptions

Among the most widely prevailing elements of the mythology relating to productivity, the following four may be most important:

1. Productivity measures reflect changes in the "efficiency" of production.
2. Changes in productivity are reasonably well measured by output per man-hour.
3. Increases in output per man-hour or per unit of other inputs invariably are desirable because they yield decreases in unit costs.
4. Increases in output per man-hour warrant parallel increases in wages per man-hour.

However, not one of these contentions can be sustained on either theoretical or empirical grounds, as will be shown.

Contrary to widespread beliefs, it is inherently impossible to measure the physical "efficiency" of manufacturing processes, or of most economic activities, for the concept is based on a false analogy. Measuring changes in the physical efficiency of a process requires comparing a combined measure of all relevant inputs with a combined measure of all relevant outputs in terms which reflect the primary purposes of the undertaking. Thus one can calculate an engine's physical efficiency with respect to energy conversion by comparing the energy content of its fuel consumption with the energy equivalent of the useful power delivered by it. But it is not possible to measure the physical efficiency of the engine as a whole, or of the process of producing it. There are no important physical common denominators for combining the input contributions of labor effort and skills, many kinds of materials and supplies, even greater varieties of facilities and equipment, and a wide array of technical and managerial activities

–in view of the obvious irrelevance of the available measures of numbers, volume, and weight, Nor are there important physical common denominators for combining the wide range of quality and service characteristics which differentiate the many available types of engines from one another.[1]

In short, there is no unitary concept of efficiency that is widely applicable in modern economies. Instead of seeking to measure the efficiency (or changes in the efficiency) of a given activity, such studies must be designed to appraise the effects of changes in various input-output relationships on specified performance objectives of the system. Nor can the rich texture of technological effects be encompassed by the crude tools developed during the many decades when the theoretical framework of economic analysis explicitly excluded such phenomena. Technological change affects more than the quantities of inputs and outputs. The concentration of economists on estimated shifts in production functions, changes in the technical coefficients of input-output matrices, and deductions of causation based on regression analyses offer but unidimensional reflections of more complex relationships–and as has been discussed, they offer estimates of technological effects which are quantitatively subject to wide errors and are analytically meaningless.

Needed Coverage of Productivity Analysis

In order to fulfill the decision-making requirements of management, productivity analysis must reach beyond customary simplified approaches to cover:

1. Changes in the level of each category of input requirements per unit of output, including materials, facilities investment, and salaried inputs as well as direct labor.
2. Changes in the proportions in which inputs are combined, both in order to take account of substitutions (for example, buying more highly fabricated components instead of making them, or replacing labor with machinery) and also in order to differentiate between changes in the productivity of major as opposed to minor inputs.
3. Differences between the productivity of inputs when they are fully utilized and when their contributions are reduced by idleness (for example, as in the case of underutilized equipment).
4. Changes in input prices attributable to alterations in their quality as differentiated from changes in the prices of unchanged inputs.
5. Changes in the composition of output and in the relative prices of various products as differentiated from changes in the volume of output involving no significant shifts in product mix.
6. Interactions among input volumes, qualities, and prices as well as product volumes, relative prices, and mix.

7. Interactions among resulting changes in total unit costs, total revenues, and total investment to determine effects on profit rates.

The following approach has been tested in a wide variety of applications over a period of years, some of which will be presented in later chapters.

Productivity Measurement Requirements

Merely comparing various input and output quantities reveals changes in ratios but does not indicate their significance. To make such findings meaningful requires an analytical framework which encompases all the inputs and outputs of the system and reveals how each contributes to overall performance. One could then work backward from specified performance objectives to identify the variables which affect them and the intervening linkages.

The significance of given input-output ratios depends not only on the analytical relevance of the categories used, but on five additional requirements whose intuitive recognition in simple production systems has often led to their being overlooked in other applications. Two of these concern the qualitative stability of each input and output category through time and their measurement in terms relevant to performance evaluation. The potential for misinterpretation of quantitative input-output changes when quality shifts are ignored may be illustrated by variations in such ratios for smelters, which may reflect variations in the metal content of ores rather than in smelter "productivity." The dangers of measuring peripheral rather than core aspects of input and output flows may be illustrated by the common use of "tonnage shipped" to measure the output of steel mills, although most production efforts beyond the furnaces seek to increase the value of products by changing the shape, and incidentally reducing the weight, of the steel being processed.

The three remaining requirements are that the numerator and denominator of productivity ratios should relate to congruent sectors of activity, that they should relate to properly linked time periods, and that the contribution of the input must be absorbed into, and affect, the output. The first requirement merely seeks to prevent such errors as comparing all the inputs of a plant with only part of its output (for example, relating total man-hours in an integrated steel mill to the steel tonnage output of the furnaces). The second counsels against using input and output data for the same period unless all the input is absorbed into the output within that period. Thus, in the case of a 6-month production cycle, output levels should be compared with material inputs 6 months earlier. The third requirement emphasizes that outputs should be compared with inputs of all factors which can be substituted for one another. Thus changes in the ratio of pig iron input to steel furnace output would be misinterpreted if no account were taken of substitutions of scrap steel inputs in place of pig iron.

The Productivity-Network Approach

One means of meeting these needs is offered by the following model covering direct inputs (figure 3–1). It identifies six components of the "network of productivity relationships." Three cover the input requirements per unit of output, not only for labor but also for materials and fixed capital. In the case of the latter, net fixed investment is compared with productive capacity rather than with output in order to differentiate between what the capital goods can produce and the extent to which they are underutilized because of market factors [1, pp. 64–66]. The remaining three links cover the proportions in which these are combined; for example, the extent to which more highly processed materials or additional facilities may be substituted for labor. Because of the possibility that capital facilities may be underutilized, these factor proportions relate labor and materials inputs to "actively utilized" net fixed investment (see Gold [1, p. 174]).

By presenting productivity relationships as a network of interactions, this approach emphasizes that a change in any component, such as output per man-hour, may be merely the *passive* resultant of changes initiated elsewhere in the network, because all components must be brought back into a working balance. For example, the partial displacement of labor by additional machines would represent an initiating decrease in the ratio of man-hours to actively utilized facilities and would lead to increased output per man-hour, even if the remaining labor continued to work at unchanged tasks and at an unchanged pace. But the adjustment process would not yet be complete. The increase in output per

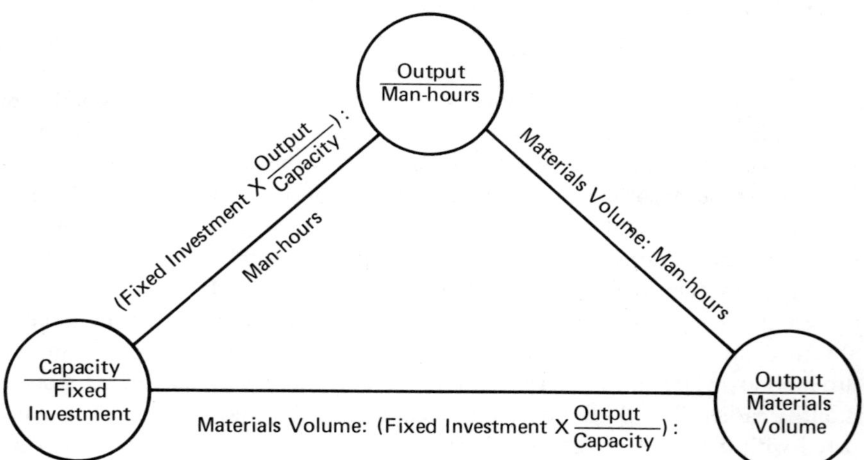

Figure 3–1. The Network of Productivity Relationships among Direct Input Factors

man-hour would require either a reduction in man-hours, if output remained at the earlier level, or an increase in materials inputs to permit the maintenance of total man-hours by increasing output in proportion to the gain in output per man-hour. In either case, the ratio of man-hours to materials inputs would decline—thus completing the adjustment cycle on the assumption that the originating replacement of labor by additional machines involved no change in materials requirements per unit of output or in the ratio of capacity to fixed investment [3, pp. 13-14].

Of course, output per man-hour may rise for a variety of reasons other than increased effort by direct labor. Among these may be mentioned the *reduction* of labor's contributions through the purchase of more highly fabricated components, the replacement of manual tasks by machinery, and the shifting of product mix in favor of one requiring less manpower. Still another set of innovations might increase output *without expanding* labor's contributions through expanding the output of given machinery or facilities without changing the number of workers tending it, either by utilizing machine capacity more fully or by increasing capacity through technical innovations.

In short, in using this model of the network of productivity relationships, it is necessary to identify the source of the innovational impact instead of assuming that it was engendered within any component registering a change. It is also necessary to trace the effects of an initiating impact in any component through the adaptive adjustments necessitated in the other components of the integrated process.

Integrating Productivity-Network Analysis into Cost and Profit Analysis

Management cannot, however, evaluate the net benefits of a past or prospective innovation solely on the basis of adjustments in the six components of the network of physical productivity relationships. The analysis must be extended to include their economic effects if it is to serve as a sound basis for decisions. To explore the cost effects of changes in unit input requirements and factor proportions, one can superimpose the structure of costs onto the network of productivity relationships [2], as shown in figure 3-2.

The effect of changes in output per man-hour on unit wage costs depends, of course, on concomitant changes in wage rates. Similarly, the effect of changes in unit material requirements on unit material cost depends on accompanying changes in the price of such materials. And the effect of changes in the productivity of fixed investment on capital charges per unit depends on the annual charges on such investment and on the capacity-utilization rate.[2] The point being emphasized in this framework is the necessity of considering *interactions* between productivity adjustments and factor prices instead of assuming that the latter remain unchanged.

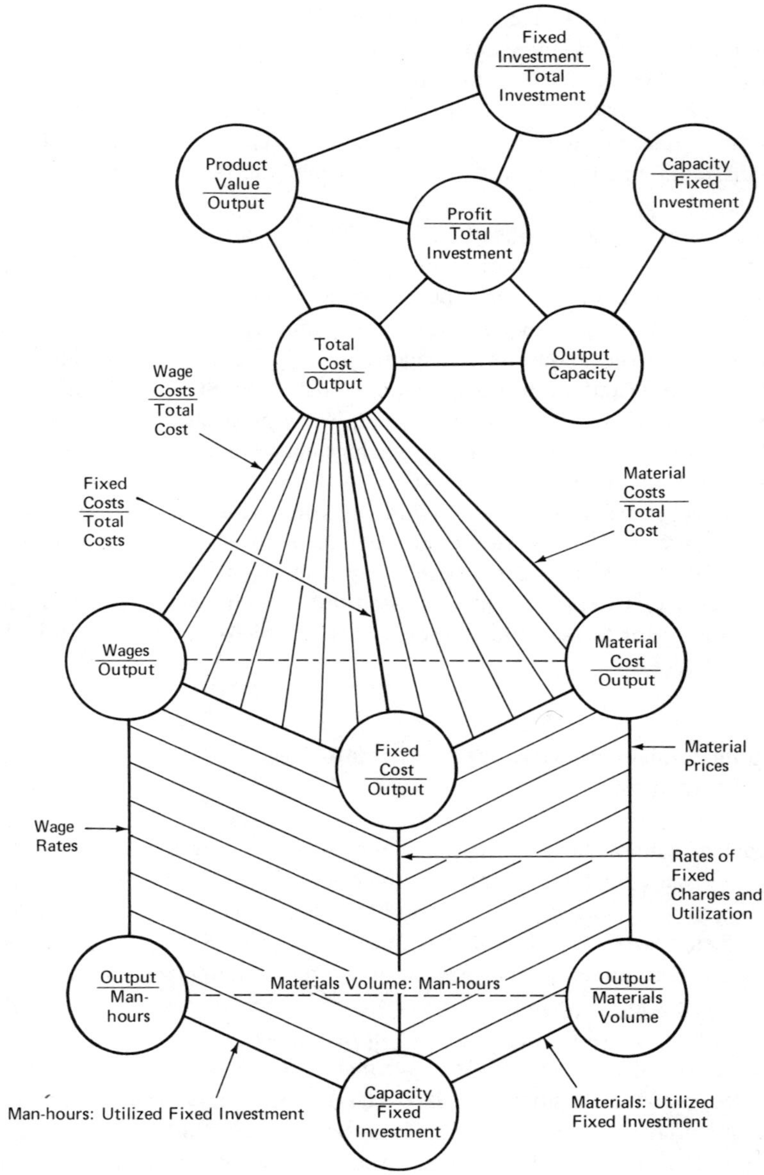

Source: Reprinted with permission from *Omega, International Journal of Management Science* 1 (February 1973). ©Pergamon Press, 1973.

Figure 3–2. Productivity Network, Cost Structure, and Managerial Control Ratios

In turn, the effect of a change in unit wage costs on total unit costs depends on the wage proportion of total costs as well as on concomitant changes in other unit costs weighted by their respective shares of total costs. For example, if wages account for less than one-fifth of total costs—as is common in U.S. manufacturing [2, pp. 185-191]—a 5 percent decrease in unit wage costs would tend to reduce total unit costs by only 1 percent. But total unit costs are more likely to increase than decrease if the innovation engendering the decline in unit wage costs involved increases in unit material and unit capital costs, which together account for more than three times the wage share of total costs in many manufacturing industries [2, pp. 137-142].[3]

Integration of the productivity-network and cost-structure models thus relates changes in "apparent" input productivities and factor proportions through factor prices to each of the unit costs. It also relates changes in individual unit costs through cost proportions to total unit costs. Hence such integration identifies the additional kinds of information required to evaluate the prospective effects on total unit costs of given patterns of changes in the network of productivity relationships engendered by technological innovations.

One point in the preceding illustration may well warrant renewed emphasis: analysis of the effects of productivity adjustments must begin with an identification of their sources, whether these are technological innovations or other developments. This is necessary to prevent overlooking other concomitant adjustments, while concentrating on those which are most controversial. Thus labor-management disputes about the extent of increases in output per man-hour and about the proper magnitude of attendant adjustments in wage rates often divert attention from the means (often technological) and costs of effecting the changes in production processes which account for all or most of the changes effected in output per man-hour.

Managerial decisions in private industry, however, obviously cannot be based on minimizing total unit costs either, in view of the overriding importance of the rate of profit in investment. Accordingly, in order to evaluate the actual or prospective effects of technological innovations, the productivity network and the structure of costs must be further integrated with some model of the determinants of changes in profitability. One such model, the *managerial control ratios model,* suggests that variations in the rate of profit on total investment are traceable to changes in, and interactions among, average product prices, total unit costs, capacity utilization, the productivity of fixed investment, and the internal allocation of investment between fixed and working capital. Thus,

$$\frac{\text{Profit}}{\text{Total invest}} \equiv \left(\frac{\text{profit}}{\text{output}}\right) \times \left(\frac{\text{output}}{\text{investment}}\right) \equiv \left(\frac{\text{product value}}{\text{output}} - \frac{\text{total cost}}{\text{output}}\right)$$

$$\times \left(\frac{\text{output}}{\text{capacity}}\right)\left(\frac{\text{capacity}}{\text{fixed invest.}}\right)\left(\frac{\text{fixed investment}}{\text{total investment}}\right)$$

According to this system of managerial control ratios,[4] it would follow that efforts to increase the rate of profits on total investment need not involve concentration on cost-reducing innovations alone. Indeed, the latter would be deemed undesirable if achieved by means that lead to reductions in product prices and capacity-utilization levels which more than offset the prospective gains in profitability derived from unit-cost reductions. Conversely, innovations might be deemed attractive if they offer prospects of increases in capacity utilization and in product prices great enough to offset any increases in total unit costs, whether due to higher-priced input factors or heavier input requirements per unit of output.

Figure 3-2 shows how these managerial control ratios may be integrated with the "network of productivity relationships" and with the "structure of cost relationships" to provide a unified framework for systemically exploring the complex of interactions linking changes in factor inputs and prices to unit costs, cost proportions, and the other determinants of changes in the rate of profits on investment. This framework may be used in analyzing past innovations, in developing innovational strategies for achieving specified future targets, or in appraising alternative innovations, even when their initial impacts focus on different parts of the system.

Changing Evaluative Criteria with Changing Aggregation Levels

The relative importance of the various physical, financial, and welfare attributes of input and output flows tends to change with the level of aggregation. Within centrally controlled systems (for example, firms), evaluative criteria tend to be derived downward from the guiding objectives of the whole through successively smaller subdivisions, and controls over resource flows tend to be developed backwards from the intended output pattern through successively antecedent stages to initial inputs. Hence all input-output adjustments must be interpreted within the context of their specified restrictions.

The preceding model may accordingly be disaggregated to permit progressively deeper penetration of plant operations in the interest of identifying the specific sources of changes observed at more aggregative levels, or alternatively, in the interest of more detailed exploration of the aggregative effects of prospective productivity or technological changes in particular operations or departments. Thus changes in the total unit costs of materials can be separated into the unit costs of each category of purchased materials, supplies, and energy. Moreover, each of these components of total unit material costs may then be decomposed into unit input quantities and their respective prices—tied into a productivity network to take account of possible substitutions among them. Total unit labor costs might similarly be separated into the unit costs of direct labor and those of indirect labor before further decomposition into their productivity-network components. And capital investment may be decomposed along parallel lines. The general process of elaborating the intraplant extension of the model is illustrated by figure 3-3.

Within a factory, department, or cost center producing one part for a marketable product, physical input–physical output relationships tend to dominate performance evaluation. Output can be measured only in terms of the number of parts meeting the required specifications. While inputs could be measured either in physical quantities or costs, the former tend to dominate performance evaluations within such component operations because the qualitative specifications for labor, materials, and equipment, as well as their prices and charges, are usually set by other units of the organization (for example, procurement, engineering, industrial relations, and accounting). Welfare constraints are also specified for the given unit through health and safety standards, insurance protection and other components of company policies, trade union agreements, and social legislation. Thus physical criteria are dominant only because financial and welfare conditions are fixed outside the given unit. Indeed, significant changes in any of these prescribed constraints would make it difficult to interpret resultant changes in physical input-output ratios without careful evaluation of their effects within a larger framework.

In evaluating the larger system which manufactures the complete product, however, cost supersedes physical quantity as the aspect of input flows to be compared with physical output within any given set of physical and welfare constraints. This reflects the production manager's freedom to improve performance not only by decreasing the quantity of each input per unit of output, but also by altering the qualitative specification of inputs, by adjusting factor proportions, and by seeking reduced factor prices—all derived from his emphasis on lowering total unit costs. But the interpretation of unit-cost adjustments presents difficulties if accompanied by substantial changes in product design or other constraints.

At the level of the firm, the primary criteria for performance evaluation changes again. Within defined physical and welfare constraints, reducing costs relative to physical output becomes less important than increasing revenue relative to costs. Moreover, increasing profit relative to total investment becomes still more important. Thus one may note a shift in performance measures from physical input–physical output to financial input–physical output to financial input–financial output at these successively higher levels of aggregation within the firm, as shown earlier in figure 3-2. This does not, of course, deny the relevance of physical input–physical output measures of performance. On the contrary, it reinforces the point made earlier that most changes in aggregates are the passive resultant of changes which actually occur at the level of component operations, and therefore, that effective managerial control of the system also requires an integrated hierarchy of differentiated measures reaching down-

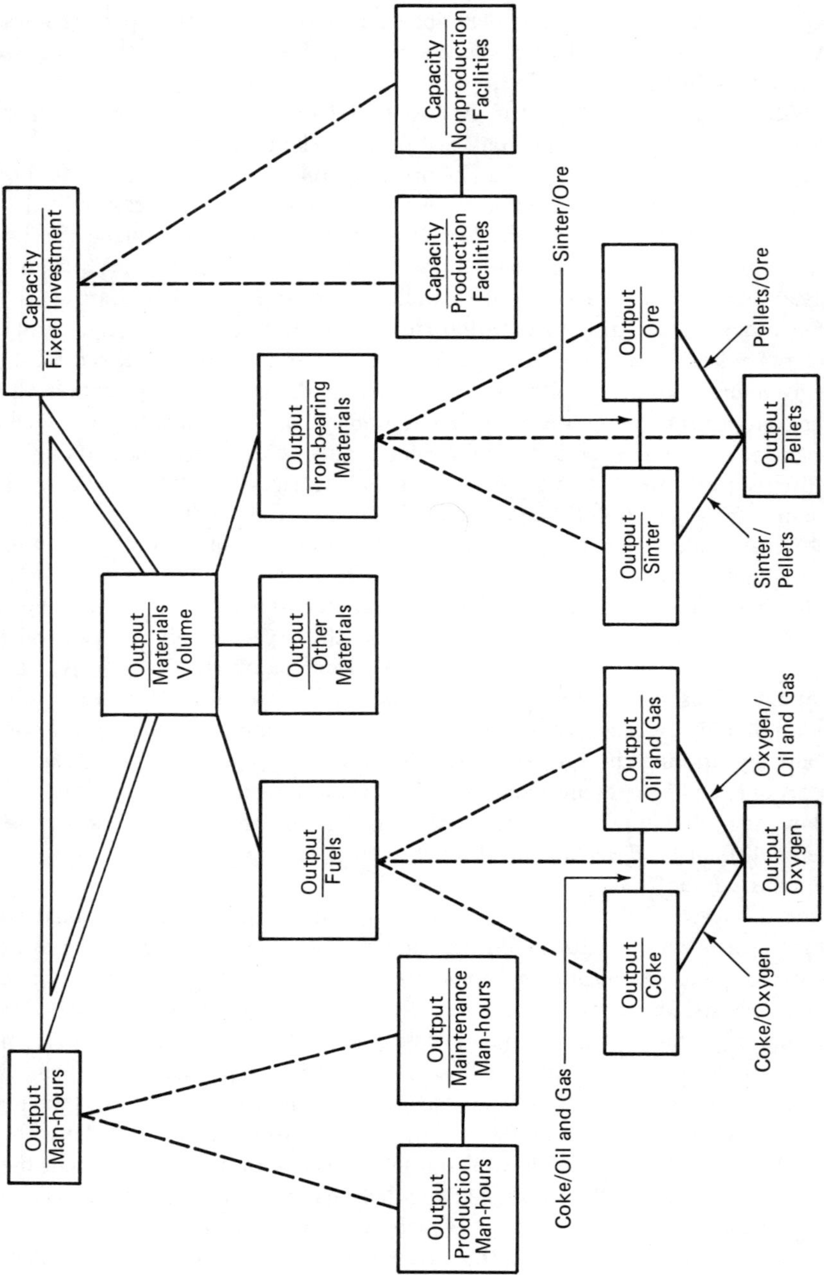

Figure 3–3. Elaborated Productivity Network for Blast Furnaces

ward from aggregate financial input-financial output measures through intermediate financial input-physical output measures to physical input-physical output measures, both in order to trace the sources of changes in the aggregate financial ratios and to plan and implement the readjustments in the underlying relationships necessary to achieve desired improvements in the aggregate financial ratios.

In short, because the variety of physical, financial, and welfare aspects of input and output flows may interact with one another, changes in any given aspect cannot readily be interpreted unless other significant aspects remain fixed. Moreover, the relative importance of these different aspects changes with the focus of the evaluator. In addition, one must recognize as well that although improvements in the input-output ratios of one sector may generate benefits at more aggregative levels, these may also be offset by (and even cause) unfavorable adjustments in other components of the larger system. Such considerations emphasize the dangers of measuring selected input-output relationships without defining relevant constraints, of applying identical measures to different levels of aggregation, and of projecting observed measures from one level to another.

Productivity Changes Beyond Plants and Firms

There has been an unfortunately widespread tendency in economics to project relationships which are meaningful at given levels of aggregation to other (usually higher) levels of aggregation where they are less meaningful and at times even misleading. Profits, for example, are directly meaningful only at the level of firms, for industry aggregates reflect some unknown combination of increases by some firms at the expense of others, and these yield no homogeneous measure applicable to the industry as a whole. Such limitations are even more true of productivity measures, for these may differ widely among products, as well as among plants and firms. As a result, industry-level measures of changes in particular input-output ratios can seldom be soundly interpreted as measures of either the effects of particular innovations or the causes of concomitant changes in costs. Indeed, they are usually vulnerable even as indicators of whether given developments are economically advantageous or disadvantageous. Yet measures of this kind often have been used to evaluate industry-wide wage claims, technological progressiveness relative to other industries and foreign competitors, and even the justifications for price increases.

It follows that commonly available productivity measures at even higher levels of aggregation tend to be still more vulnerable as additional heterogeneities—including differences among manufacturing industries and even wider disparities among other sectors of production—are swept under the rug of increasingly encompassing totals. This does not mean that all aggregative measures are useless. Rather it emphasizes that highly specialized measures must be used to serve various purposes, that some aspects of performance cannot be effectively measured at higher levels of aggregation, and that it is hazardous to rely on simplistic measures in attempting serious evaluations of productivity performance at the level of industries and beyond.

Attempts to measure the economic effects of technological innovations at levels of aggregation beyond the single firm encounter new problems arising from the variety of specialized interest groups with distinctive criteria for evaluating technological innovations and their input-output effects. Within the market economy, six such groups may be identified:

1. Resource suppliers (including trade unions, energy producers, raw material groups, and banks and financial institutions).
2. Resource purchasers (including the procurement, personnel, and finance departments of firms).
3. Resource users (including all production and fabrication departments of manufacturing firms).
4. Product marketers (sales departments of companies).
5. Product buyers (including firms as well as consumers).
6. Government agencies (including regulators and general economic policy and special welfare units).

For example, the suppliers of productive inputs are obviously interested in ratios that relate their particular inputs to the total output of prospective users. Specifically, suppliers of coal, electricity, or cotton are concerned with the effects of technological innovations on the physical amounts of these inputs required by the user per unit of his output. Reductions in such unit input requirements are usually regarded as disadvantageous by these suppliers. Providers of investment funds, sellers of machinery, and labor unions also share this emphasis on resource-oriented aspects of productivity adjustments. However, manufacturers and other users of such inputs are more deeply interested in the effects of technological innovations on the cost than on the quantity of such inputs per unit of output. Moreover, such users are more interested in the effect of innovations on the aggregated cost of all inputs per unit of output than on the separate costs for each input. This is so because the users seek to find more advantageous combinations of all inputs. In evaluating his overall operation, the manufacturer is interested more in maximizing the value than the volume of his product relative to input cost—and thus he is concerned also with the effects of the innovation on the quality of the product and its attendant potentials for expanding markets and fetching higher prices. The consumer is more interested, of course, in the effect of innovations on the service values yielded by each product relative to its price than on the sheer physical volume of total output relative to input quantities and cost (Gold [1 pp. 13-18, 40-41, 48-54], and briefly, chapter 6).

Exploring the effects of technological innovations at levels of aggregation beyond the plant and firm suggests a need to differentiate between organically integrated and artificially contrived groupings instead of continuing to apply essentially similar analytical frameworks to successively higher levels of aggregation—such as plants, firms, industries, and regions—without regard to the coherence of such systems. This need is highlighted partly because needed evaluations are focused on interrelationships between inputs and outputs, costs and revenues, and profits and investments instead of on each variable by itself, rendering comparisons meaningless unless the variables involved represent identical coverages. It is further emphasized, moreover, by the requirement specified earlier that such ratios or comparisons can be meaningful only if they relate to an integrated system of resource flows and are derived from explicit and measurable evaluative criteria.

Possible aggregation levels cover a continuum ranging from one-man operations to the entire national economy and beyond. Among them, four basic types may be singled out for examination:

1. *Control systems.* Actual networks subject to centralized control over all resource flows—as illustrated by individual firms.
2. *Specialized decisions systems.* Synthetic frameworks covering those segments of actual input-output networks which bear on the decision-making evaluations of particular input suppliers (such as trade unions) or output buyers.
3. *Group analysis systems.* Synthetic frameworks designed to analyze the position of entire clusters of competitors with essentially similar interest, such as individual industries.
4. *Descriptive groupings.* Arbitrary categories lacking analytical coherence but useful as intermediate steps in computational aggregation and disaggregation, such as individual regional totals for national industries.

These aggregation levels are presented in figure 3–4 as diversely oriented components of a generalized segment of economic activities encompassing the flow of labor, materials, and capital into several firms producing multiple products for sale to an array of buyers.

The control system is illustrated by any firm whose management controls the conversion of all inputs into outputs for maximizing specified relationships (usually financial) between total outputs and total inputs. Among *specialized decisions systems,* two kinds are illustrated: one represents evaluations by an input supplier of changes in demand for that input relative to the total output of products using it, as in the trade union model (panel C); the other represents evaluations by a buyer of changes in total inputs per unit of output among all suppliers of the given product (panel D). Each is analytically complete from the evaluative viewpoint of only one decision-making interest. Both *group analysis*

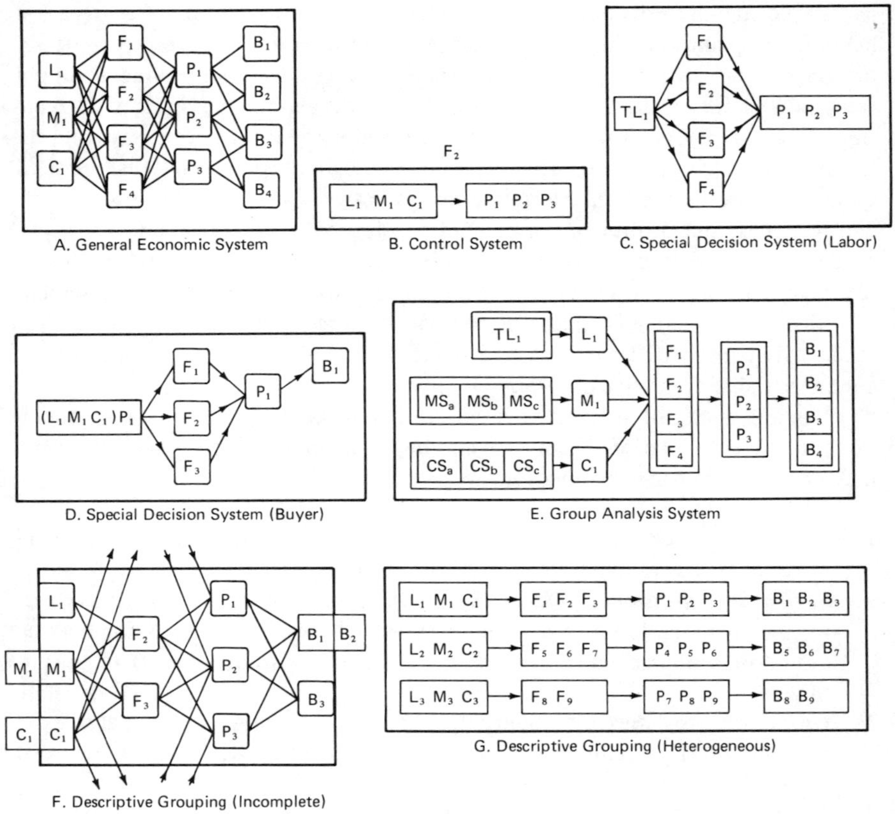

L_1 L_2: Various categories of labor inputs.
M_1 M_2: Various categories of material inputs.
C_1 C_2: Various categories of capital inputs.
F_1 F_2: Different firms.
P_2 P_2: Different products.
B_1 B_2: Separate buyers.

TL_1: Trade Union for L_1.
MS_a MS_b: Different suppliers of M_1.
CS_a CS_b: Different suppliers of C_1.
(L_1 M_1 C_1) P_1: All inputs for P_1.

Figure 3-4. Basic Types of Aggregated Systems

systems and *descriptive groupings* represent multifocal aggregates; the individual firms comprising them are each subject to centralized controls and evaluative criteria, but the group as a whole is not. In group analysis sytems, all the components have closely similar inputs and output, as illustrated by competitive firms in a homogeneous industry (panel E). As the residual category, descriptive groupings represent either incomplete or heterogeneous systems. The former are characterized by leakages into or out of the production channels linking inputs and outputs, as may be illustrated by subtotals for each region of a nationally organized industry like automobile production (panel F). Heterogeneity involves significant qualitative differences among the inputs and outputs of the firms in the group and may be illustrated by totals for each region covering all manufacturing activities or by national totals for such heterogeneous economic sectors as agriculture or transportation (panel G).

Multifocal aggregations pose special evaluative problems. In descriptive groupings which are homogeneous but incomplete, inputs and outputs may each be readily aggregated for all firms, but comparisons between them tend to be invalidated by intervening leakages. In descriptive groupings which are complete but heterogeneous, qualitative differences interfere even with the aggregation of the inputs or the outputs, to say nothing of allowing meaningful comparisons between them. Because they are both complete and homogeneous, group analysis systems, such as industries, permit the aggregation of inputs and outputs and also provide the congruence in their respective coverages needed to justify comparisons between them. But the interpretation of results is subject to two conditions. First, to provide an effective analytical focus, such systems must be designed in accordance with the purposes and evaluative criteria of a specified interest group: all competing firm managements, all suppliers of a common input, or all buyers of a common product. Second, all findings must be recognized as no more than average relationships among aggregates for the group. This means that such relationships need not be applicable to actual decision making by a particular competitor. Even more important, however, it means that such findings are difficult to interpret: one cannot automatically appraise the desirability or undersirability of a change in average input-output ratios when these may result from substitutions among input factors, changes in product mix, alterations in the relative output of different firms, or adjustments in total output. Indeed, it would be fundamentally erroneous to evaluate results in competitive industries by applying the evaluative criteria of its individual firms, such as profits, because firms often seek to enhance their achievements by undermining those of their competitors.

In short, the economic analysis of relationships between inputs and outputs may be highly vulnerable when applied to multifocal systems. This restricts the effective exploration of direct decision-making alternatives in such systems to activity sectors that can be recast into specialized decision systems. In such cases, however, each set of resultant findings would represent only one alternative interest or point of view. These alternatives could never be merged because unintegrated systems cannot have the unifying performance criteria which represent such a controlling viewpoint. In addition, the only other level of analysis applicable to multifocal systems would be restricted to homogeneous activity sectors that could be recast into group analysis systems to facilitate appraisal of the general framework of pressures (or input-output relationships) affecting each group with similar interests.

Such far-reaching implications become apparent only with the realization that beyond the level of individuals and families, control systems in Western economies are readily identifiable only at the level of separate enterprises (private firms, nonprofit institutions, and government agencies). No control systems encompass the total economies of cities, states, or regions, which usually take the form of incomplete as well as heterogeneous descriptive groupings. And control systems cover entire industries only when they have been nationalized and integrated.

On the other hand, particular regional interests might be served by synthesizing specialized decision or group analysis systems to explore input-output adjustments affecting the demand for a local mineral or for specified sectors of the local labor force, as well as others affecting the conditions of supply for certain locally consumed products. And group analysis systems might also be synthesized to evaluate adjustment patterns within reasonably homogeneous and competitive industries from the viewpoints of trade unions, suppliers of materials and capital, buyers of specified products, and the managers of the individual firms comprising the industry.

Notes

1. For further discussion, see Gold [1, pp. 6–12].
2. Algebraically, these may be expressed as follows:

$$\frac{\text{Wage cost}}{\text{Output}} \equiv \frac{\text{man-hours}}{\text{output}} \times \frac{\text{wages}}{\text{man-hours}}$$

$$\frac{\text{Materials cost}}{\text{Output}} \equiv \frac{\text{materials volume}}{\text{output}} \times \text{materials price}$$

$$\frac{\text{Fixed investment charges}}{\text{output}} \equiv \frac{\text{Fixed investment}}{\text{capacity}} \div \frac{\text{output}}{\text{capacity}} \times \left(\frac{\text{fixed investment charges}}{\text{fixed investment}}\right)$$

3. Specifically, the change in total unit cost from period 1 to period 2, compared with period 1, is given by

$$\Delta\left(\frac{\text{Total cost}}{\text{output}}\right)_{2,1} \equiv \left[\Delta\left(\frac{\text{wage cost}}{\text{output}}\right)_{2,1}\left(\frac{\text{wage cost}}{\text{total cost}}\right)_{1}\right] + \left[\Delta\left(\frac{\text{material cost}}{\text{output}}\right)_{2,1}\left(\frac{\text{material cost}}{\text{total cost}}\right)_{1}\right] + \left[\Delta\left(\frac{\text{other costs}}{\text{output}}\right)_{2,1}\left(\frac{\text{other costs}}{\text{total cost}}\right)_{1}\right]$$

4. For further discussion, see Gold [2, chapters 2 and 8].

References

[1] B. Gold, *Foundations of Productivity Analysis* (Pittsburgh: Univ. of Pittsburgh Press, 1955).
[2] B. Gold, *Explorations in Managerial Economics* (New York: Basic Books; London: Macmillan, 1971).
[3] B. Gold (ed.), *Technological Change: Economics, Management and Environment* (Oxford: Pergamon, 1975).
[4] B. Gold (ed.), *Research, Technological Change and Economic Analysis,* (Lexington, Mass.: Lexington Books, D.C. Heath, 1977).

4 Analyzing the Role of Capital in Production

Extensive experience in empirical research on the economic bases for decision making in industry suggests that one of the least satisfactory sectors of relevant economic theory and analysis is that concerned with the role of capital inputs in production. The basic shortcomings seem to be traceable, as has often been the case in other sectors of science as well as in economics, to the carry-over of concepts which are oversimplified and outdated. As a result, measurements and evaluations have been made of past relationships and suggestions have been offered for future policies which are seriously vulnerable at best and often downright misleading.

Analytical Objectives

The dominant purpose of most economic analysis in this area has been to determine the effects of changes in capital inputs on output levels. A closely associated purpose has been to explain the effects on output and unit costs of changes in the ratio of capital to labor inputs. Such studies, in turn, have provided the bases for examining changes in the productivity of capital and in total-factor productivity, as well as the apparent effects of changes in the scale of production and in technology.

A substantial thicket of publications has surrounded these core objectives. Most have offered narrowly specialized models of possible relationships among capital inputs, labor inputs, and outputs under all kinds of conditions. Some have provided empirical analyses perched precariously on arrays of dubious assumptions. What is most astonishing, however, is the paucity of serious efforts to trace the effects of actual capital inputs on the successive intervening linkages through which they bring about changes in outputs. Efforts to appraise and explain such underlying processes on the basis of speculations about their reflections in gross aggregate relationships have understandably encouraged the reification of concepts born of blackboard logic alone. The resulting literature on reswitching, putty-clay, truncation, and similar "problems" seems to offer few, if any, discernible applications to industrial or governmental decisions relating to the growth, improvement, allocation, and utilization of actual capital resources.[1]

Despite the understandable penchant of economists for concentrating on statistical aggregates, one must recognize that it is impossible to increase capital inputs in general. They must take specific forms, be applied in particular sectors, and serve specific purposes. In view of the wide range of alternatives encompassed by each of these decisions, it seems obvious that comparisons of changes in the levels of such inputs and of associated outputs can yield only descriptive results, devoid of authoritative bases for rationalizing the findings. Such studies cannot provide persuasive explanations of the wide variations in past relationships between changes in capital inputs and outputs in many industries (often hidden by emphasizing averages over extended periods), nor can they offer effective estimates of the probable results of given changes in capital (or other) inputs or in other aspects of surrounding production processes.

Accordingly, it may be argued that the prevailing dominant objectives of capital theory and analysis represent only partial elements of the more fundamental need to explore the role of capital inputs in production—the black box within which "inputs" are transformed into "outputs"—as the basis for strengthening both microeconomics and macroeconomics. This would involve more detailed examination of the nature of capital inputs, the purposes to which they are applied, the effects they have on other inputs as well as outputs, and the extent to which such relationships may differ in disparate contexts. Moreover, it would also require the design of measures more directly relevant to the resulting analytical framework.

Concepts of Capital Inputs and Prices

On the Concept of Physical Stocks of Capital

The development of capital theory has remained seriously stunted by its early conceptual foundation. One such foundation involved defining capital inputs as paralleling the other major categories of direct inputs: materials and labor. Each of these, it was assumed, could be dealt with effectively by regarding it as an aggregate of essentially homogeneous physical units—tons of coal, yards of cloth, man-hours of labor—and by regarding its contributions to production as varying with the volume of such units. Moreover, the assumption of basic homogeneity implies not only that such inputs could be properly characterized by an average price, but also that whenever the volume of such inputs could not be measured directly, it could be determined by deflating their total value by their average price.

The ambiguity of the basic concept of the physical volume of the capital stock is apparent from the widely disparate focuses of the various categories of measures proposed for it: how much there is, what physical inputs were absorbed into its construction, how much it cost, how much inputs it uses when operating, and how much revenue (deflated) it will yield during its operating life.

Although it is difficult to attach economic significance to changes in the physical dimensions of a capital stock, for example, its volume or weight, the sheer number of machines in a plant has been proposed as a measure (see Jerome [15, pp. 231-232]). A second approach has been to regard the capital stock as a summation of the physical inputs entering into building all its components, sometimes using "embodied labor" as the basis for aggregation (Adamson [1, pp. 117-119]; West [22, pp. 138-139])—an approach suggestive of Marxian analysis but also traceable to the concept of the "roundaboutness of production" introduced by Böhm-Bawerk and revived by Hayek.[2] The third approach, using the deflated cost of the capital stock, is still one of the most popular.[3] Another approach turns instead to measures of the current operating input requirements of the stock, the most popular tending to be energy consumption and the horsepower rating of the capital goods.[4] A fifth type of measure has taken two forms. An early version proposed an index of the "fixed assets of a plant or industry expressed as years of service still available" (Beach [3, pp. 11-20]). A later and more sophisticated version would represent an estimate of the value of all of the present capital stock's future net products at current (or estimated) prices to be deflated by an index of such prices.[5] One need hardly mention the lack of correlation among these differently oriented measures.

What is it that the economist really wants to know about the physical aspect of a given capital stock? If this is to be analytically relevant to the objective which guides management in acquiring a particular mix of capital goods, the answer would seem to be "its productive capacity." In short, managements are (and economic analysis should be) less concerned with how many machines there are, or how much labor and other resources went into their construction or current operating inputs, than with what the integrated array can contribute to marketable output, that is, its productive capacity.[6]

On the Homogeneity of Capital Stocks

A second critical conceptual limitation was the early emphasis on a static framework. This was especially crippling with respect to capital inputs because it distorted the time perspectives underlying both their acquisition and the evaluation of their performance. And a third limitation of long prevailing concepts in this area has been the view that the analytical framework could be broadened to take into account changes over time by allowing for adjustments merely in the quantities of the inputs and outputs covered.

Contrary to the conception which still underlies most analysis in this area, however, actual stocks of capital do not commonly consist wholly, or even largely, of homogeneous components. In most instances, they represent, instead, carefully integrated arrangements of high differentiated individual units. This results, of course, from the efforts of engineers to secure the economies of specialization by designing or selecting each facility, machine, and equipment unit to perform a narrowly limited range of functions. Indeed, plants are designed and equipped by working backwards from a planned level of capacity to produce specified product lines by means of selected technologies. Such targets then become the basis for defining successively antecedent processes, each of which is then decomposed until requirements are defined for each operation to be performed. And these latter requirements, in turn, determine the specifications for each of the various kinds of equipment to be acquired. Accordingly, one must face the question of how meaningfully the concept of an average price can be applied to such an intentionally heterogeneous array of goods. And if the significance of such a measure seems dubious, the possibility must be faced that purported measures of the physical volume of such heterogeneous arrays may likewise be meaningless.

It is obvious, of course, that most capital goods *producers* turn out numerous units of essentially similar goods within each product category during any given period and that an average price can be calculated for each such product category for each period. However, as was noted earlier, capital goods *users* (including those employing them to produce capital goods) tend to acquire highly differentiated arrays of individual facilities, machines, and other equipment so as to combine them into production lines capable of yielding distinctive mixes of marketable products. In all such cases, therefore, the most meaningful indexes of the average price of any manufacturer's stock of integrated productive facilities would seem to be the ratio of his investment in that stock to its productive capacity, or to its reciprocal, capacity per dollar of investment.

This measure also helps overcome the second of the conceptual inadequacies cited earlier: the static analytical framework. By concentrating on the capacity acquired relative to the investment required, the focus is clearly on the longer-term perspectives inherent in each. Even more important, such concentration helps us to overcome the fundamental problems represented by the third of the conceptual inadequacies noted earlier: restricting analytical provisions for encompassing changes in inputs and outputs over time to adjustments only in their respective quantities. But this is utterly inadequate with respect to capital inputs for a variety of reasons. First, because of the relatively long life of most capital goods, progressive advances in technology tend to engender significant changes in the operational capabilities of individual capital goods as well as in their costs and other characteristics. This alone would raise serious problems in measuring the change in price of a good which had itself been altered in operationally significant ways.[7] In addition, however, the extended periods between capital goods replacements tend to be accompanied by successive improvements in production processes as well as changes in product mix. Both of these tend to ensure changes from the original mix of capital goods comprising any given stock.

Significant changes in the characteristics and capabilities of individual types of capital goods pose serious problems for those trying to measure accompanying changes in price. Four expedients have been applied. One assumes that the change in price reflects inflationary pressures alone, and that the capital good itself is basically unchanged. This approach is frequently used to rationalize the continuity of price series, although its presumed justification in many cases for short periods can hardly be supported over periods of several years and even longer for most capital goods. A second approach is to assume that the change in price represents proportionate changes in the product's technical capabilities, and hence, that there has been no change in price relative to equivalent productive contributions. There are obvious weaknesses, however, in ignoring possible inflationary pressures as well as in assuming that prices can be adjusted in accordance with a product's enhanced service capabilities regardless of the magnitude of attendant changes, if any, in the cost of producing it. A third approach, which is more appealing philosophically than applicable in practice, is to attempt to estimate the economic worth of each change in the product's service features as the basis for dividing the price change between technical and market determinants.[8] The remaining alternative, which is obviously unappealing to economists concerned with measuring changes over time, is simply to regard price comparisons as meaningless whenever products have undergone alterations that have significantly changed their productive capabilities.

In addition to offering an approach which seems preferable to the preceding expedients for dealing with technological changes in individual capital goods, the proposed measure would also cope with the additional difficulties engendered by changes over time in the mix of capital goods comprising the stock of integrated production systems.[9] Specifically, by measuring the productive contribution of the integrated system rather than trying to evaluate the highly differentiated and unmarketable processing contributions of individual capital goods, and by also measuring the investment in the entire production line rather than the prices of individual machines, the proposed measure conforms to the evaluative criteria in actual use by managers—and is of primary relevance to investors as well. Thus, however a new capital good differs from its predecessor, and whatever readjustments the effective absorption of its new capabilities necessitates in the utilization of other units in the production line, the benefits considered by management in deciding to buy it are those which are realizable at the level of the production line as a whole. And such benefits would be compared with the accompanying effect on total investment as the basis for decision.

The preceding discussion also calls attention to still another conceptual limitation of many studies of capital: output relationships. These relationships usually concentrate on a comparison of incremental changes in capital and output instead of their respective aggregates. But such an approach represents still another reflection of the assumption that capital goods are as homogeneous as the investment dollars used in acquiring them. Not only is such homogeneity nonexistent at any time, but unequal improvements in individual capital goods and in various operating processes over time, combined with changing product specifications and product mix and differences in the working lives of individual units, tend to produce disparities among the throughput capacities of the numerous components of integrated production systems. Hence new investments which help to ease resulting bottlenecks may seem to yield disproportionate gains in productive capacity, not because they provide extraordinary productive contributions, but because they reduce the forced underutilization of capital goods embodying past investments. This emphasis on aggregate capital inputs and capacity rather than on incremental changes in them also helps to explain both why further incremental investments are unlikely to yield comparably generous gains in capacity and why the relationship between such incremental adjustments tends to be unstable in most industrial sectors.

On the Value of Capital Stocks

In order to assess the usefulness of alternative measures of the value of a capital stock, one must clarify the purpose which they serve and their attendant conceptual foundations. Three measures are commonly considered: current net investment, replacement cost, and the estimated value of the stock's future output.

The basic concept underlying reliance on the value of current net investment (original cost less depreciation) is that primary interest centers on the investment still embodied in production facilities. This seems to serve two purposes of major importance both to investors and to management. First, it measures a major component of the capital base used in determining profit rates. Second, it determines the proportioning of capital to other inputs, as well as the level of capital charges, with resulting effects on the magnitude and flexibility of unit operating costs and hence on the prices and net revenues which constitute the other determinant of profitability. Of course, this measure could result in misleading short-term comparisons among firms using different depreciation methods. But this would presumably reflect deliberate managerial preferences concerning the allocation of such costs over time—intentions which plainly have an important bearing on broader managerial investment and financing policies. Moreover, so long as depreciation policies differ in their time patterns for recovering investment rather than in the total allowable recovery, even interfirm differences within an industry would tend to be minimized by comparisons of mixed-vintage stocks over periods of several years.

What purpose would be served by using instead the estimated current replacement value of the capital stock? It is usually suggested that this would help minimize the effects of inflationary pressures which tend to make depreciation allocations on the basis of original equipment costs inadequate to provide for eventual replacement of productive facilities and which thereby exaggerate current profits. But such reasoning seems vulnerable to serious questions. Basically, it implies that the firm would want to maintain a replica of current productive facilities over the next 5 to 20 years or more, and also that current prices for the partially worn capital goods purchased 5 to 15 years ago would be good measures of what would have to be paid for replacing various components during that extended future. Neither of these assumptions seems to be applicable in most sectors of industry. The first ignores the continuing potent pressures for changing the content of the capital stock, especially over extended periods, because of changes in products, production technologies, and scale, as well as in relative factor prices, international and interindustry competition, and changes in the size and location of markets.[10] The second ignores the demonstrated wide cyclicality of capital goods demand and prices (Shaw [20]) and the unpredictability of long-term inflationary patterns, as well as the effects of technological changes on the very kinds of capital goods whose prices should be considered. Indeed, many of the capital goods now in place are no longer being made—preventing the determination even of current replacement prices[11]—and of course, many of those now made will similarly be unavailable when future replacements are considered. Hence current estimates of the costs of replacing present facilities in undefined future periods would seem to be subject to a very wide range of error as guides in evaluations of capital needs many years from now.

Thus replacement-cost estimates would seem to be of major practical importance only in those relatively few cases where they have a bearing on current managerial or investment decisions. One such case relates to the evaluation of those real estate holdings or accumulated stocks of marketable goods with respect to which decisions must be made either to sell now or to continue holding. Another case involves the use of some replacement costs to evaluate the competitive advantages of certain current facilities as opposed to new replacements. And a similar case concerns the use of such estimates by prospective new entrants or competitors wishing to expand capacity in choosing whether to attempt the takeover of existing plants as opposed to constructing new facilities.

Similar questions of purpose arise with respect to measuring the value of an existing stock of capital goods in terms of the estimated value of all its future products. This approach would seem to reverse the actual evaluative processes usually involved. Specifically, it is during the period prior to a capital-investment decision that management compares the investments required for alternative arrays of facilities and equipment with estimates of the net revenues likely to be attributable to their prospective contributions to production. Such estimates are based on obviously vulnerable judgments concerning the capital good's economic life, its average level of utilization, its effects on operating costs, including its own capital charges, and any resulting changes in product quality and prices. The estimated benefits may, of course, far exceed the required investment. But once the decision is made, it is the latter rather than former which defines the market value of the acquisitions, the level of capital commitments which determine operating costs, and the magnitude of the investments to be recovered–each of patent relvance to owners and managers.

What needs could be served by the inevitably wide range of estimates of the value of a capital stock based on assumptions about how much it will produce of what products for sale at what prices over its uncertain economic life? Whatever their attractions for theoretical purposes, it is difficult to believe that many managers and owners would regard such tenuous estimates as superior to actual net investment in evaluating current operating performance or alternative investments.

In short, actual net investment seems to offer a more generally useful measure of the value of a capital stock than either estimates of what it would cost to replace it, when we have no intention whatever of doing so, or estimates of what it might turn out to have been worth on the basis of hindsight evaluations 10 to 20 years from now. Net investment is more effective in meeting such pervasive needs of managers and investors as measuring input proportions and their cost effects, the capital base for evaluating profits, and the size of investment still committed and at risk. This same measure also seems more useful than its alternatives in such broader applications as analyzing trends in capital requirements, assessing the allocation of capital among economic sectors, measuring changes in net capital formation, estimating potential contributions to capital formation from depreciation, and comparing interfirm and interindustry rates of return.

Contributions of Capital Inputs to Production

Interactions with Other Inputs and Outputs

In order to develop sounder foundations for appraising the effects of changes in capital inputs on production, it is necessary to extend the list of concepts which need to be revised in order to ease continuing serious restrictions on analytical perspectives.

To begin with, even the aspects of changes in capital inputs to be considered must be broadened beyond the prevailing monopolizing concern with their sheer magnitudes. As was noted earlier, significant consequences may also flow from changes in the service capabilities of individual capital goods, as well as in the composition, operating characteristics, and output potentials of the integrated array of such facilities and equipment. Nor can such adjustments in the qualitative aspects of capital goods be shunted aside as uncommon. On the contrary, over the extended periods involved in the normal turnover of capital goods, it would be the absence of such changes that would be uncommon in many, and probably most, sectors of industry.

Another element of the unduly restricted purview of the traditional analysis of the role of capital in production involves its coverage of factor proportions. Here the sole focus is on the ratio of capital to labor inputs, and the measures concern only their quantitative magnitudes. But there can be no adequate analysis of integrated production processes while excluding all purchased materials and supplies, which generally account for more than 50 percent of total costs in manufacturing industries as a whole.[12] This is especially important because changes in capital goods frequently involve alterations in the level of fabrication, as well as in the particular specifications, of purchased materials, thereby affecting both the quantities required and the prices charged. Even with respect to labor inputs, changes in capital goods tend to engender adjustments not only in the sheer volume of man-hours, but also in the composition of labor skills and in the ratio of direct to maintenance labor, with attendant shifts in the level and flexibility of wage payments.

The parallel assumption that outputs also are affected solely with respect to their aggregate levels as a result of changes in capital inputs is equally untenable. Effective utilization of the altered service capabilities of individual capital goods, and of subsets of such goods, obviously permits and even encourages changes in the quality of individual products, in the mix of products which can be produced, and in the flexibility of this mix in response to variations in demand. Resulting changes in output cannot be properly evaluated or even measured, therefore, without taking account of such changes in its composition.

In addition to considering such possible effects on other inputs and on outputs of changes in capital inputs, it is obviously inherent in the concept of an integrated production system that changes in capital inputs may also be partly responsive to changes in the other inputs and in outputs—for example, to adjustments in the kinds, qualities, supply, and prices of available material inputs. Recognition of the need to consider the entire network of such interactions instead of arbitrarily assuming the initiating cause and the direction of influence from speculating about observed changes in aggregate relationship, however, emphasizes the importance of clarifying the purposes animating managerial decisions to alter capital inputs.

Alternative Objectives of Increased Capital Inputs

Here again, traditional analysis seems unduly simplified in concentrating on an assumed overriding drive to increase aggregate output relative to capital (or capital and labor) inputs on the grounds that this yields lower unit costs and higher profitability. But if we relax the extreme restrictions within which such theory has been developed, it is obvious that management is less interested in increasing real (physical?) output per unit of real (physical?) capital and labor inputs than in reducing total unit costs—and increases in physical productivity obviously need not yield lower unit costs regardless of attendant factor-price adjustments.

Moreover, management is clearly less interested in reducing total unit costs than in increasing its rate of profit on investment, which may be achieved despite increases in unit costs if they are accompanied by improvements in products and marketing which yield more than offsetting increases in product prices and output levels. Finally, one must recognize that managements may well increase investments merely to maintain, or even to slow the decline of, profitability in the face of even greater threats from rising factor prices, decreasing factor supplies, superior competitive products, or governmental restrictions on operating practices.[13]

In this broader context, it is apparent that capital inputs may be increased for a variety of reasons and hence can be associated with a wide range of changes in output, as well as in factor productivities, total unit costs, average product prices, and rates of return on investment. Among the most important reasons for managerial decisions to increase capital inputs are increasing capacity, reducing production costs, improving products or changing product mix, and responding to governmental health, safety, and pollution regulations. All but the last of these may result in output gains which exceed or fall short of accompanying increases in capital inputs. Moreover, all but the last of these objectives may also be achieved without primary reliance on increases in capital inputs.

For example, increases in capacity may be achieved either by adding new facilities or by improving the utilization of existing resources. Such new facilities might require more than proportionate increases in net capital investment (if undepreciated replicas of existing partially depreciated facilities were added) or less than proportionate increases in net fixed investment (if used to ease a few key-capacity bottlenecks). However, if such new facilities embody new technologies that affect the level or composition of input requirements or the design or mix of products, they might require either more or less than proportionate increases in net capital investment. But capacity increases also can be achieved by improving the quality or level of processing of purchased materials and supplies, by increasing the productivity and utilization of current inputs, by altering product designs, and by concentrating on a narrower range of more standardized products, without requiring significant increases in capital inputs.

Similarly, reductions in total unit costs might involve increases in capital inputs to mechanize manual tasks or introduction of equipment which permits the use of cheaper materials, reduces the wastage of materials and energy, or increases the proportion of output meeting quality standards. Moreover, additional capital inputs also might engender reductions in total unit costs through the economies associated with increases in the scale of production. But it is also obvious that reductions in total unit costs may be achieved by a variety of means not involving significant increases in capital inputs, including changes in material prices, shifts in the skill composition of labor, and improvements in the productivity and utilization of all inputs (including existing capital goods) through advances in production engineering and control.

Effecting product improvements may or may not require additional capital inputs, depending, of course, on the nature of the improvements. And changes in the range of product offerings also may or may not require additional capital inputs, depending on the additional economies offered by the more highly specialized equipment which could be introduced to produce a less diversified product array. But most of the governmental requirements for improving health and safety and reducing pollution do tend to increase capital inputs while maintaining or decreasing marketable output, thus generally increasing capital-output ratios.

In short, observed changes in the relationship between capital inputs and output may or may not involve changes in the productive contributions of capital. Indeed, there is no basis for correctly inferring the dominant causes of changes in aggregate capital-output ratios, and hence, there are no authoritative bases for using the past pattern of such relationships to forecast the effects on output of further increases in capital inputs alone, contrary to widespread interpretations of production functions. Rather, effective estimates of the probable results of increases in capital (or other) inputs awaits the development of fuller understanding (1) of the linkages by means of which various kinds of additional capital inputs interact with other components of the production process in different technological frameworks, (2) of the probable effects of such changes in factor proportions and productivities on costs, and (3) of the effects of such cost adjustments on the determinants of profitability or other performance objectives.

On the Concept of the Productivity of Capital

It has long been recognized that the role of capital in production is affected by variations in output levels. Because of the relatively long-term commitments embodied in a stock of capital goods, short-term fluctuations in operating levels engender comparable fluctuations in the ratio of output to capital stock (whether measured in terms of its productive capacity or its net investment). But interpreting such ratios as representing the productivity of capital involves confusing the level of contributions to production which specified resources can make with the extent to which they are utilized or left idle.

The array of capital goods comprising an integrated production line is assembled, as has been noted, in order to provide a planned level of capacity for producing specified types of products under defined conditions over an extended period of time. Alternative arrays tend to be evaluated in terms of their investment requirements relative to such capacity levels. And it is this measure—capacity per dollar of investment—which most closely accords with the concept of the productivity of capital that has greatest relevance for managerial decision making and performance evaluation. Clearly, this measure reflects the longer-term perspective in which capital goods are acquired as opposed to the shorter-term perspectives common to purchasing materials—in terms of the duration of both the financial commitments made and the productive capabilities acquired. Such integrated stocks of capital goods are assembled despite managerial awareness that output levels tend to fluctuate in most economic sectors. Hence to measure the effectiveness or productivity of such stocks of durable goods in terms of the ratio of current output to net investment would yield highly variable results without practical significance for management. Specifically, such volatile findings would not enable management to determine whether its capital stock was too small or too large, or whether its composition was undesirable, indicating, over the short run, only variations in the degree of utilization of the productive capabilities which are on hand and embodying investment.

This view accordingly suggests modification of the usual concepts of factor proportions. Instead of using the ratio of net investment to man-hours, for example, account should be taken of the partial idleness of the capital stock by measuring the ratio of "actively utilized net investment" (that is, net investment multiplied by the ratio of output to capacity) to man-hours. This would not only better reflect actual inputs absorbed into production, but also avoid the absurd finding that capital inputs per man-hour tend to *increase* when output declines and *decrease* when output recovers.

Consideration of factor proportions, however, also raises questions concerning the productive contributions made by the inputs being measured. Increased mechanization, for example, usually results in increases in output per man-hour (attributable to the displacement of labor) and decreases in output relative to capital inputs (due to the added investment in facilities and equipment). These are then commonly interpreted as demonstrating increases in the productivity of labor and decreases in the productivity of capital. But such crude comparisons of aggregate inputs with aggregate outputs without consideration of the possible changes in the role of each input in production could be used to demonstrate a tremendous increase in the "productivity" of horses in agriculture. In fact, however, closer analysis suggests that in most such instances of mechanization, parts of labor's productive tasks have been shifted to machinery, thus reducing labor's contribution to output along with a reduction in the total volume of labor inputs. But this means that the productive contributions of capital have increased. Clearly, therefore, labor's contributions per man-hour have increased less than the gain in output per man-hour, and may not have increased at all, while the productive contributions of capital goods have increased more than is indicated by the change in the ratio of output to capital inputs. Thus effective consideration of the role of capital in production and meaningful measurement of the productivity of capital require consideration not only of accompanying changes in output, but also of changes in the proportioning of the underlying productive tasks and contributions.

But what happens to the productivity of a given stock of capital goods through time? Over the first few years, commonly prevailing depreciation practices tend to reduce the net investment more rapidly than the productive capacity, progressively increasing the productivity of the net investment still embodied in the capital stock. Beyond some point, the economically effective capacity begins to decline more rapidly than the residual net investment, partly as a result of wear and increasingly as a result of changes in product design and product mix, as well as the pressures of emerging improvements in processing methods and capital goods. As a result, the productivity of the stock turns downward.[14]

This longer-term pattern is significant for two reasons. First, it emphasizes that the acquisition of new productive facilities, even those involving substantial technological advances, commonly results in an initial decline in the productivity of capital. This would occur whenever the ratio of the investment cost of the new facilities to the depreciated residual investment in the existing capital stock exceeds the ratio of the resulting increase in capacity to the existing capacity level. The importance of this outcome is frequently underestimated, especially in the case of modernization programs which are expected to decrease unit costs and thus increase profitability. In such instances, major acquisitions of new facilities may increase net investment substantially while merely maintaining capacity, and the resulting sharp reduction in the productivity of capital may substantially curtail the contributions of attendant cost savings to profitability.[15]

A second effect of this decrease in the productivity of fixed investment during the early years after new acquisitions is related to the traditional assumption that prospective buyers evaluate innovative facilities and processes by comparing their average total unit costs with the average variable unit costs of existing facilities. But this seems vulnerable both because the heavy initial depreciation charges on facilities tends to exaggerate their average total unit costs over a longer period, and because, as has been noted, management decisions would be more soundly guided by comparing the prospective effects on profit rates rather than on relative costs alone.

Attention also must be given to expected changes over time in the productivity of capital stocks subject to periodic replacements of various components. Resulting adjustment patterns tend to be shaped largely by interactions between the rate of technological progress in the relevant sector, compared with changes in input availabilities, processing requirements, and output characteristics, and by the timing of capital acquisitions relative to cyclical fluctuations and long-term trends in the prices of the capital goods involved. Technological progress tends to be positive, of course, in virtually all sectors of production. But reductions in the quality and availability of materials may offset such gains either wholly or in part. In addition, similar offsets may be engendered by safety and other restrictions on operating methods and by changes in the variety and quality of products. The prices of capital goods tend to be characterized by a wide amplitude of cyclical fluctuations, because fluctuations in demand are intensified by the relatively small size of the industries that produce capital goods as compared with the users of their products. Hence the investment cost of any given array of facilities may vary considerably over a cycle, and further effects would result, of course, during extended periods of inflationary or deflationary trends.[16]

In general, then, technological advances tend to produce progressive increases in the productivity of capital as compared with facilities and equipment embodying earlier technologies, if purchased at equal prices and operated under identical conditions. But actual outcomes are less predictable and may vary more widely among different industries and different time periods depending on adjustments in the other factors cited. In the U.S. steel industry, for example, advances in technology produced large increases in the productivity of capital from 1904 to 1947, but continuing technological advances were associated with a steady downtrend in the productivity of capital over the next 20 years, as shown in chapter 10.

Capacity Utilization and Capacity Additions

Another traditional conception bearing on the role of capital in production is that the cost advantages of maximizing capacity utilization ensures that capacity additions are made only when the rate of capacity utilization is approaching its practical peak (allowing for maintenance and so on).[17] Thus capacity additions in any firm or industry are envisioned as describing a series of steps, each riser occurring as output levels close in on the existing capacity ceiling. This may, of course, happen on occasion. But it is quite common, and may well be more widely true, that capacity additions tend to parallel output trends, with substantial gaps between them of 15 to 20 percent or more being sustained over long periods, especially at the level of industries and larger economic sectors, but also in the case of multiplant firms.[18]

Failure to recognize the causes and importance of such gaps have led to serious errors in interpreting findings of capacity underutilization. Largely because of the insidious influence of early static analysis, such underutilization continues to be ascribed almost automatically to fluctuations in demand. While this is certainly the single most important cause of variations in capacity utilization, it does not follow that it also explains consistent gaps between capacity and output. These are traceable, rather, to three reflections of dynamic forces in the economy:

1. Technological improvements in processing methods and facilities, which encourage new additions even when existing facilities are underutilized.
2. Development of new products and changes in the design and quality standards of established products which cannot be effectively produced on existing facilities.
3. Geographical shifts in markets and in the most advantageous location of in-

puts and services which offer benefits for relocation that overshadow the cost of partial underutilization of existing capacity.

Identification of such causes has several important implications. First, instead of necessarily signifying shortcomings in capacity planning, or in current pricing and distribution policies, capacity underutilization may be attributable in substantial measure to the vigor of technological and economic changes. Hence the magnitude of the average gap between capacity and output may be a better measure of progressiveness than of industrial "maturity" or "senility," tending to be much greater in the chemical and electronics industries, for example, than in bread baking. Second, current measures of capacity utilization may prove to be vulnerable indicators both of the additional increases in production which can be supplied without intensifying inflationary pressures[19] and also of the level of new capital requirements. Third, such experiential data can provide bases for revising depreciation schedules to provide more realistic reflections of the effective working lives of capital facilities.

At a still more fundamental level, such considerations invite more serious analytical inquiries concerning the optimum level of underutilization of economic resources. Clearly, full utilization would substantially hamper such reallocations as are required to adapt to those patently constructive pressures. Full utilization would also tend to minimize the competitive pressures which help to engender responsiveness to such opportunities for improving market position and profitability.

Adaptations of a Capital Stock to Changing Requirements

In what ways and to what extent can a given capital stock be adapted to changes in inputs, outputs, or production technology? It is recognized that competitive pressures tend to encourage increasing specialization of the individual facilities and equipment comprising the capital stock, as well as progressively tighter integration of successive operations—that is, increases in scale—in industrial sectors producing large quantities of relatively standardized products. But this emphasizes that industrial sectors differ widely in the adaptability of their capital stocks to the kinds of changes being discussed, thereby limiting the applicability of generalizations focused on large-scale operations.

Even such operations, however, are capable of continuing adaptations to changes in inputs, outputs, and production methods, albeit through different means, to more limited degrees, at slower rates, and probably at greater costs. Indeed, except in the case of relatively new plants, functioning capital stocks almost invariably consist of capital goods of different vintages. These reflect not only the necessary replacement of some capital goods that have worn out, but also past adaptations to external pressures, including the displacement of other capital goods made redundant by changing needs and the addition of new capital goods representing either technological advances since acquisition of the original equipment or improved adaptations to changing input availabilities or output requirements. In addition, needed adaptations also may include the underutilization of some capital goods, modifications in the tooling and controls on others, and changes in the processing techniques employing such facilities.

It should also be noted, however, that the adaptation of capital stocks to changing needs may involve adjustments reaching beyond capital inputs alone. In some cases, they may require the use of additional labor to offset the limitations of specialized machinery. Often they are likely to involve changes in procurement, perhaps requiring the purchasing of more highly processed materials or fabricated components. Moreover, possible changes in product mix also provide a measure of flexibility in adapting to changing needs.

To identify the nature of such impacts more effectively, it is necessary to recognize that even highly integrated production systems consist of numerous stages involving highly differentiated productive activities (or processes) and capital goods. But changes in technology or in inputs or outputs seldom affect all such stages. On the contrary, most such developments exert their major impacts on only one or a few stages. Hence their immediate effects on total plant operations tend to be far more limited than the expectation conjured up by the term *major technological innovations.* Over time, of course, these original effects may engender additional effects through further adaptations in operations antecedent and subsequent to those affected directly. And such expanding effects, reinforced by similar developments in competing plants, may be expected to affect factor and product markets, with eventual repercussions on producers in the form of new pressures requiring adaptations.

In short, the adaptability of existing capital stocks to changing requirements varies widely among industries and differs even within given plants depending on the nature of the adjustments to be effected. Moreover, the absorption of such external impacts may involve all inputs, not just capital, and may involve the design, mix, and level of outputs as well. Accordingly, attempts to generalize the effects of such a wide array of possible changes on an even broader array of industrial processes may yield deductions of greater interest to logicians than to decision makers in industry or in government.

Some Broader Implications of the Revised Concepts

The most important implication of these revisions in concepts is that capital inputs encompass an array of goods which are so heterogeneous with respect to the nature and levels of their contributions to production as to minimize the practical applicability of generalizations about them. This means that increases in total capital inputs may or may not increase output, decrease costs, or expand employment—in plants, in industries, or nationally. To develop more effective bases for explaining such past relationships, or for forecasting the effects of future changes, it is necessary to identify more precisely the kinds of capital inputs involved; the purposes for which they were increased; the industrial contexts in which these adjustments were made; attendant changes in the quality, mix, and prices of other associated inputs as well as outputs; and any accompanying changes in the technology and scale of the processes involved.

Another important implication is that indexes of changes in the prices of capital goods are subject to severe shortcomings, especially over periods of more than a few years. And such indexes are even more vulnerable when applied to the highly diversified stocks of capital representing the integrated production systems of specific plants and industries. This raises serious doubts about the meaning of purported measures of changes in physical stocks of capital or real capital, and it also suggests that the use of such price indexes to estimate the current or future replacement values of a firm's stock of facilities and equipment is likely to be accompanied by ranges of potential error so wide as to make it difficult to interpret the results.

It is also worth emphasizing that the technological changes which are a major source of changes in the composition and capabilities of capital inputs engender such pervasive changes in virtually all economic relationships as to undermine most of the current methodologies used in attempting to measure their effects (Burmeister [4]). There is no effective method for excluding the effects of technological changes from measures of changes in output, prices, or costs. Attempts to deflate values or costs by indexes of the general price level do not measure real values or costs, that is, what they would have been in the absence of changes in the general price level. Instead they merely measure changes in the values and costs of a given sector of the economy relative to the average changes in the economy as a whole. But the latter includes the average effects of all changes in technology experienced by the economy. Hence a finding that an industry's deflated unit costs show no decrease should be interpreted as showing that these approximated the average result in the rest of the economy rather than that it had made no real progress at all (Gold [7, pp. 203-207]). Even within individual industries and plants it is not possible to exclude technological effects from such measurements, because resulting changes in the kinds and qualities of inputs and outputs engender changes in their market prices and thus prevent measurements of adjustments independent of these technologically induced changes.

The primary focus of this chapter has been on the microeconomic aspects of the role of capital, because it is only at the level of plants and firms that one can explore the actual role of such inputs in production and thus uncover both the variety of factors affecting that role and the range of variations in such roles among plants, firms, and industries. Decisions to increase or decrease capital inputs, to alter their composition, to modify their proportioning to other inputs, or to change the methods of utilizing them must be made at a level where they can be integrated with other decisions affecting a management's guiding objectives. Such decisions cannot be made at the level of industries (except where these are nationalized or monopolistic entities), because an industry is merely an arbitrary grouping of separate plants. Nor can one assume a high degree of homogeneity among the capital decisions of firms within each industry in view of the obviously substantial differences among them with respect to size, resources, product mix, market position, locational advantages and disadvantages, technical strength, and the patterning of managerial objectives.

But such reasoning, in turn, raises serious questions about the validity of assuming such homogeneities as the analysis shifts to industry, region, and still higher levels of aggregation.[20] Such assumptions are rarely made about natural resources or material inputs because of their obvious inapplicability. Hence these inputs have generally been minimized in macroeconomic analyses—not without undermining their value. The enormous importance of capital in production, however, leaves no alternative to the development of an improved understanding of its role in macroeconomics by digging beneath the superficialities of assumed homogeneities to clarify the various and complex roles of such inputs and the disparities among their resulting effects.

In short, one can readily sympathize with the temptation to avoid the daunting complexities of allocating and utilizing actual inputs in actual industries under changing pressures. But there is little scientific achievement or social contribution in avoiding such entanglements by soaring beyond mundane realities to concentrate on interesting but largely imaginary problems. It is well to recall Oskar Morgenstern's warning that "the primary task is to discover the true nature of the underlying economic phenomena and to concentrate efforts in that direction instead of stopping short and branching out into the mathematical treatment of all ill-defined and vaguely described situation" [18]. To strengthen such insights, however, the preceding discussion suggests a need to revise some of our basic conceptions of production processes as well as some of our basic questions and evaluative criteria so as to reflect more effectively the actual economic relationships that we are seeking to understand.

Notes

1. For an excellent recent review of major sectors of capital theory, see Burmeister [4]. The tenuous relevance of most of its coverage to the urgent problems of actual capital management emphasizes the continuing gap between the focuses of academic controversy and the more mundane, but not necessarily less important, issues faced in allocating, utilizing, and evaluating actual capital inputs in actual production.

2. There was a considerable upsurge of interest in these approaches during the 1930s, centering around Hayek's *Prices and Production* [12] and including papers by Frank Knight [16] and others (for example, Hill [14] and Theiss [21]).

3. In a recent review of concepts of real capital, Hicks emphasized this as one of the two theoretically appropriate measures, but added the pithy comment, "It may not be easy to find a suitable index [of the prices of capital goods to be used for deflation], but that is not here my concern" [13, p. 208].

4. Although this has gained renewed popularity during the current energy "crisis," it has long roots reaching back to Jerome [15, pp. 205-226] and even earlier to the horsepower data collected by the U.S. Census of Manufactures.

5. This is regarded by Hicks as the only other theoretically appropriate measure of "real capital," representing its "value" sense, while the measure cited in note 3 would represent "real capital" in its "physical" sense [13, pp. 309].

6. For a detailed discussion of these problems and approaches, see Gold [6, pp. 18-30].

7. For a fuller examination of these problems, see Gold [6, pp. 25-30].

8. The difficulties of evaluating changes in service features are illustrated in Griliches [11] and Gold [6, pp. 23-30]. For one crude method of estimating such adjustments, see Gold [6, pp. 94-97].

9. It has been argued that broad indexes of capital goods prices are justified on the grounds that the factor-price changes which affect them tend to sweep through wide reaches of the economy instead of being narrowly compartmentalized by industries. While this is likely to be more true of labor than of basic materials, the more serious shortcoming of such a rationalization is that it ignores the heavy influence on capital goods' prices of technological advances in product design and manufacturing processes which are quite disparate among the wide array of industries producing capital goods.

10. For a fuller discussion, see Gold [10].

11. Even current prices for replaceable capital goods are based on limited current replacement demand and do not indicate what such prices would be if current replacement levels were sharply increased or changed in composition.

12. The cost of purchased materials and supplies has averaged more than 50 percent of the value of products for "all manufacturing" in the United States for more than 75 years, according to the Census of Manufactures. For examples, see Gold [7, p. 137] and Gold [8, p. 12].

13. For application of an analytical framework encompassing these broader considerations, and for related discussion, see Eilon et al. [5, pp. 16-39].

14. For detailed discussion, see Gold [6, pp. 135-140].

15. The relative magnitudes of these opposing pressures on the rates of profit to total investment may be illustrated by a grossly oversimplified example stipulating increases of 25 percent in net fixed investment and 20 percent in

total investment, with no change in capacity, output, and product price. This would require a 12 percent reduction in unit material plus unit wage costs merely to prevent an immediate decline in the profit to total investment ratio as a result of the concomitant increase in investment charges per unit of output and decrease in the capacity to fixed investment ratio. Thus

$$\frac{\text{Profit}}{\text{Total investment}} \equiv \frac{\text{profit}}{\text{output}} \times \frac{\text{output}}{\text{capacity}} \times \frac{\text{capacity}}{\text{fixed invest.}} \times \frac{\text{fixed investment}}{\text{total investment}}$$

$$\equiv \frac{\text{profit}}{\text{output}} \times \frac{100}{100} \times \frac{100}{125} \times \frac{125}{120} = \frac{\text{profit}}{\text{output}} \times \frac{100}{120}$$

Hence, profit/total investment would remain unchanged if profit/output rose 20 percent. Assuming a profit margin of 20 percent and fixed prices, an increase of 20 percent in profit per unit of output would require a 5 percent decrease in total unit costs. Assume cost proportions as follows: materials plus wages, 75 percent; investment charges, 20 percent; salaries, 5 percent. Then a 20 percent increase in investment charges per unit would require a 12 percent drop in unit material plus wages and no change in unit salary cost to yield the needed 5 percent reduction in total unit costs. One need hardly comment on the extraordinary difficulties confronting efforts to reduce unit-material and unit-wage costs by such proportions within a short period.

16. For further discussion, see Gold [6, pp. 135-145].

17. This discussion is focused on the relationship between capacity and capacity-utilization rates under whatever conditions are considered to represent normal practice in any context. For an interesting discussion of the economic implications of differences in conceptions of normal daily, annual, and cyclical use rates, see Winston [23].

18. Such persistent gaps have been found in various industries, including steel, cement, and paper, as well as chemicals. Such dynamic factors also help to explain the large proportion of total unemployment which represents labor out of work for less than 1 year. And although the classic findings by the Brookings Institution's investigation of the U.S. economy on the brink of the depression, that our capacity to produce had been underutilized by some 20 percent, was interpreted as demonstrating serious shortcomings in the functioning of the economy, much of this may in fact have attested to its vigor instead (Moulton, [17, p. 21]).

19. Fuller utilization of capacity involves the use of older and less efficient facilities with higher operating costs—and probably of less productive labor as well. For further discussion, see chapter 5.

20. The changing loci of homogeneities at increasing levels of aggregation and of attendant shifts in effective focuses for analysis were discussed in chapter 3.

References

[1] R.K. Adamson and M.E. West, *Productivity and Employment in Selected Industries: Beet Sugar* (Philadelphia: National Research Project of the U.S. Works Progress Administration in cooperation with the National Bureau of Economic Research, 1938).

[2] H.C. Bauman, *Fundamentals of Cost Engineering in the Chemical Industry* (New York: Reinhold, 1964).

[3] E.F. Beach, "A Measure of Physical Capital," *The Review of Economic Statistics,* February 1938.

[4] Edwin Burmeister, "Neo-Austrian and Alternative Approaches to Capital Theory," *Journal of Economic Literature,* June 1974.

[5] S. Eilon, B. Gold, and J. Soesan, *Applied Productivity Analysis for Industry* (Oxford: Pergamon, 1976).

[6] B. Gold, *Foundations of Productivity Analysis* (Pittsburgh: Univ. of Pittsburgh Press, 1955.

[7] B. Gold, *Explorations in Managerial Economics: Productivity, Costs, Technology and Growth* (New York: Basic Books; London; Macmillan, 1971).

[8] B. Gold (ed.), *Technological Change: Economics, Management and Environment* (Oxford: Pergamon, 1975, 1979).

[9] B. Gold (ed.), *Research, Technological Change and Economic Analysis* (Lexington, Mass.: Lexington Books, D.C. Heath, 1977).

[10] B. Gold, "On the Shaky Foundations of Capital Budgeting," *California Management Review,* Fall 1976.

[11] Z. Griliches (ed.), *Price Indexes and Quality Change* (Cambridge: Harvard Univ. Press, 1971).

[12] F.A. Hayek, *Prices and Production* (London: Routledge, 1931).

[13] J.R. Hicks, "Capital Controversies: Ancient and Modern," *American Economic Review–Papers and Proceedings,* May 1974.

[14] Martin Hill, "The Period of Production and Industrial Fluctuations," *Economic Journal,* December 1933.

[15] Harry Jerome, *Mechanization in Industry* (New York: National Bureau of Economic Research, 1934).

[16] F.H. Knight, "Professor Hayek and the Theory of Investment," *Economic Journal,* March 1935.

[17] H.G. Moulton, *Income and Economic Progress* (Washington: The Brookings Institution, 1935).

[18] O. Morgenstern, "Limits to the Uses of Mathematics in Economics," in J.C. Charlesworth (ed.), *Mathematics and the Social Sciences* (Philadelphia: American Academy of Political and Social Sciences, June 1963).

[19] R.R. Nelson (ed.), *The Rate and Direction of Inventive Activity: Economic and Social Factors* (Princeton: Princeton Univ. Press, 1962).

[20] W.H. Shaw, *The Value of Commodity Output since 1869* (New York: National Bureau of Economic Research, 1947).

[21] E. Theiss, "Time and Capitalistic Production," *Journal of Political Economy,* August 1932.

[22] M.E. West, *Productivity and Employment in Selected Industries: Brick and Tile* (Philadelphia: National Research Project of the U.S. Works Progress Administration in cooperation with the National Bureau of Economic Research, 1939).

[23] G.C. Winston, "The Theory of Capital Utilization and Idleness," *Journal of Economic Literature,* December 1974.

5 Determinants of Changes in Productivity Relationships

In order to develop more effective strategies for improving productivity levels, it is necessary to understand the major determinants of such adjustments and the probable pattern of results stemming from each. Among the multiplicity of factors which affect industrial operations, eight major types may be identified as having an important bearing on productivity levels and on the role of capital inputs. These are changes in (1) the scope of production (that is, the array of operations between purchased inputs and finished products), (2) the product mix, (3) the utilization of productive capacity, (4) the nature and quality of inputs, (5) the design of products, (6) the nature of technological processes, (7) the scale of production, and (8) the effectiveness of integrating and controlling operations. The last five of these are largely determined by technological improvements, thus explaining their powerful role in determining productivity levels.

Nontechnological Determinants

Changes in the Scope of Operations

The scope of production may be changed by altering the level of forward or backward integration. Thus it can be expanded by increasing the output of still more highly processed products or the purchase of less highly processed materials and supplies—and it can be narrowed by shifts in the opposite directions. Such changes tend to affect average productivity relationships because input-output ratios are almost invariably different in successive stages of production.

In general, increases in the scope of operations tend to be motivated by the desire to seek the greater productive economies and market advantages deemed to be attainable through achievement of integrated control over more of the successive stages in the fabrication process. Contractions in the scope of operations are usually associated with the desire to slough off particularly troublesome, risky, or costly sectors of production by taking advantage of the specialized facilities of would-be suppliers, especially when effective competition among them tends to ensure reasonable prices and adequate servicing of needs. It should be recognized, however, that in complex manufacturing operations that require expensive facilities and considerable technical knowledge and experience, changes in the scope of operations are likely to be made only infrequently and gradually, except as temporary expedients, because of the heavy burdens which are usually involved both in extending operations to cover additional levels of processing and in liquidating established operations and facilities. Finally, one may hazard the judgment, however, that changes in the scope of operations are more likely to increase than to decrease productivity levels, except when considerations of attendant market advantages outweigh the drive for productive economies.

Changes in Product Mix

Changes in the product composition of output affect the average productivity relationships in a plant to the extent that products require different combinations of operations and hence different levels of each input per unit of output. Adjustments in product mix may be responsive to seasonal or cyclical variations in the relative demand for various products as well as to long-term changes reflecting the progressive displacement of older products by new ones. All industries experience the latter, and most are also subject to the former.

In some industries, output recessions may shift product mix toward an increasing concentration on cheaper and more standardized products whose production processes may well be characterized by more favorable input-output relationships. In other industries, the opposite tendency may be dominant, as manufacturers seek to attract additional buyers by offering products more fully adapted to the customer's specialized preferences. In either case, however, recurrent changes in product mix obviously tend to produce similarly recurrent fluctuations in productivity relationships as opposed to affecting their long-term trends.

The introduction of new products frequently results in lower productivity levels than those already attained in the production of older products, because output volume tends to be lower, production techniques are still being developed, and price pressures are usually less severe. But increasing experience in producing such products, together with expanding output and growing competition, may well raise productivity levels in these newer sectors of output rapidly enough to approximate and even exceed the productivity levels characterizing older product lines by the time the new products achieve a major position within the structure of total output. Hence the progressive adjustment of the product composition of output need not prevent continuing increases in the productivity of operations as a whole.

Changes in Capacity-Utilization Rates

In the short run, changes in the rate of operations tend to be attributable primarily to variations in demand, for capacity tends to be more stable than output. Over the long run, changes may be expected both in output levels and in productive capacity, but there is no basis for expecting any persistent trend toward either expanding or narrowing the gap between them. In other words, capacity tends to be adjusted through time to the trend in physical output.

The effects of changes in the rate of operations on productivity levels depend on the flexibility of resource inputs, on the nature of the adjustments made in production processes, and on the focuses of the productivity measures employed. The flexibility of resource inputs depends on both the terms of procurement and the degree of specialization of input units. In the case of purchased materials, inputs can usually be readily adjusted to variations in production levels, both because procurement arrangements tend to be attuned to short-term needs and also because each category of purchased materials is internally homogeneous. On the other hand, inputs of capital goods may be regarded as representing the opposite extreme. Except in the few industries where capital equipment is rented, such facilities are generally acquired outright and hence remain available and involve costs on a continuous basis despite variations in output levels.

In the case of wage earners, the flexibility of inputs tends to be intermediate between that of materials and capital goods. Such flexibility is hardly hampered by the terms of employment, although the attendant costs of recruiting and training, together with the risk of losing good employees as a result of layoffs, may tend to moderate the amplitude of fluctuations in employment relative to those affecting production. But flexibility does tend to be limited by the degree of specialization of jobs and worker skills. Specifically, the smaller the number of workers performing identical jobs and the greater the differentiation in the skill and experience requirements of each job, the more limited will be the flexibility of employment in the face of output declines.

In short, as a result of the differential flexibility of the various categories of inputs, changes in the rate of operations may be expected to affect the factor-proportions component of productivity relationships. Such differential flexibility also affects the average productivity of labor and capital for the production process as a whole, in view of the tendency for these inputs to decline less than proportionately to a decline in output, thus reducing the ratio of total output to total input of each of these resources.[1] It should also be recognized that productivity gains from increasing capacity unilization tend to diminish and then disappear as operation rates rise progressively beyond, say, 90 to 95 percent because of some capacity imbalances among successive operations and because of the increasing difficulties of maintaining complete coordination of all production activities as margins for misalignment are squeezed. Moreover, productivity gains may reach a peak at even lower levels of capacity utilization unless increases in inputs are not characterized by declines in their quality, as will be discussed later.

Finally, it may be useful to recall the discussion in chapter 4 of the effects of less frequent but no less important changes in capacity-utilization rates resulting from capacity additions. At the level of existing plants, such increases usually take the form of augmenting the capabilities of operations which represent bottlenecks, thus serving to increase the attainable utilization rates of other operations as well as of the plant as a whole, and thereby facilitating improvements in past productivity relationships. It should be emphasized, however, that additions to capacity need not lead to increases in utilization rates and related productivity benefits. In many cases, this may represent only a temporary reduction in utilization rates until sales are increased enough to absorb the additional capacity. But in many other cases, capacity additions are made in recognition of the current or prospective need to meet market pressures that require new production facilities, either to increase productive efficiency or to produce qualitatively better or entirely new kinds of products. Such additions may sooner or later prove to be replacements—and as such, they would be represented by a short-term increase in capacity, accompanied by a decrease in utilization rate, followed by eventual reductions in capacity and accompanying potential increases in utilization rates. Of course, both kinds of capacity replacements would be expected to improve profitability, but these may or may not yield improvements in productivity relationships as well, as has already been noted in the preceding chapter.

Basic Technological Determinants

The technological changes which are most likely to affect industrial productivity relationships are largely encompassed by the following categories:

1. *Alterations in the design of products*: (a) to improve the quality of services to users (including convenience, flexibility, durability, reliability, and safety); (b) to provide new kinds of services to users; and (c) to reduce the input requirements and ease the production problems of manufacturers.
2. *Changes in the design and scale of operating processes, facilities, and equipment*: (a) to improve speed, precision, yields relative to inputs, safety, and reliability; (b) to increase capacity; (c) to permit the production of new or improved products; (d) to permit adaptation to changed material inputs; and (e) to reduce the level and alter the composition of labor requirements.
3. *Improvements in control systems*: (a) to increase automaticity; (b) to minimize deviations from desired operating conditions, flow rates, and product quality; and (c) to facilitate effective adjustments to changes in output levels and product mix.
4. *Modifications in the physical and chemical properties of material inputs, as well as the introduction of new types*: (a) to offset shortages or decreases in the quality, or increases in the price, of customary materials; (b) to minimize transportation costs; (c) to reduce waste in processing; and (d) to improve product attributes.

Such categories have proved useful in efforts to organize the helter-skelter outpouring of technological innovations for analytical purposes. At least they offer constructive guidance for penetrating beneath the not uncommon treatment of technological change by economists as though it were a homogeneous variable with generalizable sources and effects. Nevertheless, it must be recognized that many important technological developments in industry cannot be confined within any one of the preceding categories. The fundamental reasons are the technological and economic pressures for the progressively tighter integration of successive stages of operation to conserve energy and time, to reduce intermediate handling and inventories, and to promote the mutual reinforcement of adjacent control sectors. Thus the creation of new kinds of production facilities frequently entails modifications of the kinds of inputs best adapted to them as well as alterations in production-control devices and in the characteristics of resulting products.

Changes in Product Design

Changes in the design of existing products may, of corse, be slight or quite substantial. And they may be introduced either to enhance the product attributes which appeal to buyers or to facilitate production and reduce attendant costs. But the frequency of design changes involving significant alterations in production operations tends to be restricted by pressures to maximize both economies of standardization and the benefits of utilizing the skills, knowledge, and facilities already on hand.

Product design changes affect productivity relationships primarily by altering the proportions in which input factors are combined, although they may also affect needed input qualities and output specifications. But such effects are likely to be sizable only in the relatively few operations directly modified by the usual succession of limited redesigns. Hence resulting changes in productivity relationships—which may either increase or decrease particular factor productivities and factor proportions—are likely to be of modest proportions.

It should also be recognized, however, that in industries producing style goods, and in industries still subject to frequent major changes in product designs, the reduction of production costs may be considered less urgent than product improvements, with the result that greater emphasis tends to be placed on skills and facilities which are readily adaptable to shifts in product design, even if such flexibility is obtained at the cost of less favorable productivity relationships.

Changes in the Nature of Production Processes

Changes in the nature of production processes generally represent the application of scientific and technological progress. Such applications assume a wide range of forms which can be distinguished from one another only crudely. At one extreme, they take the form of a continuing stream of individually minor advances affecting narrow segments of the production process and emanating from the efforts of workmen, foremen, and engineers as well as research and development personnel. At the opposite extreme may be listed those infrequent, basic advances which result in sweeping revisions of entire production processes. Between these extremes are found a wide variety of developments affecting smaller or larger components of production processes. As among these categories of advance, past experience suggests that the more far-reaching innovations are also likely to be the less frequent—both because of the heavier burdens involved in applying them and because major advances in science and technology are likely to emerge only at comparatively long intervals. It should also be emphasized, however, that the cumulative effects of many minor advances may approach and even overshadow the consequences of more spectacular developments, and yet elicit far less managerial attention.

The objectives of such process improvements, as listed earlier, (p. 88) make it quite clear that these need not be directed toward improving productivity relationships, except when such gains promise reasonably attractive rewards relative to the risks, costs, and possible turmoil involved in their development and utilization. It should also be emphasized in this connection that advances in technological processes and associated facilities and equipment often yield significant advantages over existing operations only within very restricted conditions. Hence their diffusion rates may seem incomprehensibly slow to observers unaware of such product-specific and plant-specific limitations and of the further improvements consequently needed to expand the proportion of potential adopters to whom the innovation offers reasonably attractive net returns.[2]

Changes in the nature of productive processes probably account for the most important and pervasive changes in industrial productivity relationships. Such innovations may affect any and every component of the productivity network, with effects proportional to the scope and coverage of the advances involved.

Changes in Scale of Production

One way to increase productive capacity is to add new production units that are essentially duplicates of the original production units or plants with respect to the subdivision of tasks, the nature of the processes used, and the characteristics of the materials, labor, and capital facilities and equipment employed. Indeed this represents the traditional concept of scale in economic theory: reflecting changes in "all factors at the same time in the same degree." This would result in greater output, of course, but it would involve little or no change in factor proportions or in the productivity of inputs. As a matter of fact, such a concept of scale is irrelevant to many, and probably most, of the industrial phenomena to which economists seek to apply it: the effects of increases in the size of plants.[3] Large plants are rarely enlarged replicas of small plants. And if they were, it is difficult ot understand where the expected significant economies would come from.[4]

A quite different means of increasing productive capacity involves the revision of productive processes to achieve the economies that result from the further degrees of specialization made possible by higher levels of capacity. Moreover, it is this species of change which more properly may be designated as involving an increase in the *scale,* defined as relating to the level of planned productive capacity that has determined the extent to which specialization has been applied in the subdivision of the component tasks of a unified operation. By narrowing the range of skills and efforts required in individual tasks, specialization generally makes possible the design of more productive equipment, the development of greater facility by workmen on their assigned tasks, and the elimination of the delays usually associated with shifts from one kind of task to another. In addition, as tasks are narrowed in performance characteristics and increasingly standardized in method, the possibilities of mechanization are increased. Thus adjustments in the level of specialization may affect factor proportions as well as the productivity of different inputs.

But the practical limits of specialization tend to be determined in large measure by the level of productive capacity, inasmuch as each separate task must be performed with sufficient frequency to fully occupy the workers and equipment assigned to it—otherwise these resources would have to be assigned to several tasks in order to escape the losses involved in idleness. Moreover, it should be noted also in this connection that the productivity potentials even of mechanized processes may be raised by increases in capacity that permit the utilization of still more highly specialized and more effectively designed facilities—engineering principles apparently providing means of increasing productive capacity more rapidly than attendant construction costs with respect to a wide variety of capital facilities.

Attention should also be called to the limitation in the suggested definition of scale, implied by the words *unified operation.* This means that increases in the planned capacity of a given plant may be accompanied by a reduction rather than an increase in the scale of production if the expansion involves a proliferation of product lines, that is, if it involves a reduction in the productive capacity of the unified operations allocated to each line of products. Conversely, the scale of production might be increased without any change in total productive capacity if operations were redesigned so as to produce fewer products. But the scale of production need not be changed either by changes in the productive capacity of a plant or by changes in the variety of products manufactured unless these changes are accompanied by readjustments in the level of specialization of the unified production processes encompassed.

In short, changes in productive capacity involving adjustments in the scale of production may affect both factor proportions and the productivity of input factors at the level of individual tasks and at the level of operations as a whole. On the other hand, changes in capacity involving merely the duplication of existing production processes are likely to leave productivity levels unchanged, except to the extent that the new equipment surpasses the productivity of the stock already on hand. One may also hazard the hypotheses that increases in the scale of production are likely to be accompanied by increases in the productivity of materials, labor, and capital facilities; that, among these, the gains in the productivity of capital facilities are likely to be the greatest over extended periods of time; and that the heavier burdens of planning and control involved in increasing the scale of production are likely to require a relatively greater increase in supervisory, technical, and clerical personnel than in direct labor and material inputs.

Changes in the Effectiveness of Integrating Operations

Changes in the effectiveness with which production operations are integrated may be attributed to adjustments in plant layout, in production planning and control, in inventory management, in materials handling, and in other sectors of production management. The guiding objectives of such adjustments are to minimize input requirements relative to output by curtailing the wastage and idleness of resources. Reductions in the idleness of resources are most commonly effected by avoiding shortages and excessive supplies of purchased materials, by minimizing dislocations in the flow of work, by adjusting employment levels in accordance with fluctuations in production levels, by balancing the capacity of capital facilities at successive stages of production, and by establishing output standards on all tasks so as to facilitate the effective coordination of work flows. Resource wastage is most commonly attacked by reducing failures of material through the development of more effective procurement specifications, by reducing the volume of substandard production through better equipment maintenance and improved quality-control arrangements, and by eliminating unnecessary operations and haulage.

Such changes in the effectiveness with which production operations are integrated are likely to be frequent and numerous but of individually small proportions, except for temporary emergencies and rare overhauls of operations as a whole. The latter has occurred with increasing frequency in recent years as a result of the spreading of integrated production planning and control systems based on increasing computerization. Although productivity levels may be affected adversely on occasion, the techniques of coordination tend to improve progressively and hence to raise productivity levels. Such advances may, of course, affect both factor proportions and the productivity of inputs on particular tasks and for operations as a whole. It should be emphasized, however, that these gains are derived overwhelmingly from reductions in the idleness and wastage of resources rather than from the other sources of such advances which have been discussed.

Changes in the Quality of Inputs

Changes in the quality of inputs represent an interaction between changes in available market offerings and changes in plant needs resulting from technological and managerial efforts to increase the effectiveness with which input specifications and production requirments are adapted to one another. The quality of inputs may be defined in terms of the practical production potentials which they bring to the particular jobs for which they are employed. In general, the quality of each category of inputs may either increase or decrease, thereby tending to engender productivity adjustments in the same direction.

Improvements in the quality of materials inputs may take the form of increased strength, greater uniformity, or advances in other attributes that tend to reduce the quantity of such materials required per unit of acceptable output. But the quality of incoming supplies may also deteriorate, either as a result of shortages in the supply of higher-quality materials or as a result of managerial pressures for reduced outlays. With respect to the actual pattern of adjustments in the quality of materials inputs available in markets, two hypotheses may be hazarded: (1) that recurrent fluctuations in quality are most likely in the case of unprocessed natural materials, less likely in the case of processed natural materials, and least likely in the case of synthetic materials; and (2) that over the long run, technological progress tends to ensure an upward trend in the quality of industrial materials, with unprocessed natural materials tending to advance less than others, and unprocessed minerals even likely to decline in quality over extended periods. At any rate, improvements in the quality of materials inputs are most likely to affect productivity relationships by reducing the quantity of materials required per unit of output and thus altering factor proportions.

The quality of labor inputs may be altered with respect to the physical capacities and skills, mental abilities, psychological attitudes, educational background, job training, and experience of the workers employed. It should be emphasized that any of these factors becomes a relevant criterion for measuring the quality of labor inputs on a given job only if it significantly influences the performance levels that can be achieved. Changes in the quality of the labor inputs in any establishment are generally attributable to (1) changes in the quality of the labor available for employment, (2) changes in the effectiveness of selection and training activities, and (3) changes in the effectiveness of compensation, supervision, and other means of making the jobs attractive and of inducing labor to maximize its contributions. In general, technological progress tends to ensure gradual advances in the effectivenes of the selection and training techniques available for use, although the extent to which these improvements are applied may vary over the short run. With respect to the quality of labor available for hire, it is apparent that both increases and decreases are likely to occur over the short run as a result of changes in the volume and nature of competing demands on the labor force. Over the long run, however, past experience suggests that improvements may be expected in the quality of the labor force, in the techniques of selecting those best adapted to given jobs, and in the methods of training new employees in the best means of performing assigned tasks.

Adjustment patterns may be somewhat different with respect to a third of these major determinants of the quality of labor inputs: workers' evaluations both of the satisfactoriness of working conditions and rewards and also of the desirability of intensifying their efforts to maximize performance levels. Intermittent conflicts over output standards, wage levels, and a variety of other issues tend to produce considerable variations over the short run in employee judgments concerning the attractiveness of their jobs, with correlative effects on turnover rates and on the quality of personnel leaving for jobs elsewhere. The willingness of wage earners to intensify their job efforts voluntarily, that is, beyond the extent required by established output standards, may also vary over short periods, although probably within narrower margins. Specifically, even the intensification of efforts which might be engendered by fear of unemployment during periods of declining output tends to be tempered by seniority rules, share-the-work arrangements, and the widespread belief that increasing productivity under such conditions is more likely to increase than to decrease unemployment. Thus these worker attitudes may serve either to increase or decrease the quality of labor inputs over this short run, just as was found to be true of the other two major determinants of such quality levels. Unlike the other two, however, past experience offers little basis for assuming any significant long-term trend toward the improvement of these attitudinal determinants of the quality of labor inputs, although it is equally unlikely that such attitudes are growing progressively more unfavorable.

Changes in the quality of the capital facilities and equipment used in any plant are effected through additions to, and deductions from, the current stock of such capital goods and through the aging of the individual components of the stock. Whether new capital goods are acquired as replacements or in order to expand capacity, such additions tend to raise the average quality of capital inputs by introducing the latest and most productive types of equipment available. Deductions also tend to raise the average quality of capital inputs, inasmuch as they generally involve removal of the oldest and least efficient components of the stock of capital goods. The only major source of reductions in the quality of fixed capital inputs is the effect of wear and aging on individual units of capital goods. Hence the potential quality of capital inputs in any establishment is determined by the extent of technological progress in the developement of relevant facilities and equipment, and the extent to which such potentials are achieved is determined by the rate of turnover of its stock of capital goods. Finally, this turnover rate depends on the rate of net expansion or contraction in productive capacity (as determined by market trends), on the rate of wear and physical deterioration of facilities (as determined by the nature of the processes employed and by the tempo of production), and on the rate of obsolescence (as determined by the pace of technological advances).

Thus the quality of capital inputs may sag somewhat during periods of a few years or less, when the deferment of new acquisitions results in no offset to the effects of wear and age. But the long-term trend in the quality of capital inputs tends to be upward in all industries characterized by market growth and vigorous technological development. And even industries facing declining markets may experience a rising trend in the quality of capital inputs if such markets are still large enough to encourage vigorous efforts to advance technologically. Advances in the quality of capital inputs tend to affect productivity relationships by reducing capital-input requirements relative to the level of productive capacity, thus reducing the proportions in which actively utilized capital facilities and equipment are combined with other categories of input. But when improvements in capital inputs permit a partial replacement of labor or reductions in energy or other material inputs, different patterns of adjustments in factor proportions may result.

Summary of Direct Productivity Impacts of Changes in Industrial Operations

The changes in industrial operations most likely to account for long-term adjustments in productivity levels are advances in the nature of the processes employed, improvements in the effectiveness with which operations are integrated, increases in the scale of production, advances in the quality of inputs, especially of materials and capital, and changes in the scope of operations. Each of these categories of change is capable of engendering major adjustments in productivity levels—advances in integration and in the quality of inputs tending to be individually smaller, but also more continuous, than adjustments in the other categories. Moreover, each of these sources of long-term productivity adjustments tends to raise rather than lower productivity levels, with the possible exception of adjustments in the scope of operations, which may involve shifts in either direction through make-or-buy decisions and those involving backward or forward integration.

The changes in industrial operations which are most likely to account for short-term variations in productitivy levels are changes in the product composition of output, fluctuation in the rate of operations, adjustments in product design, changes in the quality of inputs, especially of labor and of materials, and advances in the effectiveness with which operations are integrated. All but the last of these categories may engender either increases or decreases in productivity levels during short periods. Among these categories of change in industrial operations, the greatest adjustment within short periods is likely to be that involving the product composition of output and the rate of operations, although abrupt changes may on occasion affect the quality of labor and material inputs as well. It should also be noted that most of these sources of short-term variations in productivity levels tend to affect the proportions in which factors are combined for the production operations as a whole as opposed to altering the nature and efficiency with which individual tasks are performed. Surely this tends to be true of changes in the product composition of output and in the rate of operations, the most influential of the categories reviewed. Moreover, even short-term changes in the quality of labor inputs are more likely to be attributed to significant adjustments in employee attitudes (which tend to affect productivity levels for operations as a whole) than to significant adjustments in the performance potentials of employees on individual tasks.

Thus, over the long run, productivity levels tend to follow an upward trend, while over the shorter run, productivity levels for entire production processes may be expected to fluctuate. It should be emphasized, however, that the latter result is less likely to involve changes in the efficiency with which individual production tasks are performed than changes in the incidence of idleness among the components of operations as a whole or changes in the product composition of output. Hence the productivity of actively utilized inputs is more likely to rise than to decline even in the short run, except when extraordinary reductions in the quality of inputs must be absorbed or when major changes in the product composition of output are experienced by establishments whose product lines differ significantly with respect to their productivity levels or factor proportions.

Of course, actual changes may represent the interaction of adjustments in each of several catagories, thus requiring appraisal of simultaneous pressures in various directions. Even more important, it should be recognized that although these changes affect productivity levels, they may be attended by other effects as well, and these other effects may be either more or less influential than the productivity effects from the standpoint of top management objectives. Hence industrial operations may be changed in directions involving reductions in certain productivity measures not only because of inescapable market pressures, but also because of deliberate managerial efforts to advance other objectives of the enterprise (Gold [1, pp. 109-124]).

As has already been noted, measures of apparent changes in factor proportions and in the productivity of individual inputs at successively more aggregative levels beyond the plant become increasingly difficult to interpret because of the expanding array of factors capable of influencing them. In the case of firm-level data covering multiple plants, such results would reflect any significant deviations from the past pattern of interplant differences with respect to each of the eight major types of changes in industrial operations reviewed earlier, thus requiring information about the past as well as the current status of each for every plant. In the case of industry-level data, similar information would be required not only for all plants and firms functioning in the base and in the comparison period, but also for all plants added and those eliminated since the base period. One need hardly add that these represent quite formidable requirements, even without adding the further information needed for analyzing still more aggregative data.

Constraints on the Harnessing of Productivity-Adjustment Benefits

The effects of changes in technology and in productivity relationships are determined by a succession of decisions and interactions reaching outward from the plants immediately affected to their factor and product markets. The first of these involves management choices among alternative means of utilizing the potential benefits of a given improvement in factor proportions or in the productivity of a given factor. The next encompasses resulting interactions with factor prices, and further linkages of concern to management deal with the other determinants of profitability included in the model represented by figure 3-2. Appraisal of prospective industry-level and still broader effects obviously requires consideration of a variety of other factors as well.

Two groups of factors tend to narrow the range of alternative allocations of given productivity adjustments: those tending to engender similar limitations in all industries, and those tending to produce differing limitations among industries. The first consists primarily of changes in productive capacity and physical output; their effects center on the choice between expanding productive contributions or contracting the volume of inputs. The second group is rooted in the technological differences among industries; their effects center on alternative allocations of the effects of originating productivity adjustments between modifications in factor proportions and changes in the productivity of other direct input factors.

General Effects of Output and Capacity Adjustments

Increases in the productivity of labor in any industry might obviously be utilized either by reducing employment proportionately while maintaining output or by maintaining employment through expanding output proportionately. The former need not affect either product or factor markets, except for reducing demand for labor, unless this should encounter effective resistance. But output expansion would tend to affect product markets through the increased supply to be sold and materials' markets through the increased demand for such inputs.

The increase in output would permit fuller utilization of capital facilities if they had been underutilized, but would require increases in investment if utilization levels were already optimal. And decreases in input requirements of materials per unit of output would tend to offer similar options to management, with similar repercussions in product and factor markets.

In theory, increases in the productivity of fixed-capital inputs might likewise be absorbed either through an increase in productive capacity with no change in the level of investment or through keeping capacity unchanged as a result of a proportionate reduction in the capital facilities and equipment embodying investment. But the latter option is seldom practical when the productivity gain results from technological advances which raise the productive capacity of the existing capital stock. In such cases, the durability and specialized nature of a given plant's facilities may prevent any proportionate reduction in productive facilities and the investment embodied in them except over extended periods. This means that the benefits of increases in the productive capacity of existing capital facilities tend to be offset by decreases in utilization rate to the extent that output expansion falls short of the gain in capacity. On the other hand, effecting such increases in output would tend to have carry-over effects on product markets and would also involve increased demand for materials inputs and, perhaps, for labor as well.[5]

It should also be noted that the preceding discussion of labor assumes that it is always capable of adjustment in direct proportion to changes in output. But such flexibility varies widely among industries, and hence, the more limited such flexibility, the more relevant to the evaluation of management options would be the analysis presented for increases in the productivity of capital.[6]

Specialized Effects of Technological Differences

Attention now may be turned to the second source of constraints on managerial options concerning alternative allocations of the effects of given productivity adjustments: the technological nature of the basic processes involved. In the present connection, the aspect of the nature of production processes which seems to be of greater significance concerns the comparative roles of direct labor, capital facilities, and direct materials in determining productive capacity.

Actual industrial processes cover a wide range with respect to the relative influence on productive capacity of changes in direct labor, capital facilities, and direct material inputs. One extreme might be characterized as "capital dominated."[7] This category would include processes in which production workers are engaged overwhelmingly in starting, stopping, loading, unloading, setting controls, or otherwise simply facilitating the functioning of machines and other capital facilities. And in this category, materials would play merely the passive role of providing the standardized inputs being acted upon by the machine process. Similarly, the "labor-dominated" extreme would encompass processes in which tools and other capital facilities serve essentially as accessories to wage earners, whose manual efforts and related skills represent the fundamental core of the production process—materials once again serving passively as the standardized inputs being acted upon by manual operations. One may likewise envision a "materials-dominated" extreme covering operations in which productive capacity is dominated by the resources to which labor and capital facilities are applied—both of these latter merely facilitating attainment of the production capacity determined by materials and related inputs.

The powerful influence of "factor dominance" on productivity relationships is readily illustrated. In operations approximating the capital-dominated extreme (for example, power plants, petroleum refineries, cement mills, and blast furnaces), increases in labor productivity are more likely to reduce man-hour requirements than to increase productive capacity or the productivity of fixed capital, increases in the productivity of fixed capital are likely to leave direct labor requirements per unit of fixed capital input unchanged or reduced and hence induce parallel increases in physical output per man-hour, and major increases in the productivity of the operationas a whole are thus much more likely to come from—and to be better measured by—adjustments in the productivity of fixed capital than in the productivity of labor. In operations approximating the labor-dominated extreme (for example, bricklaying, custom tailoring, and carpentry), increases in the productivity of fixed capital are more likely to reduce requirements for such equipment than to increase productive capacity or the productivity of direct labor, increases in labor productivity are likely to leave fixed-capital requirements unchanged and hance induce parallel increases in the productivity of fixed capital, and major increases in the apparent productivity of the operation as a whole are thus much more likely to come from—and to be better measured by—adjustments in the productivity of direct labor than in the productivity of fixed capital.

Moreover, both in labor-dominated and in capital-dominated fabricating processes, materials requirements tend to vary with output levels, thus tending to increase the ratio of materials inputs to labor inputs with an increase in the productivity of labor and to increase the ratio of materials inputs to effectively utilized fixed-capital inputs with an increase in the productivity of fixed capital. And in such processes, decreases in the input requirements of materials per unit of output are more likely to reduce the volume of the input requirements of materials than to increase the productivity of other factors or the productive capacity of the operation as a whole. In addition, in both labor-dominated and capital-dominated extractive processes, changes in the richness of the inputs of materials may be a determinant of significant changes in the productivity of the process as a whole, tending to be reflected by increases in the apparent productivity of both labor and fixed capital.

In operations approximating the materials-dominated extreme (for example, farming, fishing, and smelting), increases either in the productivity of direct labor or in the productivity of fixed capital are more likely to reduce requirements for such inputs than to increase productive capacity or the productivity of materials and related inputs. In addition, increases in the productivity of these dominant resources are likely to leave labor and fixed-capital requirements unchanged, thus inducing parallel increases in the productivity of direct labor and fixed capital. Finally, major advances in the productivity of the operation as a whole are much more likely to come from—and can be better measured by— adjustments in the productivity of materials and related inputs than in the productivity of direct labor or fixed capital.

In short, increases in physical output per man-hour are most likely to result from increases in the productive contributions of labor only in labor-dominated processes. In capital-dominated processes, such increases are more likely to be a reflection of gains in the productivity of fixed capital. And in materials-dominated processes, such increases are more likely to be a reflection of gains in the productivity of natural resources and related inputs. Similarly, increases in the productivity of fixed capital are most likely to result from increases in the productive contributions of the investment embodied in capital facilities and equipment only in the case of capital-dominated processes. In other processes, such increases are more likely to be a reflection of gains in the productivity of the factor dominating the process. Increases in the productivity of materials and related inputs are, in the same way, most likely to result from increases in the productivity of these inputs only in materials-dominated processes.

Although processes involving such extremes of factor dominance may still account for only a limited proportion of industrial operations, awareness of the effects of such technological constraints facilitates analysis of the relative productive contributions of different inputs in a larger set of hybrid cases involving "jointly-dominated" processes. Perhaps the most important of these is represented by operations in which the capital goods determine the volume of materials which can be processed and the quality of the materials determines the marketable output of such processes. The simplest examples would be operations involving the extraction of valuable components from raw materials (for example, blast furnaces, copper smelters, petroleum refineries, and cottonseed processing mills). Thus the capital facilities determine how much ore can be processed by a smelter, but the metal content of the ores determines how much iron, copper, or zinc can be extracted in any period. Moreover, the relative contributions of each to a change in output may be readily determined, inasmuch as the nature and magnitude of any changes in the capital goods and processing technology are clearly distinguishable from any changes in the characteristics of the materials being processed.[8]

Incidentally, one might hazard the hypothesis that industrial processes are increasingly gravitating from the labor-dominated extreme toward the capital-dominated extreme and from the materials-dominated extreme toward the jointly (materials-capital) dominated extreme. The former movement is accelerating under the impetus of computerization, added to the continuing pressures of specialization, mechanization, and rationalization. In addition, the increasing role of capital in what were once materials-dominated industries is attributable to the combination of pressures to replace labor with capital inputs and to maximize the utilization of capital inputs by reducing the idleness caused by variations in the quality and availability of the materials to be found and utilized, as exemplified by the sharply increased capital inputs of fishing fleets, mines, mobile sawmills, and irrigated farms.

Finally, it is useful to consider briefly how the generalized effects of output and capacity changes differ from the specialized effects of production processes in limiting managerial options in utilizing the effects of given productivity adjustments. With respect to the continuity of their effects through time, it is apparent not only that output tends to vary more in the short run than capacity, but also that capacity levels are more likely to change than the basic nature of productive processes over somewhat longer periods. Accordingly, the influence exerted by initial output and capacity adjustments are likely to be less enduring than those engendered by the basic nature of productive processes. With respect to their susceptibility to managerial control, it is apparent that the basic nature of productive processes is less amenable to managerial manipulation than output and capacity levels. Of course, output and capacity levels must be adjusted to market potentials and competitive forces. Nevertheless, sufficient uncertainty attends such estimates to allow considerable scope for the application of managerial preferences in many industries, especially over an extended period of time. On the other hand, the basic nature of productive processes tends to change slowly, except under the stimulus of major technological advances, which tend to be uncommon.

Notes

1. For further discussion, see, Gold [1, pp. 117-119].
2. For a fuller discussion, see Gold [2].
3. For example, Samuelson follows presentation of the traditional definition with illustrations which do not seem to accord with the requirement of maintaining fixed factor proportions [4, p. 28].
4. For further discussion, see chapter 8.
5. Incidentally, when the *productivity of capital* (defined as the ratio of productive capacity to net fixed investment) is increased through the reduction in net investment by depreciation allowances, there is a similar absence of practical options because this productivity gain can seldom be transformed into an equivalent gain in capacity combined with no change in the level of fixed investment.

6. For a more detailed discussion, see Gold [1, pp. 182–188].

7. This concept is fundamentally different from the traditional meaning of *capital-intensive.* The latter is commonly applied to plants and firms with a relatively high ratio of capital costs to total costs, as in the case of electricity-generating plants where such ratios may approximate 40 percent or more. But *capital-intensive* is also often mistakenly applied to operations characterized by large amounts of fixed investment and capital facilities, although these need not result in large ratios of capital costs to total costs. For example, this term is frequently applied to the steel industry because of its enormous capital requirements, although total depreciation and interest charges for major steel companies usually average 10 percent or less of total costs. In contrast, my use of the term *capital-dominated* refers instead to the extent to which productive capacity can be altered by changes in the capital facilities as compared with the effect on capacity of changes in labor or material inputs. For a more detailed discussion, see Gold [1, pp. 188–196, 215–230].

8. For a more extensive review of the various types of factor dominance and their effects, see Gold [1, pp. 188–196, 215–230].

References

[1] B. Gold, *Foundations of Productivity Analysis* (Pittsburgh: Univ. of Pittsburgh Press, 1955).

[2] B. Gold, W. Peirce, and G. Rosegger, "Diffusion of Major Technological Innovations in U.S. Iron and Steel Manufacturing," *Journal of Industrial Economics,* July 1970; reprinted in Gold [3].

[3] B. Gold (ed.), *Technological Change: Economics, Management and Environment,* (Oxford: Pergamon, 1975, 1979).

[4] P. Samuelson, *Economics,* 10th ed. (New York: McGraw-Hill, 1976).

6 Measurement Problems and Expedients

Economic measures are obviously necessary for planning, decision making, and performance evaluation in industry, as well as in other sectors of the economy. In addition, because necessity begets responses, a broad array of such measures have emerged into widespread use. So long as these were employed only for rough descriptive purposes, they escaped sharp critical scrutiny. But increasing reliance on such data in formulating important company and governmental policies urges careful reexamination of even the most familiar criteria with respect to their conceptual clarity, the margins within which they are amenable to measurement, and their relevance for the purposes to which they are commonly applied.

General Difficulties

In general, the major problems of measuring economic activities for analytical purposes are rooted in the nature of the phenomena to be encompassed, the requirements of rigorous statistical treatment, and the need to interpret resulting data within the context of the theoretical frameworks of economics and related social sciences. Difficulties in the first group arise from the multidimensionality of most inputs, outputs, and other elements of economic inquiry; the tendency for the characteristics of such economic elements to change through time; the difficulty of measuring some of these characteristics which seem important; and the inevitable heterogeneity of the limited number of categories into which the widely differentiated units must be gathered to facilitate analysis. Such difficulties are intensified by the requirements of statistical methodology for homogeneity within categories, comparability of data through time, representativeness of samples, and estimates of the precision of measurements. And any compromises, shortcomings, and omissions involved in coping with the preceding difficulties and requirements must somehow be considered and surmounted before resulting data can be brought into sufficient conformity with the definitions of economic and other social sciences needed to support their utilization in existing theoretical models as a basis for interpreting observed findings.

Each of these problems would be worth extended examination, especially the interplay between the simple universalistic definitions of abstract theory and the intricately differentiated texture of the variables discernible in reality. It may suffice for present purposes, however, to illustrate the fundamental nature of the inquiries to which leading economic measures of industrial activities should be subjected by reviewing some of the less widely recognized shortcomings and limitations of several of them, as revealed by efforts to evaluate changes in productivity and technology.

Output Levels

Managements need to be able to measure changes in the total physical output of their operations for a number of reasons. For example, one cannot assess the implications of increases in total revenue for growth, profitability, or effectiveness of marketing efforts without first determining the extent to which such revenue gains were attributable to greater output rather than higher product prices. Similar difficulties also are confronted in seeking to appraise changes in total costs, unless these can be compared with accompanying variations in total output. Nor can changes in input requirements be evaluated without comparing them with adjustments in total production.

For such purposes, management obviously requires measures of total output that reach beyond purely physical dimensions—such as the number, weight, or volume of various products—so as to aggregate the output of small and large, simple and complex products in terms of their economic significance. Nevertheless, there is still widespread use in major industries of such simple physical measures as tons of steel shipments and kilowatt-hours of electricity generated, despite their obvious failure to encompass the additional costly activities involved in converting raw steel into a wide range of finished bars, plates, sheets, tubes, and strip or in transmitting and distributing electrical power from generating plants to industrial and residential users.

It should be emphasized that improved measures of the total physical output of multiproduct operations have long been available and are widely employed by economists. The most common of these involves weighting the output of each product in the base and in the comparison period by its average price in the two periods.[1] Hence any change in the resulting total value of all products between the two periods must be attributable to the changes in physical output, for the other determinant of total value—product prices—remains identical in the two periods. By thus measuring the relative contributions to output of different products in terms of their relative economic values, or by the cost of all resources absorbed into each plus its overlay of profits, this approach represents an "economically oriented concept of physical output" (Gold [2, pp. 92-97]).

Such measures clearly facilitate managerial evaluations of operations by aggregating streams of physically differentiated products into unified total output flows. Among their advantages is that they can accommodate the introduction and growth of new products as well as the decline and elimination of older ones. However, they are also subject to serious limitations and problems of interpretation. First, resulting measures of output changes may obviously differ substantially from those obtained by using the technological criteria of engineers, or the weight and volume criteria of freight handlers, or the service criteria of consumers. For example, when the average mileage per tire was doubled by the addition of some chemicals to the rubber, consumers could count each tire as two in terms of use expectancy, but production managers could not do the same in terms either of costs absorbed or revenues generated. Second, the use of relative prices as measures of relative physical outputs per unit of product is clearly vulnerable both to the extent that relative profit margins differ among products (as is frequently the case) and to the extent that the ratios of value added to costs of purchased materials differ among products.

Certain other implications of this relative price-weighted measure of multiproduct output may be less apparent, however. For example, contrary to intuitive expectations, the introduction of larger and more complex products need not raise average total costs per unit of output, because the higher cost in the numerator is paralleled by a higher physical output in the denominator (resulting from the greater price weight of such costlier products in computing total output). Even more disconcerting, technological advances which lead to lower unit costs and prices for given products also engender reductions in the (price) weights given to such product units in computing total output, and declining productive efficiency leading to higher costs and prices would tend to increase the weights given to such product units in computing total output (Gold [3, pp. 205-206)].

However, perhaps the most fundamental limitation of such output measures is the assumption that each product remains unchanged through time. This may be true for many industries over relatively short periods of time, but the basic thrust of technology is to make this assumption increasingly inapplicable over widening sectors of the economy and especially over longer time periods in manufacturing, in construction, and in many sectors of the service industries. As a result, important questions arise with respect to the measurement of changes in prices and in view of the already noted critical role of price weights in determining changes in output levels.

Input Levels

Comparable problems occur in measuring inputs. One such problem concerns which dimensions of each input category should be measured: what is paid for, what is used, or what productive contributions are derived? Labor inputs, for example, might be measured in terms of numbers employed, man-hours paid for, man-hours worked, energy expended, skills applied, hazards borne, and work completed which meets quality standards. Similarly, capital inputs might be measured in terms of investments made, number or volume of equipment and facilities obtained, attendant productive capacity provided, capital charges during a period, and actual input attributable to the operation of capital goods. Such choices have to be made partly because some of these dimensions are less amenable to effective measurement than others and partly because given purposes emphasize some dimensions over the remainder. But one must recognize that the several dimensions need not vary in unison, and hence, that the measurements of one may engender only misleading inferences concerning the movements of others.

A second problem of input measurement derives from the fact that aggregation needs and difficulties are usually much greater in this area than in the area of outputs. Even plants of relatively modest size may require varieties of materials and supplies, skill classifications, and different types of equipment and facilities, adding up to hundreds of distinguishable input categories. Resulting managerial pressures to combine these into a relatively few key measures of performance have induced acceptance of various gross expedients. Lacking any meaningful physical common denominator, the variety of capital goods is usually aggregated in terms of investment values—that is, in terms of what was invested on a long-run basis rather than in terms of production capabilities obtained or contributions to current productive efforts. The diversity of purchased materials, fuels, and other supplies invites aggregation in terms of current total outlays rather than physical units. The latter are still widely used, however, to aggregate labor inputs (although total man-hours disregards wide differences in skills) and also to aggregate salaried inputs (although such total numbers lump together clerks, engineers, and executives). Resulting aggregates of major input categories are patently not comparable with one another, and their interpretation is likely to be less straightforward than is commonly recognized.

A third problem arises from such internally heterogeneous input categories: how to distinguish changes in the composition of such categories from changes in the aggregate level of any given composition of such inputs. For example, a plant with 1,000 wage earners is likely to have more than 200 jobs with significantly differentiated skills. Changes in total man-hours per unit of output are usually interpreted on the assumption that the composition of such inputs was unchanged. Ordinarily there is no effective alternative to this assumption, inasmuch as the aggregation process tends to ignore the heterogeneous specific input requirements in various sectors of production. This procedure is usually defended, especially over 2- or 3-year periods or less, on the ground that significant changes in the composition of labor inputs tend to occur only over longer periods. It is apparent, however, that the differential flexibility of various labor inputs means that fluctuations in output levels tend to alter the composition of such inputs. Moreover, the tendency for the composition of labor requirements to differ among diverse products suggests that variations in product mix would also alter the composition of inputs. Thus this common interpretation is open to serious question even in the short term. In the long run, the changing composition of labor (and of other inputs) is tacitly admitted, of course. Yet resulting adjustments in such total inputs per unit of output continue to be interpreted as though alterations in composition were invariably inconsequential.

Finally, the errors of underestimating the effects of changes in the composition of labor (and other inputs) tend to be accentuated by the fact that most plants employ substantial numbers of production specialists who frequently change the manual techniques, machine speeds and tooling, and quality standards which not only define the input requirements for each job but also affect output norms, base rates, and incentives. Hence input measurement also faces the problem of disentangling higher wage rates or factor prices for fixed-input qualities from the factor-price effects of changes in the qualitative characteristics of labor, material, or other inputs, thus paralleling the problem noted earlier with respect to output measurement.

Product and Factor Prices

Determination of the extent to which changes in the value of production are attributable to output as opposed to price adjustments depends on clearly distinguishing these from one another. However, this is made difficult by technologically induced changes in the nature of products. For example, if Product A has been modified and sells for a higher price, it may be regarded as essentially the same product (whose units represent the same "amount of output" as before) with an "inflated" price, or as an enlarged (or otherwise improved) version of the same product whose price increase merely reflects a proportionate increase in the "amount of output" (or costs absorbed) per unit of product, or as new product whose price cannot be compared meaningfully with the past price of a different product. Similar questions frequently arise with respect to input factors, as was noted earlier. To what extent do higher wage rates, for example, reflect inflationary increases for unchanged labor inputs as opposed to greater contributions through a shift to higher skills? How much of the increased cost of new equipment and facilities involves paying more for essentially unchanged production potentials as opposed to obtaining markedly greater contributions?

Efforts to resolve such difficulties are confronted by two conflicting pressures of analytical importance. The pressure for maintaining statistical comparability over time, in the interest of searching out persistent adjustment patterns, encourages underestimation of the significance of changes in the nature of the products and input factors constituting the units of measurements. On the other hand, the pressure for increasing the precision of such measures tends to reduce sharply the periods over which statistical comparability can be assured. Resulting data cannot but represent compromises, therefore, that involve errors whose significance depends on the purposes for which the measurement was made and the theoretical basis for interpreting the findings.[2]

In economic analysis (and in many accounting and statistical reports), the dominant tendency has been to assume that product and factor price changes can be evaluated on the assumption that the products and input factors have remained unchanged. This assumption is undoubtedly tenable in many cases over short periods, but it is less likely to be true over longer periods for many sectors of manufacturing, construction, and services.[3] Thus the key issue raised concerns the margin of error attributable to this assumption and its implications for evaluating the effects of technological innovations and changes in output and price levels at industry and national levels. For example, a 6 percent annual rate of increase in prices arouses widespread alarm about inflation, whereas a 3 percent rate seems to be regarded with general equanimity. Yet the question still arises: what margins of error attach to price indexes which assume that all or most products and services have remained unaltered despite enormous technological changes? Such extremely restrictive assumptions also tend to engender underestimates of the rate of growth of output in terms of attendant service values to consumers. And the deliberate exclusion by such one-sided assumptions of some of the major outcomes of technological advances may entail not only an underestimation of their effects from the standpoint of conventional criteria, but also a decreasing coverage by economic analysis of the forces reshaping the structure and functioning of the economy.

Unit Costs and Real Costs

The original conception of *unit costs* as the sum of the outlays involved in producing a discrete unit of product is clearly inapplicable in modern large-scale manufacturing operations, which usually involve the simultaneous processing and fabrication of many streams of components which are eventually assembled into a variety of products. Under such conditions, *unit costs* really represent the average ratio of total costs to total output over a given period rather than an average of the actual costs of each unit of output. At the same time, the increasing importance of indirect inputs—such as planning, control, product development, training, and supervision—further complicates the concepts of unit costs because of uncertainties concerning the incidence of their contributions among products and time periods. And similar uncertainties affect the remaining component of unit costs, representing the allocation among time periods of the charges against capital goods according to a variety of patently arbitrary depreciation formulas.

But an even more troublesome issue concerns what is meant by the average unit of product, which represents the denominator of unit costs. If such costs have been calculated as noted earlier, the output of plants producing a variety of types, sizes, and models of several product lines would presumably be expressed in terms of the statistical measure representing an implied "unit of composite product," which is patently nonexistent. Suppose, as a simple example, that a plant producing refrigerators of various sizes and with different combinations of features found that the average production cost per refrigerator had risen by 6 to 7 percent over the preceding year, while the composite average unit had changed from 6.54 to 8.32 cubic feet in volume, along with some changes in motor design, insulation, freezer space, and defrosting arrangements. Clearly, the interpretation of such findings presents continuing difficulties because every change in the composite product would undermine unit-cost comparisons from period to period as the basis for evaluating plantwide performance and because the concept of a composite product is meaningless from both the standpoint of production and sales (Gold [3, pp. 75-81]).

In order to help interpret changes in given unit costs (or product prices) over time, these are often deflated (divided) by accompanying changes in the general price level as a means of estimating changes in "real" costs (or prices), that is, in the quantities of resources absorbed into the products involved. But this technique also reflects inadequate recognition of the pervasive effects of technological innovations on the economy. Thus resource-saving innovations tend to affect factor prices, to spread from their points of origin to other firms and industries using such inputs, and to engender changes in the unit-input levels and factor prices of substitute resources. In turn, changes in the general price level represent an average of resulting price changes experienced by a large array of commodities. Deflating the total unit costs of any plant or industry by changes in the general price level can be interpreted most effectively, therefore, as merely indicating the extent to which the given unit costs have changed as compared with accompanying changes in the average cost of resources absorbed (plus profit) per unit of output in the rest of the economy.

Productive Capacity and Utilization

In most plants and firms, the level of productive capacity is a basic consideration in production planning, capital goods procurement, production-control arrangements, the design of depreciation formulas, and in other sectors of plant operations and managerial decision making. Hence most managements have in mind, or readily at hand, at least a rough estimate of the productive capacity they administer. This is particularly likely to be true on a product-by-product basis, if not in terms of a properly weighted composite of all products. It should also be noted that the basic data required for the measurement of productive capacity are usually readily available as the by-product of other plant operation and control functions, including engineering and the establishment of production and cost standards. One may conclude, accordingly, that efforts to develop more precise estimates of productive capacity are not only feasible in most plants, but also would tend to support the practical interests of management.

In theory, the precise measurement of productive capacity can be made extremely difficult if such efforts seek to encompass all kinds of imaginable but uncommon circumstances. The development of managerially useful estimates of practical capacity, however, involves less formidable difficulties than is commonly supposed. This is especially true under the following conditions:

1. If the measurement is focused on individual plants rather than on the economy at large or on major segments of it.
2. If the measurement is focused on practically sustainable capacity at present rather than on some theoretically attainable maximum under extraordinary conditions or in the future.
3. If the estimate is made on the assumption that product design, operating processes, and the general character of inputs remain unchanged; that the customary number of shifts and the normally acceptable length of work day and work week are retained; and that appropriate allowances are made for breakdowns, repairs, and maintenance.
4. If it is assumed that sufficient labor, materials, and other inputs are available to service the full utilization of present capital facilities.
5. If it is assumed that product and factor price adjustments are such as to press for the efficient utilization of all serviceable resources.

Such limitations are readily applicable to a wide range of productive activities. And if complied with, they permit the estimation of practically sustainable productive capacity with but moderate margins of uncertainty, particularly in the case of plants manufacturing one or only a few similar types of standardized products, in the case of plants manufacturing different kinds of standard products through the use of separate production facilities for each, and in the case of industries composed of plants satisfying these conditions. Only in the case of plants producing relatively small quantities of many quite different kinds of products are efforts to derive meaningful estimates of the degree of change in aggregate productive capacity faced by difficulties which may require extended specialized studies before they can be surmounted.

Productive-capacity estimates may take two forms: as an estimate of the total amount that can be produced of any given product, assuming some specified allocation of plant facilities to such output; and as an estimate of the composite productive capacity covering each specified product mix. The former of these may be expressed in purely physical terms and may be used to measure the absolute volume of capacity and relative changes in it. Because of its limitation to a single product, the purely physical measure cannot often be used to encompass the total output potential of given plants. On the other hand, such measures do permit aggregating the capacity for such production in each plant so as to yield a total estimated capacity for producing the specified product in all plants already engaged in such operations.

In the case of plants producing more than one product, the estimation of productive capacity for each product mix requires resort to techniques similar to those used in measuring physical output adjustments, which essentially involves the combination of productive capacity for each product through use of relative prices as weights. Although the results cannot be stated in terms of physical units of aggregate capacity, they can be used in two ways: to measure changes in capacity relative to some base year, and to determine capacity-utilization rates in any given year by comparing the calculated aggregate physical output of a given product mix with the capacity calculated for the same product mix, using the same price weights for both calculations. Such quasi-physical measures of capacity may be used to encompass the total output potentials or to determine the capacity-utilization rates of virtually all plants producing reasonably standardized products, whether such product lines are few or many in number.

In developing estimates of sustainable practical capacities for various product mixes as a basis for planning and evaluating performance, managements would obviously tend to specify realistic operating conditions, omitting marginal facilities, taking into account known bottlenecks, including normal maintenance, and considering only such compositions and rates of production as would accord with current costs and prices. Application of the foregoing approach to the estimation of capacity for entire industries and even large sectors of the economy, however, necessitates resort to expedients which are subject to serious weaknesses.[4] For example, different firms may base such estimates on diverse operating assumptions. In addition, considerable difficulties are involved in aggregating capacities designed to produce at least partially dissimilar products and product mixes. Moreover, it will be recalled that one of the conditions deemed requisite for the measurement of productive capacity was the availability of sufficient labor, materials, and other inputs to permit full utilization of the capital facilities. Such an assumption is reasonably acceptable in the case of studies limited to individual plants and even individual industries. As the focus is broadened to include still wider sectors of the economy, however, this assumption tends to become less tenable because the simultaneous increases in demand for such resources from many quarters may exceed the currently available supply. In such instances, output potentials must be reconsidered in terms of the availability of input factors—in short, practically attainable productive capacity may be limited by input stringencies rather than by the productive capacity of the capital facilities on hand.[5]

Some Additional Measurement Requirements

In reviewing the measurement problems associated with evaluating the effects of changes in productivity, technology, and capital, some attention should also be given to two methodological aspects of such efforts: focusing measures on the levels of aggregation most relevant to the outcomes of primary concern, and adjusting measures to the time periods most relevant to the adjustments being analyzed.

With respect to the first of these, it is obvious that although input, output, and other data can be accumulated at innumerable levels representing progressively larger sectors of the economy, many of these statistical aggregates may represent only the passive resultant of heterogeneous decisions and adjustments actually made at lower levels of aggregation. To understand such changes, and to influence them, it is necessary to identify the decision points involved as well as the objectives, incentives, and penalties considered by the decision maker. For example, since investment decisions are made at the level of the firm and the employment effects of such decisions may differ widely among industries (depending on the relative pressures of labor-displacing technologies and expanding product markets), the use of national aggregates to estimate the employment effects of adjustments in investment may be of limited value. A second implication is that commonly used variables need not be equally meaningful at different levels of aggregation. For example, profit rates are more relevant to performance evaluation at the level of the firm than at the level of the industry. Accordingly, consideration must be given to determining the most effective level of aggregation for measuring various inputs and outputs as well as product and factor prices, productivity, and capacity utilization in response to alternative analytical objectives.

The second methodological issue concerns the time periods on which various measures should concentrate in order to encompass effectively the results of the decisions and implementation efforts to be appraised. The traditional subdivision of time series into trend, cyclical, seasonal, and residual components is subject to serious analytical and practical inadequacies. In seeking to measure actual industrial operations, it is necessary to recognize the wide range of time periods within which operating variables are likely to require managerial review and decisions. Production levels, for example, may change within periods of a few weeks or less, generating comparably frequent adjustments in labor, materials, and shipping requirements. Prices are subject to change within periods of a few months in many areas of manufacturing and even more frequently in retailing. Product specifications, wage rates, salary levels, and productivity relationships are likely to change substantially over periods of a year or more. And plant capacity, basic production processes, capital equipment, and primary materials are likely to undergo major adjustments over still longer periods. Inasmuch as actual industrial operations are invariably the product of a variety of such changes recurring at different rates, economic analysis intended to evaluate different policies and efforts may well require the development of a more flexible array of time-oriented measures, as well as measures which are more precisely tailored to the specific effects of each of various sectors of decision making.[6]

Notes

1. For some purposes, the price weights might be those of the base year or the comparison year.

2. The problem may be illustrated by the controversy over treating the required addition of antismog devices to 1971 automobiles as price increases or as quality improvements. A ruling in November 1970 favoring the former was reversed in the following April, thereby affecting both price and output indexes. The question was characterized by Geoffrey H. Moore, Commissioner of the U.S. Bureau of Labor Statistics, as posing "a complex theoretical issue" (*Wall Street Journal,* April 16 and May 3, 1971).

3. For example, as discussed in chapter 4, available indexes of capital goods prices are open to very broad margins of error because of the wide variety and almost continuously changing characteristics of most equipment and capital facilities. Indexes of the prices of construction products are also highly vulnerable inasmuch as they are often found to offer indexes of the price of construction input factors rather than of resulting construction outputs. The shortcomings of price and output measures of service industries are, of course, widely acknowledged. Accordingly, recalling the shortcomings of input measurement even in manufacturing industries noted earlier, one cannot but be concerned about the emphasis placed by governments on adjustments in "*real* gross national product" in view of the vulnerability in respect to 60 to 80 percent of national output of the implicit price deflators used to adjust directly calculated gross national product for price changes.

4. Some of these were discussed in chapter 3.

5. For a detailed illustrative review of such problems as they have been encountered in actuality, see the chapters on labor and machinery in Gold [4, pp. 174-241].

6. For a more extended discussion of these, see Gold [3, pp. 11-13].

References

[1] S. Eilon, B. Gold, and J. Soesan, *Applied Productivity Analysis for Industry* (Oxford: Pergamon, 1976).

[2] B. Gold, *Foundations of Productivity Analysis* (Pittsburgh: Univ. of Pittsburgh Press 1955).

[3] B. Gold, *Explorations in Managerial Economics* (New York: Basic Books; London: Macmillan, 1971).

[4] B. Gold, *Wartime Economic Planning in Agriculture,* (New York: Columbia Univ. Press, 1969).

[5] D.A. Huettner, *Plant Size, Technological Change and Investment Requirements,* (New York: Praeger, 1974).

[6] C. Marquard, "Costs in the Electrical Machinery Industry," unpublished M.A. thesis, University of Pittsburgh, 1960.

Part II
Some Empirical Findings and Further Broadened Perspectives

7 Scale Economies: Theoretical Expectations and Empirical Findings

In the worldwide maneuvering for competitive market advantages, progressive increases in the scale of production units have been one of the major weapons in recent years. A scanning of the industrial horizon reveals an extraordinary rush toward giantism in steel mills, electric power plants, ships, petrochemical complexes, and many other sectors of manufacturing, agriculture, transport, and even distribution. This reflects a pervasive belief in the advantages of large operating units which has spread beyond engineers and the managements of firms to governments as well, leading many of the latter to join in fostering such tendencies in the hope of revitalizing their lagging industries.

Even in the midst of this stampede, however, it would seem prudent for corporate as well as public officials to reexamine the foundations of such beliefs and to undertake more careful assessments of the sources and effects of the apparent scale economies realized in the past and of those anticipated in the future. In particular, fuller information is needed concerning the relative contributions of technological and other determinants of the competitive advantages of firms operating large production units—and also concerning differences among industries in the prospective advantages and disadvantages of further increases in scale, especially in the face of possible changes in technology, markets, and resource availabilities. The potential value of such critical inquiries may be illustrated by analyzing one of the more spectacular recent examples of headlong increases in scale: Japanese blast furnaces.

The Magnitude of Scale Increases Being Examined

It was the position of the U.S. iron and steel industry in the mid-1950s, as expressed by influential leaders, that blast furnaces had already reached their maximum efficient size as evaluated by engineering and economic criteria. At that time, recently-constructed blast furnaces in the United States had a volume of less than 1,500 cubic meters, and the average production per blast furnace was about 500,000 metric tons of pig iron per year. In 1970 the United States had about 175 active blast furnaces still averaging about 500,000 metric tons of pig iron output per year per furnace, and the largest furnace in operation had a working volume of less than 2,200 cubic meters.

During the early rebuilding of Japan's iron and steel industry in the 1950s, the size of initial blast furnaces approximated those in the United States, reflect-

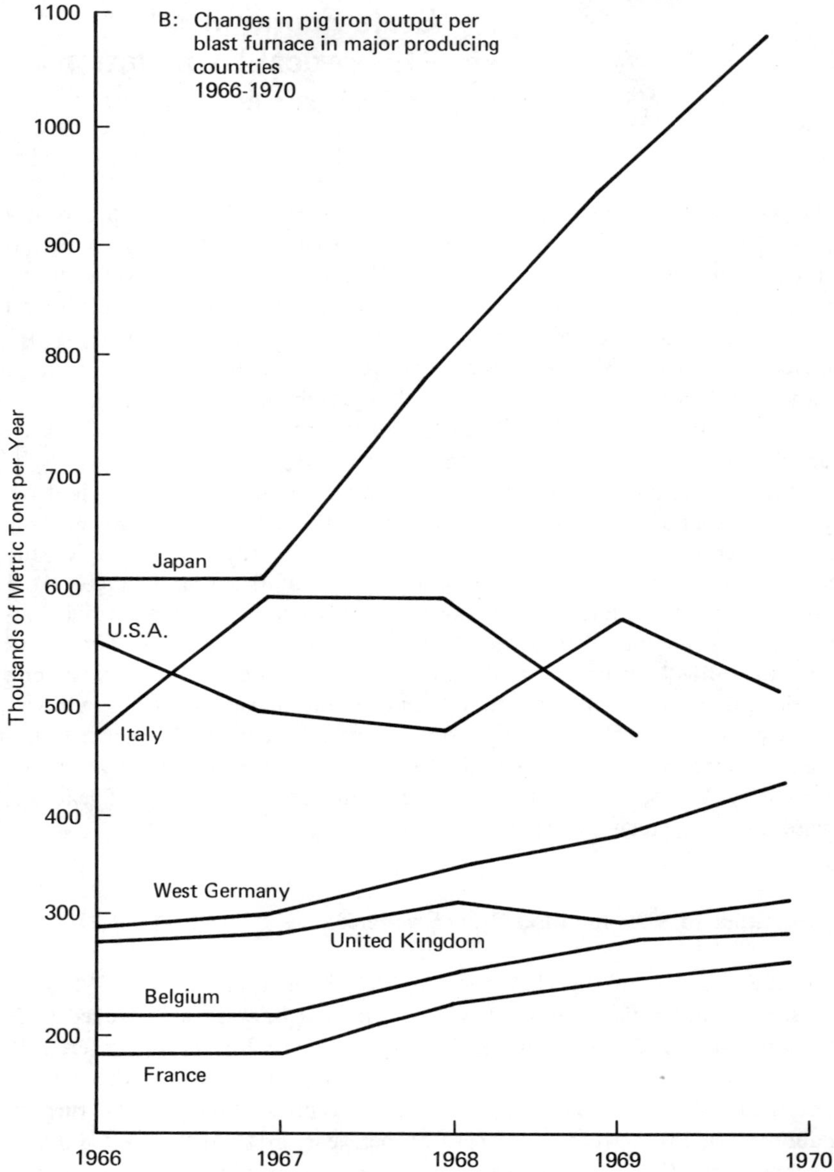

Source: *Outline of Japanese Steel Industry,* Nippon Steel Corporation, September 21st, 1971, Figures 20 and 21.

Figure 7–1. Changes in Number of Blast Furnaces and in Average Output per Blast Furnace in Major Producing Countries

ing its heavy reliance on transferred technology and purchased equipment. By 1966, Japan was producing six times its 1955 output with about 50 blast furnaces, averaging 600,000 metric tons of pig iron annually, or about 10 percent more than the U.S. average. Only 4 years later, Japan had more than doubled its output, while adding only 10 more furnaces—also increasing its average output per furnace to 1.1 million metric tons, or more than double the U.S. average (figure 7-1). In 1971 Japan had blast furnaces in operation with working volumes exceeding 4,000 cubic meters and new ones under construction or being designed with planned working volumes of 4,400 to 4,800 cubic meters,[1] or about three times what had been considered the maximum economic size in the United States only 15 years earlier (Yoshida [22]). Moreover, these new furnaces were expected to produce 10,000 to 12,000 tons of pig iron per day, or 3.6 to 4.3 million tons per year, because they were not only larger, but were to be driven to yield 50 percent more output per cubic meter of volume through high top pressure, oxygen enrichment, higher operating temperatures, stronger blast, and increased use of sintered and pelletized ore. Since then, even larger furnaces have been planned.

In order to analyze the basis for such extraordinary advances, it is useful to begin by reviewing the commonly assumed reasons for decisions favoring increases in the scale of production.

Concepts of Scale and Scale Economies

Economic Theory

Economic theory has long depicted *scale effects* (that is, the effects on minimum average unit costs of increases in the capacity of plants engaged in identical production activities) in the form of a U-shaped long-run cost function. But attempts to explore such effects realistically require significant modifications of the traditional theory.

The expectation of a U-shaped function reflects four assumptions, as shown in figure 7-2:

1. That short-term cost functions, which depict the relationship between average total unit costs and variations in the capacity utilization of individual plants, are U-shaped.
2. That the minimum points of such short-term cost functions tend to decline for successively larger plants up to some optimum size beyond which minimum costs begin rising.
3. That plants producing identical products by means of identical technologies commonly cover a wide range of sizes at any given time.
4. That the overlapping of adjacent short-run cost functions indicates the

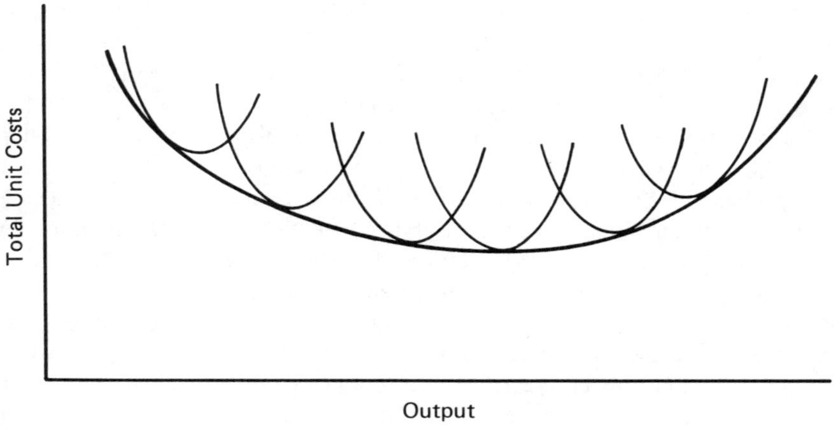

Figure 7–2. Theoretical Effect of Increasing Scale on Total Unit Costs

> diseconomies of underutilizing large plants as compared with producing the same output through fuller utilization of smaller plants.

The resulting "long-run average total unit-cost function" approximates the envelope which is tangential to the array of "short-term average total unit-cost functions" for progressively large plants.[2]

Such elementary economic concepts have been widely diffused among engineers, businessmen, and government officials and may well have encouraged receptivity toward proposals for continuing increases in scale. Unfortunately, however, analysis offers little support for the assumptions on which this theory rests.

The vulnerability of the first assumption on theoretical as well as empirical grounds has been dealt with at length elsewhere—the general conclusions being that variations in capacity-utilization rates may be accompanied by a wide range of total unit-cost adjustment patterns, even within the narrow purview of static economic theory; that the U-shaped function need not be the most common among these; and that the likelihood of its occurrence tends to decline further as the restrictive assumptions of static analysis are relaxed (Gold [6, pp. 139–148]).

As support for the more critical second assumption—that minimum average total unit costs tend to decline with increases in plant size up to some optimum and then to reverse—most textbooks rely on one basic argument. It is claimed that because of the alleged "lumpiness" of the sizes in which facilities and equipment are available, some plants are too small to fully utilize the nearest relevant size and thus have higher investment cost per unit of product at the plant's optimum output levels than plants large enough to use such facilities fully. Still larger plants would also face higher unit investment costs up to the point where they could fully utilize duplicate sets of such facilities.[3] This view would yield a horizontal rather than a U-shaped average unit-cost function, however, unless it should be further claimed that progressively larger units of equipment and facilities yield decreasing minimum unit investment costs up to some recognizable optimum size. This claim is indeed made, implicitly more often than explicitly, but economic theory provides no basis whatever for such a generalized expectation.

Realization of a significantly U-shaped long-run average total unit-cost function would also require that any decreases in unit investment cost associated with larger scale not be offset by accompanying increases in other unit costs. Such offsets tend to be uncommon with respect to unit material costs, but may be more frequent with respect to unit wage costs in view of the widely recognized problems of supervising large work forces. In addition, increases in the unit cost of salaried personnel may be quite general according to the evidence that increasingly complex systems involve a growing need for specialized staffs to plan, coordinate, control, and evaluate operations as well as maintain facilities.[4] Moreover, consideration must also be given to the relative magnitude of prospective reductions in unit investment charges as compared with possible offsets in other costs. For example, if total fixed charges approximate 20 percent of total costs,[5] investment cost per unit of capacity would have to be reduced by 40 percent through an increase in sacle in order to decrease total unit costs at full utilization by only 8 percent, even if all other unit production costs remained unchanged. In short, it would require fairly heroic assumptions to support expectations of even reasonably modest reductions in total unit costs on the basis of the theoretical analysis of scale usually presented.

The third assumption—that increases in scale involve increases in all factors at the same time in the same degree—also serves to minimize the relevance of the concept to the phenomena to which it is usually applied: plants of increasing size.[6] Larger plants are seldom enlarged replicas of small plants. If they were, it would be difficult to understand, as has already been noted, where the expected economies would come from.

Logic alone suggests that the greater the economies and subsequent diseconomies of successive increases in scale, the narrower the range of plant sizes that can survive under conditions of effective competition. With respect to the theoretical possibilities, engineering analysis suggests that within the confines of a given technology and product mix, most industrial processes tend to be characterized by relatively narrow zones within which input-output relationships are most effective. While these are obviously not always identified at the outset, it would seem to follow that every increase in scale yielding substantial improvements in performance would tend to shift the loci of effective competitive plant sizes upward rather than to broaden the range within which scale economies are too small to affect long-term survival. At any rate, the scale concept concerns differences in plant size at a moment of time, not changes over time. Nor does empirical evidence support this third assumption on any broad basis. Of course, a variety of studies have reported a wide range of plant sizes within specified industry categories as defined by statistical agencies.[7] But further analysis reveals very substantial heterogeneity within such categories with respect to the products made, technologies employed, and markets served, thereby voiding the claim of relevance to assessing the significance of scale economies.[8]

Finally, the preceding discussion of the first three assumptions undermines both the acceptability and relevance of the final assumption. Specifically, it has been suggested that the U-shaped short-term total unit-cost function is but one of a variety of theoretical and empirical patterns, that the shape of such functions may change with increases in scale, and that the range of actual plant sizes engaged in identical production activities is likely to be quite narrow in most industries. Accordingly, although underutilization of a given plant's capacity would often tend to involve cost penalties of some magnitude, it need not follow that smaller plants could generally provide similar outputs more economically at comparable levels of production.

In short, reliance on convenient assumptions in place of exploring the realities of industrial practice renders the traditional theoretical approach to scale economies widely inapplicable in concept and all but trivial in posited effects. Indeed it would not be unfair to summarize the latter as suggesting only that there is some optimal size of production unit for any given technology and product mix without specifying what it might be, what determines it, or the magnitudes of its presumed cost advantages as compared with progressively larger and smaller sizes.

Engineering Concepts

Managerial receptivity toward proposals for increasing scale tends to be encouraged not only by economic theory, but also by engineering beliefs. Thus, although the critical second assumption, noted earlier, has been found to have no effective support from economics, the supposedly hardheaded engineering literature reflects long-standing and widespread acceptance of a rule that each doubling of capacity tends to require increases in investment of only about six-tenths.[9] Further inquiry revels, however, that this expectation seems to be rooted solely in the simple-minded view that volume increases more rapidly than the enclosing surface of rectangular, cylindrical, and spherical shapes, and that the output of facilities tends to be correlated with their volume, while investment costs tend to be associated with the size of the enclosing surface. Such a relationship may hold, of course, with respect to some kinds of apparatuses and facilities, especially with respect to the cost of constructing outer shells such as tanks, furnaces, boilers, pipes, and simple buildings. But fundamental shortcomings narrowly restrict the range of its applicability.

Specifically, there seem to be few physical or chemical processes whose input-output relationships remain fixed without any boundaries. Moreover, even construction activities face growing difficulties under conditions of increasing size, strain, and deteriorative forces. In addition, large facilities often make disproportionate demands on energy inputs, functioning components, instrumentation, and so on. At the very least, these suggest that the exponent indicating the rate of increase of construction costs with gains in capacity probably covers a wide range of processes and industries beyond the supposedly universal value of six-tenths. And another implication is that the expoential value for any process is likely to change over successively higher ranges of scale.[10]

In place of the preceding, long-prevailing economic and engineering approaches, my earlier studies have suggested that scale economies are derived from the increasing specialization of functions, and hence, that *scale be defined as the level of planned production capacity that has determined the extent to which specialization has been applied in the subdivision of the component tasks and facilities of a unified operation* (Gold [5, pp. 115-117]). This means that increases in scale tend to involve changes in the size and degree of specialization of equipment, in required labor tasks and skills, in the specifications of purchased materials and components, and in technical operations, as well as in managerial arrangements and controls. Thus progressively larger plants tend to become increasingly differentiated from small plants in product mix, factor proportions, capital goods, cost structure, and operating flexibility.[11] This also suggests that substantial increases in scale tend to involve elements of technological advance and innovation as engineers and scientists explore existing technological constraints as a basis for attempting to overcome them and as they also search for possibly more favorable relationships beyond the frontiers already reached.[12] It also raises doubts about the likelihood of finding scale effects which are universal among industrial processes covering the entire spectrum of physical and biological sciences or over the entire size range of possible operating units within each.

In short, this view suggests that production functions for materials, labor, and capital goods (physical input-physical output relationships) may change in shape and level with successive increases in plant size, even without changes in product mix. But the latter, too, is likely to change, and so are production technology, organization, and management—along with the specific nature of input requirements and attendant factor prices, which together determine the shape and the level of the component unit-cost functions. Moreover, the relative effects of each of these on total unit costs will also be determined by factor proportions. Hence it would appear that major new horizons must be explored before new advances in our understanding of the generalizable and nongeneralizable elements of changes in the scale of production are likely to be achieved.[13]

In particular, although increases in scale undoubtedly yield substantial advantages in some industrial applications, such expectations may prove unduly optimistic and even misleading in others. Even engineering estimates of the effects of prospective scale adjustments are subject to wide margins of error because of the uncertainties involved in projections from past experience to a different sector of scales and associated economic and operating relationships. Nor can the distinctive effects of scale be easily determined ex post facto, for such evaluative efforts are confronted by difficult questions concerning the level of aggregation and the time period over which the evaluation should be attempted, not to mention questions concerning the influence of concomitant nonscale factors and even concerning the most meaningful critera to be employed in assessing the results, as will be illustrated in the following section of this chapter.

It should be emphasized, however, that the following concentration on blast furnaces avoids an important sector of the previously noted problems usually faced in the analysis of scale effects through minimization of the influence of differences in material and labor inputs, outputs, and basic technology.

Reasons for Increases in the Scale of Blast Furnaces in Japan

In Japan, blast furnaces cost $50,000,000 or more to construct, including necessary ancillary equipment but excluding sintering machinery and coke ovens.[14] This alone would represent a large stake in deciding to proceed with the construction of a significantly larger furnace than has ever been built and operated. As a practical matter, however, the stakes are actually much greater because the additional blast furnace capacity would normally be constructed in tandem with the steel furnaces and rolling mills needed to transform hot pig iron into marketable products. Hence any malfunctioning of the blast furnace could threaten the underutilization of a much larger array of capital facilities. On what basis, then, did the Japanese iron and steel managers decide to take such risks despite the prevailing negative view of the world-leading U.S. industry?

It is generally assumed by economists that such decisions are made through a process beginning with the presentation of engineering proposals for a larger-scale unit supported by detailed technical studies estimating the probable resulting economies in physical inputs and costs as well as in investment requirements—and also describing attendant problems and the means devised to overcome them. Management is then presumed to evaluate the prospective savings at probable levels of market demand relative to the investment required, after adding some reserve for contingencies, and finally, to decide whether the expected rates of return warrant approval of the proposal.

In order to explore whether actual decisions emerged through such a logically deduced process, extensive discussions were held with senior executives and engineers in the head offices of the six major steel companies in Japan, as well as with plant managers and engineers in at least one plant of each. Such discussions entailed quite detailed reviews of relevant technical reports, experiential data, and estimates underlying future plans. The results suggest that the actual decision processes were substantially at variance with the preceding expectations. Even more important, they provide revealing insights into the larger complex of considerations affecting these major decisions and into the changing role of technological factors through time.

Technological Criteria

As was indicated earlier, the Japanese blast furnaces constructed in the middle and late 1950s tended to parallel the sizes prevailing in the United States, concentrating around 900 to 1,200 cubic meters. Demonstrably successful assimilation of the foreign technology encouraged careful and modest extensions in scale, first by one company and then by others. Engineers currently insist that such increases had very limited footing in experimentation and careful testing. Rather the tendency was reportedly to assume that past relationships could be extrapolated over the next stage of modest increase and then to use a high ratio of engineers to labor during the early phases of operation in order to be prepared for any unexpected difficulites. And as these difficulties failed to appear, engineers were emboldened to take larger steps. The basic point emphasized, however, is that these increases in scale were not based on proposals buttressed with persuasive technical analyses.

To whatever extent it was a matter of luck, the larger units functioned quite well. Moreover, there seems to be general agreement that they resulted in lower investment cost per unit of capacity and lower unit direct operating costs, yielded by essentially unchanged crews handling larger outputs and by reductions in coke ratios (kilograms of coke per ton of pig iron). Of course, such confirmatory results tended to bolster the confidence of engineers in further extrapolations and the confidence of managers in engineering estimates.

Nevertheless, every further major jump in the size of blast furnaces involved a risk of discontinuities in past relationships. And the probability of such deviations seems to be increased by the concomitant introduction of other innovations, including high top pressure, higher blast temperatures, oxygen enrichment, and fuel injection. Gains in furnace size also involved greater blowing energy requirements and some risks to the smooth descent of the burden within the furnace. Such considerations alone would seem to justify curiosity about why managers continued to approve increases in scale, and in attendant investments, involving even greater relative increments than previously. But these decisions are rendered still less obvious by ex post facto evidence that scale economies were of rapidly diminishing proportions. For example, although direct labor costs continued to decline per unit of output, they are reported to account for 1 percent or less

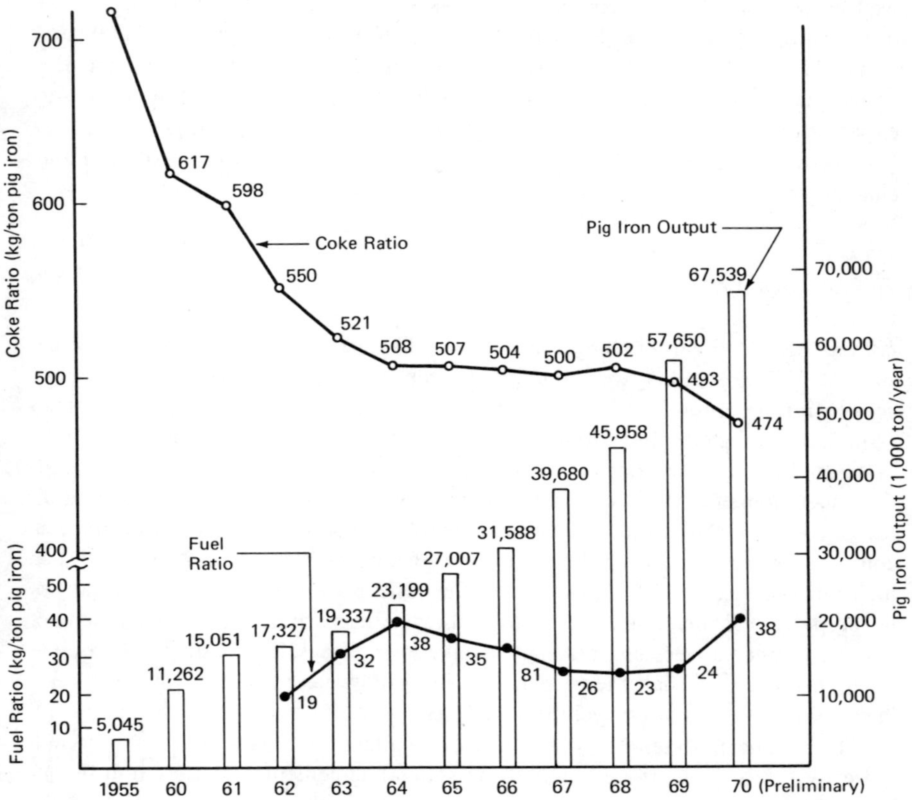

Source: *Outline of Japanese Steel Industry,* Nippon Steel Corporation, September 21st, 1971, Figure 22.

Figure 7-3. Changes in Pig Iron Output, and in Coke and Fuel Ratios in Japan

of pig iron costs (Yoshida [21, Table 5]). Moreover, between 1967 and 1970, when the average output per blast furnace rose by 85 percent, the coke ratio (in kilograms of coke per ton of pig iron) declined by only 5 percent, and even this was partly offset by a rising fuel ratio (figure 7-3).

Although the preceding data provide some helpful perspectives on scale effects in blast furnace plants, they clearly fall short of providing authoritative bases for decision making. One weakness derives from the fact that scale economies properly refer to the differences in total unit costs of alternative plant sizes, among which a choice is to be made at any given time. Resulting evaluations obviously cannot be tested effectively by making such comparisons among accumulated stocks of plants consisting of the particular plant sizes chosen in different years. The latter would also reflect the influence of changes through time in the quality of inputs, in operating methods and ancillary facilities, and in factor prices.[15] Thus continuing increases in factor prices, for example, could result in rising minimum total unit costs for progressively larger plants built in successive years without disproving the economies of larger-scale units. Another source of weaknesses, this time tending to overstate the scale economies of blast furnaces, involves inadequate recognition of cost benefits traceable to the contributions (and attendant costs) of other parts of integrated operations. Examples would include improvements in the quality and preparation of material inputs, advances in operating and maintenance techniques developed by research departments, and the not uncommon practice in Japan of assigning parts of the plant labor force to supplement the work of construction crews without fully reallocating operating cost to investment. Even reductions in coke rates are commonly reported without reference to associated increases in substitute fuels and energy inputs, such as are shown in figure 7-3 (Yoshida [21, fig. 5]).[16]

In order to help overcome such difficulties, inquiries were made among technical and managerial executives of the leading Japanese steel companies concerning their estimates of the relative conomies offered by blast furnaces of different sizes considered as possible alternatives in mid-1972. With respect to construction costs per ton of pig iron capacity, a leading specialist estimated that they become virtually horizontal beyond a daily capacity of about 5,000 tons (usually associated with a working volume of about 2,500 cubic meters) (figure 7-4). At another company, it was estimated that such capital requirements per ton of capacity level off short of 4,000 cubic meters and begin rising beyond that point. Turning to the criterion of total cost per ton of pig iron output, none placed the "minimum-cost" size of blast furnaces below 2,750 to 3,000 cubic meters, or about 1.5 to 2.0 millions tons of annual capacity. One estimated that total unit costs decreased by less than 10 percent as a result of increasing size from 2,000 to 4,000 cubic meters. Beyond that point, some doubted that further increases in size would yield any cost savings, some expected slight further cost reductions up to 4,500 cubic meters, and only one estimated that minor benefits might continue up to 5,000 cubic meters.

Two areas of general agreement among the judgments offered would appear to be of special interest:

1. That attainable cost economies tend to be of the relatively modest order of 5 percent or less beyond 3,000 cubic meters, and incremental benefits beyond 4,000 cubic meters tend to be slight and to decline rapidly.
2. That the major increases effected in the scale of Japanese blast furnaces were not attributable to any substantial technological advances.

And yet, as has already been noted, blast furnaces have been designed and are

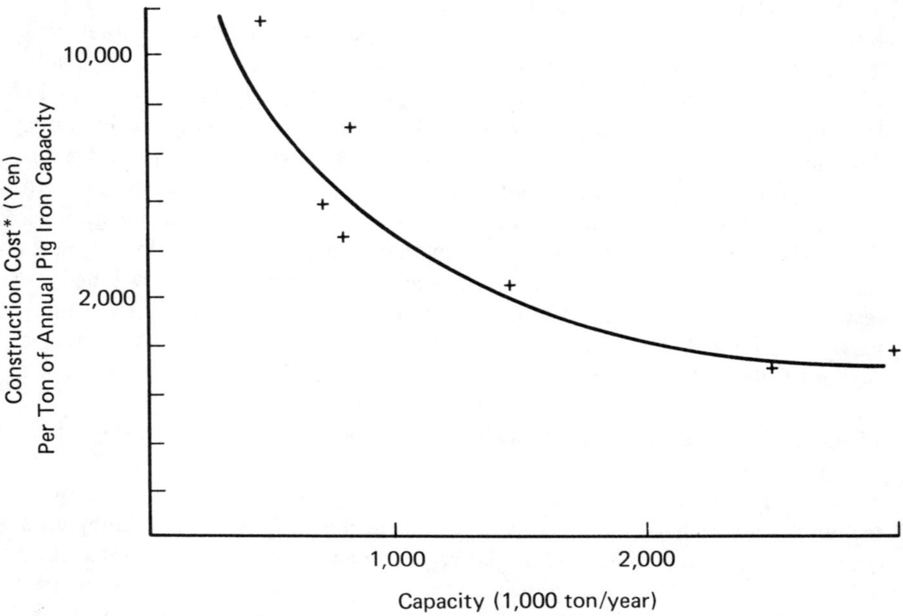

Source: H. Yoshida, *A Study of Iron-Making by Blast Furnace–Reference Data,* Kawasaki Steel Corporation, February 1972, Figure 7.

*Estimated cost of constructing complete blast furnace, including ancillary facilities, but excluding land, using estimated replacement cost at present prices.

Figure 7–4. Relation between Blast Furnace Capacity and Construction Cost

being constructed in Japan of 4,400 to 4,800 cubic meters with planned daily capacities of 10,000 to 12,000 metric tons.

Managerial Criteria

Repeated inquiries concerning why Japanese managements kept approving substantial increases in the scale of blast furnaces despite the absence of strongly supportive technical data elicited several explanations, but their common theme was that the basic drive for such increases was generated in most cases by managerial aspirations, with engineers responding to these recognized attitudes more frequently than initiating direct proposals of their own. Moreover, this also accords with the observation of Japanese specialists in management, supported by my own limited experiences, that the famous and reputedly mysterious Japanese process of "decision by consensus" usually eventuates–like ostensibly different processes elsewhere–in the development of consensus around the views deemd to be favored by senior officials.

Perhaps the most powerful force impelling management to seek increases in scale was the rapid expansion of steel demand and attendant favorable prices. With blast furnace capacity limiting the output of steel products,[17] adding large increments to capacity as quickly as possible offered gains in revenues attractive enough to overshadow the significance of any dimunition in blast furnace scale economies. Indeed, further increases in scale might conceivably be approved even if they offered no investment or operating cost economies, provided only that this would permit still larger sales at profitable prices. With respect to the relative influence of technological uncertainties and market attractions, one executive observed, "If the demand is great enough, it is worth taking the risks of increasing scale."

Another factor tending to favor increases in the size of blast furnaces was the reputed arrangement among the major Japanese producers to minimize readjustments in their relative shares of output and to prevent excessive additions to capacity by limiting the number of blast furnaces through jointly rationing the allocation of permission to build new ones. Under such conditions, it is understandable that company managements would seek to make the most of an opportunity to add capacity which might not recur for an extended period as competitors are granted allocations in turn. Such arrangements also serve to encourage the replacement of small, old furnaces with large, new units (Nakamura [11, p. 1]), while conforming to the limitations on numbers.

Moreover, both the availability of profitable markets and the pressure to make the most of available blast furnaces encouraged the intensification of efforts to maximize pig iron yield per cubic foot of blast furnace volume per day. This illustrates the inadequacy of the naive engineering view that capacity may be regarded as correlated with the volume of the shell comprising the producing unit, for Japanese engineers claimed that a 4,000-cubic-foot blast furnace would yield only 60 to 70 percent as much pig iron annually at the driving rates used in the United States as would result from Japanese practices. It also illustrates the inadequacy of the associated naive engineering view that investment costs tend to be correlated with the surface volume of the shell, for these higher yields per cubic foot of volume per day are the product of additional ancillary facilities and modifications in shell design as well as in operating practices. For example, it is argued that the major limitation on the effective size of blast furnaces derives from the size and efficiency of the blowing engines which generate the blast in the furnaces. At any rate, it is apparent that managers might well increase driving rates (yield per cubic foot per day) and the size of blast furnaces beyond minimum-cost points in the face of profitable demand. As a result, actual operating costs might understate the benefits attainable from further increases in scale if production rates and scale were limited to optimum levels.

In seeking to explain why the addition of one large furnace would be preferable to two small units, if management were assured of sufficient market demand as well as the technical feasibility of the scale increase, several reasons were offered aside from the expected direct scale economies of the furnace itself. First, the problems of internal plant logistics are substantially simplified by having fewer blast furnaces. Specifically, steel plants require a complex network of conveyers and other transportation facilities to move large quantities of materials and gas from ore beds, sintering plants, and coke ovens to each blast furnace and to move molten iron from the latter to an array of steel furnaces. Expansion through the multiplication of blast furnaces threatens disproportionate increases in transportation problems as compared with the greater simplicity of increasing capacity primarily by increasing the size of blast furnaces. For example, the very conception of 12-million-ton plants operating with ten to twelve blast furnaces is daunting to engineers and managers. Resort to larger-scale furnaces also minimizes the severe problems that would be faced in trying to alter the carefully integrated layout of existing plants in order to increase output. Second, flat land is so scarce and expensive in Japan, much of it having to be reclaimed from the sea, that decreasing the land required for blast furnaces, ancillary equipment, and the attendant complex of transportation facilities offers significant capital savings. Third, it is claimed that a smaller number of blast furnaces facilitates more effective supervision, more economical computerization, and better process control, as well as greater uniformity of product. And some also add that larger units hasten the availability of substantial increments in capacity (Nakamura [11, p. 1]).

Another powerful influence on managerial views of blast furnace scale is its relationship to maximizing the scale advantages of the entire plant considered as an integrated system. Because of Japan's lack of coal and iron ore, such supplies have had to be transported great distances. For example, the average mileage of iron ore imported by Japan icnreased from about 3,500 miles in the late 1950s to more than 6,000 miles after 1968 (figure 7-5). To reduce the costs of such long hauls, the Japanese have pioneered the construction of progressively larger ships. As the average carrier tripled in size during the 1960s, freight rates per ton of ore and coking coal decreased by 40 and 28 percent, respectively, despite general price inflation (figure 7-6.). Effective utilization of ever larger ships—major steel plants now have facilities for docking vessels of at least 150,000 deadweight tons—is said to encourage the building of larger-scale blast furnaces, and the latter in turn reinforces the trend to still larger carriers. Similar reciprocal pressures are generated between blast furnaces and steel furnaces,[18] with the latter also having had to respond to the fact that the minimum economic size of the slabbing mills which begin the shaping of steel ingots has been about 5 million tons per year (this was especially important because Japan's output was dominated by flat-rolled products). Hence managements might be expected to press for increases in the scale of blast furnaces or other components of integrated steel mills even if the particular units would not offer direct economies,

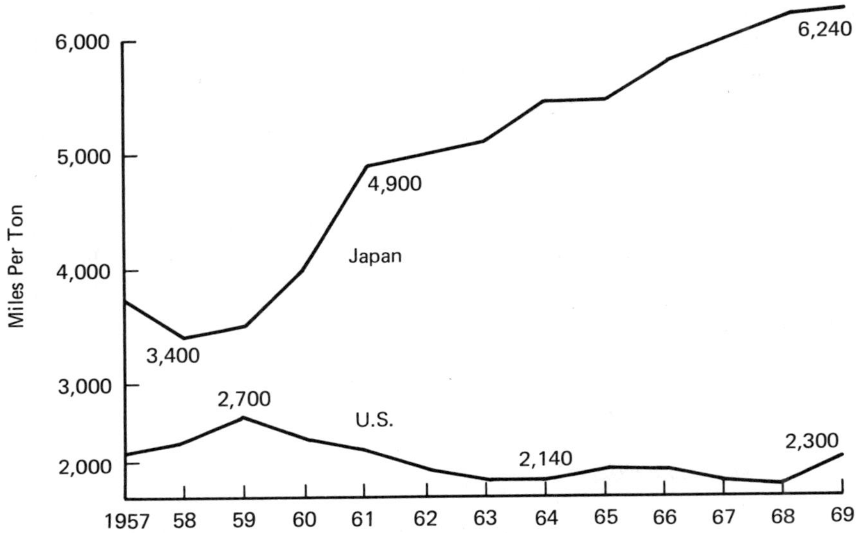

Source: See figure 7–6.

Figure 7–5. Comparison of Changes in Average Marine Transportation Distance for Iron Ore in Major Countries

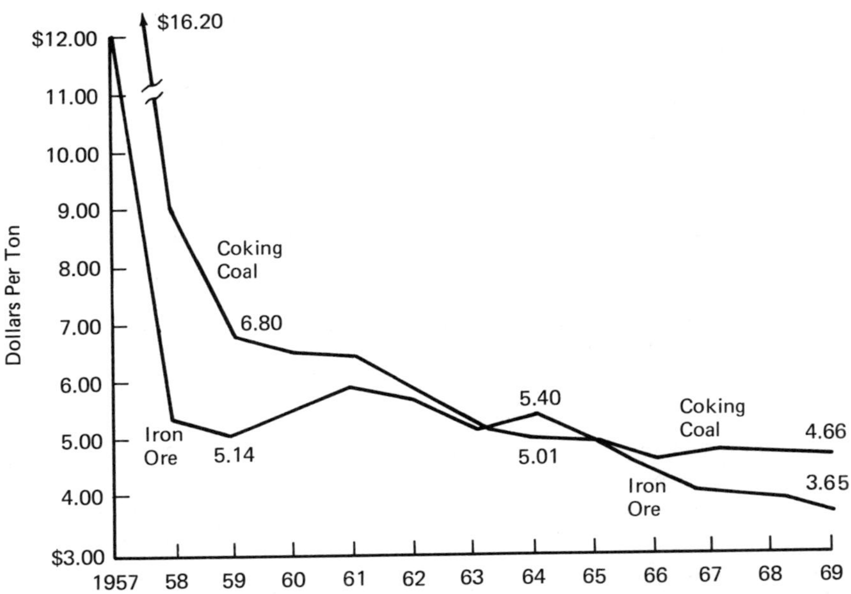

Source: *Outline of Japanese Steel Industry*, Nippon Steel Corporation, September 21st, 1971.

Figure 7–6. Changes in Marine Transportation Freight Rates for Iron Ore and Coking Coal

provided either that such efforts increase the economy of the plant as a whole through permitting more effective utilization of other facilities or that such efforts facilitate achievement of significant economies through the scaling up of other components of the integrated plant.

One additional reason for managerial support of larger-scale plants seems to be the pride derived from outdoing one's competitors in so obvious a manifestation of managerial boldness combined with technological superiority. Such evidences of leadership are not only personally gratifying to the senior executives, but also serve their basic managerial responsibility of building the morale of engineers and employees at large—for in Japan all are deeply identified with their company and take great pride in its achievements.

Conclusions and Implications

Blast Furnace Scale Effects

1. The evidence presented suggests that continuing increases in the size of blast furnaces in Japan have not yielded substantially declining average unit costs, especially beyond 3,500 cubic meters.
2. But such increases in scale have undoubtedly been rewarding through facilitating the rapid expansion of steel output needed to help satisfy profitable demand in Japan and overseas.
3. Moreover, increases in the scale of blast furnaces probably made important contributions to achievement of substantial scale economies at the level of integrated steel mill operations as a whole by supporting advantageous scale increases in other sectors and by contributing to more effective work flows.
4. Both the scale economies realized up to some size range and the apparent avoidance of significant diseconomies beyond that range have obviously been responsive to changes in technology, in operating practices, in the nature of inputs, and in product mix as well as to the economic consequences of such adjustments.
   a. Thus the increased use of sinter and pellets, resort to more powerful blasts and to top pressure, and the introduction of other fuels and increasing reliance on basic oxygen steel furnaces altered optimal technological relationships.
   b. And concurrent changes in the availability and price of input factors altered the economic weights used in calculating the relative advantages of newly available options.
   c. Accordingly, the optimal scale of blast furnaces may be expected to continue changing in response to developing economic pressures and technological potentials.

Toward Strengthening the Analysis of Scale Effects

1. Changes in any component sector of a complex network of integrated industrial operations requires adaptive readjustments in adjacent sectors and often in successively more distant sectors as well.[19]
   a. Hence, efforts to analyze scale effects in modern industry commonly require focussing on performance at the level of the integrated system rather than at the level of even large component units of equipment.
   b. The apparent effects of scale innovations also tend to change over the period required to complete the complex of readjustments triggered by them.
2. Because of the pressures for optimal integration, changes in scale may affect material input specifications, labor skills, processing methods, equipment characteristics, product specialization, and supervisory as well as technical personnel requirements.
   a. The effective tracing of such effects requires consideration of changes in the qualities as well as the quantities of each category of input and output flows and also necessitates reaching beyond such physical measures to assess their cost effects.[20]
   b. Such a rich texture of distinctive input and output characteristics also tends to narrow the range of production activities for plants which can be regarded as differing only in scale, as traditionally defined.
3. In turn, the preceding insights suggest that the traditional economic concept of scale which separates it completely from technological change is impractical. Rather it may be useful to consider a managerially oriented view of scale increases as offering a middle course toward needed technological progress between the "high risk–high payoff" potential of long-term basic research and development and the "low risk–low payoff" short-term potential of routine product and process improvement efforts.[21] Thus scale increases might be regarded as the result of efforts to reach somewhat beyond existing technological frontiers either to ease existing constraints or to uncover still more favorable operating relationships—while working with a technology which is, say, 90 percent familiar and with products which can be handled through existing distribution arrangements and are directly competitive.
4. At any rate, it seems doubtful that any generalizations can be developed concerning scale effects and optima which are both widely applicable and also of substantive importance. Instead, a wide range of analytically attractive opportunities beckons, and this involves the following:
   a. The development of categories for classifying scale-significant differences in types of economic activity (for example, manufacturing, distribution, and so on), types of technologies, types of equipment and facilities, and types of products.

b. The development of theoretical expectations for at least the more important cells within a multidimensional matrix encompassing such scale-significant classifications.

Scale Effects and Managerial Decision Making

1. The analysis which has been presented leads to the conclusion that actual scale adjustments cannot be adequately evaluated within the limited perspectives provided by prevailing economic theory or common engineering approaches.
   a. Changes in scale are obviously the outcome of managerial decisions. But adjusting the scale of production so as to minimize average total unit costs is rarely, if ever, a primary objective of management.
   b. In reality, scale effects reach beyond altering minimum unit production costs at optimum levels of capacity utilization, and management objectives cover a wide spectrum beyond merely seeking to lower such costs.
   c. Hence it need not follow—as is generally assumed—that past increases in scale yielded, or were expected to yield, significant unit-cost reductions, nor that increases in scale which failed to yield such reductions were uneconomic.
2. More penetrating analyses of past or prospective decisions involving changes in scale would seem to require a broader exploration of the relationships between the array of expected benefits and burdens of scale adjustments and the array of basic managerial objectives.
   a. Achieving attractive rates of net profit on investment is probably the single most pervasive and most powerful goal of private enterprise management, and it is apparent that reductions in average total unit production costs are a major potential source of contributions to that end. But profit rates may also be heavily affected by various other factors, including changes in product prices, the productivity of capital, the structure of financing, and the effectiveness of marketing efforts. (see chapter 3).
   b. Even in their bearing on average total unit costs, however, scale effects may be overshadowed by adjustments in factor prices, factor proportions, product mix, and market-induced variations in capacity utilization.
   c. Such determinants of profitability may also interact with managerial efforts to promote additional primary objectives, including long-term growth, maintaining or increasing market shares, avoiding severe short-term fluctuations, limiting serious risks to capital, and safeguarding managerial control.
   d. Scale increases may affect the realization of these primary managerial objectives through such means as altering the flexibility as well as the

level of total unit production costs, increasing dependence on more specialized factor markets, reducing the adaptability of the more highly specialized production system to further changes in processes, facilities, and products, and intensifying the pressures on marketing to maintain levels of demand high enough to utilize large-scale capacity efficiently.

3. The limited role of scale effects in determining the performance of the firm relative to management's primary objectives emphasizes that prospective-cost economies are likely to be but one of the factors considered by management in deciding whether or not to increase scale—with estimated effects on short-term and longer-term profitability overshadowing the physical input–physical output and unit-cost criteria emphasized by common engineering and economic analyses.
   a. As a result, identical technological and cost expectations may lead some competitors to increase scale while others reject or defer such decisions (Gold [9, pp. 230–239]).
   b. Also, increases in scale need not be diffused most rapidly at the time when their technological and cost benefits appear to be greatest (Gold [9, pp. 223–225]).
   c. Moreover, the long-term benefits of increases in scale may differ widely from their short-term benefits, thereby helping to engender further differences in the responses of various competitors. For example, adding capacity rapidly during a period of heavy demand might well yield profits justifying increases in scale even if this involves increases in unit costs and the prospect of eventual underutilization. On the other hand, the construction of large-scale facilities exceeding current demand in newly developing markets might be regarded as justified by the long-term profitability resulting from keeping competitors out through the existence of large unused capacity and using this period of market preemption to consolidate control over distribution and servicing facilities as well as customer relations. And the prospect of deferred rewards may also motivate bigger increases in scale than seem warranted by expected short-term cost economies in the case of managements forecasting increasing inflation in capital goods construction costs.
4. Accordingly, it may prove hazardous for managements to assume that increases in scale by competitors justify emulation without carefully exploring both the kinds of benefits sought by them and their results relative to the urgency of the various needs faced by the decision maker.

Notes

1. 4,400 (Fukuyama Works of Nippon Kokan KK); 4,800 (Mizushima Works of Kawasaki Steel).

2. Of course, the preceding four assumptions are in addition to the general assumptions of static economic theory (including homogeneous input factors, a single product or a fixed product mix, fixed input and factor prices, and a given state of technology) and the associated concentration on seeking the most favorable among the alternatives available at a moment of time.

3. Such a conception is basically irrelevant, of course, because all facilities and equipment are available in a variety of sizes, because builders and manufacturers are usually prepared to provide facilities and equipment in the specific sizes desired for new plants, and because plants are designed to perform optimally at planned levels of operation.

4. This widely evidenced characteristic also undermines Boulding's attempt to suggest that scale economies would be derived from the relatively fewer managerial personnel required in larger plants, for example, still only one plant manager (Boulding [3, p. 550]). This would, of course, offer only very slight savings, even if it were generally true, inasmuch as total salary costs in U.S. manufacturing average only about 4 percent, even including headquarters personnel.

5. This exceeds the average for "all manufacturing industries combined" in the United States. For cost proportions in a variety of industries which indicate how unusual fixed costs in excess of 20 percent are, see Gold [6, p. 137]. It may also be of interest to note that the financial statements of leading U.S. steel companies reveal that depreciation charges plus interest are usually less than 10 percent of total cost.

6. Indeed, Samuelson follows the presentation of this definition with illustrations which seem not to conform to the requirement of fixed-factor proportions (Samuelson [16, p. 28]).

7. For example, see Stigler's application of his survivor test to assess scale economies (Stigler [19]).

8. Smaller plants serving small isolated markets, for example, need not be under any competitive pressure to increase scale in order to reduce production costs to levels achieved in large markets elsewhere.

9. For illustrative references, proposing exponents of 0.6 and 0.7 for estimating the investment cost of larger equipment and larger plants, respectively, in the chemical industry, see Aries [1, pp. 6-7, 15], Bauman [2, pp. 39, 180-181], Crowe [4, p. 110], and Peters [13, p. 93].

10. For an excellent review of the potential sources of scale economies, including experiential as well as theoretical views, see C.F. Pratten 114, pp. 3-19]. For earlier reviews of empirical studies of scale that provide penetrating discussions of conceptual problems and the difficulties confronting efforts to undertake effective empirical testing of theoretical expectations as well as illustrations of the wide range of published findings, see C. Smith [18], F.T. Moore [10], A. Walters [20], and S. Shuman and S. Alpert [17]. Empirical estimates of exponents covering a wide array of processes are provided in Aries [1, p. 7] and Bauman [2, p. 146].

11. It would also be possible to increase scale by building a plant with a capacity equivalent to a predecessor but designed to yield a larger output of a narrower range of products, thereby permitting greater specialization of materials, equipment, skills, and production arrangements. Nor would an apparent increase in product variety reduce the level of scale significantly if it involved adjustments only in relatively minor components of the entire production process, for example, differences in color, finish, external covering, or other superficial characteristics of the product.

12. This suggests that scale changes might be analyzed more effectively if they were regarded as a sector of technological progress intermediate between the cumulative flow of small, essentially revolutionary improvements and major advances based on quantum jumps in scientific knowledge and engineering principles. Thus scale changes might well become a more clearly recognized and more common focus of technology-improvement programs, offering less risk than far-reaching research programs (because scale-improvement efforts would center closely around a core of known technology) and also larger benefits than technical-development programs seeking only modest incremental gains.

13. Even without employing this broadened concept of the nature of scale changes, Weiss's review of the published research on scale led him to conclude that it is a "still fairly blank field" (Weiss [21, p. 297]).

14. For example, a detailed estimate published in 1972 for a relatively small blast furnace (1,860 cubic meters) adds up to $31,440,000, excluding coke ovens and sintering machinery. Inclusion of the latter raises the total to $62,190,000 (Yoshida [22, Table 4-1]).

15. For estimates of the relative contributions of various factors affecting increases in blast furnace capacity aside from sheer size alone, see Nakamura [11, p. 2 and Fig. 1].

16. For an interesting review of the dramatic pattern of such substitutions in the United States during recent years, see Rosegger [15, p. 23].

17. Because Japan was more heavily dependent on basic oxygen furnaces in making steel, it needed a higher ratio of hot pig iron input to steel output than other countries like the United States and West Germany, which still had substantial open-hearth steel-making capacity and thus could use a higher ratio of scrap in the steel furnaces.

18. Since the late 1950s, basic oxygen steel furnaces have also undergone major advances in scale, increasing from heat sizes of 85 to 95 tons to 330 tons [24, p. 4].

19. For an interesting exploration of the changing results from undertaking evaluations of technological innovations at successively higher levels of aggregation, see Peirce [12].

20. Such an analytical framework was illustrated in chapter 3; for a further discussion of the effects of technological changes on input and output quality, see chapter 13.

21. For a further discussion of such strategies, see chapter 14.

References

[1] R.S. Aries and R.D. Newton, *Chemical Engineering Cost Estimates* (New York: McGraw-Hill, 1955).

[2] H.C. Bauman, *Fundamentals of Cost Engineering in the Chemical Industry* (New York: Reinhold. 1964).

[3] K. Boulding, *Economic Analysis,* 4th ed. (New York: Harper & Row, 1966).

[4] C.M. Crowe et al., *Chemical Plant Simulation* (Englewood Cliffs, N.J.: Prentice-Hall, 1971).

[5] B. Gold, *Foundations of Productivity Analysis* (Pittsburgh: Univ. of Pittsburgh Press, 1955).

[6] B. Gold, *Explorations in Managerial Economics: Productivity, Costs, Technology and Growth* (London: Macmillan, 1971; New York: Basic Books, 1971).

[7] B. Gold, "Technology, Productivity and Economics," *Omega (International Journal of Management Science),* February 1973; reprinted in Gold [8].

[8] B. Gold (ed.), *Technological Change: Economics, Management and Environmental* (Oxford: Pergamon, 1975, 1979).

[9] B. Gold, W.S. Peirce, and G. Rosegger, "Diffusion of Major Technological Innovations in U.S. Iron and Steel Manufacturing," *Journal of Industrial Economics,* July 1970; reprinted in Gold [8].

[10] F.T. Moore, "Economies of Scale: Some Statistical Evidence," *Quarterly Journal of Economics,* May 1959.

[11] N. Nakamura, *The Modern Blast Furnace: The Significance and Realization of the Large Blast Furnace,* (Tokyo: Nippon Steel Corporation, January 1971).

[12] W.S. Peirce, "The Ripple Effect: A Case Study of Pelletizing Iron Ore," *Omega,* December 1973; reprinted in Gold [7].

[13] M.S. Peters, *Plant Design and Economics for Chemical Engineers* (New York: McGraw-Hill, 1958).

[14] C.F. Pratten, *Economies of Scale in Manufacturing Industry* (Cambridge, Eng.: Cambridge Univ. Press, 1971).

[15] G. Rosegger, "Technological Change and Materials Consumption in U.S. Iron and Steel Manufacturing: An Assessment of Some Environmental Impacts," *Human Ecology,* January 1974.

[16] P.A. Samuelson, *Economics,* 9th ed. (New York: McGraw-Hill, 1973).

[17] S. Shuman and S. Alpert, "Economies of Scale: Some Statistical Evidence –Comment," *Quarterly Journal of Economics,* August 1960.

[18] C. Smith, "Survey of the Empirical Evidence of Economies of Scale," *Business Concentration and Price Policy* (Princeton: Princeton Univ. Press, 1955).

[19] G. Stigler, "The Economics of Scale," *Journal of Law and Economics,* October 1958.
[20] A. Walters, "Economics of Scale: Some Statistical Evidence–Comment," *Quarterly Journal of Economics,* February 1960.
[21] L. Weiss, "Quantitative Studies of Industrial Organization," in M.D. Intriligator (ed.), *Frontiers of Quantitative Economics* (Amsterdam: North-Holland, 1971).
[22] H. Yoshida, *A Study of Iron Making by Blast Furnace–Reference Data,* (Tokyo: Kawasaki Steel Corporation, February 1972).
[23] Company reports covering each major steel producer.
[24] *L-D Process Newsletter* (Chicago: Kaiser Engineers, October 19, 1972).
[25] *Outline of Japanese Steel Industry,* (Tokyo: Nippon Steel Corporation, September, 21, 1971).

8 Interactions between Technological Innovations and Factor Prices

Because of the widespread and powerful effects of technological innovations in industry, there is a great need, especially in market-oriented economies, to evaluate the effectiveness of changing price differentials in redirecting technological improvement efforts, as well as a need to improve assessment of the probable effects of different technological innovations on resource requirements and costs. It is not surprising, therefore, to find that much has been written about the effects of changes in relative factor prices on inducing technological innovations, or at least changes in factor proprotions,[1] nor that much has also been written about the effects of technological innovations on factor prices through intervening adjustments in factor proportions.[2]

But most of the published literature offers only highly simplified models of such relationships at levels of aggregation which preclude effective identification either of the specific technological innovations or of the specific inputs whose interactions are the purported focuses of these studies.[3] As a result, this constitutes still another sector of economic analysis in which the array of published hypothetical models is seldom relieved by serious attempts to test them—in this case, through investigations of the effects of *actual* technological innovations on *actual* factor prices or vice versa.[4]

Accordingly, the following discussion will seek to strengthen the analytical framework for tracing interactions between technological innovations and factor prices in each direction, to illustrate some actual relationships, and to suggest some hypotheses reflecting the altered expectations derived from empirical findings to date.

Effects of Technological Innovations on Factor Prices

Revising the Analytic Framework

Preceding chapters have already emphasized the superficiality of seeking to determine the economic effects of a labor-saving or other factor-saving innovation by merely tracing its effects on the given factor's price and unit costs. Production processes obviously involve integration of the contributions of all input factors, and modern technology seeks to develop increasingly effective combinations of such inputs. Hence even technological innovations which are focused primarily on one input usually require adaptive adjustments in other input factors as well, thus expanding the array of possible effects on onther factor-input levels, prices, and unit costs which should be evaluated.

What conditions determine the effects on factor proportions, and in turn on factor prices, of a technological innovation directed toward reducing the unit-input requirement of only one factor? The three most important conditions seem to be the technological characteristics of the process, accompanying changes in output levels, and managerial objectives in adopting the innovation.

As discussed in chapter 5, industrial processes may be classified as capital-dominated, labor-dominated, or materials-dominated, according to which factor is the dominant determinant of changes in capacity and productive efficiency. For example, electric power plants, blast furnaces, and petroleum refineries may be characterized as capital-dominated because the capacities of such facilities can only be altered significantly by increasing the throughput capabilities of their capital goods. Such factor dominance also affects the flexibility of the various input factors. For example, technological innovations may increase the capacity of such plants without significant increases in investment or employment (for example, by speeding up certain reactions), thus reducing the ratio of investment to capacity, but leaving the ratio of investment to labor unchanged and increasing potential output per man-hour. In such capital-dominated processes, however, increasing the effectiveness of labor efforts would not increase capacity, but would only make possible a reduction in employment levels.

The effects of a resource-saving innovation on factor proportions, and hence on factor demands and prices, also depend—as noted in chapter 5—on whether its application is followed by increasing output or leaving it unchanged. The latter would tend to reduce demand for the resource being economized, while a proportionate increase in output would leave inputs of that resource unchanged. In the case of a labor-dominated operation like bricklaying, for example, an increase in output per man-hour would obviously reduce man-hour requirements unless total output could be increased proportionately, and the latter would also involve an increased demand for bricks. But such options tend to be restricted by the technological conditions of factor dominance. In the case of a materials-dominated process like farming, for example, fertilizer-saving innovations on a given farm can only be exploited by reducing its demand for fertilizer. And a technologically induced increase in the capacity of capital-dominated facilities requiring high levels of utilization, like blast furnaces, can only be exploited by increasing output.

The third determinant of the effects of resource-saving innovations on factor inputs and their prices is management's objective in making the decision. This need not be correctly inferred from examining the results, both because results do not always conform to expectations and because one may not even guess the particular needs that management had in mind. For example, management might decide to increase investment, not to expand capacity, but to replace labor, or to economize on materials or energy, thus decreasing capacity/investment, but increasing output per man-hour or output/materials. Alternatively, management may be increasing materials input per unit of output, or investment relative to capacity, in order to improve the quality of products, thus resulting in a quite different pattern of factor proportions and attendant shifts in factor demands and prices.

In order to review all such potential changes in factor proportions systematically, use may be made of an analytical framework such as was presented in chapter 3 and summarized in figure 3-2.

Some Hypotheses Suggested by Empirical Research

Studies of technological innovations and their effects in a variety of industries suggest the following hypotheses concerning the effects of such innovations on factor prices (Gold [13]):

The direction of the effects of innovation-induced changes in factor proportions on factor prices tends to be asymetrical as among different inputs. General theory suggests that resource-saving innovations tend to reduce demand for the factor involved at any given level of product output and, hence, to reduce its price relative to what it would otherwise be. This expectation seems applicable in the case of materials-saving innovations. But decreases in man-hour requirements per unit of output are more likely to increase than to decrease hourly earnings as a result of piece rates or incentive payments or, most commonly, because of trade union demands for higher wage rates to reward increases in labor productivity—as they interpret decreases in unit labor requirements. And decreases in investment requirements per unit of capacity for new facilities in given plants and industries are likely to have no significant effect on interest rates because such partially reduced demands in narrow industrial sectors cannot play an influential role in the vast capital markets.

The timing of the effects of innovation-induced changes in factor proportions on factor prices depends on the size of the market within which the relevant factor price is determined, the coherence of that market, and the time pattern of the innovation's diffusion. To illustrate the first of these, wage-rate responses tend to be the most rapid and most nearly proportionate to reduced input requirements per unit of output because they tend to be generated through piece rates or trade union demands in the very first plants adopting a significant labor-saving innovation. On the other hand, materials prices may not respond until the innovation has diffused widely enough to force recognition of the reduced level of demand—and this may take a number of years (Gold [17, p. 131]). Moreover, it is because of the huge proportions of the capital market that the investment-saving effects of any given innovation are unlikely to produce any discernible effects. The role of market coherence may be illustrated by the tendency of labor-saving innovations to spread more rapidly than others because resulting increases in wage rates in a growing number of plants are likely to trigger trade union demands for industrywide wage increases, thus intensifying pressures for laggard firms to adopt the innovation. Ensuing decreases in materials prices, however, may tend instead to ease pressures on lagging firms to adopt materials-saving innovations. Finally, it is apparent that the timing of the impact of a resource-saving innovation on factor demand and prices depends on the time pattern of the innovation's diffusion. And this can be measured less meaningfully by the number of firms adopting it (Mansfield [28, p. 133ff]) than by the proportion of total output produced by means of the innovation over progressively longer periods (Gold [17, pp. 129–131]).

The extent of the effects of innovation-induced changes in factor proportions on factor prices may be very difficult to disentangle from the effects of several concomitant developments. One of these is the effect on such factor prices of concurrent fluctuations in the industry's output levels, or in other significant sources of demand for the factors affected, as compared with the expected effects on demand of the innovation alone. Another interacting influence may be the preinnovational trend in the prices of the input factors affected by the innovation. Thus, even major materials-saving innovations may merely moderate the rising trend of a material's price instead of reversing it (Gold [14, pp. 196–197]). Determining the distinctive effects of the innovation itself is also complicated by the frequently accompanying changes in the specific characteristics of the affected inputs. In the case of materials, for example, innovations frequently require shifts within the broad category of such materials to subgroups with altered chemical and other specifications. But the price differentials associated with such altered specifications are usually not reflected by the broader commodity groupings for which price series are generally available.[5]

Still other sources of difficulty in measuring the effects of innovation-induced changes in factor proportions are the almost invariable accompanying adjustments in product characteristics and product mix. Such changes obviously affect the measures of output used to determine both the average level of input requirements per unit of output and factor costs per unit of output. Moreover, interpretations of resulting changes in unit costs clearly depend on associated changed in average revenue per unit of output, sufficient increases in the latter rendering even increases in unit costs acceptable and possibly attractive.

Effects of Changes in Factor Prices on Factor Proportions and Technological Innovations

Theoretical Expectations and Their Applicability

The basis for most deductive analyses in this area is the concept in economic theory of a *production isoquant,* which assumes that in producing a given output, factor proportions can be shifted readily over a wide range in response to changes in relative factor prices. And this approach is then projected logically to suggest that persistent changes in factor prices tend to induce technological innovations that permit more effective utilization of factor combinations which increase the proportionate inputs of the more advantageously priced resources.

In reality, however, the actual range of such readily reversible interchangabilities—which are technologically feasible and economically equivalent—tends to be very small, even in the few industrial sectors where they exist at all. An unusually relevant example is provided by the long-dominant open-hearth process for making steel, which permits a very wide range in the ratio of hot pig iron to scrap steel inputs. Yet figure 8-1 shows that even wide fluctuations in scrap steel prices (between \$28 and \$52 per ton) had little effect on such input proportions even over quite long periods.[6] Incidentally, figure 8-1 also shows that the newer basic oxygen furnace process, which permits a narrower but still significant variation in such input proportions, seemed similarly unresponsive to the fluctuations in scrap prices.

But the overwhelming proportion of actual industrial operations have been developed under conditions of increasing industrial specialization and increasing pressure to search out optimal input-output combinations. These tend to involve

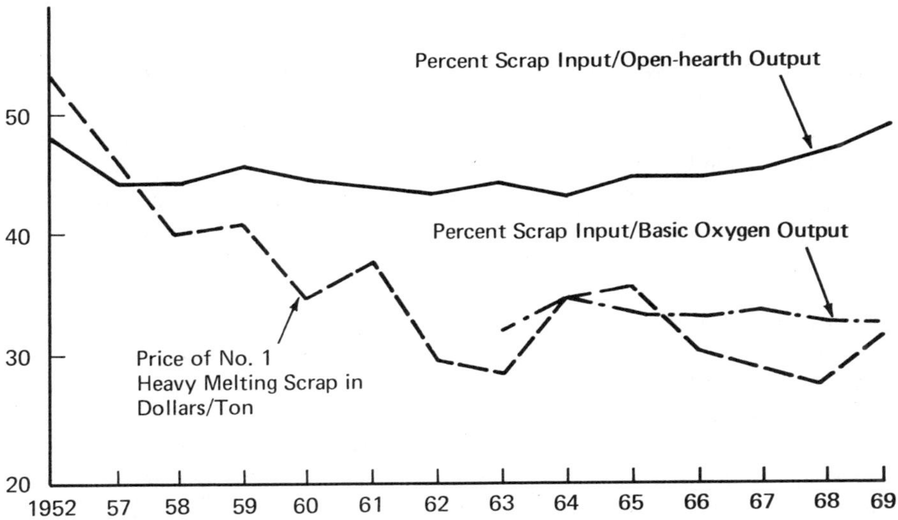

Source: Based on data in G. Rosegger, "Technological Change, Managerial Incentives and Environmental Effects," in B. Gold (ed.), *Technological Change: Economics, Management and Environment* (Oxford: Pergamon, 1975, 1979), pp. 60–61.

Figure 8-1. U.S. Scrap Prices and Scrap Input/Raw Steel Output, 1956–1969, Open-Hearth and Basic Oxygen Furnaces

very closely restricted factor proportions which reflect careful engineering and accounting determinations and are reinforced by the specialized capital facilities and production practices developed on the basis of such determinations. Accordingly, more realistic explorations of the responsiveness of industrial operations to changes in relative factor prices might give consideration to such conceptions as are reflected by the following hypotheses which have emerged from my own empirical studies.

Some Hypotheses Suggested by Empirical Research

Significant changes in factor proportions in response to changes in relative factor prices are likely to emerge only very slowly. Perhaps the most important reason for this is that significant shifts in factor proportions usually require significant changes in technologies and, hence, in capital, as well as in other inputs and associated production practices. But such technologies and related inputs are developed and employed on the basis of long-term perspectives and commitments. Hence both the incentives to, and the practical range for, responding to short-term fluctuations in relative factor prices tend to be very limited. This means that managements are unlikely even to initiate serious efforts to explore feasible adjustments in factor proportions to changes in relative factor prices until consistent long-term trends in such relative prices have become reasonably well established.

The development of new technologies to exploit significant shifts in relative factor prices is usually beset with considerable difficulties and uncertainties, but some types of input substitutions can usually be effected more quickly than others. It is often quite difficult to shift economically from one raw material to another, or even to a markedly poorer quality of the same material. As examples, one need only review the long and costly efforts to utilize lower-grade iron ore for steelmaking in the United States, or to permit shifts between steel and aluminum in producing metal cans,[7] or the current time-consuming and costly efforts even to convert electricity-generating plants from burning oil to coal. In addition, it is usually even more difficult to substitute labor for capital without incurring substantially increased costs. On the other hand, generalized methods for replacing labor with capital inputs via mechanization and instrumentation have been more fully developed, have proved more widely applicable, and therefore are more readily available as responses to unfavorable trends in wage rates. But the potential benefits of such substitutions may be sharply limited by trade union demands for higher wage rates to parallel resulting increases in output per man-hour, as noted earlier, and even for employment maintenance. Nor should sight be lost of the common tendency for reductions in direct labor through mechanization to be accompanied by at least partially offsetting increases in indirect labor, including maintenance and production-control personnel.

Managements are actually less concerned about changes in relative factor prices than in their effects on competitive position and profitability, and the connection between the latter and factor-price adjustments has several linkages capable of producing a wide range of relationships. To begin with, managers are less concerned about changes in individual factor prices than in their effects on total unit costs, as determined by the proportion of total costs accounted for by that input and also by the net effect on total unit costs of any accompanying changes in other unit costs. Thus a 10 percent increase in unit-wage costs in plants where such costs account for only one-sixth of total costs would represent less of an impact than a 5 percent increase in material costs when the latter account for more than one-half of total costs.[8] Moreover, managers tend to be less concerned about the absolute level of unit costs than about their competitive cost advantages and disadvantages. Thus changes in factor prices tending to affect all producers similarly (for example, industrywide wage-rate increases) are less likely to engender extraordinary efforts to offset them than would factor-price increases tending to disadvantage some producers compared with others. The latter may be illustrated by cases of producers relying primarily on different inputs to produce competing products, for example, makers of steel versus aluminum cans, fertilizer producers using by-product coke chemicals versus petrochemicals, textile manufacturers using synthetic versus natural fibers. Finally, it should be recalled that efforts to respond to factor-price changes by altering factor proportions through adjustments in technologies and production arrangements are also likely to affect product characteristics. Unless these promise product price and output shifts likely to yield comparable or increased profitability, such responses may be withheld.

Concluding Observations

The theoretical framework commonly applied to analyzing the prospective effects of technological innovations on factor prices and changes in relative factor prices on factor proportions and production technologies is so grossly oversimplified as to make applications to actual industrial operations difficult and even misleading. More meaningful appraisals require a comprehensive analytical framework covering interactions among all input factors, attendant changes in factor prices and unit costs, and resulting adjustments in product characteristics, prices, and output levels as well as profitability. Moreover, such analyses must take into account trends in such relationships before the impact being studied as well as for successively longer periods after it.[9]

Our exploratory studies suggest that the effects of major technological innovations on factor prices tend to be more traceable and influential—especially with respect to the particular labor and material inputs directly affected—than the reverse effects of changes in relative factor prices on factor proportions and the technologies and production arrangements which they reflect. But the speed and extent of such technological effects are likely to vary widely because of the broad range of changes encompassed by the term *technological innovations* (Gold [16, pp. 173–175]), and because of the multiplicity of managerial objectives, patterns of factor dominance, and factor and product market characteristics which may be involved. Moreover, it may be extremely difficult to disentangle such effects from the wide variety of other forces affecting factor prices, production methods, and product characteristics.

It should be emphasized, however, that these judgments need not preclude increasingly useful determinations of such effects in either direction for particular cases. Thus it would be eminently useful for industrial managements contemplating new technological innovations to undertake serious analyses of their prospective effects on factor prices as well as on input requirements in order to assess resulting cost advantages more realistically. In addition, periodic appraisals of the price trends of their major input factors would certainly offer one sector of highly relevant perspectives for managerial choices among alternative research and technological improvement programs. Similarly, governmental agencies concerned witht he encouragement of technological progress in the national interest would patently benefit from increasing empirical insights into the effects of various kinds of technological innovations under specific conditions and into the technological responsiveness of different industries to shifting factor prices—as bases for considering the desirability of seeking to modify relevant industrial decisions.

But the preceding analysis does tend to discourage hopes of achieving broadly applicable generalizations in the near future. Instead, it reinforces the conclusions emerging in other sectors of economics that, at this stage of our knowledge, an increasingly effective grasp of causal sequences and relationships requires digging beneath broad aggregates to focus sharply on what Alfred Marshall termed "the many in the one" and thus help to restore the imbalance resulting from overconcentration in recent years on studying "the one in the many."

Notes

1. Selected examples of such work include Fellner [12], Kennedy [25], Ahmad [1], Wilkinson [37], Kamien and Schwartz [22], Levhari and Sheshinski [27], and Feller [11].

2. Selected examples include Hicks [20], Gourvitch [18], Salter [33], and critiques of the latter by Brown [5], Blaug [2], Diamond [7], Doeringer [9], Sovani [35], and Kamien and Schwartz [23].

3. Illustrations of such generalized empirical studies include Mayami and Ruttan [19], Cigno [6], and Rausser [31]. There is, of course, a substantial literature concerning the effects of specific technological innovations on unit

input requirements, especially of labor, without directly considering accompanying effects on factor prices. (For surveys including such studies, see Kennedy and Thirlwall [26], Kamien and Schwartz [24], and Boylan [4]).

4. The relative scarcity of such studies is indicated by the following sparse list resulting from an extensive review of the literature by Boylan [4]: Sethur [34], Enos [10], Weinberg [36], Gold [13], Hollander [21], Dilley and McBride [8], Mansfield [28], Peirce [30], and Boylan [3].

5. For example, see chapter 13.

6. Also relevant is the fact that the ratio of purchased steel scrap to total scrap consumption averaged about 40 percent throughout the period studied (Rosegger [32, p. 60]).

7. For a detailed review of both developments see chapter 13. Such relative unresponsiveness of technology to shifting factor prices is also illustrated in chapter 9.

8. Far from representing extremes, these proportions parallel long-maintained averages for "all manufacturing" in the United States since 1900 (Gold [14, p. 191]).

9. For a review of some preogressively longer term effects of technological innovations see Gold [15, pp. 19-38]. and chapter 10.

References

[1] S. Ahmad, "On the Theory of Induced Inventions," *Economic Journal,* June 1966.

[2] M. Blaug, "A Survey of the Theory of Process Innovations," *Economica,* February 1963.

[3] M.G. Boylan, *Economic Effects of Scale Increases in the Steel Industry: The Case of U.S. Blast Furnaces* (New York: Praeger, 1975).

[4] M.G. Boylan, "Reported Economic Effects of Technological Changes," in Gold [16].

[5] M. Brown, *On the Theory and Measurement of Technological Change* (Cambridge, Eng.: Cambridge Univ. Press, 1968).

[6] A. Cigno, "Production and Investment Response to Changing Market Conditions, Technical Know-How and Government Policies," *Review of Economic Studies,* January 1971.

[7] P.A. Diamond, "Technical Change and the Measurement of Capital and Output," *Review of Economic Studies,* October 1965.

[8] D. Dilley and D. McBride, "Oxygen Steelmaking: Fact vs. Folklore," *Iron and Steel Engineer,* October 1967.

[9] P.B. Doeringer, "Factor Prices and Technological Change," *Western Economic Journal,* Spring 1966.

[10] J. Enos, *Petroleum Progress and Profits: A History of Process Innovation* (Cambridge, Mass.: M.I.T. Press, 1962).

[11] I. Feller, "Production Isoquants and Technical Change," *Quarterly Journal of Economics,* February 1972.

[12] W. Fellner, "Does the Market Direct the Relative Factor-Saving Effects of Technological Progress," in Nelson [29].

[13] B. Gold, "Economic Effects of Technological Innovations," *Management Science,* September 1964; reprinted in Gold [14].

[14] B. Gold, *Explorations in Managerial Economics: Productivity, Costs, Technology and Growth* (New York: Basic Books; London: Macmillan 1971).

[15] B. Gold (ed.), *Technological Change: Economics, Technology and Environment* (Oxford: Pergamon, 1975, 1979).

[16] B. Gold (ed.), *Research, Technological Change and Economic Analysis* (Lexington, Mass.: Lexington Books, D.C. Heath 1977).

[17] B. Gold, W.S. Peirce, and G. Rosegger, "Diffusion of Major Technological Innovations," *Journal of Industrial Economics,* July 1970; reprinted in Gold [15].

[18] A. Gourvitch, *Survey of Economic Theory on Technological Change and Employment* (Philadelphia: U.S. Works Progress Administration—National Research Project, 1940).

[19] Y. Hayami and V.W. Ruttan, "Factor Prices and Technical Change in Agricultural Development: The U.S. and Japan, 1880-1960," *Journal of Political Economy* September, October 1970.

[20] J. Hicks, "Distribution and Economic Progress: A Revised Version," *Review of Economic Studies,* October 1936.

[21] S. Hollander, *The Sources of Increased Efficiency: A Study of DuPont Rayon Plants* (Cambridge, Mass.: M.I.T. Press, 1965).

[22] M.I. Kamien and N.L. Schwartz, "Optimal 'Induced' Technical Change," *Econometrica,* January 1968.

[23] M.I. Kamien and N.L. Schwartz, "Induced Factor-Augmenting Technical Progress from a Micro-Economic Viewpoint," *Econometrica,* October 1969.

[24] M.I. Kamien and N.L. Schwartz, "Market Structure and Innovation," *Journal of Economic Literature,* March 1975.

[25] C. Kennedy, "Induced Bias in Innovation and the Theory of Distribution," *Economic Journal,* September 1964.

[26] C. Kennedy and A.P. Thirlwall, "Surveys in Applied Economics: Technical Progress," *Economic Journal,* March 1972.

[27] D. Levhari and E. Sheshinski, "The Factor Price Frontier with Embodied Technical Progress," *American Economic Review,* December 1970.

[28] E. Mansfield, *Industrial Research and Technological Innovation* (New York: Norton, 1968).

[29] R.R. Nelson (ed), *The Rate and Direction of Inventive Activity: Economic and Social Factors* (Princeton, N.J.: Princeton Univ. Press, 1962).
[30] W.S. Peirce, "The Effects of Technological Change: Exploring Successive Ripples," in Gold [15].
[31] G.C. Rausser, "Technological Change, Production and Investment in Natural Resources Industries," *American Economic Review,* December 1974.
[32] G. Rosegger, "Technological Change, Managerial Incentives and Environmental Effects," in Gold [15].
[33] W.E.G. Salter, *Productivity and Technical Change* (Cambridge, Eng.: Cambridge Univ. Press, 1960).
[34] F. Sethur, "Austrian Steel: Development and Prospects," *Journal of Industrial Economics,* June 1960.
[35] N.V. Sovani, "Improved Techniques, Costs and Prices," *Indian Economic Journal,* April-June, 1967.
[36] E. Weinberg, *Impact of Technological Change and Automation in the Pulp and Paper Industry,* U.S. Department of Labor Bulletin 1347 (Washington: U.S. Government Printing Office, 1968).
[37] M. Wilkinson, "Factor Supply and Direction of Technological Change," *American Economic Review,* March 1968.

9 Tracing the Effects of Advances in Productivity and Technology within Plants and Firms

This chapter and the next will provide some empirical perspectives on the nature and value of the insights offered by applications of the general analytical framework presented in chapter 3 (and summarized in figure 3-2).

Managerial Objectives and Feasibility of Applications

The proposed framework was designed to serve three managerial objectives: to uncover the determinants of adjustments in the past performance of the firm by identifying the primary sources of improvements and shortcomings within the complex of operations, to search out deviations in current performance from established targets in each major unit, and to develop future plans on a systematic basis covering each component in the framework.

More particularly, such analysis would permit tracing the effects of actual or prospective technological or other innovations through the system. For example, it would permit assessing the effects of actual or prospective changes in the quality, supply, price, or mix of materials or other inputs on productivity levels, factor proportions, and costs in successive stages of production. Beginning at the other end, it would permit mapping the effects of changes in product design or product mix on costs and productivity levels at successively antecedent stages of operations back to procurement, or it would permit tracing the effects of actual or contemplated changes in processes or facilities or quality standards in any given operation through successively earlier and later operating units. Thus one might readily use such an approach to appraise the effects of technological or other innovations.

Such an integrated approach tends to be especially useful in analyzing complex industrial operations because it provides realistic perspectives for evaluating shifts in tasks between operating units and for tracing possible offsets in some activities to advances proposed by others. And when employed on a multiperiod rather than a single-period basis, it permits consideration of the potential contributions of longer-term gains relative to shorter-term burdens and costs. Finally, it also permits reasonable efforts to differentiate the effects of external changes in factor and product markets from internally generated adjustments.

In various applications of this approach to actual operations,[1] all the required data have been readily available as a by-product of plant accounting, production control, and personnel records, except indexes of physical output and capacity. The former have been readily calculated, however, by weighting the output of each product in each period by its average price in that period and in the base period and then comparing the total for all products in each period with the base period total (that is, using the Edgeworth index). And indexes of capacity were developed in the same way, except that different indexes had to be developed, of course, for each basic product mix.[2]

Although the nature of outputs obviously changes from operation to operation, this presents no problems in measuring outputs, either for each unit or at more aggregative levels, so long as the nature of the products at each level of evaluation remains essentially unchanged. Much the same is true of inputs. It is obviously important, however, both to achieve complete coverage of inputs and outputs throughout the process and to gain a clear understanding of all resource flows as well as the specific boundaries of each cost center and department to be analyzed. (It has been my experience that this requires reasonable familiarity with the entire system before data categories can be effectively defined).

Integrated Steel Mill Study: Background Information

The following analysis summarizes the results of a study of the complex interwoven processes of one of the largest integrated steel mills in Western Europe: the Port Talbot Works of the British Steel Corporation.[3] A simplified flowchart of the major operations involved is shown in figure 9-1. It shows that the major materials inputs include coal, iron ore, limestone, and purchased as well as internally generated scrap. Major products include hot-rolled and cold-rolled as well as coated steel products. There are three operating departments: ironmaking, steelmaking, and finishing. In addition, there is a service department providing steam, electricity, maintenance, and other operating services, and, of course, a supervising structure of line and staff functions.

The two most important and most costly innovations during the 8-year period covered were the construction of a new harbor capable of berthing 100,000 deadweight tonnage ships, to increase the economies of access to foreign ores and coal, and the replacement of the very low nitrogen and open-hearth steel furnaces by a new basic oxygen steel making shop. Lesser innovations included the relining and enlargement of two blast furnaces, the computerization of one, and the introduction of fuel injection and oxygen-blast enrichment prior to the beginning of the study, along with the rebuilding of two coke batteries. In the finishing department, the only significant innovations were the modification and computerization of the cold-rolling mill. Thus major changes took place just prior to or during the study period in two of the three operating departments.

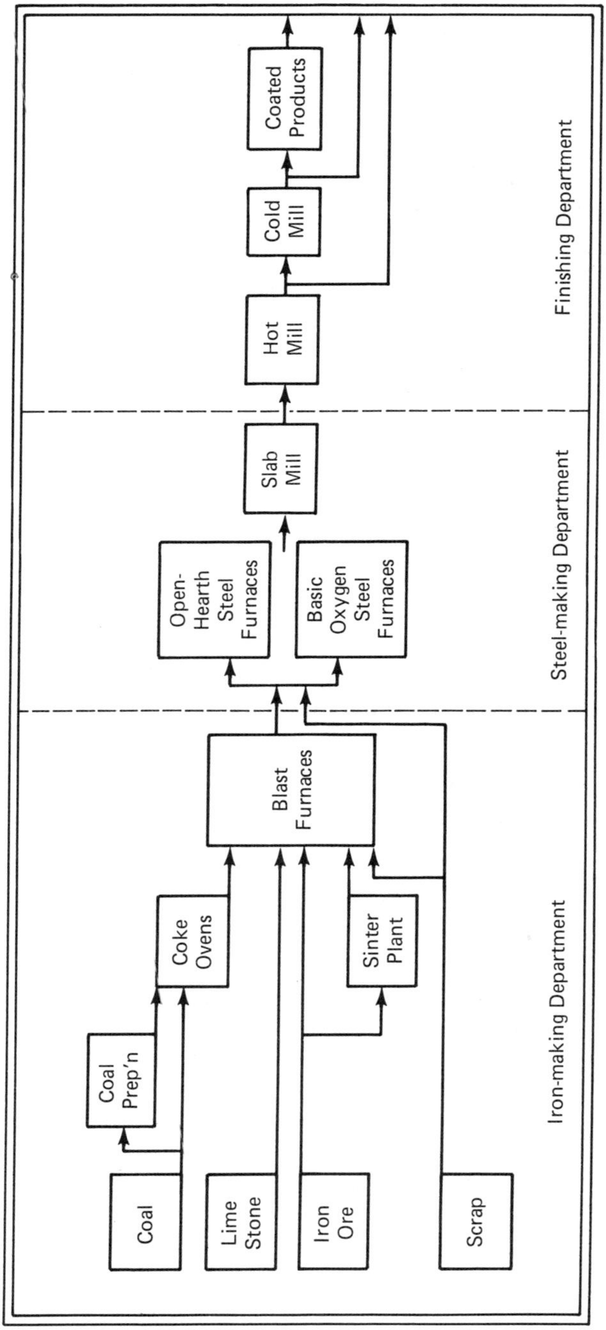

Figure 9–1. Simplified Diagram of Departments and Major Operating Units of an Integrated Steel Mill

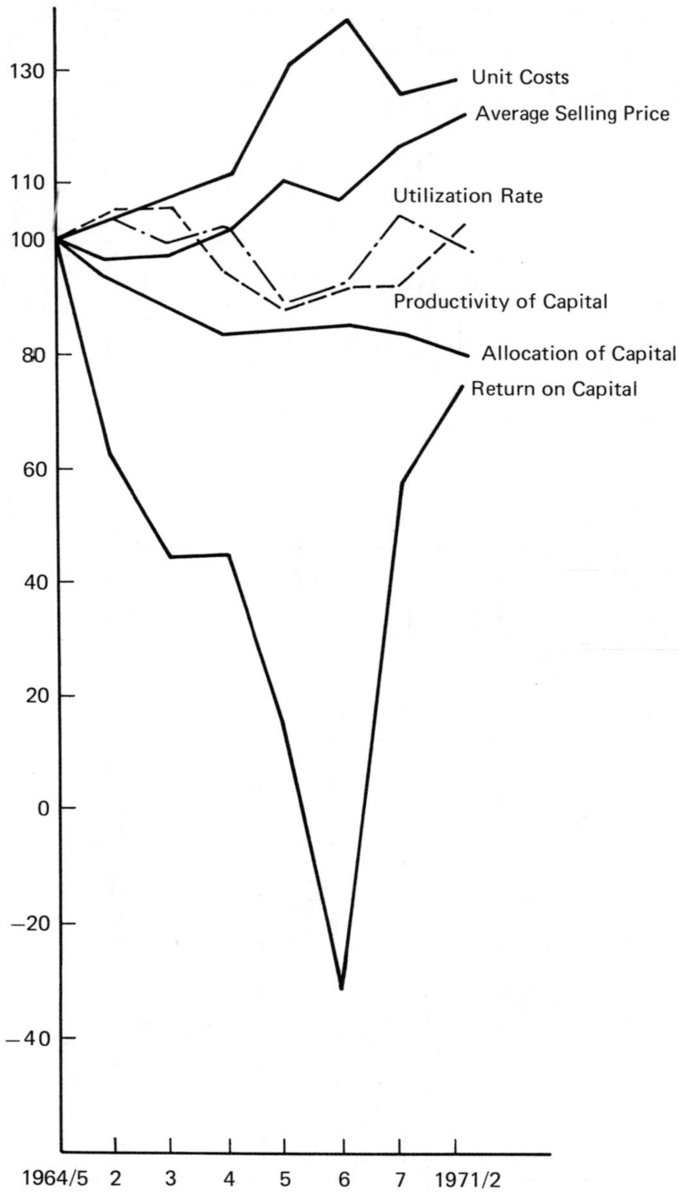

Source: S. Eilon, B. Gold, J. Soesan, *Applied Productivity Analysis for Industry* (Oxford: Pergamon, 1976).

Figure 9–2. Managerial Control Ratios: Steel Mill

Plant-Level Results: Profits and Managerial Control Ratios

Figure 9-2 shows that a steady decline in the rate of profits in total investment during the first 4 years was accentuated during the fifth only to be sharply reversed thereafter. The major reason for this outcome during the first 5 years was that total unit costs rose more rapidly than prices and this burden was accentuated during the fourth and fifth years by lower capacity-utilization rates. A sharp increase in the rate of profits on total investment during the last 2 years covered was attributable primarily to a downturn in unit costs, while prices continued to rise, and to some recovery in utilization rates. Accordingly, efforts to explain these developments may concentrate on the factors responsible for observed changes in unit costs and in capacity utilization—with materials and wages dominating the former, as shown in figure 9-3. One way to proceed

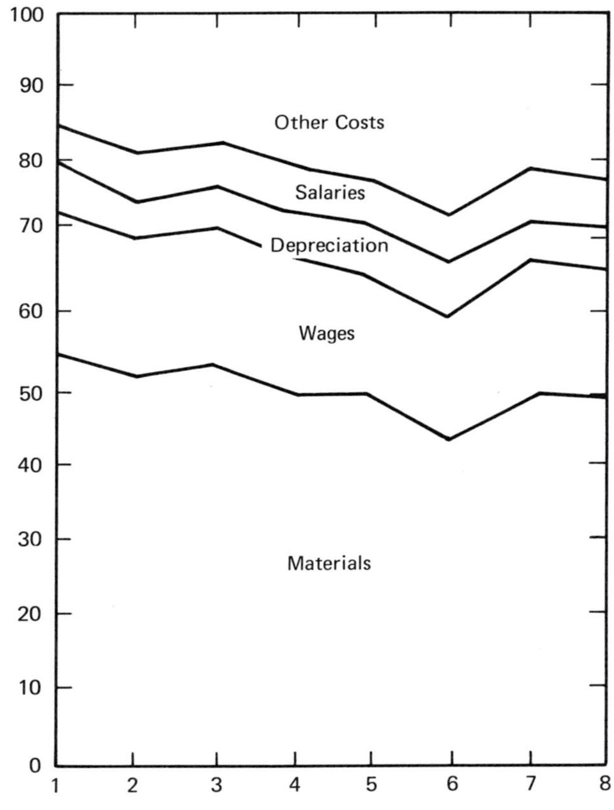

Source: Same as figure 9-2.

Figure 9-3. Cost Proportions: Steel Mill

might be to analyze changes in the average factor productivities and average factor prices at plant level (which determine such plant-level costs). But such measures would largely represent merely the passive summation of the costs actually incurred in the component departments. Hence it would appear more instructive, especially for present purposes, to examine the latter directly.

Department-Level Results: Output and Unit Costs

Figure 9-4 shows that the sharp drop in utilization rates during the fourth and fifth years was not shared equally among departments, although similarities in adjustment patterns are unavoidable among sequential components of an integrated process. It may be of interest to note here, however, that only in the sixth year was the reduction primarily due to the changeover from the open-hearth to the basic oxygen steel process. Both before that year and thereafter output was determined primarily by market demand.

Figure 9-5 compares total unit costs, unit material costs, and unit wage costs in the three operating departments. The wide differences in their adjustment patterns emphasizes the need to dig beneath plant and firm aggregates to locate the sources of differential pressures on aggregate performance as the basis for ascertaining their causes. Specifically, total unit costs rose over the 7-year period by 70 percent in iron making and by only about 25 percent in steel

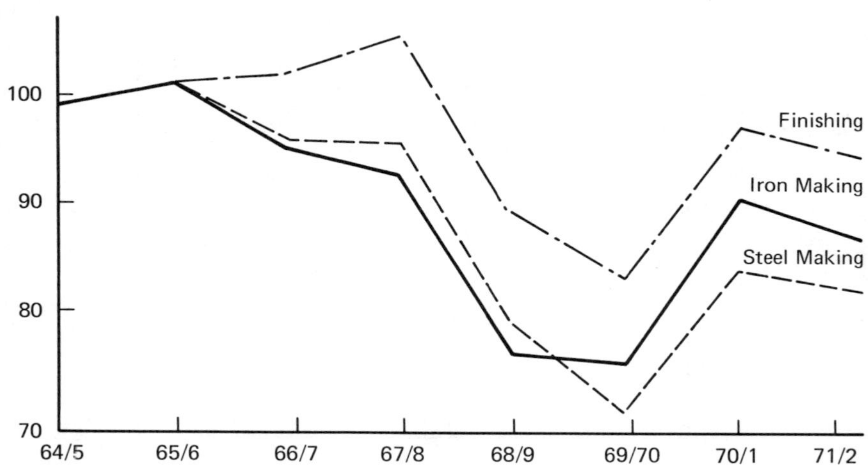

Source: Same as figure 9-2.

Figure 9-4. Output of the Iron-Making, Steel-Making, and Finishing Departments

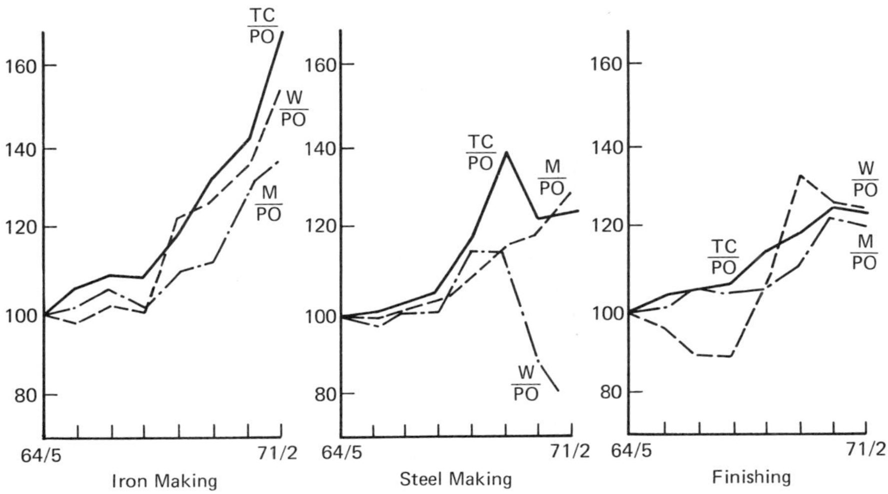

Source: B. Gold, "Analyzing the Structure of Technological Impacts: From Physical to Economic Effects," *Rivista Internazionale di Scienze Economiche E Commerciali* (Milan), February 1977.

Figure 9-5. Total Unit Costs, Unit Material Costs, and Unit Wage Costs by Departments

making and finishing. More particularly, unit material costs rose by 40, 30, and 20 percent, respectively, in these sequential departments, while unit wage costs covered a much wider gamut: rising by 56 percent in iron making, declining by 29 percent in steel making, and increasing by 26 percent in finishing.

Intradepartmental Results: Technological Changes, Productivity, and Unit Costs

As noted earlier, the major technological change during the period studied was the replacement of the open-hearth furnaces and the smaller-capacity very low nitrogen (VLN) furnaces by the basic oxygen furnaces during the fifth and sixth years. This changeover involved two major changes in materials inputs: halving the ratio of scrap to pig iron, and replacing the former 70 to 75 percent reliance on fuel oil for energy by almost complete reliance on oxygen, as shown in figure 9-6B As a result, conversion costs were expected to decline by 20 percent, assuming certain capacity-utilization rates, scrap ratios, and materials prices.

Figure 9-6A shows that such expectations were not realized. As often happens, this was due not to erroneous technological estimates, but rather to accom-

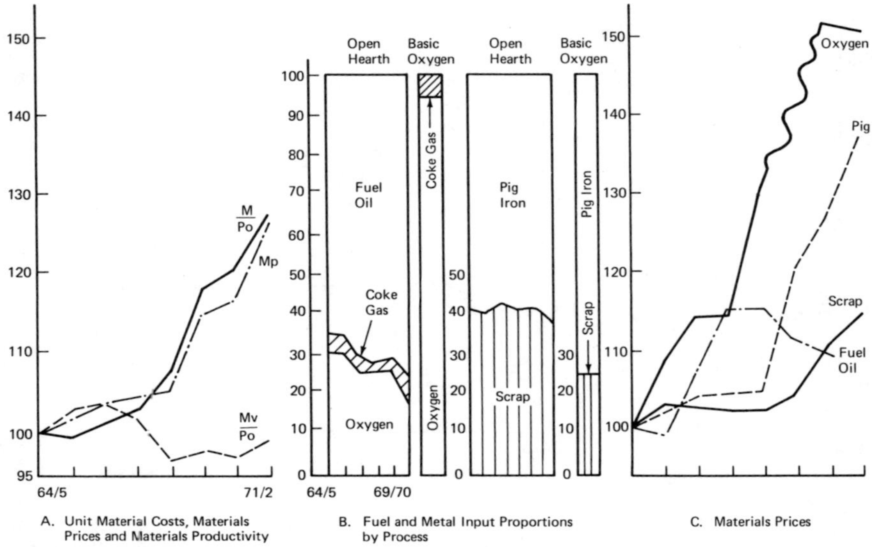

Source: Same as figure 9-5.

Figure 9-6. Unit Materials Costs and Their Determinants in Steel Making

panying economic adjustments. Although the relationship between pig iron and scrap prices had been reasonably stable for some years preceding the changeover, pig iron prices rose twice as much as scrap prices during the last 3 years, as shown in figure 9-6C. Similarly, although increases in fuel oil and oxygen prices were about the same during the first 3 years, fuel oil prices declined gradually thereafter, while oxygen prices rose by one-third. As a result, unit materials costs rose sharply instead of declining, reflecting not only the price increases just mentioned, but also the decrease in materials productivity (or increase in materials volume per unit of output, as shown in figure 9-A), due to the fact that materials inputs, like product outputs, are aggregated into a combined index of changes in total volume by weighting the quantities of each in each year by their average prices in the base and comparison years, thus responding to their disparate price adjustments.

Figure 9-7B shows that the technological innovation also had a major effect on unit wage costs, reducing them by one-third despite an increase in wage rates of 15 percent during the last 2 years. This was attributable to a spectacular tripling of output per man-hour in steel furnace operations combined with no change in labor productivity in the slab mill constituting the remaining half of the department's operations. Unfortunately, the effect of the reduction in unit wage costs was minimized by the fact that they account for only about 4 percent of total costs, as shown in figure 9-7C, while the impact of the increase in

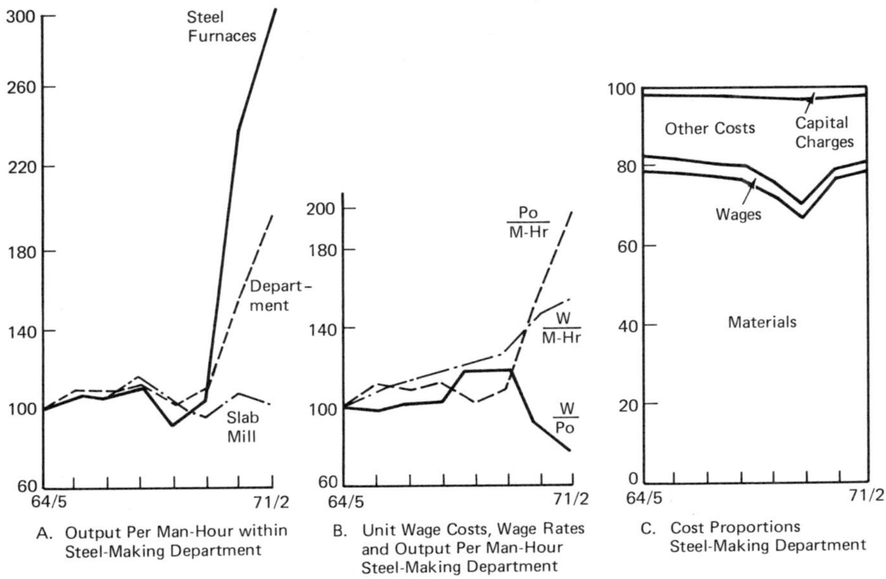

Source: Same as figure 9–2.

Figure 9–7. Steel-Making Department: Unit Wage Costs, Output per Man-Hour, Wage Rates, and Cost Proportions

unit material costs on total unit costs was multiplied by its dominant proportion of total costs.

In short, it has been possible to identify the direct impacts of the technological innovation and trace their interactions with other input factors and factor price adjustments as the basis for determining their effects on the network of productivity relationships and the structure of costs. In addition, one could easily trace these effects on steel making costs onto the unit costs of finished products and to profit margins.

It should also be emphasized, however, that such results present only the short-term effects of the innovation. Accordingly, this same analytical framework can be used to estimate the probable effects of future increases in the utilization of the new furnaces, which were capable of producing one-third more than the final year's output. Moreover, the framework can also be used to estimate the effects of prospective changes in pig iron, scrap, and oxygen prices.

Finally, presentation of the parallel analyses for each department's operating units– which is not feasible here–would permit an even more detailed mapping of the entire anatomy of plant operations.[4] For example, figure 9–8 illustrates how the general model of the network of productivity relationships can be elaborated to fit specific operations within particular departments–in this case,

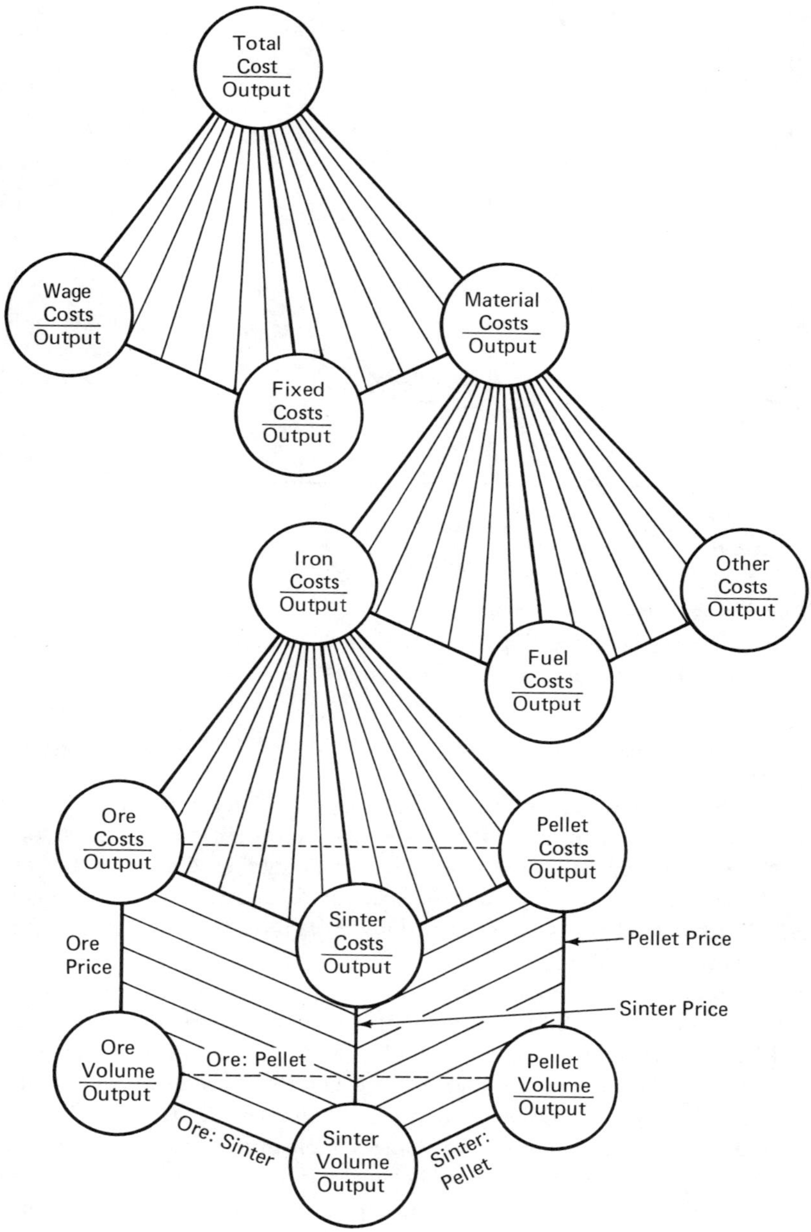

Figure 9–8. Illustrative Detailed Productivity Network and Cost Structure for Intraplant Analysis

blast furnace operations. The resulting elaborated framework would permit the tracing of all major innovations, as well as external impacts, through the entire system over the 7-year period studied, and would also facilitate development of increasingly persuasive estimates of the prospective effects of any additional innovations as well as possible adjustments in product and factor markets.

Notes

1. Other recently published applications at firm and plant levels include Eilon [1] and [2] and Hildred [3].
2. For additional details, see chapter 6 and Eilon [2, pp. 52–54].
3. The detailed study is contained in Eilon [2, pp. 75–112].

References

[1] S. Eilon, B. Gold, and J. Soesan, "Productivity Changes in a Chemical Plant," *Omega: The International Journal of Managment Science,* June 1975; reprinted in Eilon et al. [2].
[2] S. Eilon, B. Gold, and J. Soesan, *Applied Productivity Analysis for Industry* (Oxford: Pergamon, 1976).
[3] W.M. Hildred, "Productivity and Cost Effects of Innovations in Micro-Electronics Manufacturing," paper presented to the National Meeting of The Institute of Management Sciences, New York, May 3, 1978, based on Hildred et al. [4].
[4] W.M. Hildred, S.D. Nadler, and L.A. Bengston, *Innovation Accounting and Productivity Data in Electronics Manufacturing Firms: Two Case Studies,* report to the National Science Foundation, based on Grant No. PRA 76-02812, January 1978.

10 Tracing the Effects of Advances in Productivity and Technology in a Major Industry

A detailed empirical study of the actual economic effects of productivity and technological advances in a major industry offers instructive insights into the problems and intriguing potentials encountered in digging beneath the convenient assumptions and logical expectations of microtheory. More important, it also helps to clarify the network of interactions and the pattern of results engendered by technological advances.

There are a number of advantages in focusing such an inquiry on iron and steel manufacturing in the United States. The steel industry is, of course, a large and strategically important component of the structure of industries. It is also under tremendous competitive pressure both from foreign steel producers and from domestic industries producing substitute products. In addition, it faces major problems with respect to the availability and price of raw materials, energy, and capital, as well as with respect to environmental protection demands. Prehaps less widely recognized, iron and steel manufacturing and its associated industries have experienced a long and continuing involvement in a wide array of technological advances, thereby providing extended perspectives for appraising the ways in which, and extent to which, such innovations have helped to overcome some burdens while generating others.

Because of the problems confronting empirical research in this area (which were discussed in chapter 1), the original objectives of this study had to be altered in three respects. First, the traditional aim of seeking to determine *the* effects of major technological innovations was revised in favor of seeking to trace the time path of their changing effects during the course of their gradual absorption into the network of economic relationships. Second, the usual efforts to uncover the effects of particular major innovations were shifted to focus on the combined effects of the various innovations in different stages of improvement and diffusion during the successive periods covered. And finally, past evidences of the slowness with which most major technological innovations diffused in this industry,[1] as well as the distorted relationships characterizing this industry during cyclical extremes and other critical periods, urged expanding the time coverage beyond that common to most past studies. As a result, this analysis covers more than 60 years, including periods of growth and recession, wars, inflation, and labor turmoil as well as variations in the rates of technological innovation and diffusion.

Innovational Developments and Expected Effects

Major Technological Innovations Covered

The array of major technological advances brought into operation over so long a period is too extensive to list here. But it seems useful to summarize the most important of these to facilitate understanding of the types of readjustments experienced and expected benefits.[2]

1. Coal and iron ore mining and preparation: mechanization of the cutting, loading, and transport of underground coal and of iron ore; cleaning of coal; ore beneficiation and sintering; and commercialization of taconite processing.
2. Ore transportation: improvement of propulsion and navigation gear of ore-carrying ships; mechanization of loading and unloading; and changes in size of ships.
3. Coke ovens: replacement of beehive by by-product ovens; mechanization of loading and unloading; advances in scientific control of processes; and expansion in a variety of by-products.
4. Blast furnaces: increasing mechanization in materials handling and furnace charging and tapping; advances in the control of reduction processes and heat economy; improvements in refractories, oxygen enrichment and other fuel improvements; and recovery of waste products.
5. Steel making: introduction of open-hearth, electric, and basic oxygen processes; faster and better-controlled smelting and refining; longer refractory life; and continuous casting.
6. Steel rolling: increasing mechanization, speed, and power of rolling mills; introduction of cold-rolling and continuous hot strip mills; increasing process control via automation and computerization; major shifts in product mix; and improvements in product quality.

Another dimension of major technological innovations, although often defined in economic theory as entirely separate, involves changes in the scale of production. The extraordinary magnitude of achievements in this sector during the period covered may be illustrated by the following: average output per blast furnace increased tenfold after 1900; average capacity per by-product coke plant increased fivefold after 1900; average capacity per open-hearth furnace quadrupled between 1920 and 1960; average capacity per electric furnace increased sixfold after 1920. The enormous increases in the scale of coal and iron ore mines may be illustrated by the fact that the average output per iron ore mine increased sixfold after 1900.[3]

Even this limited review would seem to provide ample basis for contending that the period was characterized by a wide array of major innovations extending into all basic sectors of the iron and steel industry.

Expected Effects of Innovations

Innovations in industry are necessarily the outcome of managerial decisions. Hence in order to assess the effects of major technological innovations in the most relevant terms, it is desirable to clarify the expected effects which led managers to make the commitments and assume the risks entailed in deciding to adopt them. Among the more important of these were the following:

1. One set of innovations was expected to reduce material input requirements per unit of output through more thorough smelting, more effective combustion, reduced waste, improved heat economy, and fuller utilization of by-products.
2. Another set of innovations was expected to reduce labor requirements per unit of output through mechanization and automation as well as through increases in the scale of operations that required less than proportionate increases in manning.
3. Investment requirements relative to capacity were expected to increase because of the mechanization of formerly manual tasks, but such increases were expected to be more than offset by technological advances and economies of increases in scale.
4. As a result, the foregoing sets of innovations were expected to yield substantial reductions in unit material and unit labor costs along with somewhat more limited decreases in average capital charges per unit of output.
5. In addition, because each major innovation was expected to engender a distinctive pattern of effects, and because major innovations were introduced at irregular periods, the adjustment patterns of unit costs were expected to differ widely, thus causing substantial variations in cost proportions over time.

Attention turns next to an examination of the actual results experienced by the U.S. iron and steel manufacturing industries, to be followed by efforts to analyze the factors responsible for any observed deviations between expectations and recorded outcomes.

Actual Cost Adjustments Compared with Expectations

The primary focus of analysis—basic steel—is a broad category encompassing the commonly integrated operations of blast furnaces, coke ovens, steel making, and rolling mills. Its major inputs consist of coking coal, iron ore or pellets, and scrap as well as other fuels. Its major output consists of steel mill products along with a smaller stream of coke by-products. Thus the aggregate effects of changes in the basic steel sector can be studied without considering such intermediate products as blast furnace and coke oven gas, internally generated scrap, pig iron, and steel ingots.

In order to provide some insights into operations within this aggregate, attention will also be given to the blast furnace sector which produces molten pig iron (from iron-bearing materials and coke) to feed into the steel-making furnaces. Hence the effects of technological innovations and other changes in the antecedent operations not being considered individually–including iron-ore mining, beneficiation, and transport; the mining, cleaning, and transport of coking coal; and coke-oven operations–will be largely reflected through resulting inputs into blast furnaces.[4]

Cost Effects in Basic Steel

As shown in figure 10-1, the physical output of basic steel recorded major fluctuations around a sharp upward trend resulting in a 1967 level about eight

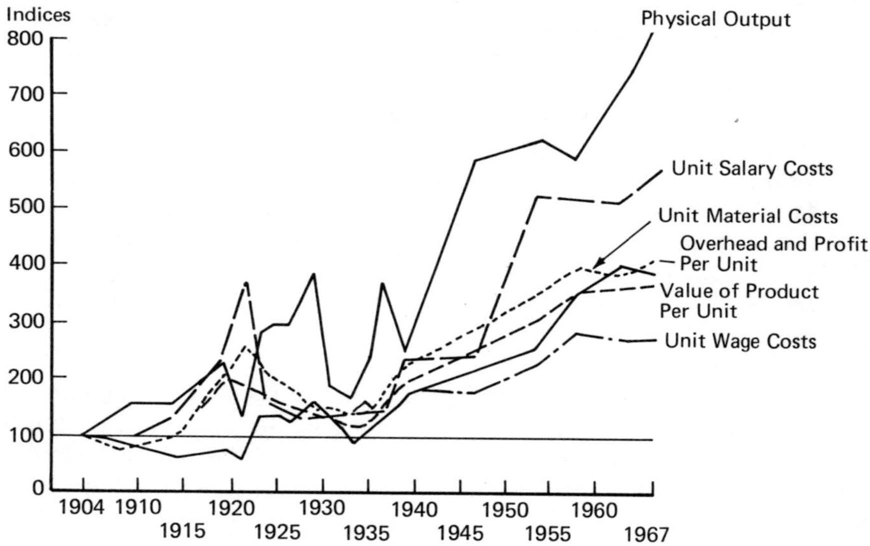

Sources: Physical output: 1904–1947 (B. Gold, *Explorations in Managerial Economics,* New York, Basic Books, 1971, p. 64); 1954–67 (U.S. Department of Labor, *Handbook of Labour Statistics,* Government Printing Office, 1972, p. 175). Wages, salaries, overheads and profits: 1904–1954 (combined totals for coke ovens, blast furnaces, steel mills, and steel foundries from *U.S. Census of Manufactures,* Vol. 2, Part II, 1954, pp. 29A-5, 33A-4 and 33A-5); 1958–1967 (estimated from data covering the same industries except steel foundries in *U.S. Census of Manufactures, 1963,* pp. 33A-7, and 1967, p. 33A-6). Materials: special estimates by M.G. Boylan to eliminate duplication in original census data. Value of product: sum of materials and value added (i.e., wages, salaries, overhead and profits).

Figure 10-1. Basic Steel: Physical Output, Unit Costs, and Average Price, 1904–1967

times that of 1904. Despite this impressive increase in output, and despite a wide array of major advances in technology as well as extraordinary increases in scale, unit costs fluctuated around a generally upward trend, except during 1919 to 1933. Indeed, actual unit costs never fell below their 1904 levels and were 2½ to 5½ times those initial levels in 1967.

Were the expected reductions in unit costs disguised by inflationary developments? Figure 10–2 presents the results of deflating the unit costs in figure 10–1 by the Bureau of Labor Statistics' (BLS) wholesale price index. Instead of declining progressively, the deflated unit costs fluctuated around an essentially horizontal trend from 1904 through 1947, rose during 1942–1954, and then remained close to these higher levels through 1967. In that year, each series exceeded its 1904 level by at least 20% except for unit wage costs, which were 18 percent lower.

In turn, figure 10–3 reveals that cost proportions were remarkably stable from 1914 through 1967, despite the numerous and variously timed major advances in technology, the substantial changes in scale, and the extraordinary range of economic conditions covered, including two wars, the Great Depression, and a variety of changes in growth rates and price levels. From 1914 through 1967, the ratio of materials cost to total product value approximated 46 percent; the wage ratio averaged 27 percent, with fluctuations ranging between 24 and 29 percent; and salaries approximated 5 to 6 percent. The residual category of overhead, other costs, and profits fluctuated around a horizontal trend at 21 percent from 1919 through 1947. Hence the only important changes in cost proportions over the 63 years covered occurred during 1904–1914, when sub-

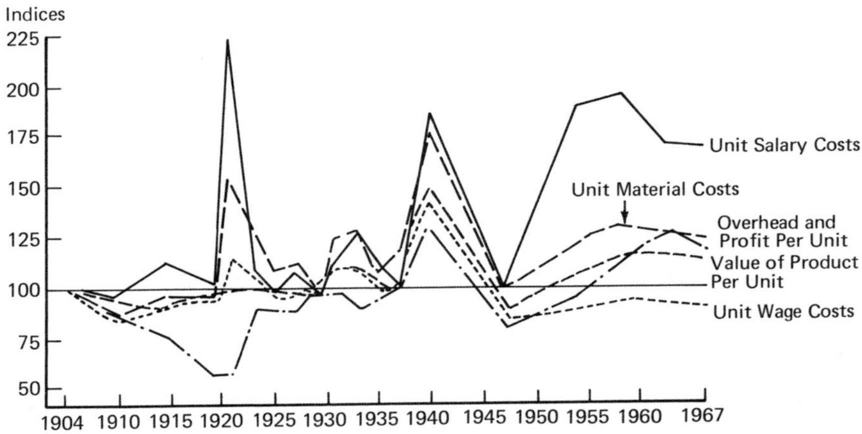

Sources: Same as figure 10–1 plus Wholesale Price Index (U.S. Bureau of Labor Statistics: *Historical Statistics of the United States,* Government Printing Office, 1960, pp. 116–117; and *Handbook of Labor Statistics,* Government Printing Office, 1971, p. 276).

Figure 10–2. Basic Steel: Deflated Unit Costs and Average Price, 1904–1967

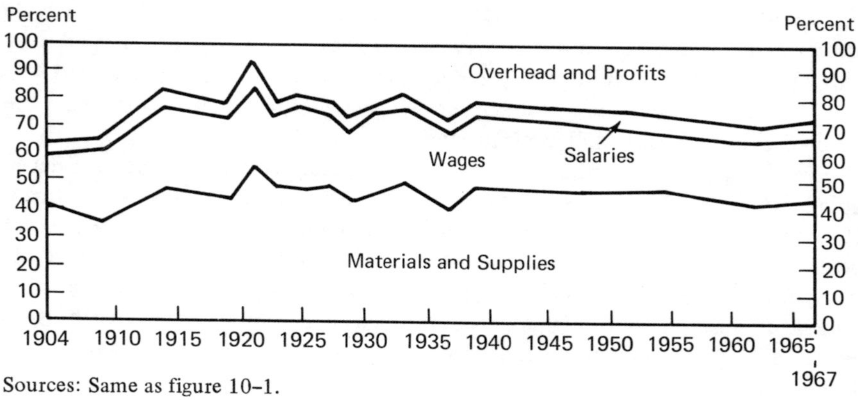

Sources: Same as figure 10–1.

Figure 10–3. Basic Steel: Cost Proportions, 1906–1967

stantial increases in the materials and wage ratios were accompanied by a sharp contraction of other costs plus profits. It should also be noted that a modest decrease in the materials ratio during the last 20 years was accompanied by an offsetting increase in the ratio of other costs plus profits (to be discussed later).

Thus cost adjustments in basic steel offered no support for the expected substantial declines in unit costs expected to result from the numerous major technological advances introduced and widely diffused. Nor does the record support the expected wide variations in cost proportions expected to result from the irregular adoption and spread of innovations focused on different inputs or from continuing major fluctuations in output levels, factor prices, and shifts in product mix.

Cost Effects in Blast Furnace Operation

In order to explore the cost changes underlying the aggregate results just summarized for basic steel, attention may be turned to the adjustments in blast furnace operations. Figure 10–4 reveals some significant differences from basic steel patterns. Physical output fluctuated sharply around a rising trend during 1904–1923, followed a horizontal trend during 1923–1939, rose by more than 50 percent between 1939 and 1947, and was horizontal again through 1954.[5] Unit costs recorded a generally rising trend during 1904–1919, a declining trend during 1919–1939, and a sharply rising trend during 1939–1954. Even during the 1930s, however, unit costs merely approximated their 1904 levels rather than displaying substantial reductions. At the end of the period, unit costs were two to four times their original levels.

In this case, deflation of the unit costs by changes in the BLS wholesale price index results in quite different perspectives. Figure 10–5 shows that unit

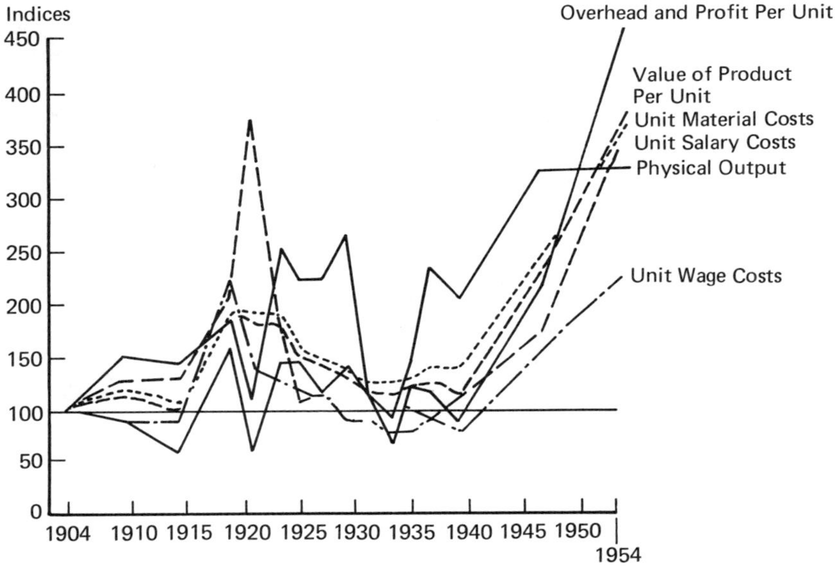

Sources: *U.S. Census of Manufactures,* Vol. II, Part 2, 1954, pp. 33A-4; Physical output: 1904-1939 (S. Fabricant, *Employment in Manufacturing,* pp. 1899-1939, New York: National Bureau of Economic Research, 1942, p. 314); 1947 and 1954 (*Annual Statistical Report,* 1954, American Iron and Steel Institute, Washington, 1954).

Figure 10-4. Blast Furnaces: Physical Output, Unit Costs, and Average Price, 1904-1954 (1904 = 100)

material costs exhibited relatively small and short-lived fluctuations around a horizontal trend during 1904-1947 before rising sharply during 1947-1954. Unit wage costs recorded sharp declines during 1904-1909 and again during 1921-1925, followed by a horizontal trend around 60 percent of its 1904 level during 1925-1947 before rising to 90 percent of that level in 1954. The remaining major category of other costs plus profits declined sharply during 1904-1914, fluctuated significantly around a horizontal trend during 1914-1947, and, like all the others, rose heavily during 1947-1954.

Although actual cost proportions in blast furnaces were quite different from those in basic steel, figure 10-6 reveals similar stability over the period studied. The ratio of material costs to product value exhibited only minor fluctuations around a horizontal trend approximating 81 percent during 1909-1947, while the wage ratio and the ratio of other costs plus profits followed similar horizontal trends approximating 6 and 8 percent, respectively. Again, significant changes were restricted primarily to 1904 through 1909, when an increase in the materials ratio was accompanied by reductions in the wage and other costs plus profits ratios, and to the final period 1947 through 1954, when decreases in the mate-

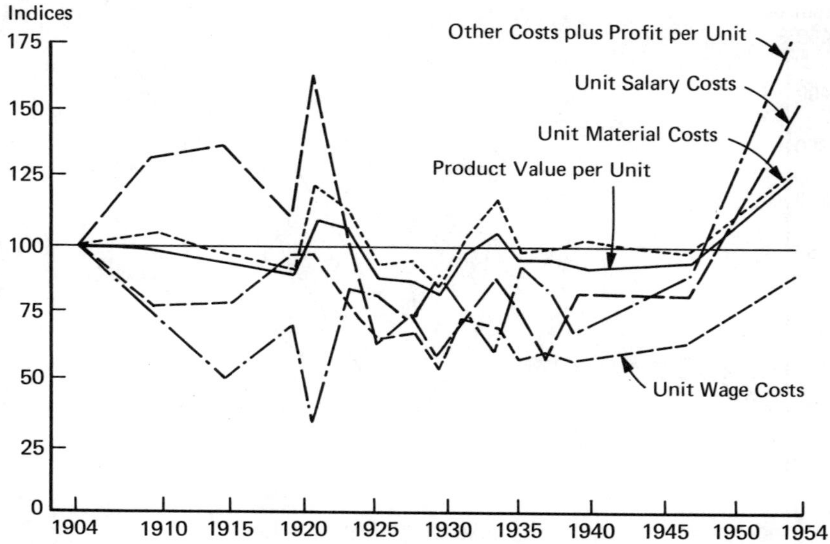

Sources: Figure 10–4; Wholesale Price Index: U.S. Bureau of Census, *Historical Statistics of the United States,* pp. 116–117 (Washington: Government Printing Office, 1960).

Figure 10–5. Blast Furnaces: Deflated Unit Costs and Price, 1904–1954 (1904 = 100)

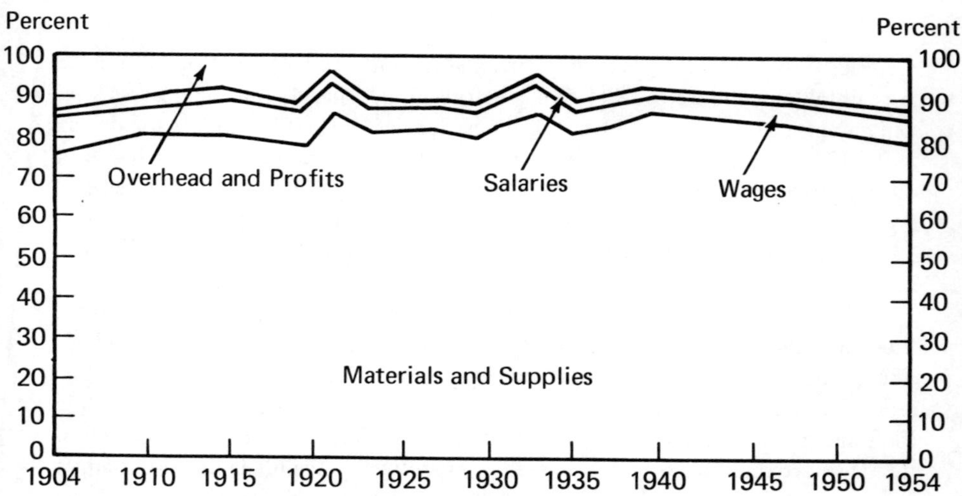

Source: *U.S. Census of Manufactures,* Vol. II, Part 2, 1954, p. 33A–4

Figure 10–6. Blast Furnaces: Cost Proportions, 1904–1954

rials and wage ratios were accompanied by increases in the ratio of other costs plus profits.

Comparing such outcomes with cost expectations, it is apparent that although advances in technology and increases in scale as well as expanded output did not yield expected reductions in actual unit costs, they did seem to have effected reductions in deflated unit costs. However, such an attribution of causation would be open to serious question inasmuch as most of the reductions in deflated unit costs occurred before 1914, that is, prior to most of the technological advances and scale increases affecting blast furnaces during the entire period studied. As for the findings relating to cost proportions, the observed stability over long periods again fails to accord with expectations.

In short, neither at the relatively aggregate level of totals for basic steel nor at the highly disaggregated level of blast furnaces did either unit costs or cost proportions behave in accordance with the expectations associated with the major technological innovations adopted and diffused during the long period studied. In order to help uncover the reasons for such deviations between expectations and results, the analysis will now dig beneath observed cost adjustments to their immediate determinants.

Cost Determinants: Adjustments in Productivity and Factor Prices

Changes in each category of unit costs are determined, of course, by changes in the quantity of the given input factor required per unit of output and by changes in the price of that factor. Accordingly, in seeking to account for the unexpected cost results just summarized, consideration must be given to whether the technological innovations reviewed failed to achieve the expected changes in physical input requirements or whether such direct benefits were offset by factor prices or other influences.

Determinants of Changes in Unit Material Costs

As was noted earlier, the primary materials inputs in blast furnaces are iron-bearing materials and coke. Over the period as a whole, figure 10–7 shows that the reduction in iron-bearing materials—including natural iron ore, sinter, and, toward the end of the period, pellets—per ton of pig iron produced declined by less than 10 percent. This reflects the fact that most of the benefits of related technological innovations were absorbed in seeking to offset the gradually declining iron content of natural ores which began to accelerate during the last 25 years, leaving only modest further reductions in the course of smelting the iron-bearing materials actually charged into the furnaces.

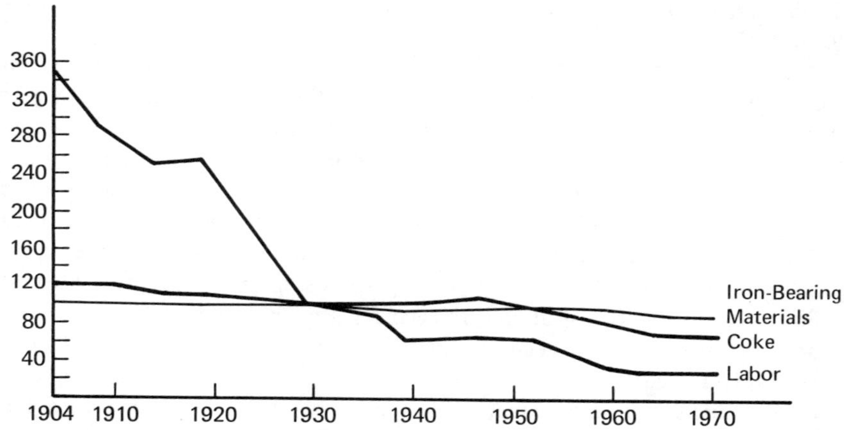

Source: M.G. Boylan, *Economic Effects of Scale Increases in the Steel Industry: The Case of U.S. Blast Furnaces* (New York: Praeger, 1975), p. 191.

Figure 10–7. Blast Furnaces: Consumption of Labor, Coke, and Iron-Bearing Materials Input per Ton of Iron Produced (1929 = 100)

Coke inputs per ton of pig iron output declined by about one-third over the period as a whole. Again it should be recalled that this relates only to the effects of developments in blast furnace operations, excluding the prior gains achieved in coal mining and coke-oven operations. Part of the substantial reduction in coke inputs per unit of output was attributable to technological advances yielding improvements in combustion and reduction processes as well as in heat economy, and these tended, of course, to reduce the total quantity of material inputs per unit of output. But an important part of the reduction in coke inputs was due rather to the substitution of other fuels and reducing agents. Thus figure 10–8 shows that although coke costs accounted for three to four times as large a proportion of total blast furnace revenues as "other materials and fuels" during the first decade, the latter had risen to almost one-half the coke proportion during the last decade.

The effects of such reductions in the unit input quantities of iron-bearing materials and coke on unit material costs were more than offset by changes in the price of these inputs. Figure 10–9 shows that coking coal and iron ore prices averaged two-thirds higher during 1923–1939 than in 1904, and that they more than doubled during 1947–1954. Hence the increases in blast furnace unit material costs presented in figure 10–4 are attributable not to the absence of expected reductions in unit input requirements, but primarily to the overshadowing concomitant increases in the relevant factor prices. It may also be worth noting that some of the reductions achieved involved shifts to substitute inputs, often involving higher prices, which served to reduce net cost savings. Moreover, the

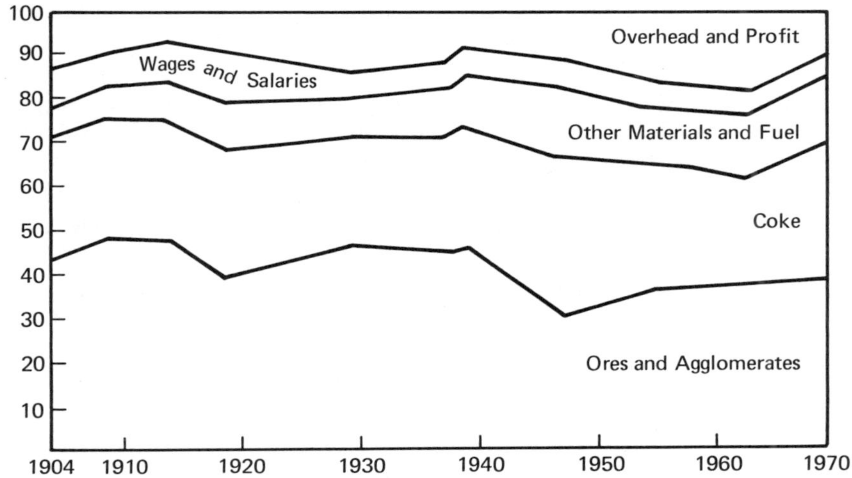

Source: M.G. Boylan, *Economic Effects of Scale Increases in the Steel Industry: The Case of U.S. Blast Furnaces* (New York: Praeger, 1975), p. 184.

Figure 10–8. Blast Furnaces: Cost Proportions—Detailed, 1904–1970

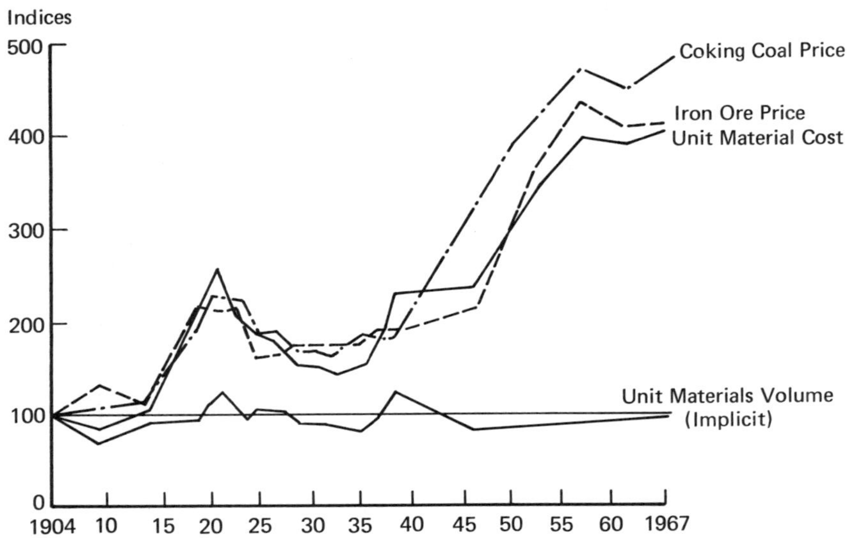

Sources: Figure 10–1; Coal price: U.S. Bureau of Mines, *Information Circular 8251,* Table A–10, p. 59; *Minerals Yearbook,* various years; ore prices: Lake Carriers Association, *Annual Report* 1967, pp. 145, 149.

Figure 10-9. Basic Steel; Unit Materials Cost, Iron Ore and Coal Prices, and Implicit Unit Materials Volume, 1904-1967

relative magnitude of reductions in unit inputs of iron-bearing materials and coke were inverse to their respective proportions of total material costs—again tending to reduce resulting savings in total unit material costs.

Essentially, the same results are found for the broader operations encompassed by basic steel. As shown in figure 10-9, the implicit volume of total materials consumed[6] per unit of total output fluctuated around a horizontal trend over the entire period, emphasizing that innovation-induced changes took the form primarily of substitutions. The most important of these involved the increasing replacement of natural ores by sinter and pellets after 1950, the partial replacement of pig iron by scrap for charging into the steel furnace as a result of increasing reliance on the open-hearth process during 1905–1920,

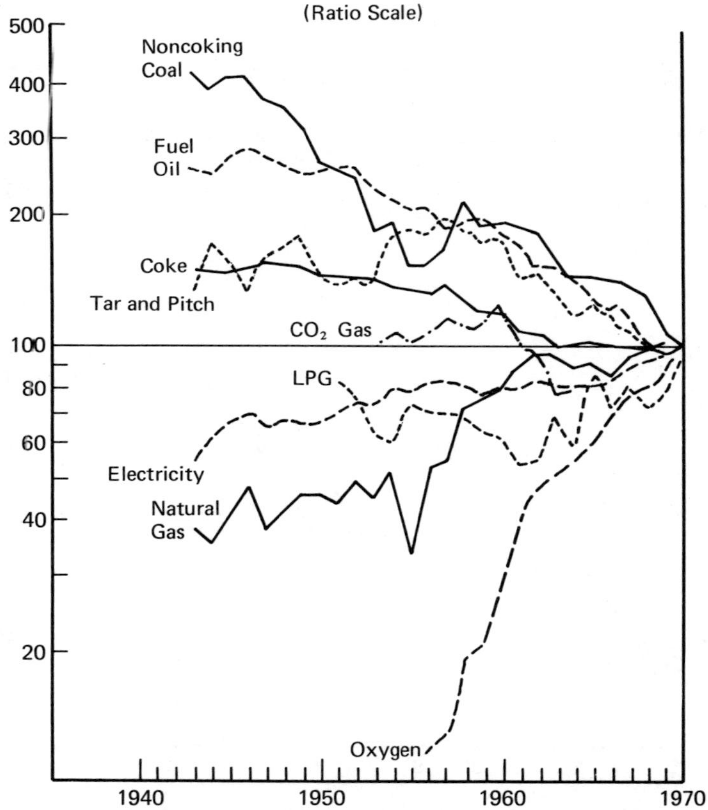

Source: G. Rosegger, "Technological Change, Managerial Incentives and Environmental Effects," in B. Gold (ed), *Technological Change: Economics, Management and Environment* (Oxford: Pergamon, 1975), p. 58.

Figure 10–10. Basic Steel: Energy Sources per Ton of Output (1970 = 100)

a limited reversal toward more pig iron with the spread of the basic oxygen process during the last decade covered, and the major shifts in energy sources involving not only the reduction in coke rates already noted and a decrease in fuel oil consumption, but sharp increases in natural gas and oxygen as well as in electricity, as shown in figure 10–10.

Because total materials requirements per unit of output remained unchanged, total materials cost per unit of output was wholly responsive to changes in the price of these materials, as shown in figure 10–9. It should be recalled, of course, that the technological changes which occurred over the period had a bearing not only on the unit input quantities of materials, but also on the weighted average price paid for them (precisely because of the changes in their composition just noted). Moreover, such technological innovations also affected other input factors as well. Accordingly, effective assessment of their effects must await examination of resulting changes in other inputs and costs.

Determinants of Changes in Unit Labor Costs

Changes in unit labor costs are attributable, of course, to the interaction of changes in output per man-hour and changes in average hourly wages. It was with respect to output per man-hour that technological changes in blast furnaces had their greatest impact on unit input requirements. As was shown in figure 10–7, man-hours per ton of pig iron output declined by 90 percent between 1904 and 1970. Even such a spectacular achievement, however, failed to yield major cost benefits.

Unit wage costs in blast furnaces declined by less than 10 percent between 1904 and 1914, as shown in figure 10–4, despite a decrease of almost one-third in man-hours per ton of pig iron. After more than doubling over the next 5 years because of inflationary pressures associated with World War I, unit wage costs were driven back to 95 percent of their 1904 level in 1929—but only through a reduction of 70 percent in man-hours per ton of pig iron over the same period. Another reduction of one-third in man-hours per ton of pig iron over the next 10 years decreased unit wage costs by only 15 percent. As a result, unit wage costs had declined between 1904 and 1939 by 20 percent, while man-hours per ton of pig iron had declined by 80 percent, reflecting a fourfold increase in average hourly wages. Man-hours per ton of pig iron decreased by another 7 percent between 1939 and 1954, but unit wage costs almost tripled as a result of another tremendous surge in wage rates. In short, man-hours per ton of pig iron recorded an impressively declining trend only to be more than offset by the even more sharply rising trend in average hourly wages.

Such relationships can be traced more directly for basic steel in figure 10–11. Although output per man-hour was seven times its 1904 level in 1967, unit wage costs were more than 2½ times their 1904 level as a result of an almost

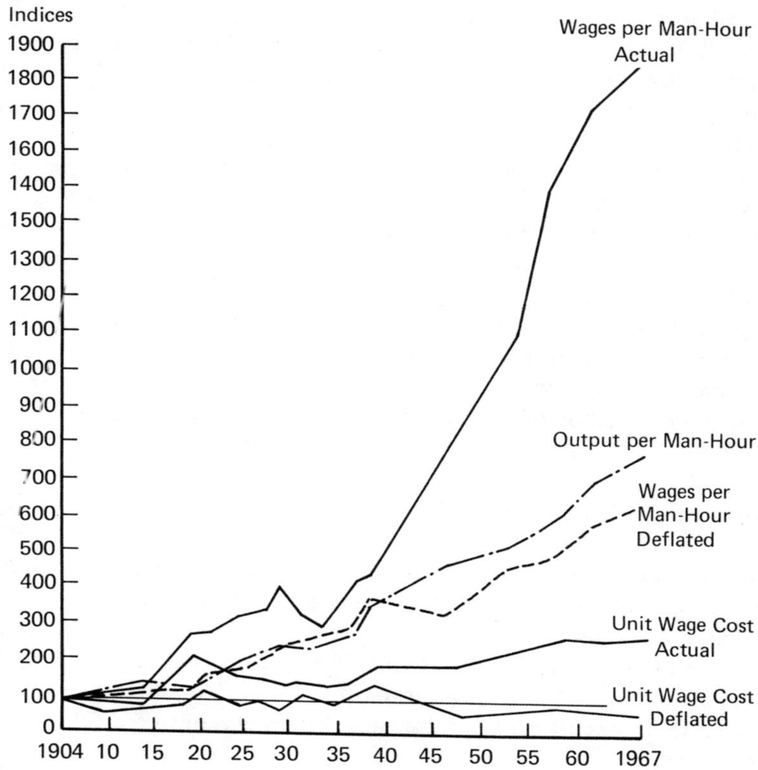

Sources: Figures 10–1 and 10–2; physical output per man-hour: 1904–1958 (B. Gold, *Explorations in Managerial Economics,* New York, Basic Books, 1971, p. 64); 1963–1967 (estimated by taking man-hour data from *U.S. Census at Manufactures,* 1967, p. 33A–6 and physical output data from U.S. Dept. of Labor, *Handbook of Labor Statistics,* Government Printing Office, 1972, p. 175).

Figure 10–11. Basic Steel: Unit Wage Costs, Output per Man-Hour, and Wage Rates, 1904–1967 (1904 = 100)

eighteenfold increase in average wages per man-hour. It should be noted that when such wage rates are deflated by the Bureau of Labor Statistics' wholesale price index the resulting trend closely parallels that of output per man-hour. This means that wage rates were fully adjusted to changes in the general price level of the economy as well as to increases in steel output per man-hour.

But this still leaves open to question the reasons for the observed impressive increases in output per man-hour. In this capital-dominated industry, labor's role has been increasingly restricted to tending facilities and equipment in accordance with technically determined procedures and operating rates. As a result, changes in output per man-hour may be regarded as determined primarily by the productivity of such capital facilities (as determined by their capacity relative to net fixed investment) and by the volume of actively utilized capital facilities teamed with direct labor (as measured by the ratio of actively utilized net fixed investment to man-hours):

$$\frac{\text{Output}}{\text{Man-hours}} \equiv \frac{\text{capacity}}{\text{net fixed investment}} \times \frac{\text{net fixed investment (output/capacity)}}{\text{man-hours}}$$

Changes in these relationships are shown in figure 10-12 and reveal two major reversals of significance to management. During 1904-1921 and 1929-1947, increases in output per man-hour were overwhelmingly attributable to increases in the productivity of fixed investment rather than to the volume of such

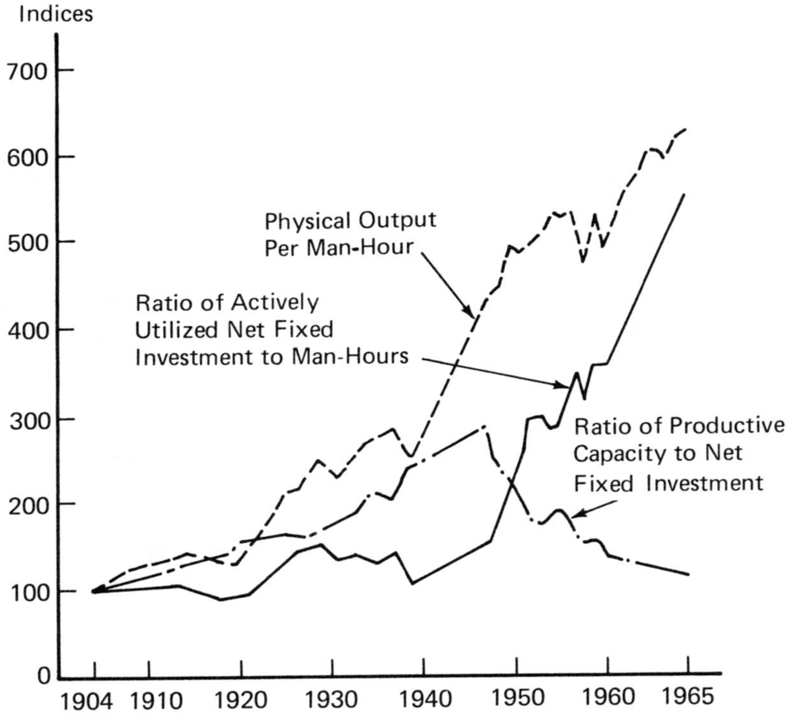

Source: B. Gold (ed.), *Technological Change: Economics, Management and Environment* (Oxford: Pergamon, 1975, 1979), p. 15.

Figure 10-12. Basic Steel: Physical Output per Man-Hour, Productive Capacity Relative to Net Fixed Investment and Actively Utilized Net Fixed Investment Relative to Man-Hours for Basic Steel Industry, 1904-1969 (1904 = 100)

actively utilized facilities per man-hour. But during 1921–1929 and 1947–1969, the reverse was true. This means that in the former periods, increases in the productivity of net fixed investment—which were due in large measure to technological advances and increases in scale—made possible greater output without larger inputs either of labor or capital. As a result, extra benefits were available which could be shared by labor and management.

In the other periods, and especially during 1947–1969, output per man-hour was kept rising only through sharply increased investments in facilities and equipment relative to employment levels, that is, through increasing the ratio of actively utilized net fixed investment to man-hours. Hence increased capital charges had to be borne before any net benefits could be counted.

But the long experience with increases in output per man-hour because of increases in the productivity of net fixed investment had established the pattern of adjusting wage rates to increases in output per man-hour. Hence this pattern continued to prevail after 1947, despite the important and costly shift in the source of increases in output per man-hour to heavier inputs of investment, with many fewer advantageous effects on costs and profitability.

Determinants of Changes in Unit Capital Costs

There were two major reasons for the sharp and sustained reversal in the productivity of capital (that is, in productive capacity relative to net fixed investment) after 1947. One was rooted in the dominance during the period of widespread efforts to modernize the industry. This involved very heavy investments largely to replace rather than to expand productive capacity. Such efforts were responsive to powerful pressures involving the adoption of new technologies, the relocation of capacity to accord with geographical shifts in markets, and the introduction of specialized equipment to accord with changes in the product composition of demand. Nevertheless, these efforts had the effect of increasing total capacity far less than net fixed investment, thereby decreasing the ratio representing the productivity of capital and tending to increase the capital costs to be borne by the only modestly increased levels of output made possible.

The other major cause of decreases in the productivity of capital was the sharp rise in the cost of new facilities per unit of capacity, as illustrated in figure 10–13. This was attributable in part to the increasing complexity of blast furnaces and other capital goods embodying advances in design and instrumentation as well as in ancillary equipment. But it was due in even greater measure, especially during the post-World War II period, to inflationary increases in wage rates and other determinants of construction costs and facilities prices (Boylan [1, p. 158ff]).

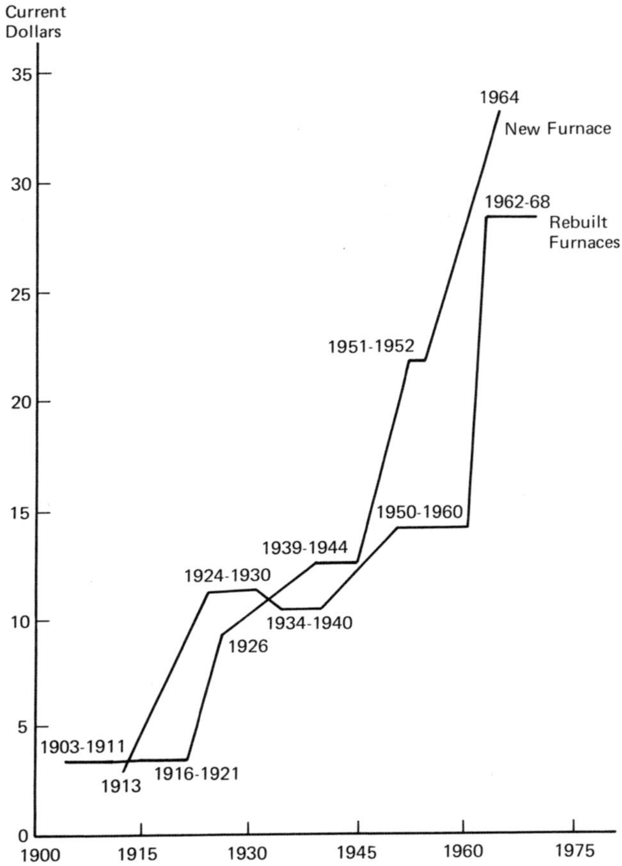

Source: M. Boylan, *Economic Effects of Scale Increases in the Steel Industry: The Case of U.S. Blast Furnaces* (New York: Praeger, 1975), p. 162.

Figure 10–13. Blast Furnaces: Investment Cost per Gross Ton of Capacity for New and Rebuilt Furnaces

Resulting Changes in Cost Proportions and Profit Margins

In order to bring these various effects within the larger managerial context of total costs at the firm level, figure 10–14 presents the cost proportions derived from the consolidated financial statements of the major steel companies for 1943 to 1972. Although these cover a somewhat broader array of operations than the basic steel category in the Census of Manufactures, comparison with

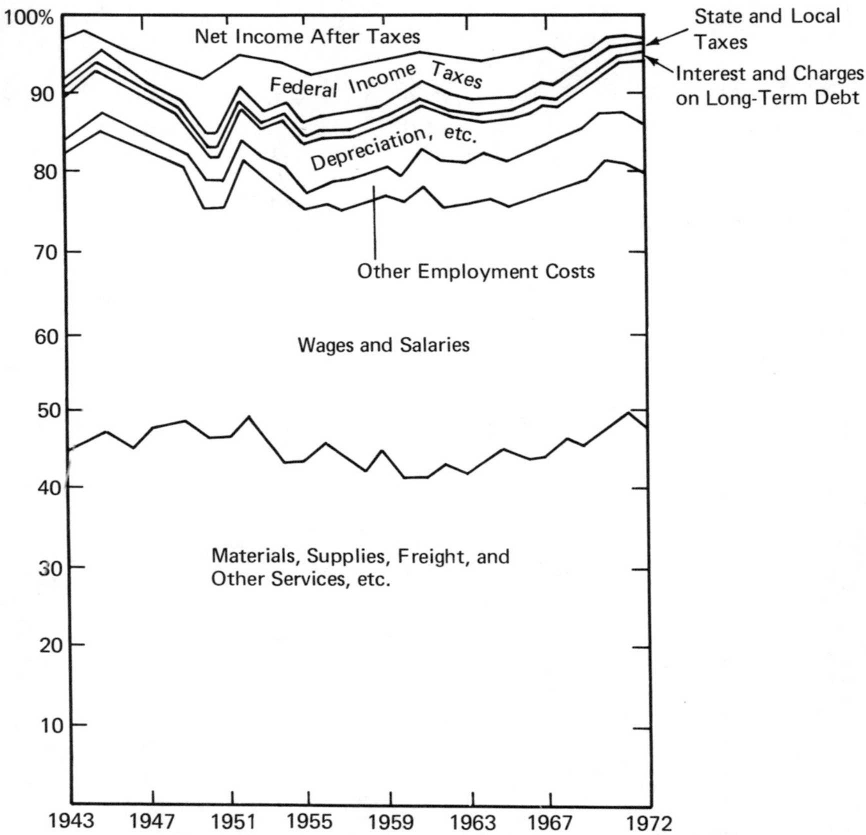

Source: Consolidated Financial Statements for Major Steel Companies *Annual Statistical Reports* (Washington: American Iron and Steel Institute).

Figure 10-14. U.S. Steel Industry: Cost Proportions, 1943-1972

figure 10-3 demonstrates essential similarity both in the relative proportions and in the trends of materials costs, of wage and salary costs, and of all other costs plus profits.

Between 1950 and 1972, the material cost ratio continued to follow a horizontal trend approximating 45 percent, although this ratio rose consistently over the last decade. Similarly, wages and salaries followed a horizontal trend approximating 32 percent, but are supplemented by a progressive increase in "other employment costs," including fringe benefits, from about 1 percent in 1949 to 4 percent in 1960 to 7.5 percent in 1972.

Within the residual category including all other costs plus profits, two major changes are discernible. The proportion of total revenues needed to cover depreciation charges and interest payments doubled from 4 to 8 percent between 1950 and 1972, reflecting the increased investments discussed earlier. And the net income after taxes proportion followed a decreasing trend; after approximating 8 percent in 1950 and again in 1955, it averaged 5 percent from 1958 through 1968 and only 3 percent during 1969 through 1972.

In short, despite impressive technological advances affecting material, labor, and capital inputs, their respective cost proportions rose, especially over the last 15 years covered. And these changes were accompanied by substantial reductions in the net profit margins which management had hoped to increase by making the heavy financial commitments and taking the substantial risks involved in adopting the various innovations.

Some Empirically Rooted Revisions of Prevailing Expectations

The preceding findings and associated analysis suggest a need for serious reconsideration of some basic beliefs concerning the effects of technological innovations which seem to be widespread among industrial managements, government officials, and engineers and economists. Most of these erroneous expectations arise, as will be seen, from common tendencies: to minimize concern with the specific means whereby changes are effected, to ignore intraplant readjustments engendered by the innovation, to ignore extrafirm readjustments traceable to the innovation, and to make evaluations within unduly short time horizons. The following discussion will be limited to five of the more important among such widespread assumptions or beliefs.

1. *The assumption cannot be justified that even demonstrably superior technological innovations are, or should be, promptly adopted throughout an industry.* As a matter of fact, gradual diffusion is far more common than rapid saturation. Indeed, as shown in figure 10-15, actual rates of diffusion have been far slower than has been recognized even by specialists. Thus, only five of the fourteen major innovations covered accounted for more than one-third of total output even 15 years after actual commercial use began, although each became dominant eventually.

Nor does this slow acceptance demonstrate the ignorance, apathy, or active resistance often assumed by outside analysts, usually on the basis of ex post facto studies. On the contrary, three quite respectworthy considerations seem to be more influential. First, various innovations obviously differ in the specific patterns of their benefits and burdens, and these patterns change as the innovations themselves undergo improvements and modifications. Second, even firms in the same industry often differ in their relative urgencies at any given time and hence differ in their evaluations of the attractiveness of particular innovations relative to the other alternatives and pressures confronting them. Third, the net attractiveness of even unchanging innovations tends to vary with alterations

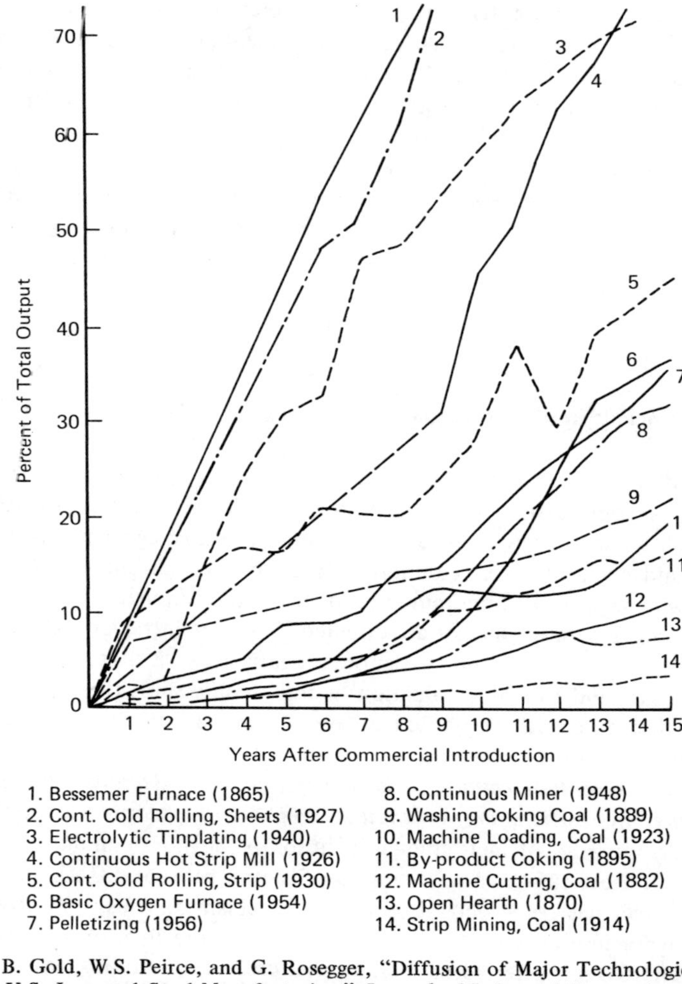

Source: B. Gold, W.S. Peirce, and G. Rosegger, "Diffusion of Major Technological Innovations in U.S. Iron and Steel Manufacturing," *Journal of Industrial Economics,* July 1970, p. 220.

Figure 10–15. Output by New Technology as Percentage of Total Output during First 15 Years after Indicated Date of Initial Commercial Use

in the firm's factor and product prices, profitability, need for expansion, and availability of capital.[7]

Moreover, it is precisely the pressures exerted by these second and third factors which shape the directions and speed of adaptations in the original innovation in order to achieve wider applicability. And in view of the human and organizational, as well as economic, costs often associated with the displacement of major technologies and facilities, it is not at all clear that impulsive responses to the initial forms of each innovation, regardless of the urgencies of each firm or the nature of prevailing economic conditions, would maximize either economic or social welfare.

2. *The assumption cannot be justified that resource-saving innovations tend to yield comparable reductions in their respective unit costs.* Such assumptions seem to be surprisingly widespread, perhaps because engineers are likely to assume that all parts of the system are fixed except for the technical changes which they are proposing, and because economists all too frequently slip back into a static framework in order to facilitate analysis. If the evaluation of such prospective effects is to be realistic, however, several intervening factors must be considered directly. To begin with, it is necessary to clarify the means whereby the expected factor saving is to be accomplished instead of merely assessing the results of the gain as given. For example, such a reduction in unit input requirements often involves a change in the qualitative characteristics of the factor involved (for example, chemical or size specifications of materials or skill requirements of labor) with attendant effects on the factor price, as was discussed in chapter 8. Alternatively, one must consider the environment in which the innovation is to be adopted. For example, if given material prices or wage rates have been rising, an innovation-induced reduction in their respective unit input requirements may serve only to moderate continuing increases in their unit costs instead of reversing such trends. In addition, the analysis should recognize the likelihood of interactions between changes in unit input requirements and factor prices.[8] For example, increases in output per man-hour tend to generate at least partially offsetting increases in average hourly wages, either through union negotiations or through piece rates. On the other hand, decreases in materials' requirements per unit of output tend to generate accentuated benefits through the decreases in materials' prices usually associated with the resulting reduced demand for such materials at each level of output.

3. *The assumption cannot be justified that technological innovations generally reduce total unit costs and prices.* Many and probably most major technological innovations involve readjustments in factor proportions and may also affect the qualitative characteristics of individual products as well as the product mix. The former may take a variety of forms, including the transfer of labor tasks to machinery and instrumented controls as well as the transfer of labor and capital input requirements to materials through the procurement of more highly processed components for products. In any case, the savings in one sector of inputs may be partly or even fully offset by the increases in other sectors, thus emphasizing the need for comprehensive coverage of changes throughout the system in order to evaluate the effects of an innovation. It should be noted in this connection that the effects of such shifts are often subject to serious misinterpretation. For example, as was noted in chapter 3, an increase in mechanization to offset the effects on unit wage costs of increases in wage rates

which exceed gains in labor productivity, as was illustrated in figure 10-11, often produces the following statistical results: an apparent increase in labor productivity combined with an apparent decrease in the productivity of capital, and an increase in unit capital costs combined with little or no change in unit labor costs (since the decrease in man-hours per unit of output is interpreted by labor as an increase in output per man-hour and hence used to negotiate an offsetting increase in wages per man-hour).[9]

Moreover, because industrial managements tend to be more concerned with increasing profitability than with reducing input requirements, they are usually entirely amenable to adopting innovations involving increases in total unit costs whenever these promise to improve products sufficiently to yield more than proportionate increases in product prices or capacity-utilization rates. Indeed, such innovations would obviously be preferred over resource-saving innovations whose prospective benefits are likely to be minimized by offsetting factor-price increases or product-price reductions.

4. *The assumption cannot be justified that technological innovations have a general tendency to increase profitability, either in the short run or over the long run.* During the early period of utilizing the innovation, expected benefits tend to be delayed or minimized because of the need for progressive adaptations of antecedent and subsequent stages of production to ensure effective integration[10] of adjustments in labor tasks, skills, and allocations—often attended by the need for new learning and sometimes involving labor-management negotiations—and because of the need to develop proper scheduling, maintenance, inventory, quality-control, and related production-control arrangements. Moreover, expected capital savings are frequently delayed until reasonably high levels of utilization of the new facilities are achieved. And the rate of return on investment may be depressed below preceding levels until a few years of depreciation help to reduce the initially higher investment requirements of new facilities relative to the largely depreciated facilities being replaced.[11]

During the later years, characterized by extensive diffusion of the innovation among producers, any net reductions in cost which have been realized tend to be passed along in the form of lower product prices under the pressure of competition to utilize capacity. For the same reason, the magnitude of the price differential which can be charged by early adopters of the innovation for resulting product improvements tends to erode as diffusion enables an increasing array of competitors to offer comparable product qualities (chapters 3 and 5).

In short, although gains in profitability are always a powerful incentive to, and a possible result, of technological innovations, they are not consistently achieved. Nor is there persuasive evidence to indicate that pioneers regularly achieve higher profitability than followers, although there have been some impressive exceptions in the aircraft, electronics, and pharmaceutical industries. On the other hand, technological innovations are commonly associated with improvements in various other aspects of performance, and they are frequently related to improvements in profitability—albeit with more uncertainty in timing, for shorter periods, and of lesser magnitudes than seem to be expected when managerial commitments are made.

5. *The assumption cannot be justified that the benefits of technological innovations are most effectively measured by reductions in real unit costs.* Such measurements are made by deflating changes in actual costs per unit of output by concurrent changes in some index of the price level. The results are usually interpreted as indicating the extent to which the relevant unit costs have changed, not because of changes in prices, but because of changes in the physical quantities of inputs used per unit of output. And it is the latter which are regarded as real costs. This approach and interpretation is reasonable, however, only in the absence of major technological innovation.

Technological changes undermine the relevance of the above approach in several ways. Three of these have already been noted in the preceding discussion: the liklihood of changes in the quality and composition of one or more major categories of inputs (that is, materials, labor, and capital facilities and equipment),[12] the likelihood of changes in the relative proportions of these major input factors, and the likelihood of changes in the quality of individual products and the mix of products. Such changes in the nature and composition of input and output flows—representing one major part of the real impacts of technological innovations—are very largely ignored by the general deflation procedure which is commonly employed. On the contrary, the latter implicitly assumes that nothing has changed except the quantities of unaltered inputs per unit of unchanged outputs.

A second basic weakness of this approach is the assumption that changes in the general price level are attributable to factors having nothing to do with technological change, such as the level of economic activity and changes in monetary and fiscal policy. But this is patently untrue in modern economies subject to pervasive pressures for technological innovations. In such economies, most, if not all, sectors of industry are continuously engaged in developing, introducing, and diffusing a wide variety of innovations, albeit at widely varying rates. And, as has already been noted, such innovations engender progressive adjustments in factor and product prices, as well as in physical input and output flows. Hence changes in the general price level reflect the effects not only of aggregate changes in economic activity and money supplies, but also of the average effects of technological innovations in industry at large on factor and product prices.

Hence the results of deflating the average total unit costs of an industry through dividing them by concurrent changes in an index of the general price level requires a quite different interpretation from that which is usually provided. Such a procedure really involves a comparison of changes between the individual industry and the rest of the economy. Because the latter has also been affected by technological changes, the deflated unit costs of the given industry which result represent not the actual change in its real unit costs over the period studied, but only the differential change in its relative unit costs as compared with average changes in the economy. The importance of this change in interpretation is indicated by reference to the findings in many industries (Gold [3, pp. 185–191])—including those presented earlier in this chapter—that deflated unit costs have recorded a horizontal trend over long periods despite demonstrably major technological innovations. Instead of accepting the common interpretation of such a finding as representing the absence of significant impacts on real unit input requirements, this should be interpreted rather as indicating that the cost effects of technological and other innovations merely kept pace with the average level of such effects in the economy at large. To repeat the well-worn though apt cliché, in technologically active modern economies, individual industries must be reasonably active themselves merely to keep pace with others.

In short, a horizontal trend in deflated unit costs over extended periods, such as were shown in figures 10-2 and 10-5, does not signify an absence of technological progress or an absence of benefits from such progress. To extend the preceding analysis one step further, such a relationship could mean not only that economies in the industry have roughly paralleled those in the economy as a whole, but also, alternatively, that the industry has withheld the benefits of its differentially greater physical input economies from consumers to be shared by its input factors through higher wage rates, salary levels, or profit rates, or that these input factors have received relatively lower payments in order to help absorb the burdens of the industry's differentially smaller economies as compared with other industries. Indeed, the deflated total unit costs of any industry could deviate from a horizontal trend over extended periods only if there were a progressively expanding margin (either upward or downward) between its factor prices and profits and those in other industries—a condition likely to be undermined over time by the mobility of resources and by competition from substitute products (Gold [2, pp. 130]).

6. *But the apparent vulnerability of the preceding widely accepted expectations concerning the effects of industrial research and major technological innovations should not discourage continued promotion of these major sources of economic and social progress.* On the contrary, recognition of such findings should help to prevent the potentially inhibitory effects of using inappropriate criteria to judge their results. As a matter of fact, most of the engineering estimates of direct gains with respect to physical inputs and physical outputs were realized. The burdens caused by decreasing supplies of high-grade raw materials were largely offset; their unit input requirements were reduced through less wastage, the development of by-products, and more effective utilization of what was consumed; and pollution levels were kept declining from the peaks associated with Bessemer converters and beehive coke ovens. Labor requirements per unit of output were contracted sharply, while hazardous and brutally arduous work was increasingly replaced by tasks that place greater emphasis on

skills and knowledge. Improved facilities, equipment, and instrumentation made possible extraordinary advances in product quality and variety as well as in productive capacity and in the precision with which operations could be adapted to changes in inputs, outputs, and production levels.

Hence the vulnerability of the preceding expectations was rooted in the assumptions that economic benefits would directly parallel such physical improvements. Reliance on such assumptions, however, is evidence of a failure to supplement expert engineering evaluations of immediate physical readjustments with expert production-management estimates of subsequent physical readjustments in associated sectors of operation and, far more important, with comparably expert economic analyses of the probably effects of the unavoidable interactions of both sets of physical readjustments with short- and longer-term supply and demand pressures in input factor and product markets. Such additional analyses would help to develop more realistic estimates of the magnitude and time patterns of the net benefits of alternative innovations as well as the advantages and disadvantages of pioneering as opposed to following competitors. Moreover, such economic analyses may also contribute to the planning of future research and innovational efforts by identifying supply, demand, and price trends in factor and product markets which foreshadow developing pressures and opportunities.

Over the long run, keeping up with competitors with respect to technological progress seems to be essential to survival. Acceptance of this view need not, however, counsel progressive increases in R&D commitments. Instead, the rising cost of such efforts, their increasing specialization, and their very modest rate of major successes in many industries suggests the development of new R&D strategies in steel and other basic materials industries. These would involve such choices as the following: narrowing the sectors of specialization, changing the ratio of inhouse versus contract research, and altering the relative emphasis on internally generated innovations versus licensing (see chapter 14).

Finally, it should be emphasized that although the economic benefits of technological innovations that can be captured by individual firms tend to be smaller and shorter lived than seems to be widely expected, such rewards may still compare favorably with alternative sources of differential advantages over competitors. And yet this raises the question of whether such incentives are large enough to encourage a level of investment in technological progress which accords with national social welfare objectives. After all, most of the benefits which flow through, and then past, the innovating firms and industries accrue to society at large in the form of higher real incomes per capita, more effective utilization of scarce resources, industries which are more competitive in domestic and world markets, less onerous work, and a generally stronger and more secure economy. But such findings as have been presented here identify a variety of factors tending to limit the returns which are expected to motivate industrial managements to make the large investments and assume the heavy risks involved in major research programs and technological innovations. Accordingly, these results may also warrant consideration in the course of any review of the adequacy of public policies concerned with encouraging further technological progress in particular sectors of industry as well as in the economy as a whole—such as is presented in Chapter 17.

Notes

1. A study of the diffusion rates of fourteen major innovations in the U.S. rion and steel industry and related coal- and ore-mining operations revealed that, as shown in figure 10-15, only five accounted for more than one-third of their relevant sectors of output even 15 years after initial successful commercial applications.
2. For the dates of initial commercial utilization of the leading innovations and their early rates of diffusion, see figure 10-15.
3. Based on data presented in Nelson [7].
4. The sequence of operations in iron and steel operations was shown in figure 9-1.
5. The U.S. Census of Manufactures ceased publishing separate data for blast furnaces after 1954.
6. Determined by dividing changes in the index of total material costs per unit of output by an index of changes in the prices of the various materials, weighted by their respective shares of total material costs.
7. For extended discussion, see Gold [5].
8. One should not concentrate, as Salter [9] did, solely on technological responses to change in factor prices without also going on to consider the subsequent repercussions on factor prices. For further discussion and related empirical findings, see Gold [3, pp. 193-197] and also chapter 8.
9. For an early discussion of this problem, see Gold [2, pp. 126]. For a reference to later publications dealing with this problem, see Nelson [7, pp. 32-33].
10. For a tracing of such necessary adaptations even beyond the plant adopting the innovation, see Peirce [8].
11. For further discussion, see Gold [4, pp. 23-24].
12. For further discussion, see chapter 13.

References

[1] M.G. Boylan, Jr., *Economic Effects of Scale Increases in the Steel Industry: The Case of U.S. Blast Furnaces* (New York: Praeger, 1975).

[2] B. Gold, "Economic Effects of Technological Innovations," *Management Science,* September 1964; reprinted in Gold [3].

[3] B. Gold, *Explorations in Managerial Economics: Productivity, Costs, Technology and Growth* (New York: Basic Books, 1971).

[4] B. Gold (ed.), *Technological Change: Economics, Management and Environment.* (Oxford: Pergamon, 1975, 1979).

[5] B. Gold, W.S. Peirce, and G. Rosegger, "Diffusion of Major Technological Innovations in U.S. Iron and Steel Manufacturing," *Journal of Industrial Economics,* July 1970; reprinted in Gold [4].

[6] B. Gold, W.S. Peirce, and G. Rosegger, *Economic Effects of Technological Innovations in U.S. Iron and Steel Manufacturing, 1900–1960* (forthcoming, 1980).

[7] R.R. Nelson, M.J. Peck, and E.D. Kalachek, *Technology, Economic Growth and Public Policy* (Washington: The Brookings Institution, 1967).

[8] W.S. Peirce, "The Effects of Technological Change: Exploring Successive Ripples," in Gold [4].

[9] W.E.G. Salter, *Productivity and Technical Change* (Cambridge, Eng.: Cambridge Univ. Press, 1960).

11 Competing Technologies and Costs: An International Comparison

Efforts to develop policies for dealing with import threats to the competitive position of the U.S. steel industry were heavily influenced by the 1977 *Report to the President on Prices and Costs in the U.S. Steel Industry* by the Council on Wage and Price Stability (hereafter, COWPS report [1]). This alone would warrant careful examination of its findings and conclusions, but such scrutiny is also urged by the report's skeptical conclusions concerning the effects of major technological advances and the potentials of modernization. In addition, the resulting absence of constructive perspectives failed to provide any basis for a coherent policy concerning the future development of the industrial base of the U.S. economy within the context of world economic development and trade.

Relevant Findings and Implications of the COWPS Report

Summary of Major Findings

The COWPS report provides a recent review and analysis of studies bearing on the relative construction and operating costs of Japanese and American steel mills. Its major findings relevant to the objectives of this book are as follows:

1. Average total production costs per net ton of finished steel products (excluding returns to equity) are $61 lower in Japan than in the United States (p. 60).
   a. This is attributed almost wholly to Japan's $55 advantage in labor costs. (p. 55).
   b. Similarly, it is noted that the $40 to $45 difference in net cost per ton shipped between Nippon Steel and "the most efficient U.S. plant" was "remarkably close to the labor cost differential of $5.92 per man-hour times 7–8 man-hours per ton in 1976" (that is, $41.44 to 47.36) (p. 78).
2. Current "best practice" in the U.S. steel industry is estimated to save only about $45 of operating cost per net ton of finished product compared with the average of the six largest producers, while other estimates cited range between $25 and $20. The latter even assumes that such a "best practice" firm would use "large basic oxygen furnaces, large blast furnaces and 100 percent continuous casting" (pp. 77–78). These estimated savings would come primarily from reducing man-hours per net ton of finished steel from

8.2 to between 6.4 and 6.6 (saving \$19.55 to \$22.00) and from reducing energy and coke costs by \$6 to \$7 (p. 77).

3. Compared with the current average costs of a fully integrated carbon steel plant, a new "greenfield" plant would reduce operating costs per net ton by about \$60 while increasing capital charges by \$177, assuming that the new capacity would cost \$800 per ton, resulting in a total cost per net ton of \$417 compared with the current average of only \$300 (pp. 79-82). The report adds that "it is inconceivable that there are 6 million tons [that is, less than 6 percent] of capacity currently in production which require operating costs (exclusive of capital charges) of \$417 per net ton" (pp. 79-82).
   a. By way of comparison, it is estimated that a greenfield plant in Japan would reduce operating costs per net ton by \$30 while increasing capital charges by \$119, assuming that the new mill would cost \$540 per ton of capacity.
   b. Incidentally, the report claims that "nearly 60 percent of the U.S. disadvantage in greenfield production costs derives from higher construction costs of the new plant," that is, from the "inability of the U.S." construction sector to erect plants as quickly and cheaply as the Japanese (p. 84).
4. The alternative of expanding U.S. steel capacity by "rounding out" existing plants (that is, through a "balanced expansion of steelmaking and finishing facilities") was estimated to reduce production costs by about \$40 per net ton of finished products relative to the average for existing plants while increasing capital charges by about \$100, assuming a cost of \$450 per ton for the added capacity, resulting in total production costs per ton of \$360, or \$60 more than the current average.

Implications of the COWPS Findings

The first of the preceding findings implies that the widely recognized advances in Japanese technology and scale have yielded production cost advantages of only 2 to 3 percent—almost all the remaining differences being attributable to higher U.S. wage rates. This meager estimate of the benefits of technological advances is reinforced by the second of the preceding findings, that introducing "best practice" in U.S. mills would reduce operating costs per net ton of finished product by only \$20 to \$45, or by 8 to 14 percent. And the third and fourth of the preceding findings couple the preceding pessimistic views of technological potentials with recognition of the heavy impacts of inflation on the cost of new facilities to suggest that the U.S. steel industry's competitive cost position would be severely weakened rather than strengthened by constructing large, modern plants utilizing the best technologies available, and that it would even be disadvantaged, though less severely, by large-scale efforts to modernize and expand existing plants.

Some Alternative Perspectives on the Effects of Advances in Technology and Scale

During the past 25 years, the most important technological advances affecting steel production costs have been increases in the size and efficiency of blast furnaces; increases in the use of basic oxygen furnaces as well as in their size; increasing use of continuous casting; increasing applications of mechanization, automation, and computerization; the increasing use of very large ships for transporting needed raw materials; and major improvements in the extent and effectiveness of pollution-control efforts. These have obviously affected raw material, energy, labor, and capital requirements along with associated costs. In order to estimate the magnitude of such effects and their bearing on modernization and expansion options in the United States, it may be helpful to begin by exploring results in Japan, where these advances have been introduced more rapidly and more fully than elsewhere. Attention will then be given to the implications of such findings for assessing the potential effects of similar advances in the U.S. steel industry.

Some Effects in the Japanese Steel Industry

The major expansion of the Japanese steel industry occurred during the 1960s. Raw steel production rose from only 24.4 millon tons in 1960 to 102.9 millon tons in 1970 and to 131.5 in 1973, with an estimated capacity of about 150 in 1975 (COWPS [1, pp. 100, 145]). Accordingly, explorations of the effects of the technological and scale advances embodied in new facilities may be concentrated on the period since 1960. It is also relevant for comparison purposes to note that the Japanese plants in 1960 were reasonably comparable with those in the United States, in considerable measure because much of the technology in the first generation of postwar Japanese plants was based on U.S. practices. For example, the average output of pig iron per blast furnace in Japan was very close to the U.S. average as late as 1966 (as shown in chapter 8), and its ratio of steel production from basic oxygen furnaces in 1960, as shown in figure 11-1 was still small enough (11.9 percent) to be comparable with the U.S. ratio of about 6 percent (American Iron and Steel Institute [3]).

Newly built blast furnaces in Japan have continued to increase in size and in the intensity of production per unit of volume. Inner volume increased from 1,146 cubic meters in 1958 (Chiba No. 2) to 3,363 in 1970 (Mizushima No. 3) and 5,070 in 1975 (Oita No. 2); and output per cubic meter nearly doubled by 1973 (figure 11-2). One result of these and other technological changes in blast furnace operations was to reduce average coke consumption per ton of output from 619 kilograms in 1960 to 434 in 1973, that is, by 30 percent, and to reduce the total fuel rate per ton by about 20 percent (figure 11-2). But even these Japanese estimates of gains underestimate the effects of technological changes,

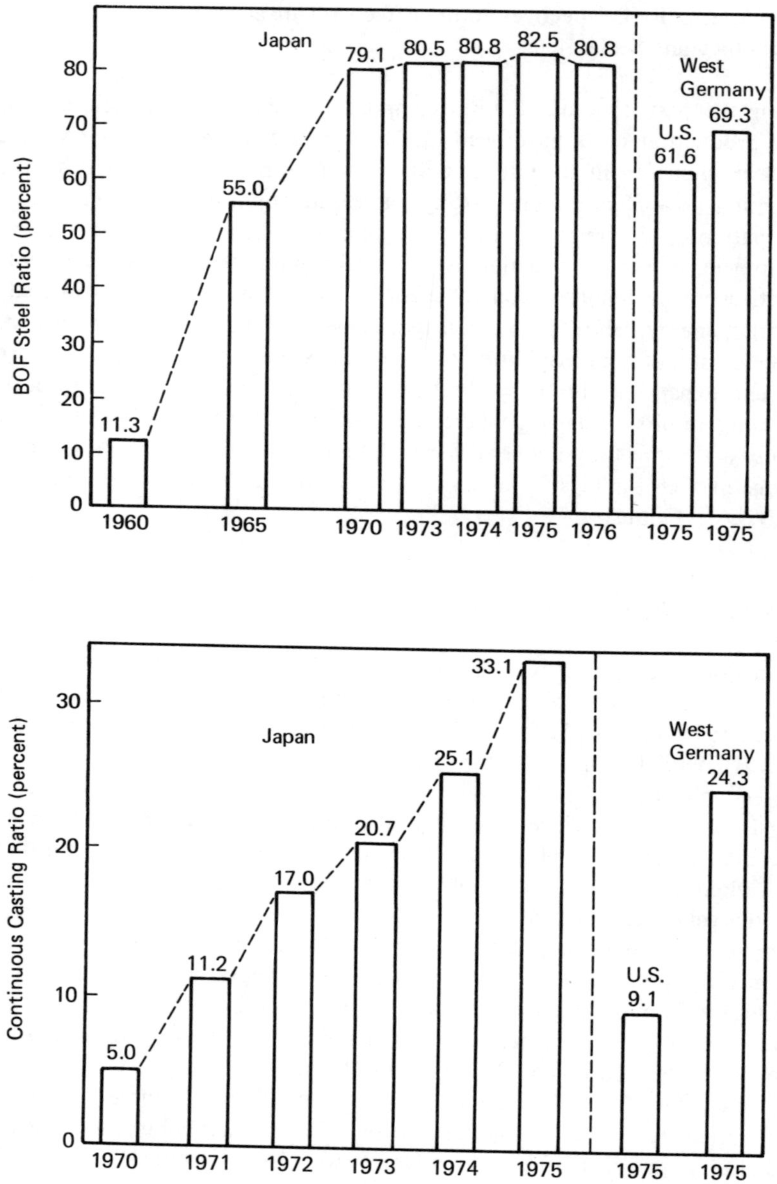

Source: T. Kono, Nippon Steel Corporation [2].

Figure 11–1. Reliance on Basic Oxygen Furnaces and on Continuous Casting in Japan, United States, and West Germany in Selected Years

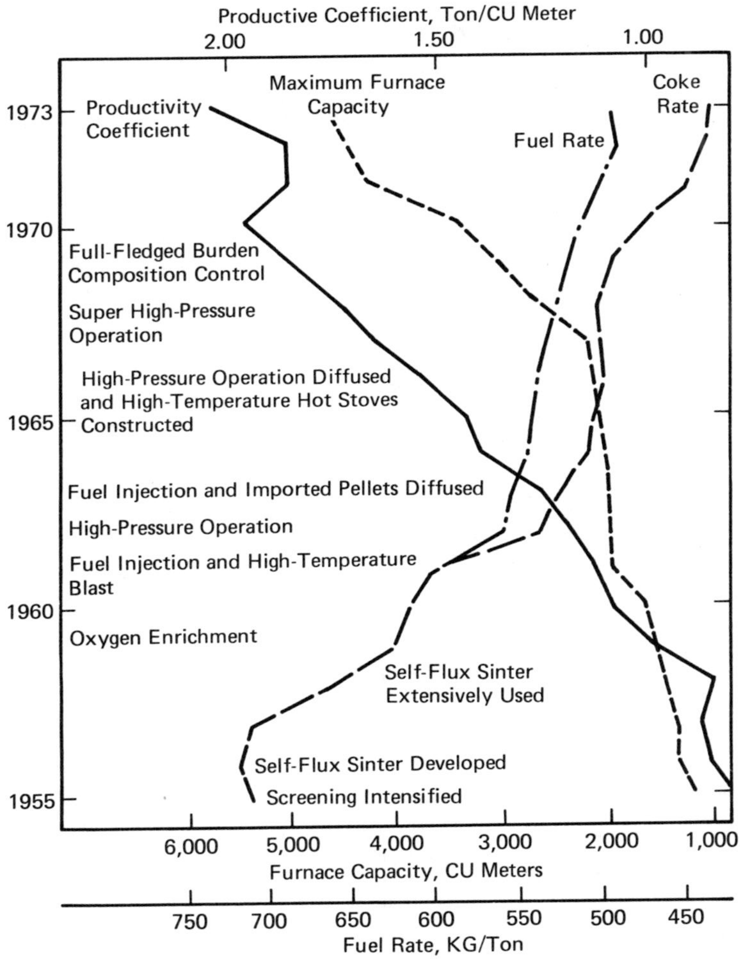

Source: Same as figure 11–1.

Figure 11–2. Changes in Japan's Blast Furnace Operating Performance (Productivity Coefficient, Fuel Rates, and Furnace Capacity), 1955–1973

because they relate to industry averages rather than to the results of best practice.

The extraordinary expansion of the Japanese steel industry also facilitated rapid increases in the ratio of steel output provided by basic oxygen furnaces from 11.9 percent in 1960 to 82.5 percent in 1975 and in the ratio of continuous casting output from 5.0 percent in 1970 to 33.1 percent in 1975 (figure 11–1). Some indication of the resulting effects of these and other technological

Table 11-1
Estimated Man-Hours per Ton of Finished Product Capacity in Major Japanese Steel Works, 1975-1976

	Capacity		*Employment*			*Capacity*	*Man-Hours*	*Man-Hours*
	Raw Steel, Tons (1)	*Finished Yield, Tons (1) × 0.862 (2)*	*Plant, Number (3)*	*Contract, Number (4)*	*Total, Number (3) + (4) (5)*	*Total Employment Tons/Man (2) ÷ (5) (6)*	*Capacity, Man-Hours/Ton 2,000 ÷ (6) (7)*	*90 Percent Capacity, Man-Hours/Ton (7) ÷ (.9) (8)*
Yawata	11.9	10.26	20.0	15.08	35.08	292	6.85	7.61
Kimitsu	10.9	9.39	7.9	5.96	13.86	677	2.95	3.28
Mizushima	12.8	11.03	12.0	9.05	21.05	524	3.82	4.24
Kashima	11.0	9.48	12.0	9.05	21.05	450	4.44	4.93
Oita	8.0	6.90	3.7	2.79	6.49	1,063	1.88	2.09
Fukuyama	15.4	13.27	9.7	7.31	17.01	780	2.56	2.85

Explanatory Notes: (1) Raw steel capacity is 90 percent of nominal capacity to accord with AISI "production capability"; (2) yield ratio based on new calculations in T. Kono, "Comments on Production Yield," in [4], exceeds the estimated ratio of 0.751 in the COWPS report (p. 53) by 15 percent; (4) contract labor proportion of total employment for five major steel companies is 43 percent (*Steel Labor Handbook–1977*, Japan Federation of Iron and Steel Workers' Unions); (7) agreed normal 1870 annual working hours plus 120 average overtime hours.

advances are provided by Japanese estimates that total energy consumption per metric ton of raw steel had declined by about 15 percent in 1973. Moreover, total man-hours per net ton of steel products had declined from about 45 in 1960 to 8.5 in 1973, or by more than 80 percent (figure 11-4).

It is important to note again, however, that the preceding data are industry averages rather than reflections of the full effects of technological advances in new plants. For example, a comparison of steel-making capacity adjusted for final product yield of 0.862 with employment, after allowing 43 percent for contract labor, yields estimates of full capacity output per man-hour in 1975-1976 ranging between 2.95 and 4.44 for Kitmitsu, Kashima, and Mizushima and only 2.56 for Fukuyama. At 90 percent of capacity utilization, assuming no reduction in employment, the first group would range between 3.28 and 4.93, and Fukuyama would rise to 2.85 (table 11-1). (1) These represent levels 42 to 65 percent below the industry averages for 1973. Moreover, my recent field study suggests that efforts are being intensified to extend integrated computer controls so as to reduce energy and man-hour requirements much further.

Comparison of Japanese Data with COWPS Estimates for Japan and the United States

The preceding substantial benefits of technological and scale advances in the Japanese steel industry are less apparent from the estimates of raw material and labor usage rates in table III-3 of the COWPS report [1, p. 53]. This is due partly to differences in the measures used and partly to differences in the levels of aggregation used.

For example, it is quite possible that Japan uses more coking coal, more purchased scrap, and more purchased electricity per ton of raw steel production. But this does not mean, as might be inferred by some, that its fuller utilization of major technological advances has yielded no productivity benefits, nor that fuller adoption of such advances in the United States would yield little or no advantage. Actually, average coke rates per ton of blast furnace output in 1974 were only 437 kilograms compared with 609 for the United States, or 28 percent less (figure 11-3). Japan does, however, use a higher ratio of hot pig iron (produced by the coke-consuming blast furnace) than the United States precisely because it has more fully adopted the advanced technology of basic oxygen furnaces, which typically use lower ratios of scrap than the older open-hearth process.

Similarly, the Japanese may use more purchased scrap per ton of raw steel output, although they obviously use less total scrap per ton of such output. This, too, represents the effects of their fuller adoption of continuous casting and other technological advances which result in higher yields of finished product—as recognized at the bottom of COWPS table III-3—and hence in less home-

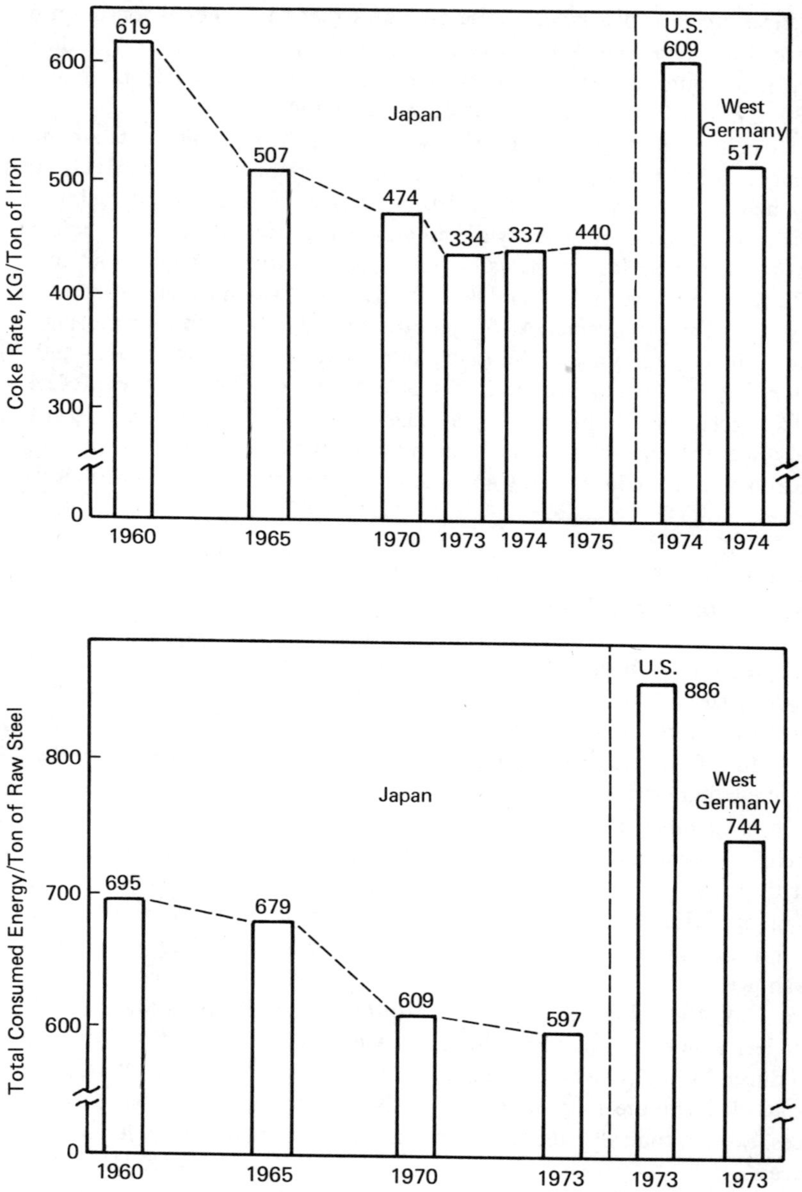

Source: T. Kono, Nippon Steel Corporation [2].

Figure 11-3. Steel Industry Energy Consumption and Coke Rates in Japan, United States, and West Germany in Selected Years

generated scrap. Moreover, although this table estimates that the Japanese use more fuel oil and electricity as well as coking coal per ton of raw steel production, it should also be noted that the Japanese estimate that their total energy consumption per ton of crude steel in 1973 was 30 percent less than in the United States (figure 11-3).

The estimate in COWPS table III-3 that the Japanese use about one-sixth more man-hours per ton of raw (or finished) steel than in the United States is more difficult to account for. It may, of course, reflect a temporary deviation from more representative levels due to the extraordinarily low level of capacity utilization in 1976 (71.1 percent; COWPS [1, p. 145]) combined with the limited downward flexibility of employment levels in Japanese practice. Because Japanese employees are rarely idle, however, the output measure may be misleading because it ignores such alternative work contributions as new construction, which continues even when capacity is underutilized, modernization, and accelerated maintenance. Another possible explanation may be that office-employment ratios are higher in Japan, and the COWPS estimate emphasizes its coverage of all employees. But neither of these possible influences would seem to be relevant in assessing the potential effects in the U.S. steel industry of adopting the major technological innovations so widely utilized in new Japanese plants. Hence only the adjustment of Japanese data to the U.S. product mix would seem explanatory—and it is not at all apparent how much of the sharp reversal of the productivity relationship for 1973 shown in figure 11-4 is attributable to this consideration.

In general, plant-level man-hours per ton of plant capacity would seem to provide a more meaningful basis for assessing the potential effects of such technological and scale advances in the United States than total man-hours per ton of actual output for an entire industry subject to quite different restrictions on employment levels. Accordingly, it may be useful to recall my earlier estimate for leading plants of 2.85 to 4.93 man-hours per ton of finished product at 90 percent of capacity (table 11-1), or between 50 and 72 percent less than the American Iron and Steel Institute (AISI) average for the U.S. industry at its highest productivity levels in 1973 and 1974 (figure 11-4). To this should be added the reminder that intensive efforts were apparent at each of the plants I visited in 1977 to further reduce plant man-hour requirements per ton of output by 25 to 40 percent, in addition to rationalizing office operations. It may be worth noting in this connection my sense of shock at observing the Oita plate mill operating without a single worker on the floor at the time. The difference between seeing even 10 to 15 workers and none may have induced an overreaction on my part because it illustrated at least a temporary achievement of the implicit target being doggedly sought by systems engineers at each of the other major plants in Japan.

Still another perspective on the potential benefits of new facilities is offered by estimates of the effects of scale increases on unit production costs. Cockerill

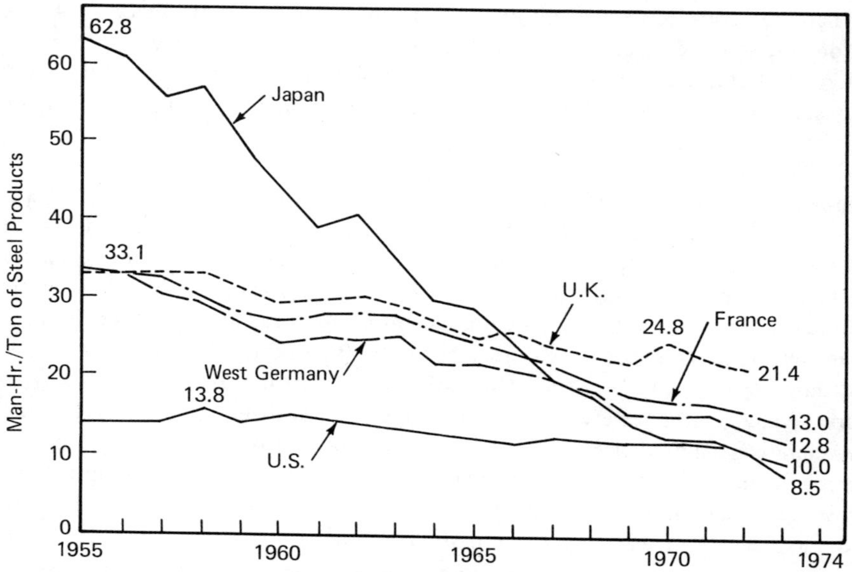

Source: American Iron and Steel Institute.

Figure 11–4. Steel Industry Man-Hours per Net Ton Shipped in Selected Countries

and Silberston [5] estimated in 1973 that integrated steel plants with annual capacities of more than 7 million tons in the United States should have production costs per unit of output 15 to 20 percent higher than Japanese plants of the same size, but about 15 percent lower than U.S. plants of 3 million tons capacity, with the comparable cost advantage of large Japanese plants approximating 20 percent. It is extremely difficult to generalize about the effects of such differences, both between countries and within countries, because of a variety of dissimilarities among plants which can affect costs markedly. Because such estimates represent the results of careful inquiries among knowledgeable specialists, however, they do at least indicate that new facilities may be expected to yield benefits not only from utilizing new technological advances, but also from any accompanying increases in scale. The hitherto untapped potentials of both may be greater in the United States because technologically advanced plants of more than 7 million tons capacity already account for about one-half of Japan's steel output, while such large plants account for only about one-sixth of U.S. output, and because even these have not yet fully utilized the major technological innovations widely used in Japan.

In short, the technological advances and increases in scale embodied in new Japanese mills during the past decade apparently have yielded substantial reductions in the levels of raw material, energy, and labor inputs per unit of output. Hence, although their wider adoption in the United States need not, of course, offer parallel benefits, it would be astonishing indeed if such adoptions were entirely devoid of significant improvements in productivity.

Implications for Prospective Modernization and Expansion in the United States

Examination of the prospective benefits of adding new facilities to modernize and expand the productive capacity of the U.S. steel industry obviously requires reviewing the probable effects of particular additions not only on unit input levels and factor prices, but also on capital requirements and the ability to supply available markets. In addition, effective analysis must also consider the consequences of doing virtually nothing. And the effects of alternative options on the competitive position of the U.S. steel industry must be considered not only as of the present, but also as they would be 5 to 10 years from now.

Potential Savings of Raw Materials, Energy, and Labor

The estimates of potential savings from new technology cited in the COWPS report approximate 20 percent for man-hours per net ton of finished steel products and 12 percent for energy and coke costs. Resulting savings in total operating costs for plants utilizing all best practices range from $20 per ton (or 6.5 percent below the associated estimated average for integrated carbon steel plants) to $25 per ton (or 8 percent below the accompanying estimated average) to $40 to $45 per ton (or 12 to 16 percent below alternative accompanying estimated average) [1, pp. 72-78].

Such estimates fall short of the differences between U.S. and Japanese input factor utilization levels cited earlier in this chapter. These indicated a difference of more than 30 percent per ton of crude steel in total energy consumption in 1973, even at the level of industry averages, with the gap at that time between the best plants in Japan and in the United States probably wider still. Moreover, the Japanese have accelerated their energy-conservation efforts in steel plants since then, suggesting the practicability of further reductions.

With respect to man-hour requirements per net ton of steel shipments, the Japanese have already surpassed the savings estimated as maximum potentials in the COWPS report and are working intensively to reduce present levels by another 25 to 40 percent. For example, Ogishima officials noted their objective of reducing employment from the original level of 20,000 for the Keihan Works to 6,000 for an equal capacity.

The largest of the three estimates of potential cost savings in the COWPS report was developed in two ways. One showed that it approximated the average cost per net ton shipped by Nippon Steel (after allowing for the differential in wage rates between the United States and Japan); the other showed that it approximated Inland Steel's average cost per net ton of shipments. Although these are eminently useful comparisons, it is difficult to understand why they are regarded as best-practice potentials instead of being recognized as the actual achievements of facilities built more than 10 years ago, on average. Moreover, Inland Steel's superior performance was achieved without the technologically most modern and large-scale blast furnace, which it is in the process of building now, as well as without various additional new facilities which it deems essential to expanding capacity and improving performance (Securities and Exchange Commission [8]). As for Nippon Steel, its results cover the operations of nine plants, only two of which—accounting for less than one-third of company capacity—were built within the past 12 years (*Nippon Steel Annual Report, 1976*).

A variety of significant innovations have been developed within the last few years, and many processes and facilities have been improving in efficiency. Accordingly, in setting technological performance targets for new facilities unlikely to come on stream within less than 3 to 5 years, it would not seem unreasonable to aim at "best-practice" goals at least 15 to 20 percent beyond those achieved by relevant facilities already in operation somewhere and at "average-practice" goals within 5 years close to current best-practice performance.

New Construction Costs in Japan and the Factors Affecting Them

New steel mill facilities in Japan have long required substantially less investment per ton of capacity than in the United States, but their costs also have been rising, partly because of increases in wage rates, partly because of demands for increasingly sophisticated machinery and controls, and most recently, because of rising pollution-control standards. Thus, according to the estimates given to me in interviews, Fukuyama cost \$80 per ton in the "precomputer age", and Kimitsu, Kashima, and Kakogawa cost \$200 to \$250 per ton, while recent additions to these latter have been costing \$330 to \$500 per ton. Ogishima officials gave me an estimate of \$400 per ton for building the first half of their planned 6.0-million-ton plant, but their competitors claimed that it probably would cost \$450 to \$500 per ton. About 20 percent of this total was for pollution-control systems and equipment, which is claimed to yield the best results in the world and which is certainly most impressive to the observer.

Steel mill construction costs in Japan were less than 40 percent of U.S. levels per ton of capacity until the last few years. Indeed, one Japanese construction engineer returning from an extended visit to ARMCO's new Middletown facilities claimed that he could have built them in Japan for 20 percent of what they cost here. And current costs are still estimated to be at least 40 percent less than in the United States. My systematic questioning of Japanese engineers and managers concerning the sources of these savings elicited the following array of obvious as well as less obvious factors:

1. Lower wage and price levels in Japan result in cheaper building materials and equipment as well as lower wages for construction workers, who are generally paid at levels similar to those of production workers.
2. Unremitting pressure is exerted to minimize costs of construction per unit of capacity through evaluating both advance estimates and actual performance facility by facility rather than for the entire plant or project as a whole, and consistently cross-checking comparative costs among plants to identify laggards. Moreover, construction tends to be faster because there is less labor trouble, because the steel companies supervise all or most construction—avoiding the extra costs and delays involved in using general contractors and an array of consultants—because Japanese construction crews are expected to work harder and lose less time in unproductive activities, and because most of Japan tends to be free of interruptions from severe weather.
3. There is also aggressive pressure to increase the actual capacity squeezed out of purchased equipment after as well as before installation. Suppliers are expected to provide equipment which exceeds the capacity contracted for by at least 5 to 10 percent if they are to hope for repeat orders. Head office and plant engineers are then expected to keep expanding capacity after installation by 3 to 5 percent each year through developing modifications in design, tooling, accessories, and operating methods and through increasing utilization rates. When I was examining the blast furnace at Ogishima, my guide said, "This may look like a blast furnace to you, but to our engineers it is a piece of laboratory equipment."
4. Larger-scale facilities can apparently be built at less cost per unit of capacity up to sizes which have only been reached in recent years with respect to some facilities, but which have still not been reached with respect to others.

Mill site preparation tends to be more expensive than in the United States, of course, when shortages of flat land necessitate either large earth removal operations or building on land dredged from the sea. In the case of the latter, however, some projects seem to have been aided through government programs concerned with deepening ship channels and harbor improvements.

Finally, it should also be noted that some construction costs may be understated in Japan, especially in the case of additions to or modifications of existing plants, through charging such work to plant operating costs. This is especially interesting because the use of plant employees for such purposes is not at all uncommon during periods of recession, when such employees are not needed for production but are not laid off either, and because such practices tend to exaggerate operating costs per ton of product shipped when capacity-utilization rates decline.

Some Implications of Japanese Experience for New Construction in the United States

One major potential contribution to reducing steel mill construction costs in the United States which can be derived from Japanese experience relates to the need for more continuous and aggressive pressure on design, construction, and production engineering for substantial improvements in performance. Extensive research on the United States steel industry for more than 20 years has left me with the impression that most companies have been less demanding of innovations and improvements in such technical sectors of performance than in Japan, that engineers have accordingly eased into a less driving work pace, and that resulting contributions have been more modest. Nor was there much comfort in discovering at a meeting of more than 200 steel engineers in December 1977 that my stating such critical views drew no disagreement—only expressions of frustration and illustrations of the discouragements faced by more aggressive innovative efforts. Such situations may develop because of the absence of the stimulus to process and construction innovations which would be offered by numerous major plant projects, or they may reflect a declining interest in squeezing more capacity out of existing facilities when capacity is so seldom strained, or they may be due to a reluctance to generate trade union frictions by altering prevailing production practices. Moreover, they even may be rooted in a belief that intensified marketing efforts are likely to be more rewarding, less expensive, and less troublesome than production improvements.

Other possible means of reducing steel mill construction costs suggested by Japanese experience include seeking to increase the degree of steel company involvement in supervising construction operations, soliciting construction and equipment bids from foreign as well as domestic sources—to expose them to the international competitive pressures with which our steel companies must cope—and altering the timing of construction projects and equipment purchases to take advantage of the wide cyclical fluctuations in such demands. It may be of interest to note in this connection that one of the Japanese officials told me that his company was buying some equipment for a new facility from Germany because it was being offered at a lower price than was available from Japanese manufacturers. With respect to timing, I have often heard references to U.S. Steel's expansion projects during the 1930s despite its excess capacity, which resulted in low prices whose benefits were enjoyed for more than a decade thereafter.

An even broader and more important potential contribution to strengthening the future competitive position of the U.S. steel industry can be derived from Japanese experience. The principle involved was expressed by a Japanese steel official when I asked why his company and others kept expanding despite current underutilization of available capacity and despite increasing resistance to their exports from their major markets in the United States and Western Europe. He said, "The question is simply: to be or not to be. To survive in this very competitive industry, we must keep moving ahead. This means better processes and products, higher productivity and lower costs than other producers. And there are limits to such possibilities in old facilities and equipment." Hence the constant pressure not only on workers and engineers, but in all functions and at all levels of management. Hence, despite the high cost of new facilities cited earlier, every Japanese plant I visited is actively involved in expansion efforts, although attendant increases in capital charges may well exceed immediate savings in operating costs, using calculations similar to those made by COWPS for the United States [1, pp. 80-83]. It may well be, as has been suggested elsewhere (Gold [6]), that effective entrepreneurship often involves undertaking capital projects that prove successful not because attractive benefits were generally apparent before initiation, but because management effected whatever additional technological, market, and financial adjustments proved necessary to adapt resulting production capabilities to changing and often unpredictable opportunities.

Some Implications for COWPS Appraisal of Greenfield and Round-Out Options

As the entire analysis in this chapter suggests, my basic doubts about the COWPS judgments concerning the expansion options available to the U.S. steel industry center on the assumptions underlying the estimates used. Specifically, I believe that the incorporation of already available technological advances will yield greater savings in round-out and greenfield projects, and also that investment costs and attendant capital charges will be lower. Moreover, I cannot help feeling that similar judgments must account for the current and planned expansion projects of Inland Steel, Bethlehem Steel, and other companies.

I am also concerned by the overemphasis on present values and relationships in an analysis focused on policy decisions necessarily covering the next decade in view of the periods required for planning and constructing major new facilities. Surely the productivity gaps between most existing plants and major new facilities will increase with time in view of the more limited benefits to be obtained from retrofitting major innovations into old facilities. Unless inflation rates are expected to abate, new facilities will cost progressively more if we keep deferring their construction. Indeed, a major source of Japan's current competitive advantage is its having built a huge amount of large-scale, technologically advanced plant before the recent surge in inflation. Moreover, I cannot believe that steel demand will stop growing in the United States and world.

Under such conditions, the virtual cessation of modernization and expansion in the U.S. steel industry would, in my opinion, represent a catastrophic error in policy. It would tend to result in a progressive loss of competitiveness by an already old and further aging stock of plant capacity. It would encourage further reductions in the industry's research and development efforts, except for product improvements not requiring significant changes in processes and facilities. This would further accelerate the obsolescence of our capacity because of its declining ability to respond to shifts in the product mix and quality standards of market demand (Gold and Boylan [7]). And the likely outcome of such tendencies would seem to be increasing U.S. dependence on imports from an increasingly cartelized world steel industry, with serious resulting impacts not only on our steel industry and on steel prices in the United States, but also on the competitive positions of steel-using industries in this country and on raw material and equipment suppliers to the domestic steel industry.

The essentially hopeless outlook of the COWPS report reflects an overconcentration on the disadvantageous aspects of the U.S. steel industry's position. One cannot help being struck by the dramatic contrast between this approach and that of the Japanese in the 1950s. Lacking virtually all needed raw materials, without any modern production facilities, and with only the most meager resources of engineers and skilled workmen experienced in contemporary steel technologies, the Japanese considered it quite feasible to undertake a program of development and expansion designed to challenge the world leaders within 15 years. In 1977, on the other hand, the COWPS report examined a steel industry with perhaps the best supply of raw materials outside the U.S.S.R., with production facilities probably better than those of all countries but Japan, with an unsurpassed aggregation of technological expertise and skilled labor, and with the largest and most affluent market in the world, only to imply that the outlook for the American steel industry was hopeless, for nothing but progressive deterioration can result if neither modernization nor expansion is considered economically feasible.

A more balanced view would, in my opinion, recognize that, except for that of Japan, the current position of the U.S. steel industry is more favorable than that of any other country, and its long-run prospects outshine all, including those of Japan. Accordingly, it would appear more constructive to begin the development of national policies relating to our steel industry by urging consideration of a commitment to making it equal or superior to the leading steel industries of the world within the next 10 years. And the next step would be to determine what the steel companies, their plant builders and equipment suppliers, and their trade unions as well as steel users and the government could contribute to achieving such a national objective. In short, my question would be not "Could we?" nor "Should we?" but "How can we?"

Note

1. It may be of interest that my estimates of 450 to 677 tons per wage earner for Kimitsu and Kashima tend to be supported by the statement of Jean Van Asbroeck, marketing chief for Cockerill Steel, the largest steel producer in Belgium, that "his company produced only 200 tons per man, compared to productivity of 255 tons per man achieved by National Steel in the U.S. and a huge 524 tons per man turned out by the modern Japanese mills" (*European Community,* (OECD), November-December 1977, p. 9).

References

[1] Council on Wage and Price Stability, *Report to the President on Prices and Costs in the U.S. Steel Industry, October 1977* (Washington: U.S. Government Printing Office, 1977).

[2] Tsutomu Kono,[a] *Letter to Friends in the U.S. Seeking Prosperity for the World Steel Industry* (Tokyo: Nippon Steel Corporation, August 1977).

[3] American Iron and Steel Institute *Annual Statistical Reports* (Washington: American Iron and Steel Institute, various years).

[4] Tsutomu Kono,[a] *Comments on Production Yield Discussed in the U.S. Council on Wage and Price Stability Report: Prices and Costs in the U.S. Steel Industry* (Tokyo: Nippon Steel Corporation, February 1978).

[5] A. Cockerill and A. Silberston, *The Steel Industry: International Comparisons of Industrial Structure and Performance* (Cambridge, Eng.: Cambridge Univ. Press, 1974).

[6] B. Gold, "On the Shaky Foundations of Capital Budgeting," *California Management Review,* Winter 1977.

[7] B. Gold and M. G. Boylan, "Capital Budgeting, Industrial Capacity and Imports," *Quarterly Review of Economics and Business,* Fall 1975.

[8] Securities and Exchange Commission, *Form S-7* (detailing Inland Steel's plans for raising $100 million through a new equity issue), March 1976.

---

[a]Mr. Kono is General Manager of the Corporate and Economic Research Department of Nippon Steel and the author of numerous highly perceptive analyses of the steel industries of United States and of other countries as well as of Japan.

12 Economic Evaluation of Technological Development Alternatives

Increasing competition from overseas has generated widespread concern in the United States about possible means of strengthening the technological capabilities of a growing array of domestic industries. This has led to considerable discussion about the relative potentials of modernization—involving adoption of the best technology currently available here or abroad—as compared with efforts to develop revolutionary new technologies through intensified research and development programs. Choices between these major alternatives, as well as among the numerous possibilities within each, are often guided initially by expected gains in technical efficiency. But the competitive position of an industry (or firm) represents an economic evaluation of its performance. Hence, in appraising alternative possible advances in an industry's technological capabilities, overriding emphasis must be given sooner or later to the prospective economic effects of the advances.

To examine such potential economic effects systematically requires reaching beyond the simplified measures which have dominated the published literature to a more encompassing analytical framework, such as was presented in chapter 3. The following discussion will seek to illustrate the applicability of the foregoing approach to one of the key focuses of current controversies about how to strengthen the technological capabilities of domestic industries: the steel industry. In addition, this discussion will concentrate on technological potentials for reducing production costs rather than on seeking to deal with potentials for improving product attributes.

Some General Perspectives on Actual Costs and Related Mythologies

Cost proportions obviously differ among steel companies in the United States, mostly because of dissimilarities in their activities beyond operating steel mills, but also to some extent because of certain disparities within such operations. Nevertheless, it would seem to suffice for present purposes to focus on the average magnitudes of the major cost categories in manufacturing steel products. Purchased materials account for about 45 percent; wages and salaries, for 35 to 40 percent, including fringe benefits; and depreciation and interest combined, for 6 to 8 percent.[1]

Such proportions obviously contradict the long pervasive economists' conception of steel as an outstanding example of a "capital-intensive industry," meaning one that has a high ratio of fixed capital charges to total costs. This erroneous conception is largely attributable to technological ignorance. It is true, of course, that the steel industry requires enormous amounts of capital facilities and equipment involving huge investments. These account for only a minor proportion of total costs, however, because the embodied technology yields comparably enormous productive capacity and requires huge inputs of materials and labor. On the other hand, these capital inputs play a far greater role in determining productive efficiency and total unit costs than is reflected by their own cost levels. Indeed, the steel industry should rather be characterized as a "capital-dominated industry," meaning that changes in the capacity of its mills and in the attainable productive efficiency with which they utilize labor, material, and investment inputs are overwhelmingly determined by the technology, scale, and modernity of its capital facilities and equipment.[2]

The assumption that steel is a capital-intensive industry implies that cost proportions and total unit costs would tend to vary significantly with variations in capacity utilization levels—as shown in traditional U-shaped short-run cost curves—with total labor and material costs tending to vary directly with output levels, while total fixed capital charges remain unchanged.[3] Empirical findings in chapter 10, however, demonstrated that such cost proportions have varied only within a remarkably narrow range despite extraordinary adjustments in capacity utilization and general price levels. Even more surprising was the finding of relative stability in cost proportions over long periods despite the irregular timing of major technological innovations impinging first on one input factor and then on another. Perhaps most disappointing of all to many technological specialists may be the additional empirical finding that a succession of major technological innovations in the steel industry, and in other industries as well, failed to yield the almost invariably expected reductions in total unit costs, even after costs were adjusted for changes in the general price level. A number of reasons for these disappointing results were discussed earlier. At this point, however, the most relevant implication of these evidences of the apparent insensitivity of costs to major technological and market impacts is to reinforce still further the preceding warnings about the dangers of oversimplifying the relationship between such impacts and their economic consequences.

Potential Sources of Economies in Labor Inputs

Adjustments in unit costs are largely traceable, of course, to changes in the quantity of each input per unit of output, in its quality and price, in its proportioning relative to other inputs, and in the mix of products. Technological analyses of prospective innovations often concentrate only on whichever of these determinants is directly affected, and most economic analyses reflect similarly restricted focuses. However, the widespread disappointment of industrial managements with the actual benefits derived from major technological innovations relative to the expectations which triggered their adoption urges fuller consideration of the interactions involved in achieving their effective integration into the larger system.

Wages represent the second largest proportion of total costs, accounting for about 25 to 30 percent. The impressive technological potentials for reducing such inputs is suggested by the fact that man-hours per unit of output in large, modern Japanese steel mills are already much less than one-half the U.S. average. Moreover, as was also noted in the preceding chapter, these plants are actively engaged in seeking to reduce such requirements by an additional 25 to 40 percent within the next 3 to 5 years. Past gains have been achieved primarily through increases in the scale of operations and in the utilization of continuous casting and progressively wider applications of mechanization and computerization. The new targets are expected to be reached through the continuing extension of these very same means, that is, even without contemplating any revolutionary new technologies. Hence, in order to justify substantial commitments for such radical and inevitably risky development programs, they would have to offer potential reductions of at least 75 percent below current unit man-hour requirements in the United States.

What would be the effects on labor costs if comparable technological innovations could be introduced in the U.S. steel industry? This would obviously depend in the first instance on whether production workers and their trade unions were willing to accept reductions of one-half to two-thirds or more in man-hour requirements per unit of output. Although the United Steel Workers have long professed the principle of accepting all technological advances, field research reveals increasing resistance in existing plants to innovations threatening even relatively modest reductions in employment. Such resistance could be expected to intensify, of course, when confronted with innovations involving sharp reductions in manning, expecially if unemployment levels remain high.

The labor cost effects of such innovations would also depend on accompanying changes in wage rates. In recent years, trade unions have demanded increases in wage rates in proportion to reductions in man-hours per unit of output,[4] as well as in proportion to increases in the cost of living. Under such conditions, even if unions permitted a doubling or tripling of output per man-hour, unit wage costs would tend to rise rather than decline.[5] It is instructive to recall in this connection the finding in chapter 10 that between 1904 and 1967, output per man-hour in the U.S. steel industry rose nearly eightfold, but unit wage costs more than doubled, nevertheless, because average hourly wage rates rose nineteenfold. More serious still, such innovations are likely to increase total unit costs even more than unit wage costs because of the charges generated by the additional capital investment commonly necessary to achieve significant increases in the output per man-hour of this capital-dominated industry. Finally, estimates of the prospective effects of technological innovations on unit wage costs must also allow for the relatively inflexible but progressively increasing "fringe benefits"—to cover vacations, unemployment, pensions, insurance, and so on—that were found in chapter 10 to have added 45.7 percent to total wage payments for hours actually worked in 1975 as compared with a 23.5 percent addition in 1960.

In view of such discouraging prospects for achieving substantial reductions in unit labor costs in existing plants, despite the availability of tested technologies for sharply decreasing unit labor requirements, even revolutionary technologies might prove devoid of significant labor cost benefits. It is possible, of course, that potential results might be more promising if such innovations were embodied in new plants and in new locations, instead of attempting to retrofit them into existing plants with highly developed resistances to technological advances in the form of established work rules, skill classifications, and incentive-pay arrangements. But managements might well wish to seek some persuasive reassurances against such offsets to prospective benefits before committing substantial resources to the development of new technologies whose effective utilization could increase the competitiveness of the U.S. steel industry.

In considering the prospective contributions of further technological innovations to reducing employment costs, attention should also be called to the significant opportunities available for reducing requirements for salaried personnel. Their numbers in the U.S. steel industry rose from 17.9 percent of wage employees in 1950 to 34.4 percent in 1975 (Gold [5, p. 180]). Increasing mechanization and computerization of a wide array of clerical functions as well as some staff functions would probably make it possible to reduce such inputs by one-half or more within a few years without requiring any major technological advances.

Potential Sources of Economies in Material and Fuel Inputs

It may be recalled that purchased materials and supplies account for about 45 percent of total costs in the U.S. steel industry. Slightly less than half represents outlays for iron-bearing inputs, including iron ore, agglomerates, and scrap, while the remainder pays for coal, other fuels, and electric power. Appraisals of technological potentials in this area must encompass their prospective effects not only on total energy and total iron-bearing input requirments per unit of output, but also on the mix within each category, because various degrees of substitution are technologically feasible which may or may not be advantageous depending on relative factor prices. It should also be recalled in this connection, from the discussion in chapter 8, that because relative factor prices are often highly variable over time, while the facilities embodying new technologies are often relatively inflexible and long-lasting, the factor prices used in appraising such potential innovations should seek to reflect long-term trends rather than current relationships. Finally, as will be illustrated later, even more aggregative levels of evaluation would be necessary when changes in the composition of direct inputs also affect results in subsequent stages of operation.

In considering technological improvement potentials with respect to energy inputs, it may be useful to begin with the gains already achieved by modern Japanese mills, as summarized in the preceding chapter. Japanese coke rates have been more than 30 percent below the U.S. average since 1973, and their total energy consumption per ton of steel has been even more advantageous. Nevertheless, the Japanese have intensive efforts under way in this area as well to reduce energy inputs further. Their past differential gains were achieved primarily through increases in the scale of blast furnaces and basic oxygen furnaces, through more rapid adoption of the latter as well as of continuous casting, and through increasing computerization to improve heat economies at various stages of operation. Moreover, significant additional gains are expected through further extensions of these methods. Over the longer run, substantial gains are also expected from intensive programs to increase the continuity of successive steel operations and from research seeking advances in rolling at lower temperatures. In view of these large gains, which have already been achieved abroad, and the additional gains likely to result from the further extension of available technologies, efforts to develop revolutionary new technologies would have to promise reductions of at least 50 percent below current energy requirements per unit of output in the United States in order to justify substantial resource allocations.

What would be the effect on energy costs if technologies yielding similar reductions in energy requirements could be introduced in U.S. steel mills? With respect to reducing the physical levels of coal and other energy inputs per unit of output, there is no reason, in principle, why Japanese achievements could not be duplicated. But the construction of larger-scale facilities would require huge investments, of course, as would the further diffusion of continuous casting. Moreover, it takes considerable time to learn how to operate such facilities with maximum efficiency, and it also requires highly motivated labor to provide continuous close conformance with technical instructions. If such requirements could be met, major reductions in energy requirements per unit of output would appear to be attainable even before exploring the additional potentials offered by revolutionary new technologies.

But the cost effects of energy-saving technologies also depend on the prices of the inputs involved. Efforts to develop cost-saving combinations in the United States during 1940–1970 resutled in sharp reductions in inputs per unit of output of coke, fuel oil, non-coking coals, and tar and pitch, but these were accompanied by increasing inputs of oxygen, natural gas, and electricity.[6] Although such substitutions were encouraged by the relative prices of these inputs during that period, it is obvious that shifts in relative prices would readily reverse the economically most desirable direction of such adjustments in the composition of energy inputs.

Some technologies provide sufficient flexibility to permit reasonably prompt and fulsome adaptations to such price gyrations—for example, permitting shifts among different types of fuel injections into blast furnaces. But other technologies are less adaptable. For example, analysis in chapter 9 of the effects of replacing open-hearth furnaces with basic oxygen furnaces in a large British mill revealed that unexpected reversals in the relative prices of fuel oil as compared with oxygen and of scrap as compared with pig iron (costs) contributed to sharply increasing unit material costs over a period of years instead of yielding the expected substantial decreases. Thus, too, recent increases in natural gas prices have discouraged some U.S. development work on direct reduction processes, although these remain quite attractive in regions endowed with plentiful, cheap supplies of such fuel. Similarly, recent sharp increases in the price of noncoking coals have discouraged long-continued and costly efforts by U.S. steel companies to develop an effective form-coke process. And termination of the high-temperature gas reactor project of Gulf Atomics and Shell seems to have suspended U.S. interest in proposals for a nuclear steel-making facility which would have utilized the high-temperature gas expected to be available as a reasonably priced by-product of such a nuclear power plant to fuel a direct reduction operation.

With respect to iron-bearing inputs into steel mills, technological achievements and potentials seem much more limited in squeezing out more of the iron actually contained in each of the iron-bearing materials used than in altering the mix of inputs so as to minimize the total costs of such inputs per unit of hot metal output. For example, the increasing availability of reasonably priced fine ores encouraged the development of improved methods of sintering them, leading to a rapid increase in the ratio of sinter to natural ores as blast furnace feed in the United States during the 1950s and early 1960s. Since then, pellets have accounted for a steadily increasing share of such inputs, forcing declines in the proportions accounted for by natural ores and sinter. This development is especially interesting because pellets are priced substantially higher than domestic natural ores per iron unit contained. But their unexpectedly large contribution to increasing the iron-producing capacity of blast furnaces yields investment and cost benefits which more than offset their higher price—in addition to yielding other benefits.[7] Nevertheless, new sinter plants continue to be built in areas where access to reasonably priced foreign fine ores utilizing cheap water transportation offers continuing advantages over higher-priced domestic pellets available only after high transportation costs.

In short, technological potentials for reducing the cost of purchased materials and supplies in the U.S. steel industry seem to be more promising with respect to reducing the level of energy than of iron-bearing input requirements per unit of output. But substantial cost advantages may also be available through developing technologies which would permit effective adjustments in the mix of energy inputs and iron-bearing inputs in response to significant future shifts in the relative prices of alternative sources within each of these categories.

Potential Sources of Economies in Capital Inputs

As was noted earlier, capital inputs affect the competitive position of the U.S. steel industry not only through their bearing on the level and flexibility of total unit costs, but even more important, through their controlling influence on the quantity, quality, and mix of both potential outputs and resulting input requirements. All such effects derive from the scale and technological modernity of the facilities and equipment embodying fixed investment, the rate of utilization of such facilities, and the rate of charges against such inputs to recover the investment and pay suppliers for its use.[8] Among these three sets of factors, the potential contributions of technological advances would seem to be greatest with respect to the first and least with respect to the last.

The economic theory of scale benefits is open to serious criticisms, and so are most of the published empirical studies of such effects in various industries, as was noted in chapter 7. It seems clear, nevertheless, that up to some point, increases in scale (properly defined) do yield significant cost savings in various industrial operations. Such benefits in the steel industry seem to have been most apparent in the form of reductions in capital investment and man-hour and fuel requirements per ton of capacity for various major operations and for entire integrated plants. Here again, Japanese experience suggests that substantial reductions with respect to each of these inputs may be achieved by increasing the scale of operations in U.S. mills. Although modern Japanese steel mills are 50 to 100 percent larger than even the leading U.S. mills, it is quite possible that the economically optimal scale using current technologies may be smaller in some U.S. operations than the largest Japanese units. Such differences may arise either because the latter have at times placed greater emphasis on expanding capacity rapidly than on achieving the lowest possible costs, as was discussed in chapter 7, or because many U.S. plants expect larger fluctuations in output and hence lower average levels of capacity utilization, with attendant diseconomies tending to offset the economies of still larger scale.

In addition to the potential benefits of larger-sized units, however, significant scale benefits may also be attainable through greater specialization of plants in two directions: sharply reducing the array of products within each major product line, which often involve only slightly differentiated specifications, and reducing the wide range of product lines manufactured by most integrated steel mills. These represent two of the most serious barriers to major advances in the achievement of more nearly continuous steel mill operations, as well as fuller realization of the technological capabilities of production facilities.

Graduating beyond the custom tailoring of thousands of products to concentrate on a few dozen with longer runs under standard conditions would reduce operating costs in virtually every stage of production in addition to increasing yields, reducing inventories, and permitting improvements in distribution and customer servicing. Moreover, resulting price reductions, combined with the development of more widely applicable standard products, might well gain broad customer acceptance of them, especially if reinforced by the continued availability of more specialized products only at substantially higher prices. In short, this may well represent a less formidable technological frontier with more far-reaching implications for improving the competitiveness of a major sector of the U.S. steel industry, not only against steel imports, but also against competition from other industrial materials, than a variety of technologically more exotic possibilities.

Significant benefits may also be revealed by analyzing the potential cost savings from narrowing the range of product lines produced in each mill combined with designing mills of different sizes in order to seek higher utilization rates in various geographical areas. There is, of course, nothing new about such possibilities except the need to replace past rough-cut judgments in making such decisions with more sophisticated analyses both of the technological possibilities for each plant and also of the optimal distribution of the total capabilities of multiplant companies between large "base-load" plants—to borrow the electric power system analogy—and a network of more highly specialized complementary plants.

Improvements in unit capacity costs may also be effected through reducing plant construction costs, increasing the throughput of existing facilities, developing new technologies, and reducing equipment prices. The Japanese have managed to halve U.S. unit capacity costs through advances in each of these areas, but efforts to adopt their methods with respect to the first three factors would require numerous changes in our managerial policies and trade union practices, as reviewed in the preceding chapter. Equipment prices are affected not only by domestic wage rates, but also by the scale of the plants producing such equipment and by the extent to which the equipment has been standardized. Hence substantial reductions in such equipment prices are likely to devleop only if encouraged by a large-scale program of modernization and expansion in the U.S. steel industry combined with increasing acceptance of more highly standardized components in building such additions, or by increasing reliance on imports of such equipment.

Potentials of Revolutionary New Technologies

Turning at last to the potentials of revolutionary new technologies, it may be useful to present some evidence concerning the prospective effects of even successful developments. Past studies amply demonstrate the large ratio of failures among the relatively basic research undertakings which spawn eventual successes, as well as the long periods of costly efforts involved in transforming the few promising outcomes into commercially applicable products. But there seems to be less awareness of the findings in chapter 10 that even successful innovations are diffused far more slowly than is commonly believed, that the rate of early adoption does not provide reliable guides either to subsequent adoption rates or to ultimate levels of application, nor that evidence does not support the frequently assumed tendency for more recent innovations to diffuse faster.[9] This suggests that unless revolutionary technologies are developed to the point of effective commercial use with inordinate rapidity, unless they offer patently outstanding competitive advantages, and unless their diffusion is also accelerated to extraordinary rates, they are unlikely to have any substantial impact on the competitive position of the U.S. steel industry within the next 10 to 15 years.

Such perspectives certainly do not suggest that efforts to develop revolutionary technologies should not be promoted. On the contrary, the very future of the domestic steel industry over the long run depends on intensive programs to develop such advances, for the deterioration of basic research and development capabilities would ensure its accelerated obsolescence and competitive decline.[10] The fundamental implication of the foregoing discussion is rather that such efforts msut be combined with a more immediate program to modernize and expand the domestic steel industry through effective utilization of already available technologies and relatively straightforward extensions of them. To do nothing—as is implied by the COWPS report[11]—or to wait until some miraculous new technological advances are developed (which could not be reasonably duplicated by foreign competitors in relatively short order) is likely to prove catastrophic not only for the U.S. steel industry, but also for related industries and major geographical areas.

Concluding Observations

1. Beginning with the physical input–physical output network of the analytical framework presented in chapter 3, the preceding analysis suggests that:
   a. The largest prospective reductions in unit input requirements seem to center around labor and energy, but significant gains in the productivity of capital also seem attainable.
   b. Major gains in these sectors have already been achieved by foreign steel producers, thus requiring the expectation of truly far-reaching further reductions below current U.S. input rates to justify long, costly, and risky efforts to develop revolutionary technologies surpassing those which are available.
   c. Technologically attainable major reductions in man-hour requirements per unit of output may prove unrealizable in practice, however, if labor

resists attendant sharp reductions in employment levels and unless production workers can be motivated to maximize attainment of high technological potentials through strict adherence to technical operating instructions. Problems of this sort have already been demonstrated by the inability of the Finsider plant in Taranto (Italy) and the Usinor plant in Dunkerque (France) to duplicate the achievements of the Japanese mills on which they were modeled.

d. Technologically attainable reductions in unit energy requirements do not seem to face comparable resistances, but reductions in capital requirements per unit of output are likely to be offset at least partially by investments needed to meet rising pollution-control standards.

2. Moving up the analytical framework to include factor-price interactions with prospective reductions in unit-input requirements suggests that:
   a. Even if a major reductions in unit man-hour requirements could be effected, trade union demands for proportionately higher wage rates would tend to offset most or all of the expected decrease in unit wage costs, thus tending to result in even higher total unit costs than before (because of the accompanying increases in investment usually required in this industry to make possible substantial reductions in labor inputs). This obviously intensifies the difficulties of improving the competitive position of the U.S. steel industry inasmuch as it is already burdened by wage rates substantially in excess of those prevailing in Japan, in much of Western Europe, and in such developing sources of steel exports as South Korea and Brazil.
   b. Reductions in unit energy or in unit iron-bearing requirements, however, are more likely to induce decreases than increases in their respective prices, except in cases where cartel controls are introduced. This means that reductions in such input requirements are likely to be fully transmitted to their respective unit costs and may even be accentuated by accompanying factor-price reductions resulting from decreases in the demand for such inputs.
   c. Steel-making facilities, costs, and equipment prices have tended to rise sharply for a long period of time in the United States[12] as well as elsewhere, in most cases more than offsetting accompanying gains in their production capabilities due to technological advances, and thus tend to make this an unlikely source of significant reductions in unit capital charges or even in unit capacity costs. This tends to reduce the likelihood of decreasing the current substantial U.S. disadvantage in unit capacity cost relative to the Japanese. But a continuation of such inflationary pressures would suggest that current additions to capacity are likely to be less costly than those to be built 3 to 5 years from now.
3. Moving further up the analytical framework to consider potential interactions among average prices, average total unit costs, output levels, and product mix suggests that:

a. Increasing concentration of plants on a substantially narrowed range of products might yield increases in capacity utilization and reductions in costs sufficient to permit such decreases in price as would engender gains in competitive position.
b. Such plant specialization might also help to reduce unit capacity costs by limiting needed equipment capabilities—and it might well further the automation of plant operations, thereby contributing to reduced manpower requiremetns as well.

4. Thus the most promising short-term targets of technological advances seeking to improve the competitive position of the U.S. steel industry by reducing its costs relative to foreign producers would seem to center around reducing energy requirements.
   a. Substantial gains could also be achieved in labor costs if technological advances were somehow to be accompanied by major changes in currently prevailing trade union attitudes toward adjusting employment levels and wage rates so as to leave reasonable net benefits to the developers and adopters of such advances.
   b. Significant cost gains might also be achieved in the utilization of capital investment through increases in the scale and specialization of plants as well as through major technological advances, but only if these could be effected without more than offsetting increases in the cost of such resources.
5. Finally, there can be no doubt of the importance of initiating efforts to develop revolutionary new steel technologies, for numerous recent advances suggest that additional advances are in the making and are in fact being actively pursued in Japan and elsewhere. Hence even commitments to such efforts would merely involve competing with others similarly engaged, instead of assuring eventual superiority. It should be emphasized, however, that effective company participation in such efforts, without which the prospects for successful commercial application would be very small indeed, would seem to require major changes in government policies which currently constitute a formidable array of disincentives to taking on such long, costly, and risky commitments.[13]
6. But the revitalization of the U.S. steel industry requires more than the earliest possible introduction of the best technologies and facilities already in use elsewhere combined with the initiation of programs to develop revolutionary new technologies to surpass the achievements of competitors.
   a. It also requires major changes in the past government attitudes and policies, which have discouraged and actively hindered maintenance of the industry's past world leadership.
   b. Major changes would also be necessary in the policies of steel companies, in the practices of trade unions, and in the cost efficiency of our construction and capital-equipment-producing operations.[14]
   c. Nor are these problems peculiar to the steel industry. Hence broadly

encompassing efforts to meet the foreign challenge in this basic sector may also help set the pattern for developing constructive measures for dealing with emerging challenges from abroad to a wide array of our industries.

7. More generally, it should also be emphasized that:
   a. There has been a dangerous continuation in recent years of the long-established tendency to evaluate progress in American industries by comparing current performance with past levels, instead of recognizing that increasing international competition requires comparison with foreign achievements as well, lest our advances over the past fall short of those being attained abroad.
   b. There has been a dangerous tendency to project academic conceptions and ideals of market competition into international trade, despite their patent inapplicability to prevailing realities:
      i. In most parts of the world, the technological progress of industries is no longer being left to the profit-motivated efforts of individual entrepreneurs; rather it is being directed and supported to a considerable degree or even fully by central governments stressing employment, foreign exchange, security, and other nonprofit objectives. Such motivations are quite likely to encourage allocations to technological development greater than those justified by the profit expectations of individual entrepreneurs exposed to competition with such government-supported producers.
      ii. For these same reasons, lower-priced imports need not, and often do not, represent lower production costs or greater productive efficiency. Hence, American producers must face the possibility that even costly advances in their technological capabilities may yield little or no market advantages if foreign exporters can match any resulting price decreases through increased help from their governments.
   c. There has been an excessive reliance in policymaking on abstract economic theory and highly aggregative statistical studies of the economies of research and development, of scale increases, of market concentration, and of various other aspects of developing and utilizing technological advances in industry. Increased research focused on individual industries and even on particular product groups seems essential if sufficient understanding is to be achieved of the numerous and highly significant differences among them to guide practically relevant diagnoses of needs and recommendations for dealing with them.

Notes

1. For illustrations of differences between cost proportions as determined from company financial statements and those reported for the Census of Manufactures category of "basic steel," see Chapter 10, figures 11-3 and 11-14.

For another estimate of cost proportions in the U.S. steel industry, see Council on Wage and Price Stability [2, p. 60].

2. For further discussion, see chapter 5.

3. For a detailed discussion of the reasoning involved and its shortcomings, see Gold [3, pp. 121–151].

4. Labor prefers, of course, to use the reciprocal measure—output per man-hour—because of its implication that any increases in output are attributable to the efforts of the man-hours, although this tends to be uncommon in capital-dominated industries. For further discussion, see Gold [4, pp. 14–15].

5. Changes in wage costs per unit of output are obviously determined by the relationship between changes in wages per man-hour and in output per man-hour. Hence, a 10 percent increase in the latter, which is accompanied by a 10 percent increase in the former, leaves unit wage costs unchanged. But a further increase in wage rates to compensate for a concomitant rise in the cost of living would obviously result in higher unit wage costs than before the innovation.

6. For further discussion and actual data, see figure 10–10 and Rosegger [9, pp. 58–59]. For a detailed review of shifts in blast furnace fuel inputs in the United States over extended periods, see Boylan [1, pp. 108–111].

7. For a general review of pellet effects, see Peirce [8, pp. 149–168]. For a detailed review of changes in blast furnace feed in the United States and their effects, see Boylan [1, chapter 5]. For a discussion of the widespread underestimation of the economic effects of technological innovations because of the pervasive reliance on methodologies which ignore qualitative changes in the nature of the inputs and outputs involved, see chapter 13.

8. The bearing of these factors on fixed capital charges per unit of output may be illustrated algebraically as follows:

$$\frac{\text{Fixed capital charges}}{\text{Output}} = \frac{\text{fixed investment}}{\text{capacity}} \div \frac{\text{output}}{\text{capacity}} \times \frac{\text{fixed charges}}{\text{fixed investment}}$$

$$(\text{Unit fixed capital charges}) = (\text{unit capacity costs}) \div (\text{utilization rate}) \times (\text{rate of fixed charges})$$

9. For a more detailed review of such findings, See Gold *et al.* [7].

10. For fuller discussion, See Gold and Boylan [20].

11. Discussed in the preceding chapter.

12. For example, see figure 10–13, Boylan [1, pp. 162] and Gold [5, p. 177].

13. These are discussed in chapter 17.

14. For further discussion, see chapter 17.

References

[1] M.G. Boylan, *Economic Effects of Scale Increases in the Steel Industry: The Case of U.S. Blast Furnaces* (New York: Praeger, 1975).

[2] Council on Wage and Price Stability, *Report to the President on Prices and Costs in the U.S. Steel Industry,* (Washington:, U.S. Government Printing Office, October 1977).

[3] B. Gold, *Explorations in Managerial Economics: Productivity, Costs, Technology and Growth* (New York: Basic Books; London: Macmillan, 1971).

[4] B. Gold (ed.), *Technological Change: Economics, Management and Environment* (Oxford: Pergamon, 1975).

[5] B. Gold, "Factors Affecting Capital Requirements in the U.S. Steel Industry," *Tekko-Kai* (Tokyo), September 1977. English translation in *Hearings on World Steel Trade, Serial 95-37* (U.S. Congress, House Ways and Means Subcommittee on World Trade, 1977). Also see "Analyzing versus Forecasting Industrial Prospects: The Case of Steel," *Iron and Steelmaker,* March 1977.

[6] B. Gold and M.G. Boylan, "Capital Budgeting, Industrial Capacity and Imports," *Quarterly Review of Economics and Business,* Fall 1975.

[7] B. Gold, W.S. Peirce, and G. Rosegger, "Diffusion of Major Technological Innovations in U.S. Iron and Steel Manufacturing, *Journal of Industrial Economics,* July 1970. Reprinted in [4].

[8] W.S. Peirce, "The Effects of Technological Change: Exploring Successive Ripples," in Gold [4].

[9] G. Rosegger, "Technological Change, Managerial Incentives and Environmental Effects," in Gold [4].

13 Interindustry Repercussions of Major Technological Innovations

This chapter presents a preliminary exploration of an underdeveloped sector of the economic effects of technological innovations. It has three objectives: to review some basic limitations of most past studies, to suggest some concepts and analytical approaches for improving coverage of the fuller range of such effects, and to provide some empirical illustrations of the additional insights which may be obtained.

Some Basic Limitations of Past Studies

Most economic analyses of technological innovations have focused on the innovation as the initiating cause and have then sought to determine resulting changes in the relationship of physical input to physical output quantities and in total unit costs (or particular components of them) in the firms or industries adopting them. Such undertakings commonly suffer from four major shortcomings:

1. They tend to ignore, or give only peripheral attention to, accompanying changes in the qualitative characteristics of the inputs and products affected, thus subjecting their productivity and cost evaluations to the possibility of serious errors.
2. They fail to explore the surrounding matrix of further effects represented by the impacts of the given innovation on the sectors supplying the industry's inputs and purchasing its outputs, thus limiting insights into resulting changes in their product and factor prices, markets, and other operating characteristics.
3. They ignore the internal and external pressures that triggered adoption of innovations under study and thereby assume, instead of determining, the actual specific objectives of such decisions, which define the most relevant criteria for evaluating results.
4. They provide limited (or no) perspectives on the implications of such major technological innovations for broader economic and social problems and related public policies.

Some General Concepts and Approaches

On the Significance of Qualitative Changes in Inputs and Outputs

Changes in the qualitative characteristics of inputs and outputs tend to be ignored because of the measures employed. These commonly involve deflating changes in the value of products by changes in their average price to measure changes in output levels and similarly deflating changes in the cost of materials, labor, and capital goods by changes in the average price of these categories to determine changes in input levels. Such expedients obviously imply that only the quantities of products and inputs have changed, leaving their qualitative characteristics essentially unchanged. But virtually all major technological innovations violate such assumptions. Most require changes in the kinds and specific characteristics of at least some purchased materials and capital goods, and sometimes in labor skills as well. And most innovations also lead to, or necessitate, changes in the service attributes of at least some products, not to mention the product mix. Clearly, the more numerous and significant such alterations are in the qualitative dimensions of inputs and outputs, the wider are likely to be the margins of error of traditional measures of the productivity and cost effects of technological innovations.

Moreover, innovation-induced changes in the qualitative characteristics of inputs and outputs may have even greater effects on the industries supplying their inputs, and on those purchasing their products, than the commonly measured changes in input and output quantities and product prices. Because competition tends to minimize the prices paid for identical goods available from alternative sources, endowing products with distinctive attributes is one of the most promising means of gaining price and other marketing advantages over competitors. This explains the heavy emphasis on product improvements in the research and development programs of a wide range of capital and consumer goods industries, and even of basic industrial materials industries such as metals, chemicals, and fibers. It is also reflected in the fact that technological innovations are likely to be adopted even if they result in higher rather than lower total production costs per unit of product, provided that they yield product-service attributes for which purchasers are willing to pay prices, and buy quantities, offering attractive returns to the producer.

Resulting changes in the qualitative attributes of products, however, may generate pressures for adaptive technological and other adjustments by purchasers engaged in further processing and fabrication operations. These may involve changes in the nature and composition of other inputs, in processing methods, and even in the design of particular products and the resulting product mix—leading in turn to possible changes in production costs, product prices, and market potentials. Thus innovation-induced qualitative changes in product characteristics may give rise to a train of responsive innovations in one or more of the successive stages of the structure of production, reaching from raw materials producers to manufacturers of final consumer goods.

But technological innovations are also likely to involve adjsutments in the qualitative characteristics of one or more of the inputs to the changed processes. In order to fulfill such altered requirements, suppliers may have to revise their own product designs, production methods, and even some input specifications. And this chain of backward pressures engendered by the innovation may similarly be transmitted by the immediate supplier to his own suppliers and even further back.

It follows, therefore, that innovational decisions in any firm may be triggered not only by internally generated proposals for reducing costs or improving products, but also by pressures from suppliers to utilize qualitatively improved materials, components, or capital goods and by pressures from purchasers to satisfy their newly modified procurement specifications. Hence, a comprehensive approach to exploring the interindustry ramifications of major technological innovations must encompass the complex network of interactions involved in the absorption and progressive diffusion of such impacts within particular sectors of the economy.

Expanding the Analytical Framework

In order to guide systematic explorations of the broader repercussions of major technological innovations, the analytical framework must reach out toward seven different channels of change, each capable of transmitting pressures in either direction (as shown in Figure 13-1):

1. The first encompasses successively higher levels of aggregation within the firm—from the operating stage directly affected, through antecedent and subsequent stages, to total plant (or firm) performance.
2. The second covers resulting effects on competing plants (and firms) through to results for the industry.
3. The third traces effects backward to input suppliers and their respective industries.
4. The fourth traces effects forward to product buyers and their industries.
5. The fifth covers "sidewise" pressure on product buyers and their industries.
6. The sixth traces the cumulative effects of these forward, backward, and sidewise pressures on regional and national problems as well as related public policies.
7. The seventh concerns the eventual effects on consumer desiderata.

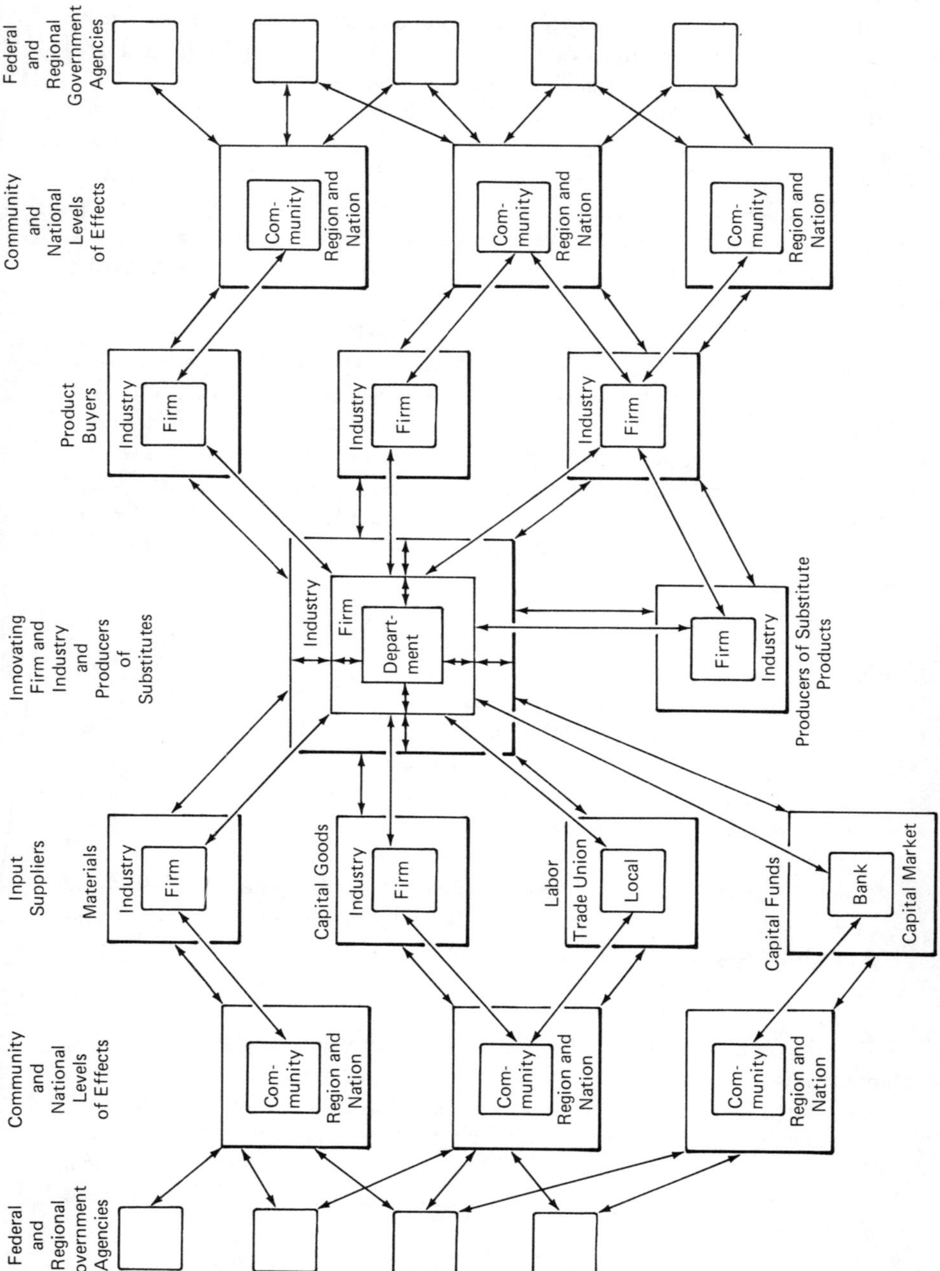

Figure 13-1. Illustrative Framework for Tracing Technological Effects

Some Analytical Problems

Identifying significant changes in the qualitative characteristics of inputs and outputs at successive stages of transmission and tracing their economic effects often requires considerable knowledge of the relevant technologies. Shortcomings in this respect may well lead to minimizing and even overlooking the effects of innovations involving major qualitative changes which are not readily apparent to the technically unsophisticated observer, for example, changes in the physical and chemical properties of materials.

Efforts to trace the effects of given technological innovations are commonly confronted by several frustrating difficulties, as was noted in chapter 10. The innovations themselves are subject to progressive development as they are adapted to an increasing variety of applications. It is often difficult to disentangle their direct effects from the secondary and tertiary effects resulting from subsequent adaptive reactions over time. Moreover, over the extended time periods usually involved in achieving widespread diffusion even of major innovations, many firms and industries are likely to have several substantial innovations in various stages of utilization. Still further difficulties are obviously caused by the concomitant effects on economic measures of the unceasing adjustments in product and factor markets attributable to many influences quite unrelated to technological innovations.

Finally, competitive pressures often encourage such continuous exchanges, and even cooperative efforts at times, between suppliers and customers as to seriously hamper efforts to determine the directions of technological pressures. Indeed, exploratory inquiries frequently yield overlapping claims to making "key" contributions to given innovations.

On the Major Effects of Interindustry Technological Repercussions

Intraplant Transmission of Qualitative Effects

Within a plant, attention must be centered first on effects in the stage of operations immediately affected by the innovation. One set of required determinations centers around possible changes not only in the quantity and average price of each input category, but in the specific physical, chemical, and other specifications of each material, purchased component, machine, and facility affected by the innovation, as well as in labor skills, technical staffing, and supervision. Another set centers around possible changes in the qualitative specifications of the individual products of that stage, in their respective production costs, and in the overall product mix. Efforts must then be made to trace the effects of observed input changes on earlier operations and the effects of output changes on subsequent operations.[1]

The critical problems to be confronted are of two kinds. One involves adjusting price and quantity measures for changes in the qualitative attributes of inputs and outputs in order to make generalizable economic evaluations at certain levels of aggregation (for example, changes in factor prices, in particular productivity relationships, in unit costs, and so on).[2] The second problem involves the opposite requirement of continuing to focus on the particular qualitative changes affecting each input and output so as to trace its distinctive impact on preceding or later stages of production.

Intraindustry Repercussions

Although some studies of the economic effects of technological innovations have been focused on the industry and others on the firm or plant, few publications have sought to clarify the tenuous relationships between these levels of analysis. To explore these, it is useful to begin by asking in what ways the pioneering adoption of a major innovation by one or a few firms is likely to affect the operations and results of other firms in the industry. Resulting pressures may be combined into three groups:

1. *Technological Pressures,* including pressures for increasing diffusion of the basic innovation, for increasing research and development efforts to improve the innovation and to facilitate its adaptation to particular plant conditions, and for cooperation both in developing relevant product and other technical standards and in coping with any accompanying safety or environmental problems.
2. *Market pressures,* including pressures on particular material, energy, and capital goods supplies and prices; competitive pressures on the prices of affected products; and pressures to cooperate in dealing with resulting trade union demands for changes in wage rates and working conditions.
3. *Governmental pressures,* including pressures for maintaining effective competition, pressures for safe working conditions, pressures for meeting environmental standards and for ensuring product safety, pressures for natural resources and energy conservation, and pressures for safeguarding national security.

The extent and effects of each of these pressures can be determined only by studying it directly. Such effects cannot be inferred from changes in industry-level data for productivity, cost, price, and profit changes for a variety of reasons. The plants comprising an industry may obviously differ in product mix, scale, modernity, resources, and location, thus altering industry results over time with changes in the level and composition of output even without any new innovation. Moreover, any given innovation may be attractive only to particular sectors of the industry and would diffuse through such sectors only gradually, meanwhile yielding benefits to early adopters that are at least partially offset by the competitive disadvantages of the laggards. It is accordingly difficult to avoid concluding that productivity, cost, and profit measures at the level of an industry may deviate widely from these same measures for individual plants within the industry, and that such deviations are likely to be even greater with respect to the effects on such measures of technological innovations which are only partially and unevenly diffused.

Effects on Product Purchasers and Input Suppliers

The quantitative and qualitative effects of major technological innovations on purchasers of the affected products are obviously transmitted through resulting changes in their prices, prospective supply, and service attributes. In the case of purchasers using such products as inputs to further processing and fabrication efforts, any change in price might affect the purchaser's unit production cost and input mix, and changes in total supply would permit increased output if this input had been a limiting factor. But changes in the service attributes of the product might have far more widespread effects on the purchaser's operations, including the quality and mix of other material, energy, labor, and capital goods inputs; research and development efforts; processing techniques and scale economies; pollution and safety requirements; and product design, mix, costs, and prices. Such price changes and any accompanying changes in the quality of the final products also might have significant effects on this producer's competitive position relative to producers of substitutes for his products.

Somewhat similar carry-over effects may be transmitted back from the innovating firms to the suppliers of their inputs of materials, components, and capital goods. In this case, however, the primary influence is likely to be the change in the qualitative characteristics of the inputs to be provided. Meeting such requirements may often necessitate changes not only in research and development activities, but also in processing techniques, equipment and facilities, pollution control and safety measures, labor skills, quality controls, energy needs, and even the sources and specifications of their own inputs. Moreover, such shifts in the needs of the innovating firms may also affect the competitive position of suppliers in different locations as well as of traditional suppliers relative to suppliers of substitutable inputs.

In this connection, attention may also be given to the potential effects of major technological innovations on the relevant labor markets and associated trade unions. Such effects may include adjustments not only in total employment levels and the composition of skill requirements, but also in working conditions, incentive and other payment arrangements, and jurisdictional overlaps among traditional trade union boundaries. Transportation services to and from the innovating firms may also be affected, of course, with respect to the mode used and the volume of movements to be handled.

Other Effects of Public and Governmental Concern

Public and governmental concerns with the effects of technological innovations cover a network of different economic and social focuses at aggregation levels ranging from individual localities to the entire nation and over progressively longer time periods. In all cases, they tend to be concerned with the cumulative effects of such innovations over all affected firms in a region or in the nation rather than with results in particular industries.

The communities surrounding innovative plants, or those supplying their inputs or purchasing their outputs, tend to be concerned primarily with the effects of major technological innovations on local employment and wage levels; on related changes in health, safety, and pollution problems; and on prospective tax contributions. The major economic agencies of the state and federal governments tend to be concerned with resulting changes in the growth, continuing competitive strength, and internal competitiveness of the relevant industries; the trend, stability, and skill composition of their labor requirements; their needs for domestic and imported natural resources and energy; their contributions to, and needs for, capital formation; and their involvement in foreign trade. Other agencies concentrate on environmental effects, product safety, the adequacy of technological improvement efforts, minimizing the wastage of natural resources and energy, facilitating the adaptation and improving the utilization of transportation services, and so on.

The key point to be emphasized is that the development of such a broad analytical framework as has been presented for tracing the effects of major technological innovations is designed merely to provide a systematic basis for considering the possible repercussions from any specified innovation. The extreme diversity encompassed by the term *major technological innovations* ensures that particular cases may require the further development of this framework in certain directions, just as many others may confine their significant effects to only a few of the many channels which have been noted. Moreover, all such evaluations may be expected to change significantly over extended periods as the innovation is diffused, as its impacts on product and factor markets are gradually absorbed, and as resulting market adjustments engender responsive technological and other readjustments in the input-supplying and product-purchasing firms which produce new counterpressures on the original innovating firms.

Accordingly, two efforts to trace such repercussions will be presented to help illustrate the richness of the interactions which may be confronted in seeking to extend analyses of the effects of major technological innovations beyond the innovating plant, firm, or industry and thus to lay the foundations for deeper probing of their ramifying effects.

Illustrative Empirical Explorations of Interindustry Repercussions

Attention will be given first to the successive transmissions of the effects of a major change in the qualitative attributes of a product. The second case illustrates a more complex network of interactions between producers, customers, and competitors.

Tracing the Effects of Pelletizing Low-Grade Iron Ore

Basic Innovation and Its Objectives. The innovation to be examined involves the concentration and pelletizing of low-grade iron ore for sale to the steel industry.[3] Its development was supported by two different sources. Facing the eventual depletion of its high-grade iron ores, the state of Minnesota began financing research more than 50 years ago to upgrade its poorer ores and thus help to preserve the economic base of its mining areas. Recognition of the rapidly decreasing availability of such high-grade ores, especially because of the swollen demands of World War II, led a number of steel companies to undertake intensive development efforts and to make heavy investments in the development of commercial-scale pelletizing plants. Their objective was not merely to provide additional supplies of iron ore, for ample iron ore could be obtained from overseas; rather their primary objective was to revitalize existing sources of iron ore in order to preserve the economic viability of their inland plants, which accounted for most of the nation's capacity.

In short, the critical objective was not to reduce the unit cost of producing iron ore. And the critical result was a change in two of the qualitative characteristics of the product: increasing its iron content and changing its form from variously sized lumps of natural ore to uniformly sized pellets.

Effects on Iron-Ore Production. The direct input effects of the innovation included heavily increased investments in new mines, new pellet plants, and energy production. In addition, employment was increased, new skill requirements had to be met, and a new array of burdensome waste disposal and pollution-control problems had to be dealt with. On the output side, changes were only inadequately reflected by changes in total tonnage and in average iron content of shipments from the 51.5 percent of natural ores to about 61 percent.

Moreover, even if prices are measured on the sophisticated basis of "contained iron units" rather than sheer weight, pellets were about 25 percent more expensive than natural iron ore and were also more expensive than overseas ores delivered at coastal ports, thus bespeaking the importance of their changed qualitative characteristics. As for the mining region, a tremendous economic boom and concurrent sharp increase in tax revenues were also accompanied by growing environmental controversies.

Effects on Transportation. Because pelletization did not require shifts to new geographical areas, its major effects on transportation were due to resulting changes in the qualitative characteristics of the product. First, the adaptability of pellets to the effective use of conveyor belts, unlike natural ores, reduced the costs of handling to and from ships, as well as the costs of loading and unloading. Moreover, this trait also encouraged two major changes in ship design. One involved increasing ship size, because conveyors, unlike stationary loading bins, could be extended further out from the dock and thus avoid the problems of unbalanced loading of ships with wider beams. A second important design change involved the introduction of self-unloading ships, to take advantage of the easy flow of pellets onto a conveyor on the bottom.

In addition, pellets also decreased the costs of transportation. This was due partly to their iron content per unit of volume. Faster loading and unloading also increased the number of trips which a ship could make during the shipping season, and this was further enhanced by the free flow of pellets in cold weather, when natural ore freezes. Finally, the introduction of larger ships involved an increase in immediate investment but not longer-run investment, inasmuch as fewer of these were needed to handle the demand for pellets. Nevertheless, these reductions in transportation costs per iron unit were still insufficient to offset their higher production costs, as indicated by the fact that the price of pellets per iron unit delivered in Lake Erie ports was still more than 25 percent higher than that of natural ore.

Effects on Blast Furnace Operations. The most spectacular effects of pelletization were in blast furnace operations and were derived entirely from the qualitative changes in pellets as compared with natural ore. Among these, increases of 50 to 100 percent in the capacity of existing blast furnaces (depending on their proportions of pellets to total iron-bearing inputs) were obviously most important. Interestingly enough, it has been calculated that only one-fifth of this gain was attributable to the higher iron content of the pellets, four-fifths being due to the increased efficiency of smelting resulting from the shape of the pellets.[4] It should be emphasized that this capacity effect was largely unanticipated and hence represented a generous further reward to the risk-taking involved. In addition to resulting reductions in capital charges per unit of pig iron output, the increased use of pellets sharply reduced coke consumption per ton of pig iron output and also reduced unit input requirements of flux, sinter, and flue dust. Because coke and sinter processes are heavy polluters, the reduction in input requirements helped to ease environmental-control problems, as did the reduced volume of slag to be handled and disposed of.

As a result of such benefits, pig iron production costs per ton were reduced enough to more than offset the increased costs of concentrating and pelletizing the low-grade iron ores. Moreover, the decrease in the energy requirements of the blast furnace more than offset the increase in energy requirements in mining and pelletizing. In addition, the reduction of pollution problems in the urban areas where most steel plants are located helped to offset the increased pollution problems in the less densely populated mining areas. Finally, the sharply reduced investment requirements for additional blast furnaces, resulting from the increased capacity of existing facilities made possible by pellets, just about offset the expanded investments entering into mining and pelletizing.

Some Broader Effects. Perhaps the most important effects of the concentration and pelletizing of these low-grade iron ores, however, were the incalculable benefits of saving not only the economic base of the northern mining areas, but also major components of the economies of the large, inland steel-producing centers, including Chicago, Cleveland, and Pittsburgh. Before the commercial success of pelletizing had been demonstrated, it was widely expected that most of the steel industry would have to move close to ocean ports, investing huge sums in new sites while winding down operations and employment and gradually abandoning heavy investments in established steel centers.[5]

Such readjustments would also have required heavy investments in the development of overseas mines and in expanding shipping to handle such expanded imports, in addition to severely undermining the Great Lakes shipping industry. One need hardly mention the accompanying increased susceptibility of operations to foreign supply and price pressures or the attendant implications for trade and foreign exchange balances. Instead, successful pelletization has curtailed the earlier trend to increased dependence on overseas ores. Additional benefits of broader significance include the encouraging example of advancing technology to help offset the depletion of high-grade natural resources and help conserve energy as well.

Some Reverse Technological Pressures. As was noted in the earlier general discussion, such innovational pressures often engender counterpressures. Thus the substantial advantages of pellets have increased the demand for them and have also encouraged efforts to further enhance the qualitative determinants of their benefits and reduce their costs. Such increases in demand have intensified earlier pressures to increase the size of ships and the use of self-unloaders. Moreover, the resulting pressure to maximize utilization of more expensive ships has intensified efforts to expand the shipping season through the use of larger icebreakers and other means. Such efforts have also been reinforced by the fact that taconite mining and pelletizing operations now continue year-round and by the desire of both the pellet producers and the steel mills to reduce the inventories necessitated by the suspension of shipping during winter.

Such demand pressures also have encouraged the more recent successful concentration and pelletization of nonmagnetic iron ores. Another result has been the construction of large, new pelletizing plants promising further economies in production. Pressure has also continued for improving pellets in size, strength, and certain other respects as well. On the other hand, increases in the volume of such operations have also intensified governmental concern with attendant environmental problems, especially those associated with the disposal of the enormous volumes of tailings left after removal of the iron from these low-grade ores.

Some Technological Interactions between Metal Producers and Can Makers

Another illustration of the interindustry ramifications of technological innovations will trace the highlights of interactions engendered by a series of innovations involving greater and lesser changes in the qualitative attributes of the products affected. The immediate focus will be on resulting demands generated by the rapidly growing beer and soft drink container market. Proper evaluation of the effects of such innovations requires clarification of the objectives of the interacting interest groups: can makers obviously sought to increase the share of metal cans relative to bottles, steel producers obviously sought to provide all the metal stock required by can makers, and aluminum producers first sought to enter this market and then to gain an increasing share of it.

Double-Reduced Tin Plate. Introduction of an additional rolling process enabled the steel industry in the early 1960s to reduce the thickness of tin plate by about one-fourth while also strengthening it. This required some increase in steel mill investment and costs, but much less than the resulting increase in the output (and capacity) of can-making stock measured in units of area. The result was an increase in steel revenues per ton of such tin plate, but a reduction in the price to can makers of the square feet of stock needed to make 1,000 cans, without requiring any significant changes in can-production operations. Thus it strengthened the competitive position of can makers vis-à-vis bottles and yielded some derived benefits to steel producers. However, it also introduced new technical problems for the latter, for the thinner double-reduced tin plate was more likely to crack because of the stretching involved when it was bent otuward at both ends to form the flanges used to produce the double seams for affixing the tops and bottoms.

"Easy-Open" Top. Aluminum cans had no place in the beverage container market because of inability to produce a sufficiently tight side seam for the body of the can. But in 1962 an "easy-open" top made of aluminum was developed which won wide consumer approval and thus provided a partial entry for aluminum, replacing the steel top of three-piece steel cans (body, top, and bottom). Of course, can makers incurred an additional cost for this qualitatively altered component, but enjoyed further increases in sales. Such market responsiveness triggered more than 6 years of intensive, highly technical efforts by can makers as well as aluminum and steel producers to develop still better tops. Despite successive improvements by the latter, however, steel tops continued to lag competitively.

Two-Piece Aluminum Cans. As a result of development efforts by aluminum companies beginning in the late 1950s, 1964 saw the widespread introduction of two-piece aluminum beer cans. These were produced by a new process which cupped and then stretched a flat piece of aluminum into a complete seamless cylinder open at the top. This qualitatively different can was produced at high speed and with much less labor, resulting in total can production costs which were competitive with three-piece steel cans despite the higher cost of aluminum stock per can. As a result, they gained a rapidly increasing share of the beer can market at the expense of growth rates for steel cans and bottles.

Although the product was identical in size and function, its qualitative differences required can makers to invest in new production facilities and develop new operating quality control and supervisory arrangements. Moreover, can makers were now faced with the problem in capacity planning of assessing probable future changes in the relative demands for steel and aluminum cans and in the relative prices of both kinds of can-making stock.

"Tin-Free" Steel. In order to improve its competitive position, steel producers succeeded in developing a "tin-free" steel for beverage cans in 1968, which involved replacing the tin coating with chromium. Not only is chrome cheaper than tin, but it can also be applied in a thinner coating, thus yielding a double economy which more than offset the modest additional facilities investments required by steel producers. This qualitative change reduced the cost of steel can stock to can makers, but required new technologies for sealing the side seam of can bodies, inasmuch as traditional soldering was effective only with a tin coating. Fortunately, efforts to develop such innovational methodologies had already been under way for some years because of growing concern about the absorption of lead from the solder, especially in soft drink cans which were heavily used by children. As a result, two competitive solutions had already emerged—cementing and welding—but neither was regarded as entirely satisfactory when applied to the steel canning materials used in the past. However, both proved acceptable when applied to the newly available tin-free steel.

Thus two additional significant qualitative changes were made in beverage cans, involving adjustments in the input requirements, equipment, and production methods of steel producers as well as can makers. As a result, the competitive position of steel cans was improved somewhat, although aluminum cans kept expanding their market share.

Two-Piece Steel Cans. Expanding commitments to two-piece beverage cans intensified efforts by can makers to develop such machinery for steel. This became commercially successful in 1973. But resultant gains in steel's competitive position from the reduction in steel requirements per can were at least partially offset by shifts in can sheet requirements back from double-reduced to single-reduced tin plate and back from tin-free to tin-coated sheet. The former was caused by the need for thicker initial stock to permit the greater stretching (technically, drawing and ironing) involved in producing two-piece cans, the latter because tin provides the superior lubrication required for such greater stretching. In addition, this process again increased steel production quality requirements with respect to the control of nonmetallic inclusions and size and thickness variations. Another by-product effect on steel producers has been the increased demand by can makers for steel made by the new "continuous casting" process rather than the old "ingot then slab-rolling" process. Two-piece steel cans can be made from stock produced by the latter process, but only if the steel has been "aluminum-killed." Inasmuch as this involves a price premium, whereas continuously cast steel does not, can makers have understandably demanded the latter for installations producing two-piece cans. Moreover, it should be noted that the expansion of continuous-casting capacity has involved heavy investments, costly training and learning periods, and significant defect rates.

As for can makers, the development of two-piece steel cans involved the prospects of having to invest in a substitute array of new machinery, to accept the risks involved in building larger-scale operations, and to make more difficult choices between additions to steel can or aluminum can capacity on the basis of guesses about future price relationships. The scale issue arises from the fact that two-piece can plants require roughly double the investment per unit of capacity, but can offset this with lower operating cost if scaled to produce at least 250 million cans annually through continuous two-shift operations. Hence shut-downs due to operating problems or decreases in demand can prove very costly, and such risks are aggravated by the fact that many can plants are built to serve individual breweries and consequently suffer with the latter when market shares among brewing companies change, even though total demand continues to increase. Moreover, the ready substitutability of steel and aluminum cans ensures that a differential change in the price of one would force can plants committed to the higher-priced material to absorb any resulting cost disadvantages.

Environmental Pollution Pressures. In recent years, a new form of pressure affecting competition among beverage containers has become important: governmental measures to reduce littering. The original dominance of returnable bottles prior to 1940 has been reduced progressively under the impact of metal cans and, to a more limited extent, one-way bottles. But recent legislation in Oregon and elsewhere requiring deposits on all beverage containers has, initially at least, reversed this long trend. This may be due to the better organized arrangements for collecting and reusing returnable bottles, along with the greater familiarity of store keepers with the process. If so, comparable improvements in preventing metal can littering may restore their market share where such restrictions are in force.

At any rate, it emphasizes the importance of other qualitative characteristics of the competing beverage containers. For example, an average of twenty refills per returnable bottle reduces its costs and energy requirements per use to very favorable levels in comparison with single-use metal containers. The higher metal value of aluminum cans permits payment of a larger reward for returning empty cans to some collection point for recycling than would be warranted for steel cans. On the other hand, steel cans can be separated from general municipal refuse collections more easily than other containers through the use of magnets, and already functioning processes for detinning such cans seem to demonstrate commercial feasibility.

Other Implications. In general, then, even this microcosm of industrial activities centering around the packaging of beer reveals an intricate array of technological interactions between can makers and their suppliers within the larger framework of competition from bottles, changing consumer preferences from draft to bottled to canned beer, changing distribution patterns from taverns to supermarkets, and changing governmental concerns with environmental issues. In the case of most of the innovations reviewed, the effects on the operations of the product buyers were attributable at least as much to changes in the product's qualitative attributes as to changes in its price. Moreover, almost every technological innovation served as a direct stimulus to engendering further adaptive or offsetting technological innovations.

As for some broader implications of these developments, it may be of interest to mention the progressive shifting of beer consumption from taverns to homes, the recent emergence of plastic containers as a new competitor, renewed efforts to replace tin as well as chrome with chemical coatings to avoid expensive cartel pressures on the former and supply-threatening political pressures on the latter, and a developing trend toward brewers running their own captive can-making plants as a result both of the consolidation of beer production into fewer and larger firms and the development of compact, high-capacity, largely automated, two-piece can plants.

Concluding Observations

In short, most past evaluations of the economic effects of major technological innovations have been inadequate and even misleading because of their neglect of the qualitative aspects of resulting changes in inputs and outputs, although a large part, and often most, of resulting economic benefits have derived from modifications in such qualitative characteristics. Moreover, such shortcomings become even more serious when efforts are made to trace the interindustry repercussions of technological innovations, because changes in such qualitative attributes have often necessitated more widespread adjustments than changes in factor and product prices in the operations of input suppliers, product buyers, and producers of substitute products. Indeed, the need to adapt economically to such qualitative adjustments in needed inputs and available outputs may be one of the most influential triggers of interindustry technological interactions and the research and development programs underlying them. Moreover, the identification of changes in the qualitative attributes of inputs and outputs are an essential component of efforts to account for observed adjustments in resource requirements, factor prices and production costs, the level and mix of products, and the service values obtained by consumers.

One of the critical requirements for overcoming such past inadequacies is to gain a more thorough understanding of the relevant technologies at each stage through which the effects of innovations are to be traced. This is necessary both in order to focus on the most likely channels of interaction and in order to help evaluate the limitations of simple price and quantity measurements in appraising economic effects. It is widely believed in industry that most of the economic benefits to the innovator of qualitative improvements in products have only a very brief half-life as competitors develop parallel advances and then bargain them away to gain or maintain competitive position. This emphasizes the importance of recognizing that the old focus of economists on determining *the* effects of technological innovations must be shifted to determining *the time pattern of changing effects* attributable to such innovations. Such a posited pass-through of economic benefits also raises the question of what happens to the qualitative improvements which engendered them. In most cases, these do not disappear but rather are passed along as real gains in the service values obtained by consumers which are not adequately reflected by product prices and in the social benefits of access to new resources, resource conservation, and the development of safer and more attractive working and living environments.

Notes

1. For empirical illustrations of such efforts, see Eilon et al. [3, chapters 4-6].

2. For illustrations of alternative, but still crude, approaches to making such measurements, see chapter 6, Griliches [6], and Gold [4, pp. 92-97].

3. For a more detailed analysis, see Peirce [7].

4. For detailed analysis, see Boylan [2, chapter 7].

5. For example, see Barloon [1].

References

[1] M. Barloon, "Steel: The Great Retreat," *Harper's Magazine,* August 1947.

[2] M.G. Boylan, *Economic Effects of Scale Increases in the Steel Industry: The Case of U.S. Blast Furnaces* (New York: Praeger, 1975).

[3] S. Eilon, B. Gold, and J. Soesan, *Applied Productivity Analysis for Industry* (Oxford: Pergamon, 1976).

[4] B. Gold, *Foundations of Productivity Analysis* (Pittsburgh: Univ. of Pittsburgh Press, 1955).

[5] B. Gold (ed.), *Technological Change: Economics, Management and Environment* (Oxford: Pergamon, 1975, 1979).

[6] Z. Griliches (ed), *Price Indexes and Quality Change* (Cambridge, Mass.: Harvard Univ. Press, 1971).

[7] W.S. Peirce, "The Effects of Technological Change: Exploring Successive Ripples," in Gold [5].

Part III
Some Approaches to Advancing Productivity and Technological Capabilities

14 Intrafirm: Alternative Strategies for Advancing Technologies

Since about 1950, there has been increasingly pervasive acceptance throughout the industrialized world of the view that technological innovations are one of the primary determinants of relative competitive strength. This has generated pressure for progressively heavier commitments for research and development programs by nations as well as by individual firms. But the outcomes of such undertakings have often been regarded as disappointing, leading to a significant waning in recent years both of enthusiasm for, and of allocations to, technological development efforts. Because of the serious implications of such revised perspectives, it would seem useful to reexamine the role of technological innovations in promoting competitive position, the availability of alternative strategies for effecting technological advances, and the bases for choosing among them and for evaluating results.

Technological Advances as Sources of Competitive Advantage

Investments in technological development programs may be expected to offer five kinds of primary benefits:

1. Attaining competitive advantages through new or better products or processes.
2. Obtaining knowledge which can itself be sold advantageously.
3. Keeping up with, or avoiding injurious lags behind, competitors.
4. Minimizing prospective differential disadvantages involving inputs, transport, and so on.
5. Providing the image of highly progressive management.

Most enthusiastic supporters of expanding research and development efforts expect the outcomes to be concentrated in categories 1 and 2. But such expectations are bound to be unrealistic for several reasons and hence can only serve to underestimate the positive gains derived from such programs.

Efforts to develop significant technological advances in products, processes, and input requirements are usually under way in most competing firms of substantial size. Of course, some have larger programs, and staffs may also differ in experience and abilities. But the penetration of the unknown (or the solution of hitherto unsolved problems) involves a considerable amount of groping, with success seemingly more frequently attributable to luck than to the sheer magnitude of investments or to objectively demonstrable differences in staff quality. Accordingly, even the "best" staff and most generous budget can be expected to lead the pack only once in a while. And in most such cases, the advantage is likely to be of only modest proportions and quite limited duration. Moreover, even demonstrably superior products and processes tend to gain market shares relatively slowly (Gold et al. [2, pp. 220–223]) as a result of competitive marketing efforts and the inertia of buying habits. Hence even these occasional "successes" of technological development efforts are seldom likely to produce spectacular benefits. And most advances in knowledge, even when patented, seem to command but modest returns, contrary to the impression conveyed by the relatively small number of well-known exceptions, including nylon, float glass, and certain drugs.

The foregoing also indicates why the largest and most consistent yields from technological development efforts are likely to take the form of the defensive competitive gains in the preceding categories 3 and 4. Despite the enormous value of such contributions to maintaining an effective competitive position, however, they tend to be underappreciated by industrial management and wholly ignored by investors, the government, and the public at large. This may be because such defensive benefits are often regarded as but partial offsets to past shortcomings and tend to be associated with relative losses (even if decreasing) rather than with positive gains. Hence even the hoped-for category 5 benefits depend increasingly over time on the actual harvests in the first two categories.

In addition to reorienting prevailing perspectives concerning the probable loci and magnitudes of the prospective benefits of technological development efforts, it is also necessary to recognize the limited role of technological innovations within the complex of most managerial strategies for promoting the objectives of an enterprise. One effort to clarify this role suggested the following hypotheses (Gold [1, pp. 222–225]):

1. Most top managements have a reasonable stable order of preference among the means of improving or maintaining profitability, growth, market position, security of assets, stability of operations, and a favorable public image.
2. Their first preference is generally for continuation, or only moderate intensification, of familiar operations involving little risk to established organizational structures and patterns of resource allocation (for example, modest improvements in products and distribution arrangements, small additions to productive capacity not involving major innovations in processes, and reductions in production costs via gradual improvements in techniques and facilities, as well as progressive reductions in waste).
3. The generation or pioneering adoption of major technological innovations is likely to rank low because it tends to involve heavy investments, substantial risks and readjustments in existing organizational arrangements and budgetary allocations affecting many functions and operating divisions.

4. That such lower-ranking preferences are seldom resorted to except (a) when more favored means prove inadequate, (b) when extramarket factors (for example, governmental pressures or subsidies) alter the relative potentials or costs, (c) when technological advances by competitors threaten mounting disadvantages, or (d) when continuing internal technological development programs yield unexpectedly substantial potentials.

Thus technological progress is universally recognized as essential to the maintenance of an effective competitive position over extended periods. But in the here and now, it is generally subordinated to a variety of other means whereby management seeks to safeguard or improve its performance relative to competitors—at least until such preferred weapons prove inadequate.

Alternative Strategies for Advancing Technology

The preceding review of the potential benefits of technology-improvement efforts, and of managerial preferences relating to changes in production operations, provides a basis for examining alternative strategies for seeking such benefits. Most discussions of such alternatives concentrate on two strategies: programs seeking a stream of small, evolutionary advances in products and processes, and those aiming at individually major gains. The former are generally considered to involve small risks in return for a high probability of successive small payoffs without long delays. The latter represent a strong contrast, involving the risk of much larger resources in return for a low probability of large payoffs after relatively long periods.

As a practical matter, however, two additional alternatives warrant careful consideration. One of these involves concentration on seeking the economies of production offered by increases in the scale of operations. In this case, risks may be presumed to be far less than when seeking major new discoveries because the technology involved is presumably 85 to 95 percent known, the staff is experienced in the specialized fields encompassed, and the prospective innovations would presumably fit most existing procurement, marketing, and organizational arrangements instead of posing new problems in several or all such areas. Estimations of prospective benefits would tend to be of at least moderate proportions to trigger such developmental efforts. And results might well be expected within shorter periods than would generally be consumed in bringing major new innovations to fruitation.

The technical literature on scale economies seems to be dominated in part by theoretical models which are so obviously oversimplified as to engender but limited confidence on the part of managers faced with heavy financial commitments in seeking to build well beyond experiential frontiers. And the other major component of such literature consists of analyses of performance by actual plants representing different levels of capacity, usually built in different

Table 14–1
Selected Characteristics of Alternative Strategies for Advancing Technology

Alternatives	*Development Cost*	*Success Probability*	*Time to Fruition*	*Likely Rewards*	*Associated Disruptions*
Evolutionary improvements	Low	High	Short	Small	Small
Licensing	Low	High	Short	Moderate	Small/Large
Scale increases	Moderate	Moderate	Moderate	Moderate	Small
Major advances	High	Low	Long	Large	Large

years (reflecting possible advances in technology) and often designed for dissimilar product mixes. Such studies may yield useful insights, of course, and yet be of little value to managements having to choose among alternative scales in specifying the characteristics of a plant to be built at a given time without effective foreknowledge of future changes in technologies or markets. Moreover, available studies, and even estimates from engineering design firms, rarely shed much light on the possible effects of constructing units which are 50 to 100 percent larger than current maximums rather than the common extensions of only 5 to 10 percent. Nor can the effects of such major jumps, which might yield major competitive advantages, be convincingly derived by extrapolating "freehand" beyond known frontiers.

The last of these major alternatives consists simply of buying licenses to use whatever technological advances achieved by others seem to offer significant improvements in competitive position. Such purchases tend to involve no risk, inasmuch as they usually relate to improvements that have already been shown to work effectively, and they presumably offer reasonably attractive returns within relatively short periods after decisions have been made to acquire them.

In comparing these alternative strategies, five characteristics seem important: relative costs of development, relative likelihood of commercial success, relative time to achieve such success, relative magnitudes of resulting market rewards, and the extent of attendant costly disruptions in organizational arrangements, capital allocations, materials requirements, labor relations, and marketing patterns. The crude summary of such characteristics in table 14–1 suggests that licensing and scale increases fall between the extremes of concentrating on evolutionary and extraordinary advances. Hence the development of practical policies for advancing technology might more commonly be broadened to encompass portfolios of all four strategies in varying combinations.

Factors Affecting the Choice of Strategies

In choosing among such alternative strategies, little more than a starting point is provided by the vague, though ostensibly sophisticated prescription of "decision making under uncertainty" that one should seek the most favorable combination of prospective net gains weighted by the probabilities of success. Beyond that, it is necessary to recognize the influence of the technological and market characteristics of the particular industries under consideration. In addition, attention must be given to the resource constraints, managerial preferences, and guiding objectives of the individual firms making such decisions.

For example, in consumer goods industries accustomed to very modest rates of technological advances and whose markets are strongly responsive to product differentiation, distribution and sales innovations, management might concentrate technological improvement efforts heavily toward seeking evolutionary improvements. Such tendencies might be further reinforced by the limited technical knowledge of most buyers, which makes it possible to moderate the potential penalties of lags in major technological innovations through the intensification of marketing efforts and the introduction of lesser but distracting improvements.

In industries subject to rapid technological advances and selling to technically sophisticated buyers, on the other hand, it may prove more rewarding to make heavy commitments to the development of major innovations.[2] This would be encouraged by the likelihood of substantial advances by one competitor or another at relatively frequent intervals and by the rapidity with which market shares tend to shift toward the successful innovator—and hence, by the urgency of catching up with advances by others without prolonged delay.

In industries producing largely undifferentiated products with slowly changing technology and hence operating in markets which are responsive to price differentials among competitors, the more promising course may involve allocating substantial proportions of technological improvement efforts to cost-reduction efforts. Oddly enough, however, serious research exploring the potential cost benefits of increases in the scale of production seems to have been very limited as compared with speculations about scale effects rooted primarily in abstract economic theory or in engineering mythology.[3]

While the preceding categories are obviously illustrative rather than comprehensive, they serve to suggest one set of factors tending to differentiate the primary thrusts of technological development programs among various sectors of industry. Technological improvement efforts may also be expected to differ among firms within such industrial sectors. In part, this may be due to substantial differences in the volume of resources available for such undertakings. Firms with limited resources, for example, are obviously less likely to reach beyond modest, low-risk, short-term projects than those with more ample resources. The experiential biases of management also affect the emphases of such programs, with technologically oriented executives being more likely than those with marketing or finance orientations to support ambitious technological targets. Still another influential factor is the definition of the firm's objectives in establishing these programs (Gold et al. [2, pp. 234-235]). Depending on the areas of competitive pressures, the loci of discerned opportunities, and the satisfactoriness of its current market position, firms may undertake technological improvement programs with casual prudence or with desperation, and they may stress "keeping up," "catching up," or "getting ahead." Indeed, apparent anomalies, represented by firms with limited resources undertaking high-risk efforts to achieve major advances, often reflect managerial judgments that this is the only remaining feasible approach to maintaining survival or to breaking through prevailing barriers to achieve market shares necessary for reasonable profitability.

Choices among alternative strategies for improving technology also require consideration of some additional advantages and disadvantages of each. For example, concentration on small evolutionary improvements serves not only to limit the costs and risks involved in such developmental efforts, but resulting modest changes also facilitate orderly adjustments of labor requirements, capital facilities, materials inputs, and marketing arrangements, whereas major technological advances might well involve turbulent, costly, and time-consuming adjustments in several of these areas. On the other hand, such an evolutionary course minimizes the firm's ability to catch up quickly with the major advances which emerge every so often even in sectors of long-dormant technologies.

Efforts to secure the economies of increases in the scale of production seem to be attended by a more tangled array of advantages and disadvantages. For example, it is widely recognized that such economies may decline rapidly as output levels fall progressively further below capacity levels. What seems to be less widely recognized is that the short-term penalties of such underutilization may also engender long-term benefits when large-scale facilities are sited in new markets, because of what may be termed their "preemptive" effect. Specifically, the existence of such heavy excess capacity is likely to discourage the entry of competitors for an extended period, thereby enabling the pioneers to develop a firm grip on distribution channels, user services, and local buying preferences. On the other hand, it is obvious that the exploitation of scale benefits through the construction of new facilities becomes rapidly known throughout most industries, and also that the associated technological advances involved can usually be emulated without excessive delays by leading competitors. Attendant scale benefits may, nevertheless, accrue to the innovators for as long as even knowledgeable competitors are inhibited from adding massive new facilities because their capacity already exceeds demand in their primary markets, or because their construction costs are sufficiently greater to minimize the prospective net economies of the new levels of scale.

Among the prospective advantages of seeking major innovations, one must consider not only the direct advantages to the successful innovator of a new or substantially better product or process, but also possible returns from selling its technology to other producers. And still another benefit may be the head start of the pioneer over competitors in seeking further advances along the lines already explored. The most obvious source of discouragement, of course, is the vexatiously prolonged uncertainty lasting right up to the point of final efforts at commercialization and threatening the loss of the entire cumulative investment until that last hurdle is surmounted (Jewkes et al. [4]). But even such an initial success leaves uncounted the subsequent possible costs of redeploying labor, replacing capital facilities, and modifying procurement and distribution arrangements.

Licensing as an Alternative

The preceding general review of the advantages and disadvantages of the alternative direct paths to developing technological improvements provides a basis for evaluating the remaining option: licensing innovations from their developers. As has already been noted, this usually involves no risk about the nature of the prospective benefits and little risk about their general magnitude or when such returns may be expected to begin. Hence the most critical short-term issues usually center around the direct cost of licenses and the burdensomeness of any attendant restrictions on the licensee.

A recent survey of Japanese experiences with licensing in the steel and electronics industries suggests that they have found this a most rewarding strategy over the past 15 years for "catching up." Moreover, in some industries, such as electric power and chemicals, many firms apparently plan continued heavy reliance on licensing "to keep up" for some time into the future. The experience to date is regarded as overwhelmingly favorable because virtually all important innovations have been made available with minimal delay, few restrictions, and on admittedly reasonable terms. In evaluating resulting benefits, the Japanese seem to give heaviest weight to three: (1) to the savings in time, permitting rapid overtaking of the world leaders in the industries involved; (2) to their consequent ability to concentrate their best scientific and engineering talent on devising commercially valuable incremental improvements on the basic innovations licensed from abroad, in contrast to the heavier concentration of talent in the licensing countries on the innovation's foundations, "beginning by standing on the foreigners' shoulders," as one respondent phrased it; and (3) to the advantages of assessing the best developments in all countries before choosing whichever seems most attractive, instead of having to make do with whatever their own programs manage to create.

What factors account for such widely reasonable pricing of licenses to use technological advances? This question becomes even more interesting if the results of our preliminary inquiries should be sustained—that, in a wide array and perhaps most cases, the income from licenses does not cover even the costs of the successful innovations involved, much less the full cost of the underlying programs with their seemingly unavoidably heavy yield of useful but uncommercializable knowledge.

Three explanations of such licensing behavior by innovators seem to be most common.[4] One argues that most innovations in technologically sophisticated industries are likely to offer only temporary advantages at best, and hence, that it is sensible to get as much return from them as possible before their proprietary value disappears altogether. Acceptance of this viewpoint tends to vary directly with the extent of estimated competitive efforts in the given technological sector. Thus the heavy emphasis on major innovational targets in a number of leading Western industrial nations ensures the actual or threatened competition that motivates each to rush its new wares to Japan and offer it on terms attractive enough to discourage waiting. A second interrelated argument sees low-priced licensing as a means of minimizing incentives for other companies to undertake, or to continue, costly efforts to duplicate the given innovation, lest the latter lead not only to eroding the proprietary value of the original innovation, but also to intensifying competition to surpass the original.

But the third explanation points to a quite different kind of motivation: the organizationally induced defensiveness of many administrators of technology-improvement programs. Such executives are confronted both by frequently expressed doubts about the economic justification of their operations and also by the readiness of production and sales departments to take credit for all realized cost reductions and revenue increases, even when rooted in developments originated by the technology-improvement program. As a result, many of these technology-improvement departments have intensified their efforts to generate as much direct income as possible through selling licenses, perhaps unduly encouraging speed and lower pricing in the offering of newly emerging advances.

However, such explanations merely generate doubts about the wisdom of having undertaken the major technological developments being offered for licensing on such attractive terms to the buyer. If the differential advantages of successful advances are subject to rapid erosion, why undertake costly, risky programs to seek such successes? Such a commitment becomes doubly questionable as long as competition renders it probable that successes by others will be available for licensing without undue delay and on reasonable terms. And the aggressive pressure for prompt licensing by the innovating technical department may reflect interdepartmental competitiveness which may undermine overall company performance by inhibiting: cooperation in transferring innovations into operating departments; objective evaluation of outside developments offered for licensing; and concentration on technological development targets more likely to improve company operations than income from licensing.

From the standpoint of a company considering the possibility of increased reliance on licensing, the key bases for decision center around whether competition among innovators is likely to ensure ready access to significant advances on reasonable terms. Under such conditions, licensing offers such advantageous options as

1. Concentrating invariably limited research and development resources on a

narrower range of projects, thus permitting more intensive efforts to outdo others, while protecting against the possibility of serious penalties from sudden, unexpected gaps in varying sectors of the firm's technological frontiers.
2. Moderating increases in research and development allocations in favor of developing or intensifying offsetting competitive advantages in marketing, distribution, or other functional areas.

Of course, the extent to which such conditions are met varies widely among industries and hence encourages comparable differences in the degree of reliance on licensing. But prevailing practice is changing under the pressure of two developments. On the one hand, the rapid expansion of technological frontiers in most industries, combined with the mounting costs of exploring them, urges increasingly serious consideration of including licensing as an important component in designing cost-effective research and development portfolios.[5] And on the other hand, growing experience is serving to develop increasingly standard arrangements for buying and selling licenses. Taken together, these trends may also encourage greater specialization in the research and development efforts of all but the largest firms to capitalize on their differentially greatest strengths.

Where licensing fits into a technology-improvement portfolios depends, of course, on the particular sectors of the given industry in which competition among innovators has produced—and is likely to maintain—the ready availability of most significant advances on reasonable terms. Conversely, this would also identify the areas in which companies must depend on internally generated improvements and hence the problems to whose solution might be allocated the additional resources saved through increased reliance on licensing. Moreover, the role of licensing would also depend on the longer-run prospects for the competition necessary to ensure continuing availability of advances. Although interindustry differences may be substantial, there seems to be a powerful trend toward increasing innovational efforts in most industries and in an expanding array of countries. In addition, even if such competition should diminish gradually in some sectors, alert monitoring would probably permit a shift to inhouse development programs in time to minimize any continuing serious penalties from major changes in licensing availabilities.

Conclusions

1. There is no empirical evidence to support the claim that increasing allocations to technology-improvement programs generate consistently greater growth or profitability in all industries. But this does not mean that such efforts are wasted or should be curtailed. Rather it emphasizes the importance of broadening the evaluative criteria used so as to encompass other economically valuable contributions as well.

2. Increasingly critical analysis of all corporate resource allocations means that technology-improvement programs are also likely to be scrutinized more closely with respect to the relative returns (of all kinds) derived from each major component of such portfolios (West [5]). Hence the originally dominant tendency to do everything in house may be expected to give way to increasing consideration of such external contributions as licensing and contracting out.
3. Interindustry differences in the relative effects on company performance of new products, improved products, lower-cost production, transportation economies, substitutions among material inputs, and improvements in occupational safety and community pollution emphasize the need for reconsidering the organization of technological research and development efforts to assure comparably differentiated allocations among such disparate targets, instead of shifting such allocations continuously in response to successive exigencies.
4. Despite the frequently offered "prudent" advice to concentrate on "catch-up" or defensive technology-improvement programs, there is little evidence of the practicality and economy of such a strategy. To be able to catch-up quickly, one usually has to be thoroughly familiar with the problems, techniques, blind alleys, and ideas in the emerging domain. And if the costs of achieving such familiarity have been borne, they should yield leadership gains every so often (Gold [1, pp. 227, 234]).
5. In considering research on the economies of scale, attention should be given not only to a far more thorough analysis of the specific potential effects of large increases, but also to the possibility of concentrating such efforts in cooperative industrywide institutes.

Notes

1. For a somewhat different conception of the role of "defensive" R&D, see Goldring [3].

2. Some conceptual bases for planning both evolutionary and major innovational program are discussed in Gold [1, pp. 232-233].

3. For a more detailed discussion, see chapter 7.

4. For a broader review of licensing strategy from the standpoint of the innovator, see Young [6].

5. This would supplement the other common approach to harnessing expertise in a wider array of specialized fields, that is, contracting with research firms with demonstrated expertise to conduct some company projects.

References

[1] B. Gold, *Explorations in Managerial Economics: Productivity, Costs, Technology and Growth* (New York: Basic Books; London: Macmillan 1971).

[2] B. Gold, W. Peirce, and G. Rosegger, "Diffusion of Major Technological Innovations in U.S. Iron and Steel Manufacturing," *Journal of Industrial Economics,* July 1970; reprinted in B. Gold (ed), *Technological Change: Economics, Management and Environment* (Oxford: Pergamon, 1975, 1979).

[3] L.S. Goldring, "Defensive R&D as a Management Strategy," *Research Management,* May 1974.

[4] J. Jewkes, D. Sawers, and R. Stillerman, *The Sources of Invention* (New York: St. Martin, 1959).

[5] A.S. West, "How to Budget R&D Expenses," *Chemical Engineering Progress,* January 1970.

[6] V.E. Young, "Invention Licensing Strategy," *Research Management,* November 1972.

15 Intrafirm: Strategies for Broader Performance Evaluation

Presumably all organizational arrangements and managerial policies are subject to improvement. In order to assess the magnitude and urgency of needed improvements, however, it is necessary to evaluate current performance. How well can this be done? Are there major sectors of operations where performance evaluation is so inadequate as to undermine recognition of improvement potentials and even encourage potentially misguided decisions?

To this day, the most important contributions to performance evaluation and associated managerial control efforts have come from accounting. General accounting, cost accounting, and their extensions into budgeting have provided a firm foundation for measuring the financial aspects of resource allocations and flows, including their cost and investment components. But effective performance evaluation also requires a parallel flow of information concerning the contributions derived from such outlays. Whenever it has measures of outlays without congruent measures of resulting contributions—whether for component operations, for intermediate time periods, or even for entire systems—management cannot evaluate performance effectively and hence is poorly positioned in seeking to improve it. Indeed, under such conditions, the emphasis on maximizing performance relative to the measurable cost targets may leave little incentive to improve any aspects of performance which are not equally amenable to being appraised and rewarded.

The following discussion seeks to identify some important sectors of such shortcomings and suggest approaches toward helping to overcome these weaknesses.

Some Shortcomings in Performance Evaluation

The challenge of sounder performance appraisal centers around three problems:

1. How to measure multidimensional performance meaningfully.
2. How to evaluate the effectiveness of such performance.
3. How to assess the value of resulting contributions to organizational performance relative to its absorption of organizational resources.

Although some headway has been made in dealing with each of these needs in many areas of intraorganizational operations, much remains to be done before performance appraisal can begin to approach the objectivity and precision of the budgetary allocations with which it should be interacting.

Evaluating Staff Functions

Continuing increases in the size and complexity of organizations has fostered the development of a wide array of specialized staff functions designed to facilitate planning, coordination, control, and performance evaluation. It is not uncommon to find such staff activities proliferating in number, claiming increasing resources, and exercising substantial influence on managerial policies and the effectiveness of operations as a whole. Measuring their costs obviously presents no difficulties. But how well can we measure the effectiveness of their own operations or relate their outlays to resulting benefits?

Consider the accounting department, for example, the most measurement-oriented of staff functions. It is simple enough to identify excess idleness and errors in recording and computation as well as failures to meet established deadlines for reports. But how are other dimensions of its performance to be evaluated, including the speed of reporting deviations from expected results, the comprehensiveness of its reports, the analytical value of its responses to special management inquiries, the penetration of its diagnoses of the causes of performance variations, and the soundness of its estimates of the prospective effects of alternative actions? Moreover, one might also wish to consider the department's initiative in probing emerging shifts in past relationships, in adapting measures and standards to changes in product design, operating arrangements, and input quality, as well as in calling important or unexpected developments to the attention of appropriate executives.

Recognition of the importance of identifying such collateral responsibilities has been encouraged by programs of "management by objectives."[1] But the means of appraising the effectiveness with which such objectives are achieved remain less clear. To what extent could the department's current manning and budget be reduced without significantly impairing needed performance? To what extent has the department achieved the productivity advances that operating departments are under continuing pressure to produce? And most important—and most difficult—of all is the problem of estimating the value to the organization of the performance contributions made relative to the resources consumed. For example, one might ask how convincingly firms have been able to measure the financial benefits of computerizing their accounting operations relative to the considerable costs involved.

There is no reason, of course, to concentrate on the accounting department more than other departments. Similar questions could be asked about all other staff functions, including personnel, industrial relations, executive development, corporate planning, and even such seemingly less vulnerable departments as engineering and research.[2] My query does not concern the usefulness, or even the necessity in most cases, of such specialized activities, rather I am concerned only with the ability to appraise and control resource allocations to such functions by evaluating their corresponding contributions—to decide whether more should be expected from them in return for current budgetary commitments or whether larger allocations should be made in order to secure certain additional contributions. Clearly, such contributions of staff functions have only a roundabout, and often only a gradually realized, effect on aggregate performance. Hence it would be meaningless to try to evaluate each staff function in terms of its demonstrable effects on the profit levels or other overall achievements representing the combined contributions of all departments interacting with changing external pressures. This leaves us with two highly practical questions: Wthin what margins can the contributions of staff functions be determined: within 10 or 25 percent or only within a still wider range? How effective can budgetary-adjustment decisions be with respect to activities whose contributions are subject to such substantial uncertainties?

Such questions are plainly of little importance to small firms, but, in large firms with substantial staff operations absorbing major resources, inquiries of this sort may be very practical indeed.[3]

Evaluating Line Functions

Although the tasks of line functions tend to be more sharply defined and their performance more directly reflected by resource flows, all three of the basic performance appraisal problems just mentioned apply to these activities as well.

In the case of procurement operations, the basic tasks obviously include the acquisition of all needed materials, supplies, purchased components, and equipment in accordance with defined quality specifications, in quantitative flows which vary with production and inventory needs, and on terms which minimize total net delivered costs plus inventory costs. Accordingly, measurements of performance would obviously cover such aspects of operations as the amounts procured relative to the amounts required, the proportion of receipts found below specifications, inventory levels relative to requirements, the magnitude and duration of shortages of any needed supplies, the prices paid for goods, and the amounts paid for their delivery. Such measures would describe various outcomes of the past procurement efforts, but they would still omit consideration of such possibly even more important aspects of performance as alerting management to possible future procurement difficulties, suggesting possible changes in "make or buy" or inventory policies, and informing the engineering staff about shifts in supply availabilities and prices which might permit cost savings or product improvements.

Moreover, evaluation of the effectiveness of the procurement department also requires analysis of the problems which had to be overcome and the costs of these operations. Did changes in specifications require searching for new sources of supply? Were supply requirements subject to unexpected and sharp variations? Were any needed materials or transport facilities in short supply? Were past relationships with suppliers such as to ensure sympathetic responses to this organization's needs? And again one faces the further critical questions relating to the costs of what was achieved and the value of such results to the organization. Is there evidence of greater increases in achievements than in outlays? How much more could be accomplished if budgetary allocations were increased by 10 or 20 percent? Since the objective cannot be to minimize procurement costs regardless of benefits to the organization, inability to make such comparisons may lead either to excessive expenditures in this department or to curtailing potential contributions to the performance of the whole.

Similar problems attend efforts to appraise the performance of the sales department. Here, too, it is simple enough to measure how much of each product was sold, to whom, and at what price.[4] But sales performance should also encompass informational and analytical responsibilities. It should call attention to shifts in buyer preferences, in competitive offerings, and in prospective demand levels. And it could analyze the causes of lost sales as a basis for suggesting changes in product design, the range of product sizes and types, pricing policies, financing terms, delivery arrangements, and service provisions. Assessments of the effectiveness of sales activities would have to supplement measures of actual results with evaluations of the range, quality, and price of its products as compared with competitive offerings. Consideration would also have to be given to changes in the needs of its regular customers, to any losses of such customers to competitors, and to any gains involving the penetration of new markets. Only then can the further problems be faced of estimating the value of such achievements to the organization for comparison with attendant costs.

In the case of production units within a manufacturing plant, performance is usually measured in terms of the average unit cost of the number of product units meeting defined specifications. And such specifications are derived backwards, of course, from the specifications of the final product and the planned subdivision of production tasks among successively antecedent operations. But evaluating the effectiveness of such operations involves some additional problems. In most production operations, basic routines are overlaid with a variety of deviations from normal conditions. Shortages of materials, machine breakdowns, misplaced tools, and accidents are commonly regarded as random factors for which standard allowances can be made with reasonable conformance to actual results over periods of perhaps several months. But two other kinds of deviations from prevailing norms must be considered in a different light.

Alert supervisors and their technical assistants are expected to be searching constantly for ways to improve efficiency, to reduce wastage of materials, to curtail avoidable equipment idleness, and to reduce manpower requirements. Toward such ends, they may experiment with modifications of existing production flows, tooling, personnel allocations, maintenance procedures, inspection arrangements, and motivational efforts. When successful, these innovations should yield progressive improvements capable of lasting indefinitely. A quite different source of nonrandom deviations from routine conditions may take the form of intermittent reductions in operating efficiency rooted in localized and temporary labor-management tensions.

In large units, and even more in multiunit operations, both kinds of deviations may escape higher management awareness for extended periods—even months—as periodic cost statements simply cumulate all results over a period of weeks, yielding net variances from cost standards which may easily be attributed to random variations rather than to managerial improvements or deficiencies. Such delayed awareness of the actual causes of observed changes in cost performance may have certain undesirable effects. It may defer recognition and reward of unusually alert and innovative managers, thereby tending to discourage such initiatives, or it may encourage some managers to keep these additional potentials cloaked to prevent revision of the operating standards by which their future performance will be judged, preferring to keep such potentials in reserve to offset possible future contingencies. Or it may delay the introduction of staff industrial relations specialists, as fearful managers avoid calling attention to labor problems which they are still hoping to cope with in time.

In short, two factors tend to introduce an important gap between changes in the performance of component production operations and their recognition by higher management through the interpretation of regular financial reports: the relative infrequency of accounting reports relative to the flexibility of working arrangements and conditions, and the tendency of higher management not to regard variances from standards as significant unless they are unusually large or quite prolonged. Although the resulting delay in recognizing new advances as well as new problems may be of only limited significance in companies with strong market positions in relatively stable industries, others facing sharper competition in more volatile markets may find such lags burdensome.

Evaluating Performance in Service Organizations

Performance evaluation may be unsatisfactory even at the level of operations as a whole in the case of governmental and other non-profit organizations which provide services, such as schools, health facilities, social service agencies, universities, philanthropic foundations, and religious organizations. In such cases, the basic problems center around measuring output as the basis for evaluating the effectiveness of performance and measuring the value of the services provided relative to costs.[5]

It is apparent, of course, that the trade-off between the quality of service to each recipient and the numbers served may cover an extremely wide range in schools and in many other organizations providing ostensibly standardized services. Instructional expenditures per student can be adjusted over a wide spectrum by altering class size, ranging from individual tutorials to lecturers with microphones addressing crowded ampitheaters. The critical point here is that the same expenditures may be associated with services to client numbers which may well vary inversely with the quality of the services rendered. Hence simply measuring the outlays involved provides no valid basis for estimating the contributions made. Under such conditions, serving more clients despite an unchanged budget obviously need not imply more effective performance, nor would an increase in budget to serve the same number of clients ensure a comparable increase in contributions to clients as opposed to permitting some erosion in the effectiveness of performance.

A different challenge to output measurement and performance evaluation is encountered when an agency provides a variety of services, some of which are costlier than others in resource requirements per client and some of which may be construed as having a greater social utility than others. The proverbial military doctor who can attend to hundreds of soldiers in a few hours by handing out either pink pills or white after asking the patient what troubles him stands in marked contrast to the elaborate physical examinations available to small numbers in different situations. Similarly, evaluation of the performance of a community social service center which provides recreation for children, lectures for adults, family counseling help, and mental health services obviously requires consideration not only of the quality of service in each category, but also of the relative value placed on each category of service by the agency's sponsor or by some other authoritative body. Here again, one cannot evaluate the effectiveness of the agency, the effects of a decrease in budget, or the effects of an increase in the number of clients serviced unless more effective means are devised for appraising the composition of services provided relative to the costs involved.

In the case of public and other nonprofit service organizations, such difficulties are not even constrained by the availability of profit data to help assess economic viability. But even in the case of private firms offering professional services which have such market measures, such as medical groups, law firms, and consulting organizations, it is obvious that there can be considerable variations between net income levels and the quality of services provided, and the gaps between them can keep expanding over extended periods before deteriorating quality finally becomes apparent to long-established clientele. Such variations in the quality of services rendered may arise from changes in the competence of the staff, in the time and cost pressures on them, or in the quality of supervision over their efforts. To detect such tendencies before they engender increasing, and not easily reversible, penalties in the form of client reactions may well require performance evaluation efforts that are more penetrating, more comprehensive, and more frequent than customary financial statements.

Evaluating Provisions Made for Future Benefits

One of the major problems of public agencies as well as private firms is derived from the pervasive heavy emphasis on short-term performance as compared with longer-term results. Current investment in undertakings expected to yield benefits only some years from now is widely regarded by investors and voters both as withholding benefits that could be provided now and also as offering less attractive returns to current financial inputs because of the uncertainties involved than would result from a greater emphasis on the short run. Hence most managers and politicians tend to place a high discount on long-deferred benefits in shaping their policies and decisions.[6]

Nevertheless, business and public operations must involve commitments into the future. Whether such commitments are given any weight in the assessment of the organization's performance, however, depends on whether there is any formal recognition of their magnitudes and purposes. Oddly enough, however, such recognition tends to be minimal and even nonexistent in many financial statements, thus again limiting effective evaluation of performance.

Among the common commitments which tend to yield benefits for business organizations only over a periods of some years may be included expenditures for development of future markets, of future sources of raw materials, of future improvements in products and process, of employee and managerial abilities, and of future additions to capacity. Such undertakings may require quite substantial resources. Yet skimping on such longer-term efforts may endanger the future of the organization, especially in industries characterized by strong competition and rapid innovation. Taken together, these considerations identify another sector involving the need to evaluate attendant performance and contributions relative to the resource commitments involved. Shortcomings in the former need to be identified so as to trigger either reductions in the resources allocated or changes in the programs and personnel involved. But mere recording of the financial outlays involved is patently insufficient to make possible the managerial evaluations necessary to ensure economical as well as effective promotion of such defined objectives.

Perhaps even more serious than the inadequate evaluation of longer-term projects may be the tendency—especially during periods of intensified economic pressure—to curtail allocations to such developmental efforts in order to improve the more readily recognized and widely reported measures of current performance. Attendant reductions in research and development, as well as in the other programs mentioned earlier, are often not even identifiable in commonly issued financial statements. Hence the depletion of such future sources of profitability and growth—surely an important form of company assets—may be unclear enough to minimize the likelihood of recognition and resistance by those concerned with longer-term performance. Similar pressures are encountered, of course, by public agencies which are well aware of the unpopularity of increasing current expenditures and associated taxes in the interests of long-deferred benefits.

In short, this additional sector of needed performance evaluation emphasizes not only the penalties of uncertainty concerning the effectiveness with which current tasks are being performed, but also the dangers of inadequate appraisal of the extent to which responsibilities essential to the longer-run functioning of the organization may be slighted or even wholly neglected.

Some Suggestions for Improving Performance Evaluation

Performance appraisal has long remained a dormant component of performance-measurement activities because of the prevailing belief that the aspects of performance to be measured in any organization are obvious, as is the interpretation of findings. But, as has already been illustrated, the growing emphasis on rigorous analytical bases for decision making throughout the administrative process has revealed a variety of pressing problems in this area. This has not diminished the importance of continuing to improve techniques for measuring recognized performance attributes accurately and promptly. However, it has generated a need to reconsider what else should be measured, what such findings should be compared with for evaluative purposes, and how these comparative results should be interpreted.

Toward Improved Measures of the Results of Performance

There is no need, of course, to belabor the continued need for prompt and accurate recording of all financial outlays with respect to each sector of organizational activity, of the quantities of physical resources obtained through their expenditure—including various kinds of materials, manpower, and capital goods—and of the quantities of various intermediate or final products turned out, as well as of the revenues obtained from selling the latter in the case of private organizations. But the effective measurement of performance clearly requires penetrating beneath these generalized aggregates to the specification of those attributes of the physical inputs and outputs, as well as those attributes of the associated costs and revenues, whose adjustments are capable of affecting resulting contributions to the organization as a whole.

The nature of such contributions obviously varies with the kind of organization being considered and among its numerous line and staff components. But in most cases, the responsibilities of each component may be regarded as consisting of a core of standard tasks and a superstructure of additional potential contributions.

The former usually involve an array of essentially repetitive tasks to be performed in accordance with defined or at least reasonably clear "understandings" of the minimum expected quantity and quality of specified products or services. And such expectations include allowances for dealing with common variations in operations. Hence even this routine aspect of performance measurement implies a need to assess the extent to which operating conditions deviated significantly, either favorably or unfavorably, from the normal variations allowed for. Moreover, it also implies a need to determine the extent to which various kinds and degrees of deviations from normal variations in operating conditions would be expected to alter the expected quantity and quality of inputs during any period. And, by way of illustration, it might be noted that such extraordinary deviations might relate, in the case of manufacturing units, to changes in the specifications or mix of products, in the supply or quality of inputs received, in output levels, in maintenance requirements, and in the cooperativeness of labor. In short, even seemingly normal physical and cost results in standard tasks may hide unusually meritorious or inadequate performance—and failure to recognize either may dull incentives to continuing improvement.

To add further emphasis to such problems of measuring output, attention might also be drawn to the difficulties involved even in the apparently simple task of measuring changes in the output of multiproduct plants. Managerial appraisals obviously require measures capable of aggregating the output of small and large, simple and complex products in terms of their economic significance. As was noted in chapter 7, measures for such purposes have long been available and are widely used by economists, although still uncommon in industry. But even these are subject to significant shortcomings.

The superstructure of additional potential contributions should encompass at least three elements: making arrangements for achieving continuing improvements in the performance of its standard tasks, calling attention to any prospective problems or opportunities in order to initiate advance planning to deal with them, and suggesting means of improving performance in related sectors of operations on the basis of experience with interactions. None of these is reflected by common output and cost measures. Yet they could engender important contributions to future performance. Moreover, such effects are likely to be encouraged effectively only if these potential contributions are identified as a part of assigned responsibilities, if related achievements are assessed regularly, and if the results are recognized as entering into subsequent performance evaluations and rewards.

In addition to such general requirements for improving performance measurement, attention should be drawn to some illustrative specialized needs in order to indicate something of the fuller texture of problems which may be confronted. With respect to activities providing a reasonably standardized kind of service, such as schools and training programs, the qualitative characteristics must be specified in considerable detail and the fulfillment of such standards must be tested frequently before changes in the numbers served can be accepted as a measure of performance. Where a variety of services in provided, serious efforts must be made to define their relative weights (in terms of resource requirements and service values) before output can be measured appropriately in the face of shifts in composition.

Perhaps the most difficult problems of output measurement concern services with a large component of apparently nonstandardized problem-solving responsibilities such as public, industrial, and governmental relations. These would seem to require both an adequate standby "fire-fighting" capacity as well as adaptability for dealing with any of a wide range of problems. And yet the pressure for increasingly effective use of limited resources has led toward closer coordination of these seemingly diverse functions by concentrating most resources on selected primary problems and seeking to reduce emergencies in these sectors through continuing educational and preventive programs, thereby also clarifying key performance-appraisal cirteria.

The last illustration calls attention to still another sector of specialized problems in measuring outputs: how to assess activities much (or all) of whose contributions are to emerge beyond any given evaluation period. Major examples involving physical results include programs for facilities construction, raw material exploration and development, and research and development on products and processes. Major service functions with a strong orientation toward future benefits include market development, executive development, corporate development, and the maintenance of financial reserves both to withstand unexpected setbacks and to support promising innovations. In most of these areas, especially those involving services, such limited performance appraisal efforts as are employed tend to focus on the industriousness of those engaged. It may facilitate more effective evaluation, however, to attempt to define specific time patterns of achievement targets for all such programs—in rough imitation of those for facilities-construction projects—specifying "milestones" for successive time periods. Then the results should be compared with such targets for each evaluation period.

Toward Improved Evaluations of the Effectiveness of Performance

Although the processes of measuring the level of performance, appraising its effectiveness, and estimating its value relative to attendant costs overlap one another partially, their central objectives differ sufficiently to warrant separate treatment. Appraising the effectiveness of performance involves three components: comparing actual outputs (whose measurement has just been discussed) with what are considered to be meaningful standards of performance, measuring changes in the inputs absorbed, and comparing changes in performance levels with those in input levels.

If basic tasks and operating conditions have not changed, current results may be compared either with past results or with the results planned for the period covered. If the basic tasks have not changed but operating conditions have changed, actual results might be compared either with those of competitors, when feasible, or with estimated potentials under the conditions encountered based on careful evaluation of the special problems encountered. But efforts to apply such expedients would necessitate developing sound grounds for planning future targets, for assessing the prospective effects of various major changes in operating conditions, and for evaluating the performance of competitors with due allowance for significant differences.

In developing such analytical foundations for appraising changes in comparative performance, attention also must be given to determining the extent to which apparent changes in the effectiveness of performance were due to internal achievements or shortcomings as opposed to external developments beyond the control of the operating sector being evaluated. The latter includes the effects not only of extraorganizational changes in factor and product markets and governmental constraints, but also the effects of changes in higher-level decisions within the organization. Among these might be included changes in products, processes, facilities, and output levels, along with changes in the nature and quality of materials inputs, cost allocations, and the payment arrangements and working conditions negotiated with trade unions.

There are two reasons for attempting such differentiations as an integral part of performance evaluation. One is the obvious need to assess each unit's performance only within the limitations on discretionary efforts imposed by externally determined constraints and to highlight attendant shifts in burdens among different operating units as the basis for altering their respective performance targets. The second and even more imporatnt reason is to clarify for higher management the full implications of changes made by it and its share of responsibility for subsequent changes in the performance of various internal units and the organization as a whole.

And a final requirement for developing sounder bases for performance appraisal is rooted in the preceding consideration. In any thoroughly integrated system of operations, adjustments in the nature or effectiveness of performance within any sector may affect the nature and effectiveness of performance in immediately adjacent and perhaps more remote sectors. Hence measures of performance and evaluations of its effectiveness should be designed so as to fit together into a structure permitting evaluations at successively higher levels of aggregation and permitting disaggregation of such overall evaluations through successively smaller subsectors. Thus, for example, the evaluation of one processing unit ought to parallel evaluations of other processing units, and these should fit together into the evaluation of total processing operations and so on.[7]

The second component of assessing the effectiveness of performance introduces problems of measuring changes in the inputs absorbed. One of these concerns which dimensions of inputs should be measured for this purpose. Another difficulty arises from the internal heterogeneity of input categories, which poses the problem of distinguishing changes in the composition of such categories from changes in the aggregate level of any given composition. A third problem centers around attempting to aggregate differential adjustments in a wide variety of materials and supplies, skill classifications, salaried expertise, and types of facilities and equipment. All were discussed in chapter 6 along with practical expedients for dealing with them.

The remaining component of the processes of appraising the effectiveness of performance involves attempting to combine the changing levels of achievement with respect to the various dimensions of desired performance, attempting to combine the differential changes in the levels of all kinds of inputs—recognizing that some of these adjustments may involve substitutions among input categories—and finally, comparing the resulting summary measures of changes in contributions and changes in resource absorption with one another. Each of these steps is confronted by substantial difficulties, of course. But it is important to recognize the penalties which may be exacted by continued reliance on admittedly inadequate expedients. Concentration on just one or two of the more readily measurable aspects of performance is bound to encourage neglect of all others which, though given verbal emphasis, clearly have little bearing at the point of reward-determining evaluations. Accordingly, it may be necessary either to provide clear indications of at least the rough order of relative weights attached to various aspects of performance—and to reinforce these in the course of making and explaining subsequent evaluations—or to avoid the obvious disparity between assignments and evaluations by forthrightly narrowing the specification of performance requirements.

As for comparing relative adjustments in inputs and outputs as the basis for appraising changes in the effectiveness of performance, or in the "productivity" of operations, closer analysis reveals a number of requirements that have to be met if observed changes in such comparisons are to be interpreted correctly. Among the most important of these is the existence of an analytical framework which encompasses all the inputs and outputs of the given operating area and provides a theory of how it functions. Others reviewed in chapter 3 concern the congruence of activities covered by the input and output measures used, the qualitative stability of the tasks and resources entering into the measurements, and the provision of time lags between inputs and outputs which accord with the time required to transform the former into the latter in the given operation.

Toward Improved Appraisals of the Value of Performance Adjustments

Although the elements of the performance appraisal process which have been discussed serve a number of intermediate purposes, the eventual objective of such efforts is supposedly to compare the value of each operating group's contributions to the performance of the organization as a whole with the cost of the resources absorbed by the group. Resulting comparisons might then serve as guides to the reallocation of resources so as to maximize fulfillment of defined goals.

Such an objective, however, is difficult to attain. The widespread development of larger and increasingly complex organizations reflects the improvements in performance made possible through the subdivisions of gross undertakings or tasks into components which are smaller and more homogeneous in their requirements and, hence, more amenable to the development of more highly specialized knowledge and skills which tend to yield improvements in performance. As a result of such a distribution of responsibilities, most departments record heavy costs and no income, while sales departments record heavy incomes and small costs. Yet it is obvious that such comparisons do not indicate the desired directions of resource reallocations.

What is needed instead is a framework which keeps track of the physical outlays and contributions as well as the financial outlays and contributions reflecting the flow of resources through the organization. The development of accounting has provided an increasingly detailed tracing of the financial aspects of such flows. But this falls short of managerial needs because it fails to keep track of the attendant variations in the level and composition of the accompanying physical resource flows. And yet most organizations can accomplish their purposes only by transforming financial inputs (investments and borrowings) into physical inputs (materials, labor, and capital goods), by transforming physical inputs into physical outputs, and by transforming physical output into financial returns (either directly through the sale of products and services or indirectly through the provision of public services which engender support for renewed financial inputs), as shown in figure 15-1.[8]

According to this illustrative model, the performance of private firms would be measured by the relationship of financial returns to financial inputs, that is, of revenues and profits to costs and investment. But variations in such ratios of financial outputs to financial inputs would be the outcome of antecedent variations in the ratio of financial inputs to physical inputs (representing the result of material and capital goods procurement efforts and of labor and salaried hiring activities), in the ratio of physical inputs to physical outputs (representing the results of production activities), and in the ratio of physical outputs to financial outputs (representing the results of sales activities).

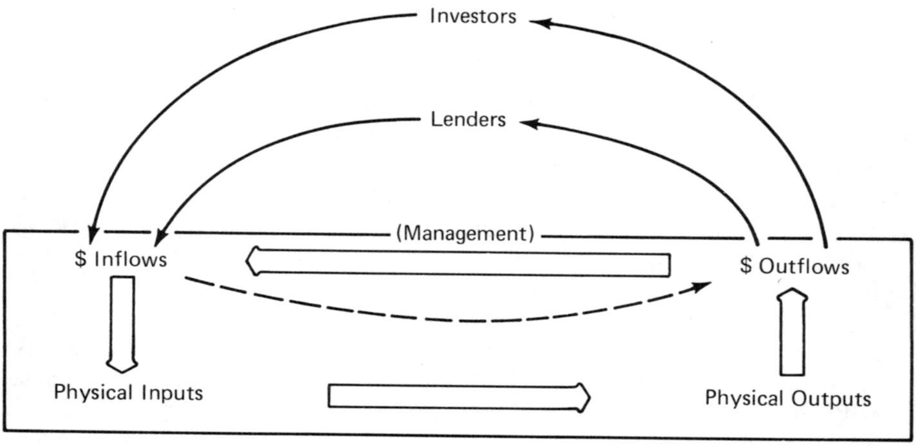

Figure 15–1. Physical and Financial Flows within the Firm

Lest there be any misunderstanding, the basic purpose of this illustration is not to argue in favor of some particular grouping of functions, but simply to emphasize that the very nature of the relevant measures of performance must change to accord with the changing nature of the tasks in successive stages of organizational activity. An additional purpose of this illustration is to stress the need to recognize that prospective adjustments within any intermediate stage of operations cannot be evaluated properly except by tracing their expected effects both back through the antecedent stages leading to financial inputs and forward through the succeeding steps leading to financial outputs, thereby seeking to evaluate any internal adjustment in terms not merely of its effects at the point of change, but on the basis of its effects throughout the system. Thus cost-reducing innovations within manufacturing sectors may have to be rejected if they are found to involve changes in product design or quality likely to have adverse market effects. And innovations found to involve shifts to more expensive inputs may nevertheless prove attractive if expected to engender offsetting gains in product prices and sales volume, as was noted in chapter 3.

The preceding point also suggests the general approach to elaborating such an analytical framework for application to organizations comprised of numerous subdivisions of line operations as well as substantial arrays of staff functions. In the case of the former, the basic guideline is provided by the fact that subdivisions are usually designed and function as specialized components of recognizable task clusters and associated organizational units responsible for producing intermediate (and eventually final) products which encompass the processing and other contributions of these specialized subunits.[9] In the case of staff units, the objective might well remain the same: to determine the sectors of line operations which its efforts are supposed to help and then to trace its effects on such sectors. But it is likely to be much more difficult to do this both because many staff operations are intended to improve many sectors of operations and because such effects are more difficult to separate from the influence of many other simultaneous activities. Nevertheless, it is not easy to avoid the conclusion that unless serious efforts are made to evaluate such functions, the result is likely to be a loss of control over staff sectors which have accounted for an increasing level of employment and costs in wide sectors of public as well as private organizations.

One remaining problem of performance evaluation concerns those operat-tions whose contributions are intended to be realized in large measure beyond the current evaluation period. An earlier reference divided these into two groups: those yielding physical outputs in the form of new facilities, new sources of raw materials, and new improvements in products or processes; and those yielding future benefits in the form of executive development, new market development, and the maintenance of strong financial capabilities for supporting innovational efforts or for easing the impact of unexpected market adversities. Once again, it may be argued that if there is no overt recognition of the extent of such commit-ments to safeguard or develop the future of the organization and the magnitude of resulting prospective benefits, managements may be encouraged to minimize such commitments in the interest of utilizing available resources to maximize the short-run performance which tends to be highlighted by traditional financial reporting. To help minimize the pressures favoring such myopia, consideration might be given to supplementing current financial statements with statements and exhibits specifying the magnitudes of commitments which have been made for maintaining or expanding productive capacity, supplies of needed inputs, markets, and trained labor as well as executive replacements—and the magnitude and timing of expected results. Such supplementary information would certainly provide additional valuable perspectives for investors seeking to evaluate prospec-tives performance. And if the inclusion of such material became at all common, it might well generate pressure against management policies whose overemphasis on short-term results would thus be brought to the notice of investors.

Some Organizational Implications

Serious efforts to overcome the pervasive inadequacies of performance appraisal in public as well as private organizations are likely to require considerable resource commitments over extended periods of time in order to accumulate the specialized knowledge, to refine the needed techniques and to integrate resulting physical with financial criteria and findings. This should occasion no surprise in view of the heavy costs commonly entailed in developing comprehensive cost-accounting and budget control systems in complex organizations, and in view of the even more difficult problems faced and the more meager accumulation of experience available as yet in developing the needed additional elements of an integrated performance appraisal system which have been discussed.

Equally important is the necessity of recognizing that these additional tasks require categories of expertise different from those provided by accounting expertise alone. The need to define the critical dimensions of, and bases for evaluating, short- and longer-term performance in each major line and staff function with respect to its prospective contributions to the effective functioning of the whole encompasses a broad range of knowledge and experience. Even the most promising personnel prospects for assuming such responsibilities would have to supplement past backgrounds in accounting, industrial engineering, economics, operations research, or other already established professional fields to develop penetrating insights into the characteristics of many different kinds of performance while retaining a unified conception of their respective roles in promoting more aggregative objectives.

In turn, acceptance of such broader conceptions of the dimensions of performance appraisal, along with the attendant needs for a different array of specialized personnel capacities and for independence from the operations being evaluated, suggests the possibility of introducing a new managerial function responsible for performance appraisal throughout the organization, including accounting and perhaps budget controls as component parts of this larger sector of responsibilities.

Why should such efforts be organized as a separate function? Why should not such needs be discharged by the supervisors of each operating unit? These questions have been raised repeatedly as each new managerial function has been separated from the totality of responsibilities encompassed by the original conceptions of management. Why were line responsibilities as a whole progressively subdivided into separate components such as procurement, production, and sales? Why were general management functions further subdivided into specialized responsibilities dealing with engineering, personnel, and finance—only to be further subdivided to established distinctive groups concerned with research, industrial relations, executive development, accounting, budgeting, and corporate planning?

In virtually all such instances, specialized functions were established reluctantly and only after strenuous efforts to avoid the attendant fragmentation of established organizational groupings and their associated powers.[10] To overcome the influential opposition of such prevailing arrangements, it was necessary to demonstrate the following with respect to each prospective new grouping of functional responsibilities:

1. That current levels of relevant achievement were inadequate relative to recognized pressures.
2. That substantially improved performance seemed attainable through reliance on personnel with more highly specialized training and experience.

3. That such specialists would tend to be less capable of performing most of the other tasks encompassed by the broader functional group from which separation was being proposed.
4. That centralizing such a new responsibility would ensure closer conformance with the objectives of the organization as a whole as well as greater consistency and effectiveness than dispersing such specialists among existing organizational units.

Similar advantages may be offered by a centralized performance appraisal function, but the argument for establishing such an organizational group would have to be considered anew by each organization. And at this early stage in the consideration of such a possibility, it is difficult to meet some of the preceding conditions convincingly.

Of course, similar problems were faced in connection with the other specialized functions which have achieved wide acceptance by now. The superiority of specialized knowledge and experience could hardly be recognized in the absence of such recognized specialists. And their development could hardly be encouraged so long as the performance of individuals was appraised and rewarded on the basis of a wider array of tasks. Nor was consistency likely to be considered important by supervisors dealing with each of their component tasks on whatever improvised basis suited their own purposes and pressures. In short, such specialized managerial functions have developed gradually through a process of mutual reinforcements as initially limited recognition of new needs encouraged comparably limited efforts to meet them, and as the growing success of the latter engendered expanding recognition of these needs and of the means of dealing with them more effectively.

Accordingly, little more can usefully be attempted at this time than to call attention to the extent and potential costs of prevailing inadequacies in the evaluation of performance in most private and public organizations, to review some of the primary tasks involved in seeking to overcome such shortcomings, and to indicate some of the means whereby needed improvements might be effected. In addition, consideration of the necessarily broad scope of a comprehensive system for appraising all sectors of performance from the standpoint of the functioning of the organization as a whole, combined with the unusual array of specialized personnel required for such an undertaking, has suggested the possibility that effective discharge of these wide-ranging and important responsibilities might warrant their assignment to a new managerial function.

Notes

1. The "management by objectives" movement is usually traced back to Drucker [3]. Increasing experience with efforts to apply it to individual companies led to a series of explanatory textbooks, including those by Odiorne [14],

McConkey [11], and Humble [10]. In turn, studies of the problems encountered and the results achieved have been presented in a variety of personnel, management, and general business journals (for example, Cherrington and Cherrington [2] and Owens [15]). Such experiential and research reports have been usefully reviewed and supplemented recently by Carroll and Tosi [1]. Despite increasing experience with this approach during the past decade, they conclude that "the measurement of performance is still a difficult problem" and also that research on such programs "has provided few practical guides for actually carrying out the goal-setting and performance-review aspects of the MBO [management by objectives] process" [1, pp. 15-16].

2. For an excellent review of the problems which have been encountered by efforts to evaluate research performance, see Edwards and McCarthy [4]. Broader discussions of the problems involved are provided by Gold [6, p. 419], Gold [8], and chapter 14.

3. The essentially introductory state of work in this area is illustrated by McConkey [12] and Wagman [16].

4. Such an introductory set of measures is suggested in Humble, [10, p. 67].

5. For an initial approach to this problem area, see McConkey [13].

6. Indeed, increasing reliance on the "net present value" approach to capital budgeting formalizes this bias, see Gold and Boylan [9].

7. Various aspects of these problems were discussed in chapter 3 and are considered at greater length in Gold [5, pp. 48-54].

8. In the case of government service agencies, such a model might be altered by showing taxpayers as the source of financial inputs and clients as the recipients of the physical output of services.

9. This approach is illustrated and associated problems are discussed in Gold [7, pp. 19-31 and 157-160].

10. For a discussion of such processes, see (Gold [6, pp. 397-398]).

References

[1] S.J. Carroll, Jr. and H.L. Tosi, Jr., *Management by Objectives: Applications and Research* (New York: Macmillan, 1973).

[2] D.J. and J.O. Cherrington, "Participation, Performance and Appraisal," *Business Horizons,* December 1974.

[3] Peter Drucker, *The Practice of Management* (New York: Harper and Row, 1954).

[4] S.A. Edwards and M.W. McCarthy, "Measuring the Performance of Researchers," *Research Management,* January 1973.

[5] B. Gold, *Foundations of Productivity Analysis* (Pittsburgh: Univ. of Pittsburgh Press, 1955).

[6] B. Gold, "The Decision Framework for Major Technological Innovations," in K. Baier and N. Rescher (eds.), *Values and the Future* (New York: Free Press, 1969), pp. 397–398; reprinted in Gold [7].

[7] B. Gold, *Explorations in Managerial Economics: Productivity, Costs, Technology and Growth* (New York: Basic Books; London: Macmillan 1971).

[8] B. Gold, "What is the Place of Research and Technological Innovations in Business Planning," *Research Policy,* Summer 1973.

[9] B. Gold and M.G. Boylan, "Capital Budgeting, Industrial Capacity and Imports," *Quarterly Review of Economics and Business,* Fall 1975.

[10] J.W. Humble, *How to Manage by Objectives* (New York: Amacom, 1972).

[11] D.D. McConkey, *How to Manage by Results* (New York: American Management Association, 1965).

[12] D.D. McConkey, "Staff Objectives Are Different," *Personal Journal,* July 1972.

[13] D.D. McConkey, "Applying Management Objectives to Non-Profit Organizations," *SAM Advanced Management Journal,* January 1973.

[14] G. Odiorne, *Management by Objectives* (New York: Pittman, 1964).

[15] J. Owens, "Values and Pitfalls of MBO," *Michigan Business Review,* July 1974.

[16] B.L. Wagman, "An Approach to Measuring the Productivity of Staff Functions," *Public Personnel Management,* September-October 1974.

16 Factors Stimulating Technological Progress: Some Japanese Experience

Japan's spectacular surge into the ranks of leading industrial nations during the past 15 years has gained widespread, if sometimes grudging, admiration. But there is still inadequate recognition of one of the most remarkable features of this achievement: that it resulted in large measure from the Japanese outperforming the United States and Western Europe in the very areas in which their superiority seemed most secure—in industrial technology and productive efficiency. Disregard of this significant advance helps to explain the successive reactions of surprise as strong Japanese competition has emerged in industry after industry. And it may well foreshadow serious disappointments for those who are confidently predicting that Japan's industrial development has now peaked and that the progressive weakening of its competitive strength will prevent even the maintenance of its current industrial capacity.

As a basis for considering such future potentials more effectively, this chapter will first review the factors that seem to have contributed most to Japan's extraordinary technological progress, with particular reference to steel mills and their computerization. Attention will then turn to the likelihood that such factors will help to continue Japanese leadership in these and related sectors of industrial operations as well. The analysis represents the author's personal judgments based on extensive field research on steel operations in the United States, Western Europe, and Japan.

Major Sources of Japan's Advances in Steel Computerization

Until the late 1960s, the Japanese steel industry was dominated by technologies licensed from foreign producers, especially Americans. Since then, the Japanese have made increasingly significant innovative contributions of their own. These include increases in the scale of ships, blast furnaces, and entire steel mills, as well as advances in the basic technologies of sintering, iron making, steel making, continuous casting, several sectors of finishing, and pollution control. In the application of computers within the steel industry, progress had long been dominated by the United States, reinforced by the preeminence of its domestic computer manufacturers in providing needed hardware and by their cooperation in developing needed software. Within the last few years, however, the Japanese have surpassed the United States and all other Western countries in the computerization of most steel operations. What were the most influential factors responsibile for this success in a sector of technology with an immense range of applicability to other industries?

The Role of Top Management

No contribution to the development and application of computerization in the Japanese steel industry was more important than the strong and unwavering support of top management, which was rooted in four distinctive elements of Japanese managerial philosophy.

One of these involves a deep commitment by all management personnel to building the power and prestige of Japan. This urges not only the sacrificing of any profit opportunities involving company actions that might tarnish the national image in the eyes of foreigners, but also the undertaking of even costly efforts to minimize continuing dependencies on foreigners, especially with respect to important technologies. A second basic element emphasizes long-term performance targets over short-term criteria, in strong contrast to the overwhelming pressure in U.S. capital markets on maximizing short-term results. A third characteristic of most Japanese industrial management seems to be a strong commitment to increasingly comprehensive companywide planning and centralized control. And still another reflects the especially powerful personal drive of senior managements to achieve ego-satisfying superiority over domestic and foreign competitors in any sector of performance, financial or otherwise.

It is to such underpinnings in managerial philosophy that one must look for explanations of a variety of policies and actions which differ from those commonly encountered in Western steel companies. For example, Japanese steel companies use a much higher ratio of engineers to wage earners than their competitors and make much more aggressive demands on them for *continuing* improvements in all facilities and operations. Head-office and plant engineers are expected to keep increasing the capacity and efficiency of all facilities and equipment by 3 to 5 percent each year through developing modifications in design, tooling accessories, and operating methods as well as through increasing utilization. It is within the context of such general pressures on engineers for progressive long-term achievements that programs for expanding computerization have been developed and applied. On the other hand, extensive research on the U.S. steel industry for more than 20 years has left me with the impression that most companies have been less demanding of engineering innovations and improvements than in Japan—and I have had the same impression in Western European steel companies.

The basic managerial objectives just mentioned also seem to account for the fact that Japanese steel companies make larger allocations for research and development than their competitors and seek a different pattern of results. Although it is difficult to obtain demonstrably valid data on R&D expenditures in Japan—such information being regarded as a critical component of competitive strategies—available estimates range two to four times the percentage of sales revenue found among leading U.S. steel companies, with the higher figure seemingly the more likely. This deeper commitment is associated with two other distinctive characteristics: a greater emphasis on seeking major process improvements, and a fuller support for developing the scientific foundations of key processes. The former differs, of course, from the dominant emphasis on product improvements in steel research in the United States, and the latter contrasts with the greater American emphasis on more immediate, "practical" improvements based in considerable measure on engineering ingenuity and a substantial intermixture of improvisation and trial and error with experimental research.

It is interesting to note in this connection that Japan's impressive advances in high-quality, high-yield rolling through computerization are apparently attributable to such a long-run process-oriented research program begun in the 1950s. It involved reviving basic research on the theory of plasticity, which had been initiated and later abandoned by the Max Planck Institute in Germany. When I asked why this was done at a time when Japan's steel industry was still both small and backward, the answer given was that they realized that the technology being purchased from abroad had already been in use for a long time and hence must be approaching obsolescence. Therefore, Japan would obviously have to develop a next-generation technology through fundamental research if it were to gain an effective competitive position in international markets.

Another factor stimulating advances in computerization was early recognition by top management that an integrated network of computers offered the most promising means of fulfilling its long-term commitment to increasingly comprehensive planning and centralized control. As a result, the basic framework of their computerization systems was designed, even in the early stages, to encompass all company operations. This basic framework then served several valuable pruposes: it defined the conceptual constraints within which all lower hierarchical levels of application had to be developed so as to ensure compatibility with larger system; by continuously highlighting the missing blocks in the systems, it provided a holistic rather than a localized view of the relative desirability of alternative next steps in completing the system; and it helped to maintain strong management pressure for continued progress by identifying the gaps still limiting their exercise of fully integrated control as well as the scope of detailed planning.

Such a "top-down" approach is almost the opposite of the essentially "bottom-up" approach commonly found in Western steel companies. This has usually been initiated by developing process controls for individual operations and then trying to integrate such controls for various sequences of operations. Sufficient progress at these levels tends to be followed by efforts to develop production-control schedules for major subsectors of a plant and then for an entire mill. Eventually, this would be followed in multiplant companies by developing integrated production-planning programs covering all mills by relating their respective capabilities and assigned commitments to incoming orders.

Complete development of either the top-down or the bottom-up system would require covering all the same applications, of course, including allocations of orders, materials, equipment, and manpower as well as associated financial resources over periods of some duration. But the bottom-up approach tends to necessitate more frequent redesign of programs developed independently for different operations and for different plants when efforts are eventually made to integrate them with one another to achieve successively higher levels of hierarchical control. Moreover, the bottom-up approach also tends to be more sporadic in coverage as a response to the changing pattern of pressures and initiatives generated by different operating units—and in turn, it tends to lose momentum as each specific project is completed and decisions must be awaited choosing among competing proposals for the next stage of allocations in the absence of an existing overall development program. Perhaps most serious of all, the bottom-up approach tends to face repeated difficulties in persuading each successively higher level of management to approve the extension of computerization to more aggregative levels, instead of being assured of the powerful support of top management combined with their pressure for continuing progress, as has been more characteristic of the Japanese approach.

Implementation of the Japanese approach may be illustrated in two ways. First, systems design and computer specialists have been an integral part of the teams assigned to design new plants. Hence the potentials of computerization have been one of the basic considerations entering into capacity, process, equipment, and layout decisions instead of having to be retrofitted later bit by bit to arrangements originally made without considering computerization possibilities. Second, computer programs for specific operations have seldom been developed by simply having computer specialists observe, analyze, and then prepare programs for them. Rather, leading Japanese steel companies have made considerable investments in the more roundabout and longer process of requiring some specialists in the operation to undergo intensive training in systems analysis and computerization methods and also requiring some computer specialists to undergo intensive training in the given operation, often including a period of active experience. Together they form a team, all of whom have a reasonable degree of overlapping competencies rather than comprising an array of one-sided specialists. The resulting full accommodation of operating experience has helped to minimize both work-force skepticism and the number of needed exceptions to programs.

The Role of Government

A second major source of impetus to advanced computerization in the Japanese steel industry was the elite status given to the industry in the government's program for economic development and export expansion. This helped to ensure availability of the enormous investments needed for the industry's unprecedented construction of giant new mills. In order to appreciate the critical importance of such government support, it may be worth recalling the extreme difficulties encountered by private steel companies in the United States and Western Europe in efforts to raise capital for new integrated plants solely on the basis of their limited profit prospects as compared with those of other industries. Thus only one new integrated steel mill has been built in the United States in more than 12 years (with a capacity of less than 6 million tons), while the Japanese built eight, averaging nearly 10 million tons of capacity each.

In turn, the construction of a succession of new facilities encouraged application of the newest advances in all relevant technologies, including computerization. Incorporation of such innovations as integral elements of new facilities offered substantially greater benefits, of course, than could be obtained by attempts to retrofit them to facilities designed and laid out without such modifications in view. Moreover, the realistic prospect of additional plants to be built sustained the stimulus to developing further major advances in processing methods and facilities in contrast with the erosion of such encouragement in countries where limited prospects for new plants precludes early application of such advances.

The government's emphasis on the development and continuing improvement of the industry's international competitive strength also reinforced heavier managerial commitments to basic research and development as well as to the employment of larger engineering staffs than would have been justified by an overriding demand for maximizing short-term profitability.

Another major contribution of government policies toward the steel industry—including the prestige of having been designated as an elite industry, its rapid expansion with attendant opportunities for accelerated advancement to positions of responsibility, and its commitments to intensive technological development—was that the Japanese steel industry was enabled to attract the best technical and other graduates from leading universities. Such an inflow of young talent for more than a decade has endowed the industry with an invaluable stock of innovative capabilities. Not for decades have the career possitilities offered by the steel industries of the United States and Western Europe been regarded by new graduates as comparably superior to available alternatives. This does not mean that Western steel industries have failed to employ able technical and managerial recruits. But it does suggest that they may already have lost valuable ground competitively to the Japanese in this important foundation stage of future technological progress.

Two additional sources of governmental aid to the Japanese steel industry's technological development also warrant recognition. The first derives from the government's interesting bifurcated policy on competition, the objective of which is to maximize the international competitive strength of its industries rather than to maximize competition in itself. This results in stressing the maintenance of strong competition among domestic producers in domestic markets during periods of brisk economic activity, while also supporting cooperation among such producers in facing industrywide problems. The latter includes acceptance of their joint efforts to penetrate foreign markets as well as to prevent any destructive competitive behavior in domestic markets during recessions. In addition, the government has also encouraged domestic producers to cooperate in dealing with common technological needs, including, for example, overcoming certain pollution problems and pooling the operating data of different facilities to accelerate progress in the computerization of rolling mills. And the remaining form of government aid relevant to the current discussion concerns its active support of expansion of its computer industry. Although this has centered on the development of computing machines and their components, an associated concern with ensuring applicability to an increasing range of practical industrial operations seems to have encouraged extensive efforts to explore and fulfill steel industry needs.

The Role of Organizational Relationships

Technological progress and computerization in the steel industry also benefited from the unusual character of organizational relationships in large Japanese firms, which derive essentially from the national culture.

In the case of technical and managerial personnel, the most important of these distinctive arrangements has been the widely recognized assurance of lifetime employment and the less widely recognized common practice of reasonably frequent shifts in assignments among plants, among departments, and even between line and staff instead of emphasizing narrow vertical career lines. Together these tend to stress loyalty to the company rather than to component units and thus help to reduce interdepartmental barriers to the cooperation required for effective development and utilization of computerization and other major innovations. Indeed, as was noted earlier, computerization teams are often formed by transferring operating engineers to them and later transferring systems engineers into line positions. Western managers are often quick to note that such reallocations require costly new learning with each transfer, but it may be worth considering such counterclaims as the following: that most positions require relatively limited amounts of specialized learning; that the additional benefits of experience beyond, say, 3 years may be increasingly small and the tendency to rigidify existing practices increasingly large; and that much may be gained from the periodic introduction of newcomers likely to look at prevailing arrangements with the freshness derived from a different experiential background and also likely to examine suggested innovations with greater objectivity.

The kinds of wage-earner resistance to technological innovations which are frequently encountered in Western steel mills and other industries tend to be minimized in large Japanese plants by the combination of lifetime employment security and payment systems that base differentials on years of service rather than skill levels. Under such conditions, computerization or other improvements in operations pose no threats either to employment security or to earning levels. They usually require learning new methods, of course, but this is apparently often regarded as stimulating by a relatively well-educated work force because it leads to a reduction of customary routines and to an ego-satisfying involvement with recognizedly more advanced technologies.

The motivations of managerial personnel and of wage earners just reviewed have also tended to be very strongly reinforced by the close identification of each individual's interests with their common interest in enhancing the performance of the company. In the course of increasing industrialization and urbanization, the deep commitment of the individual to his group relationships—which is at the core of Japanese culture—has involved a growing identification with the company as the most immediate substitute for the now dispersed and attenuated *Grossfamilie.* The resulting personal pride in company accomplishments, and especially in outdoing competing companies, provides an important further impetus to welcoming improvements.

The Role of Increasing Output

The remaining primary source of major contributions to the accelerated progress of computerization in the Japanese steel industry, and of other technological innovations as well, was the rapid expansion of its capacity. Most company analyses of the economic benefits of computerization show savings in labor costs as accounting for between one-half and two-thirds of the total and increases in salable product capacity, via improvements in yield, as accounting for most of the remainder.

Thus computerization helped the Japanese industry to cope with early labor shortages and eased the effects of rapidly rising wage rates on unit labor costs. And the later manpower savings could be fully exploited, despite lifetime employment guarantees, only because decreases in labor requirements per unit of output were more than offset by expanding output.

Similarly, increasing the yield of final products from a given level of inputs helped not only to reduce variable costs per unit of output, but also to expand practical capacity without comparable increases in investment. But the latter benefit, too, could be fully realized only because output was expanding fast enough to maintain high levels of utilization of the increments in capacity.

Such special supporting conditions have obvious implications for the lagging performance of the U.S. and Western European steel industries with respect to computerization during the past decade. When computerization threatened reductions in labor requirements or the downgrading of skills, trade union resistance tended to shrink the proportions of probable labor-cost savings far below those suggested by technological considerations alone, especially in situations where unemployment levels were already a source of political sensitivity. And inasmuch as steel output levels were seldom restricted by capacity in the United States and Western Europe during this period, the attractiveness of achieving further increases in capacity for which there would be no demand was obviously limited.

In short, a significant part of the greater progress of computerization in the Japanese steel industry represented a response to substantially different conditions rather than a fuller exploitation of practical potentials which were equally available to the steel industries of the United States and Western Europe. And this fact obviously has important implications for assessing the prospects for continuing rapid advances in the computerization of the Japanese steel industry.

Future Prospects for Computerization in the Japanese Steel Industry

Developments in recent years have obviously affected each of the four major sets of factors which contributed so heavily to rapid advances in the computerization of the Japanese steel industry. Nevertheless, three such developments seem likely to continue exerting positive pressure for a continuation of such leadership, albeit somewhat less aggressively.

Changes in the Role of Management

There is no evidence of changes in management's overriding commitments to the national interests of Japan, to the predominance of long-term performance objectives over short-term criteria, or to achieving increasingly comprehensive companywide planning and integrated control. Hence all these stimuli to maintaining leadership in the further development and fuller application of technological advances, including computerization, remain undiminished. Only the urgency of managerial pressures to achieve competitive superiority may be easing somewhat.

One reason for the latter is that worldwide acknowledgment of their great competitive strength has inevitably reduced their early driving need to achieve such recognition. Such achievements also gradually dissipated the need to "prove oneself" within Japanese society, which burdened the young executives who were prematurely catapulted into senior positions by General MacArthur's dismissal of the top echelons of Japanese industry during the period of occupation. Moreover, the rising average age of Japanese industrial leaders may also be associated with a reduced willingness to assume major risks. As one official told me, "We built our first new mill when our senior management was in its forties and our second when our management was in its fifties. They are now in their sixties and we may not build a third for quite some time."

In short, managerial pressure for technological superiority will undoubtedly continue, although it may be moderated somewhat relative to the frantic efforts of the past decade. It is less likely, however, that management's drive for increased computerization will be similarly eased, in view of their intensified need for comprehensive planning and effective controls to adjust effectively to shifting pressures in both domestic and international markets.

Changes in the Role of Government

The early powerful support of the government for the rapid expansion and technological advancement of the Japanese steel industry has been largely curtailed because it no longer enjoys high priority in the nation's eocnomic development program. This means that the government no longer encourages the addition of major new facilities and hence no longer facilitates the industry's access to large additional investment funds from domestic capital markets. In addition to withdrawing such positive supports, the government has also imposed an array of capital-absorbing pollution-control requirements which equal or exceed those of other major steel-producing countries. Moreover, the government has even pressed the industry to moderate exports to its major U.S. and Western European markets so as to ease complaints from their governments.

Such shifts in governmental policies obviously tend to eliminate past stimuli to those forms of technological advances whose effective utilization would require the construction of large, new mills. And revocation of steel's status as an elite industry, combined with the scaling back of its growth prospects relative to past rates, has undoubtedly reduced its ability to attract the best current university graduates.

But the burdensome effects on the industry of these changes in governmental policies have been much less significant than the positive contributions of its earlier support. Having already acquired the enormous facilities and other resources which have established it as the third largest producer and by far the leading exporter in the world, the Japanese steel industry is now quite capable of financing the more modest rates of growth planned for the next decade without requiring help from its government. The resulting shift from building additional giant, new plants might, of course, reduce commitments to some sectors of potential technological advances. But it will certainly intensify efforts to achieve advances in the wide range of technological sectors promising increases in the capacity and efficiency of existing plants, among which computerization developments offer major potentials. Finally, although a reduced inflow of outstanding young recruits is bound to have a limiting effect on innovational capabilities over the long run, this diminuendo is not likely to be significant during the next two decades because of the industry's disproportionately heavy absorption of such talent during the past 15 to 20 years. Nor is it obvious that U.S. and Western European steel producers are proving more successful in outbidding other employers for the most promising of university graduates.

Changes in the Role of Organizational Relationships

Numerous references have been made recently in Western business journals to a developing erosion of the values binding Japanese workers and managers to the interests of their companies. But the very meagerness of the evidences cited–limited to a minuscule number of companies, mostly of minor significance–suggests that such interpretations are exaggerated, perhaps representing wishful efforts to sustain the Western belief that such relationships are inherently untenable.

It is true, of course, that recessions and the prospect of reduced rates of growth have forced Japanese industrial leaders to consider means of adapting to such changing conditions. Few, however, have doubts about the importance of maintaining the cohesive organizational relationships which have enabled their firms to avoid the internal frictions that have undermined the competitive strength of Western industries. And such loyalties to the company and to co-workers are likely to remain strong so long as the reciprocal obligations of lifetime employment security, participation in relevant performance-improvement efforts, and sharing in resulting benefits are fulfilled. Accordingly, Japanese managers have made recognizedly strenuous efforts to meet their employment obligations even during the recent severe recession experienced in a number of industries, while initiating adjustments to prospective declines in long-term employment requirements by reducing current new additions to the permanent work force.

Thus the unique loyalties and mutually reinforcing relationships which have characterized large Japanese firms seem to have remained essentially intact, ensuring continued encouragement to, and acceptance of, performance-improving innovations inlcuding computerization for considerable periods in the future.

The Changing Role of Output Pressures

Contrary to some public statements in Japan and widespread hopes abroad, Japan's steel capacity is likely to keep expanding for at least the next 5 years and probably beyond. Visits to the modern steel mills in Japan reveal that each is actively involved in expanding its production potentials as well as improving its productive efficiency. Capacity may accordingly rise by 30 million tons on a raw steel basis without the construction of a single new integrated plant, relying instead on rebuilding older facilities, squeezing more out of their modern facilities, and "rounding out" to overcome any existing bottlenecks.

The normal incentives to such improvement efforts tend to be strongly intensified by the fact that Japan enjoys an important advantage over all other major steel-producing countries as a result of having built numerous large-scale, technologically advanced plants before the recent severe inflation in the cost of new facilities, which has led most other countries to defer new plant construction. This means that any recovery in world steel demand is likely to be differentially favorable to the utilization of these low-cost Japanese mills. It also means that further technological improvements in the performance of already technologically advanced and large-scale Japanese plants would enable them to add capacity far more quickly and at much less cost than would be possible for foreign producers having either to upgrade old plants or to build new ones. Accordingly, in view of the already noted emphasis of Japanese management on long-term perspectives, there is every reason to expect undiminished, and perhaps even intensified, efforts to develop such performance-improving technologies.

In the case of computerization, improvement targets continue to center around reducing unit labor requirements, increasing capacity relative to investment requirements, and extending and improving comprehensive planning and control systems—plus a newly intensified emphasis on energy conservation and on reducing manpower requirements in offices. It is quite possible that potential future savings from such advances may be smaller than in the past, but there can be little doubt that remaining potentials seem quite impressive.

For example, it has already been noted that reductions in production manpower requirements per unit of output have been the major source of savings from past computer applications in most Japanese steel mills. Yet, as was noted in chapter 11, every Japanese plant seems to be actively engaged in seeking to reduce such unit labor requirements by 25 to 40 percent. Indeed, such efforts are being accelerated to avoid having to increase hiring when steel demand picks up and also to ease the cost effects of continued increases in wage rates.

Additions to the capacity of integrated steel mills are currently estimated to cost about \$500 per annual ton in Japan (as compared with roughly twice that in the United States.) Hence advances in computerized planning and control would offer investment savings on the order of \$200 million for every 5 percent increase in the practical capacity of an 8-million-ton plant—an incentive obviously large enough to warrant quite intensive efforts.

Japanese steel mills have always placed heavier emphasis on reducing energy costs than most other producers because of their almost complete dependence on costly imports of fuels. But the multiplication of energy prices in recent years has led to a redoubling of Japanese efforts to economize on energy, with computerization playing a major role in such efforts.

In short, there is ample reason to anticipate a continuation of major efforts by the Japanese to remain in the forefront of a wide range of technological development efforts in the steel industry in order to safeguard, and perhaps even bolster, their competitive strength in international markets. It is even likely, in view of the industry's strategic place in the structure of Japanese industries, its importance as a source of employment and foreign exchange, and its prestigious technological leadership, that any significant weakening of its international position would quickly engender renewed governmental programs to restore its preeminence.

Some Concluding Observations and Implications

1. The Japanese steel industry outdistanced its competitors in computerization, as well as in other sectors of technology, because of a combination of supporting factors, including certain distinctive values of its management, certain economic goals and policies of its government, certain psychological characteristics of its personnel, and the stimulus of extraordinarily rapid growth. Together these factors led to the mounting of larger, more basic and more persistent programs to improve the efficiency of steel processes and facilities as well as the more effective planning and control of all operations.

2. In considering possible means of stimulating similarly accelerated advances in computerization and other forms of technology in the United States and in other countries, one must begin by recognizing that some of the early contributing factors in Japan are no longer operative, and that others are so deeply rooted in the Japanese culture as to defy transfer. Among the remainder there are two which seem to represent the most important sources of restrictions on possible future efforts by Western steel producers to duplicate or surpass these Japanese achievements. One involves the pervasive pressure against the long-term decision-making perspectives necessary for improving the technological capabilities of an industry with production facilities so massive and so complex as to require at least 5 to 8 years to build new plants and at least comparable periods to develop major processing advances to the point of effective commercial applicability. The second involves the increasing pressure of trade unions against employment-threatening technological advances and in favor of offsetting any increases in output per man-hour with comparable increases in wage rates.

In general, therefore, the interest of Japanese steel producers in promoting various forms of technological advances would surely be modified if their expected benefits were to be curtailed by governmental regulations, trade union pressures, or shifts in the availability of inputs or in the level of market demand.

And conversely, substantial improvements in currently perceived benefits may be necessary to motivate Western steel managements to intensify their efforts to develop major technological advances in their production processes and facilities.

3. Before concluding, it is important to recognize a fundamental difference between the requirements for maximum progress in computerization as compared with those for most other forms of technological advances. The latter tend to be directly applicable to, and to concentrate their major effects within, particular subsectors of complex production operations. Their prospective advantages and disadvantages can best be understood and evaluated, therefore, by managerial and technical specialists in that area. They are the ones expected to appraise the alternatives available to them and to recommend whichever among these seem to offer especially attractive results according to their criteria. Top management awaits such recommendations from various parts of the organization and makes independent choices among them on the basis of their relative attractiveness. Long experience with this approach in dealing with various technological innovations has inevitably led in many firms to decisions about computerization projects in the same way.

Computerization, however, represents an essentially *general* process of technological advances rather than an array of separate innovations. It may, of course, be applied beneficially to particular operations. But its major potentials derive from providing a means of progressively increasing conformance with optimal operating conditions not only within individual operations, but also between successive operations and among all parts of an entire system. Hence its most effective development, application, and utilization require recognition of these comprehensive potentials by top management and its commitment to the planning and gradual implementation of an integrated program of computerization covering at least entire plants and preferably the entire firm. This would provide a framework for active participation by top management in the guidance of computerization applications on the basis of plantwide and companywide perspectives, instead of limiting its role to choosing among an array of individual computer-application recommendations from below which reflect differences among various organizational units in the innovativeness of technical staffs, in the receptivity to change of their immediate managers and even in the cooperativeness of their work crews.

Recognition of this distinctive characteristic of computerization and the resulting assumption by top management of an active role in promoting computerization on an increasingly encompassing basis probably represents the single most important factor accounting for the more rapid and more comprehensive application of computerization in the Japanese steel industry.

4. Finally, this study tends to confirm the findings in chapter 10 and my previous studies that most managerial evaluations of the economic effects of technological innovations tend to be seriously inadequate. For example, most

steel company evaluations of computer applications in Japan as, well as in the United States and Western European countries tend to exaggerate benefits by comparing current inputs, outputs and costs with what they would have been under earlier manual operations. But this ignores the accompanying but separate contributions of changes in processes, facilities, instrumentation, maintenance practices, and product specifications as well as product mix. And computer benefits also tend to be exaggerated by using estimates of cumulative savings, which keep rising because even the input reductions of past years are multiplied by progressively rising factor prices, while accompanying increases in product prices are ignored.

On the other hand, some significant contributions of computers are ignored. For example, not one of the estimates provided by firms in this study included the savings in capital derived from increasing the capacity of existing facilities —hardly a minor consideration in view of the high cost of new capital facilities. Nor did any of the estimates include the savings from the faster transfer of improved practices to other plants made possible by computerization. Also ignored in all cases was the valuable feedback stimulus to research and to production engineering of the analyses involved in seeking to develop optimal programs for various operations. Perhaps most interesting of all, no serious efforts were encountered to evaluate the contributions of integrated computerization to increasing the effectiveness of company planning and control despite its obviously critical bearing on overall performance.

It should be emphasized, however, lest these final comments be misunderstood, that the need to develop more effective measures of the effects of major technological innovations, including computerization, is at last beginning to be recognized and that the newly available techniques for doing so are accordingly beginning to be applied (Gold [2, pp. 59–112] and Gold [3, pp. 197–228]).

References

[1] S. Eilon, B. Gold, and J. Soesan, *Applied Productivity Analysis for Industry* (Oxford: Pergamon, 1976).

[2] B. Gold, *Explorations in Manageral Economics: Productivity, Costs, Technology and Growth* (New York: Basic Books; London: Macmillan 1971).

[3] B. Gold (ed.), *Research, Technological Change and Economic Analysis* (Lexington, Mass.: Lexington Books, D.C. Heath, 1977).

17 Productivity and Technology-Improvement Efforts: Deterrents and Potential Remedial Policies

There are very good reasons for congressional and public concern about the technological capabilities of industries in the United States. But these are not widely understood as yet because much of the discussion so far has centered around vague generalizations and mistaken conceptions of the actual problems to be dealt with.

Clarifying the Bases for Improving Technological Capabilities

Measures and Determinants

It is true, of course, that the United States does not dominate all fields of technological progress. But it never did. And so one could always cite some sector in which others had gained the leadership without thereby demonstrating any pervasive weakness in domestic achievements. It is also probably true that the United States is accounting for a decreasing proportion of total scientific and technological progress in the world. But to expect anything else seems naive in view of the increasing industrialization and rising education levels of many countries. On the other hand, some might derive comfort from the absence of persuasive evidence that U.S. technological capabilities as a whole have been surpassed, or even closely approached, by any other nation.

In any case, such generalities are meaningless. There is no effective measure of overall technological capabilities which can be used either to compare different countries or to evaluate changes over time within one country. Rather it is necessary to recognize that technological capabilities tend to be highly specific. Thus our aircraft and computer industries lead the world, our footwear and textile industries seem to be in a much more vulnerable position, and recent ostensibly knowledgeable discussions about our steel industry reveal the most astonishing confusion about the international ranking of its technological capabilities. Accordingly, meaningful evaluations must be made on an industry-by-industry, or even on a product-by-product, basis.

Similarly, there is no single or direct measure of technological capability. Evaluations of technological capabilities in any industrial sector must encompass such key determinants as (1) the level of advancement of its basic and applied technical knowledge, (2) the size and quality of its technical manpower, (3) the modernity and capacity of its production facilities, (4) the skills and productivity of its labor, (5) the supply and quality of its raw materials and fuels, and (6) even the usefulness and attractiveness of its product designs. Nor can such elements be combined to arrive at an overall measure even of relative technological capability.

In view of such complexities, what are the bases for the negative judgments about U.S. technological capabilities which seem to dominate current public discussion? Most seem to be based on such economic aspects of performance as prices, production costs, and even sheer output trends. It is obvious, however, that such deductions may be highly erroneous because these aspects of economic performance are responsive to a wide array of factors not necessarily associated with the level of technological progress. Hence effective evaluations of technological capabilities require analyzing *both* the technological and economic aspects of performance and then tracing their interactions. Only then can we assess the prospective economic benefits of alternative improvements in any of the technological determinants of performance and also uncover any nontechnological sources of observed changes in economic performance.

That reliance on erroneous evaluative criteria can encourage mistaken diagnoses is illustrated by the recent upsurge of public concern about the adequacy of U.S. technological capabilities. This seems to have been triggered primarily by the increasing flow of imports of manufactured goods into our markets, with attendant threats to domestic firms and employment levels. Lacking specific knowledge about the particular industries and circumstances involved, many observers have assumed that increases in imports must be attributable to lower prices, which reflect greater productive efficiency, derived in turn from superior technology. But most imports priced below domestic products gain their advantage from lower wage rates, and others are traceable to special cost-reducing subsidies or aids from their governments, designed to increase employment or earn needed foreign exchange. Cases in which lower import prices reflect lower production costs attributable to more efficient production facilities are relatively few, and those clearly attributable to superior technologies are even more scarce.

Of course, concern about increasing imports has helped to attract needed attention to the inadequacy of recent advances in the technological capabilities of some major industries. But the national objective should reach beyond the limited goal of regaining technological superiority in the relatively few industries in which foreigners have caught up with, or even surpassed, domestic producers. Instead, all domestic industries should be responding to the national need to overcome shortages of natural resources, to keep raising standards of living, to continue reducing threats to health, safety, and national security, and to promote other important social goals.

Basic Needs and Primary Responsibilities

In order to design national policies to further the development of the technological capabilities of industry, it may be useful to begin by clarifying the basic needs to be considered and the locus of primary responsibility for dealing with each.

With respect to the first two determinants of the technological capabilities of industry—the level of advancement of general scientific knowledge and the adequacy of effectively educated technical manpower—the United States still enjoys world leadership. In view of increasing progress abroad, maintenance of these advantages probably requires further increases in support of basic scientific research. Our large, existing educational establishment, however, suggests that any further advances in this sector may depend more on raising performance standards than on adding facilities. At any rate, responsibility for leadership in these areas must, of course, remain with the government, supported by philanthropic agencies and academic specialists.

Labor productivity is obviously one of the most important determinants of technological capabilities, and it may well be the one in which past U.S. advantages over foreign competitors have been declining most rapidly. Many factors are obviously involved in determining man-hour requirements per unit of output, including the modernity and scale of production facilities, which have already been mentioned as managerial responsibilities. But the magnitude and effectiveness of labor contributions to output also involve factors, including the continuity and extent of effort, the steadiness of conformance to prescribed work methods and quality standards, and the receptivity to improvements in operations, which are determined in large measure by trade-union policies and wage-earner attitudes.

With respect to purchased supplies, individual firms plainly have no choice but to seek cheaper or better input materials and minimize avoidable energy consumption. But their technological capabilities can also be affected substantially by governmental efforts to increase supplies of such needed inputs, to develop effective substitutes, to encourage conservation, and to help prevent, or minimize, the effects of artificial price and supply controls by foreign producers. Similarly, although individual firms must take primary responsibility for expanding their markets through product improvements, attractive pricing, and energetic sales efforts, they must rely on government to promote growth and stability of the domestic economy, to restrict unfair competition from imports, and to secure entry into foreign markets for our exports on comparable terms.

But the most important sources of direct improvements in industrial productivity and technology are management decisions concerning allocations to advance the technical knowledge embodied in its processes and products and to improve the modernity and scale of its production facilities. Even industries which are still world leaders may have to increase outlays for such purposes in view of intensifying competition from abroad. And such needs are all the greater for industries already facing strong challenges from foreign producers. But the responsiveness of managements to such pressures are obviously determined by their perceptions of the relative profitability of alternative resource commitments compared with the magnitude of the investments, risks, delays, and other burdens involved—always bearing in mind that improvements in productivity and technology usually represent only a small sector of the array of alternatives to be considered. Hence reduced rates of progress with respect to productivity levels and technological advances in wide sectors of industry are probably attributable in large measure to managerial judgments that the attractiveness of prospective returns from such undertakings have declined relative to other resource commitments—and such judgments can be heavily influenced by government and trade-union policies as well as market developments.

Practical Decision Options and Criteria

In order to consider means of encouraging managerial decisions that seek advances in productivity and technology, attention will be turned first to the basic options available to management in promoting such gains, then to the dominant factors influencing their choices, and finally to the means whereby trade unions and the government could encourage greater commitments to such improvements.

Available Options

Not all the factors which were identified in chapter 5 as direct sources of changes in industrial productivity levels are primarily controlled by management decisions. Changes in capacity utilization, product mix, and the supply and quality of available labor and materials tend to be dominated by changes in market conditions—and to dominate short-term changes in productivity relationships in most industries. Thus, as was indicated earlier, because of the limited downward flexibility of labor and capital inputs, recurrent increases in capacity utilization tend to be accompanied by increases in output per man-hour and in output relative to net fixed investment, up to the point where further increases require resort to less efficient facilities, to the employment of less efficient labor and lower quality materials, and to exceeding optimal production schedules. Over the longer run, the most influential of these external pressures on productivity levels, aside from broad economic conditions, are likely to be changes in the availability and quality of materials and fuels, declines tending partially or wholly to offset contributions toward higher productivity from other sources.

Among the decisions affecting productivity levels which are controlled by management, two tend to be dominated by nontechnological considerations: labor relations and the span of operations (reflecting backward or forward integration or diversification into new kinds of production). The latter take the form of very infrequent decisions involving large, long-term investments with attendant risks, which are heavily influenced by procurement and marketing considerations, with resulting changes in productivity levels (whether increases or decreases) given lesser weight. On the other hand, labor-relations decisions rank among the most important influences on productivity levels. Their primary focuses in the short run are obviously to provide effective incentives for maximum sustainable efforts to increase the volume and improve the quality of production. Toward that end, there have been widespread management agreements to raise average wage rates in proportion to increases in physical output per man-hour, often supplemented by increasing allowances to cover changes in the cost of living, time off for illness and vacations, contributions to unemployment and pension benefits, and various forms of insurance. The primary additional focus of industrial relations over the longer run is increasingly being recognized by management as gaining unrestricted acceptance of technological innovations. Although managements have already provided costly benefits to encourage such acceptance, it is not all clear that these have intensified labor's efforts to increase production and quality. Even more serious are currently increasing evidences of resistance to technological innovations which threaten existing employment and skill levels. Needless to say, such rising costs and restricted benefits represent one of the important elements in managerial evaluations of the attractiveness of prospective investments in seeking further improvements in productivity levels and technology.

Managerial decisions offering reasonably continuous short-term gains in productivity levels through technological developments center around programs of short-term research, development, and other innovational projects seeking incremental improvements in the utilization of materials and energy; in the efficiency of existing facilities and equipment; in the integration of production operations; and in the design of products, although the latter may also be motivated by efforts to increase their attractiveness to buyers even at the expense of reducing productivity levels. Such programs usually entail relatively modest financial commitments combined with small risks. But they are also likely to yield only small gains in productivity, and even smaller market rewards, in view of the likelihood of similar efforts by competitors.

Only three major areas of managerial decisions affecting productivity and technology remain: modernizing existing plants through the purchase of new equipment and facilities embodying technological improvements, building new plants harnessing increased scale economies as well as technological advances, and establishing longer-term research and development programs seeking major advances in products, processes, and production facilities and equipment. Modernization programs would involve moderate investments, as compared with new plants, would entail small technological risks, and would offer the moderate rewards of helping to reduce lags behind technologically superior competitors, although the retrofitting of advanced technologies within the constraints of existing facilities seldom permits the full harnessing of the new potentials.

Building new plants which embody major advances already employed by competitors would obviously require larger and longer-term investments and would involve increased market risks and perhaps some technological risks as well (depending on the extent to which effective operations depend on the acquisition not only of hardware, but also of experiential skills and knowledge). If successful, however, such new plants would be expected to catch up with the current technology of competitors, and hence, offer higher rates of return than modernization projects after completion and the attainment of high levels of utilization. Long-run research and development programs seeking major advances usually involve still greater risks and progressively heavier commitments, but they offer much larger and longer-lasting potential competitive advantages.

In short, these last three constitute the most important sources of substantial advances in productivity levels and technology controlled by management decisions. And the increasing potential magnitudes of their respective contributions tend to be paralleled by increases in the magnitude, duration, and riskiness of the financial commitments required.

It is important to recognize that firms and industries may differ widely not only in their evaluations of the relative profitability of major improvements in productivity levels as compared to other managerial efforts, but also in their evaluations of the relative attractiveness of different kinds of productivity and technological advances. As was discussed in chapter 14, the latter would reflect differences in the rate of technological progress in the relevant industrial sector, the technical sophistication of most customers, and their responsiveness to improvements in the technological capabilities of products as compared with increases in the attractiveness of product designs and reductions in product prices. Other factors tending to induce differences among firms and industries in their commitments to improvements in productivity and technology might include the relative urgency of expanding output and adjusting to lower-quality materials or to shortages of energy or needed labor skills. Moreover, even within a given industry, firms may differ in their readiness to rely on gaining significant competitive advantages through advances in productivity and technology as opposed to concentrating on such other means as marketing innovations, changes in pricing strategies, shifts in financing, and so on. Such differences may reflect the past expertise of top management, past experience with these various alternatives, or emulation of the tactics of leading competitors.[1]

Considerations such as the foregoing may help to explain why the relative emphasis on advancing productivity levels and technology has differed among industries and will continue to do so. And they may also help to explain why the relative emphasis on such gains tends to fluctuate over time among firms in the same industry. But they do not explain evidences of a seemingly widespread tendency toward a decreasing rate of progress in industrial productivity levels in the United States over a period of years.

Decision Criteria

In attempting to identify the factors which seem to have contributed to the general slowing down of such progress, attention will be given first to the determinants of relevant decisions in individual firms and then to factors tending to discourage commitments seeking to improve productivity and technological capabilities in industries at large.

Presumably most managements seek to allocate available resources so as to promote attainment of the firm's objectives, among which the maintenance or improvement of profitability is usually given the heaviest weight. From the standpoint of the latter, alternatives are widely evaluated by comparing expected contributions to net profits through increased margins between revenues and costs with associated investment requirements—with future yields discounted.[2]

Increases in revenues may be achieved by various combinations of their four determinants: increasing productive capacity; easing output restrictions due to shortages of needed materials, energy, or labor; reducing (increasing) product prices enough to stimulate offsetting increases (decreases) in sales; and increasing the attractiveness of products, and hence customer demand, through improvements in design and quality. And reductions in cost may obviously be achieved by decreasing the volume of inputs per unit of output, by shifting to lower-priced inputs, or by appropriate substitutions of some inputs for others.

Small improvements in both revenue and cost determinants are attainable through relatively low-cost and low-risk allocations to product modification, materials engineering, and production engineering. But such efforts are likely to yield diminishing improvements in productivity and even lesser benefits in cost reductions within given plants using established facilities and equipment. Physical productivity gains tend to decline as past rates of idleness and wastage are progressively reduced, as fuller use of equipment capabilities is achieved, and as shortcomings of coordination and control are minimized. Moreover, resulting cost savings are likely to fall short of paralleling some productivity gains because of factor-price increases. Thus increases in output per man-hour tend to engender increases in hourly wage rates, and the tightening of quality and dimensional specifications for materials in order to reduce the quantity required per unit of output often involves at least partially offsetting increases in price. Conversely, shifts to cheaper materials often result in increasing the volume of such inputs required per unit of output. Incidentally, this latter expedient may also undermine product quality, with possibly unfavorable repercussions on sales volume and prices.

But larger gains in revenues and cost savings require more basic advances in product development, in production technologies, and in operating facilities and equipment, as well as in their utilization, through the modernization of existing plants and the construction of new plants embodying advances in scale and technology. As was noted earlier, however, these tend to require greater financial commitments and to involve larger technological as well as market risks. Moreover, although the projects which prove successful are likely to yield more generous rewards, these tend to become available only after extended periods of waiting, thus shrinking the "discounted present value" of such eventual gains.

It is important to recall at this point that the higher past trends in productivity resulted from adding the contributions of these major advances to those of smaller improvements. Between these two sources of further gains, it is probable that there has been less of a decline in the continuity of efforts to achieve such smaller gains than in those seeking more substantial advances. It is unlikely, therefore, that past rates of progress in the productivity and technological capabilities of U.S. industries can be regained, much less surpassed, unless the sources of major advances are reinvigorated.

Widespread Deterrents to Seeking Major Advances in Productivity and Technology

Maximizing Short-Term Performance

One of the most powerful deterrents to such undertakings is the prevailing emphasis on short-term profitability combined with the high costs and risks of long-term research and the construction of large, innovative production facilities. Increasing weight has been given to short-term profitability for a variety of reasons. One of these has been the growing use of formal capital budgeting methods which provide for the explicit discounting of future returns, and which have tended to shorten investment horizons further in recent years as discount rates have risen.[3] A second reason has been the increasing role in stock ownership and trading of institutions under great pressure to maximize short-term returns and with little basis in terms of personal involvement for long-term commitments to any given firm, as a result of which reductions in profitability tend to engender prompt stock price penalties and attendant pressures on management.[4] And a third reason has been increasing uncertainty about longer-term economic prospects in a wide array of industries, often less than fully reflected in quantitative discount rates.

Such pressures have tended to encourage concentration on projects which can be completed more quickly and which involve relatively smaller financial commitments—rather than face the prospect of declining profitability over an extended period as increasing resources are absorbed into long-term undertakings which yield no additional revenues until some come to profitable fruition. With respect to research, this has tended to favor immediately applicable over more basic advances, emphasis on modest product improvements rather than achievement of major advances in key processes, and catching up with actual or threatened achievements by others rather than attempting adventuresome pioneering.[5] With respect to the adoption of innovations developed by others, an emphasis on short-term profitability tends to favor waiting until both technological and market risks seem to have been substantially reduced. As for building large, new plants embodying innovative technologies, such pressures make it more difficult to obtain needed financing if substantial revenues are not likely to be forthcoming within 3 to 4 years, especially in industries subject to substantial fluctuations in capacity utilization.

Prospective Offsets to Expected Cost Benefits

Another widespread deterrent to commitments to improving industrial productivity and technology has been the diminishing prospective economic benefits even from successful advances in production technologies and facilities.

Because unit wage cost differences have been a significant source of competitive advantages in many industries, prospective gains in this area have been a major stimulus to technological development efforts in the past. Such undertakings are being discouraged, however—as was noted in earlier chapters—by increasing trade-union pressures in two directions: to resist technically feasible reductions in employment levels, and to raise hourly wage rates in proportion to any permitted decreases in man-hour per unit of output. Expected unit wage cost benefits tend thereby to be largely or wholly eliminated, even though man-hour inputs are most often being decreased not through intensified production efforts by labor, but rather by substituting capital for labor through technological advances involving new processes, larger-scale facilities, and increased automation. Under such conditions, the accompanying increases in fixed capital charges tend to result in raising rather than lowering average total costs per unit of output, especially in industries subject to substantial fluctuations in output.[6] It should be recognized, however, that the potential benefits of major technological innovations in reducing unit labor costs might be substantially more promising if they were to be embodied in new plants in new locations instead of attempting to retrofit them into existing plants with highly developed resistances in the form of established work rules, skill classifications, and incentive-pay arrangements.

The possibility of increasing the productivity of capital has been another source of stimulus to projects seeking to improve processing technologies and to achieve greater economies of scale. Substantial advances have been achieved on both fronts in a wide range of industries, but expected benefits have fallen significantly short of expectations because of the long-established rising trend in capital goods prices, construction costs, and interest rates. As for decreasing material and energy requirements per unit of output, technological advances have been largely offset by the decreasing quality and rising price of many natural materials and fuels and by the increasing investments required to utilize these technological advances.

The repeated references to increasing capital requirements above merely reflect the widespread tendency in virtually all industries toward the increasing dominance of capacity levels and productive efficiency by the modernity and scale of facilities and equipment, as was discussed in chapter 5. There are few production industries in which labor dominance continues, except for handicraft operations, and equally few in which materials are dominant. Both these have tended to move at first toward "joint dominance," as in automobile assembly plants, machine tool factories, and metal smelters—but with virtually all further changes tending to increase the role of facilities, equipment, instrumentation, and computerized controls. Accordingly, this must be a primary focus of efforts to improve industrial productivity and technology.

One more factor tending to reduce the potential economic benefits of efforts to develop technological advances is the government's heavy participation in profits when such efforts are successful, combined with its withdrawal from sharing the losses likely to result from many (and perhaps most) efforts to advance major industrial technologies significantly.

Government Regulatory Activities

Efforts to advance industrial productivity and technology also tend to be deterred by various government regulatory activities. Few government regulatory activities are universally regarded as devoid of benefits. Their consideration here will be limited, however, to their possible bearing on the apparent decline in industrial programs to develop and apply major advances in productivity and technology.

Environmental pollution controls represent one of the important sources of such deterrents. Such negative pressures do not derive from the principle of reducing pollution, but rather from the level of the standards set, the speed of required progress, and the methods of implementation. It is obvious that pollution controls will divert some investment and technical manpower from programs to increase productivity and the effectiveness of production technology. The relevant question concerns how much of such diversions is desirable from the standpoint of the national welfare, considering the latter to include the maintenance and improvement of industrial competitiveness and associated employment and income levels. Clearly, the higher the standards set and the shorter the period allowed to achieve compliance, the greater such diversions are likely to be, leaving reduced resources to improve productivity and technology. Moreover, the less integrated the demands of various governmental agencies for controlling air and water pollution, as well as related health and safety standards, the more wasteful are industry's responses to such separate demands likely to be.[7]

Another deterrent derived from pollution controls is the long, drawn-out, and costly process of analyzing and evaluating the prospective environmental impacts of new plants. Delays of 1 or 2 years, and even longer in some cases, combined with additional outlays for special studies unrelated to plant requirements, may represent formidable additions to the burdens to be overcome before deciding to go ahead—and thus further reduce the likelihood of such a decision, or at least delay it in favor of other options thereby rendered relatively more attractive.

One of the important sources of improved technological capabilities in recent years has been increasing the scale of operating units, whether ships, power plants, cement mills, petroleum refineries, pulp plants, or steel mills. Effective development and utilization of such facilities, however, have tended to encourage increases in the size of the firms operating such units and, hence, increasing dominance of many industries by a relatively small number of firms. In other countries, the harnessing of these potential increases in efficiency and competitive advantages have been actively supported by the governments. In the United States, however, our official commitment to maintaining effective competition in industries has been interpreted as requiring resistance to whatever may be considered "excessive" concentration at different periods by different officials. This has tended to discourage efforts to realize the full potentials of scale increases, lest successes reduce the number of competitors and thus invite government objections or even penalties.

Patent policies, which were originally intended to encourage technological advances, have not only been offering decreasing incentives to such efforts, but have actually begun to exert a negative influence in some areas. One major problem has been rooted in the vulnerability of patent decisions, in part because of the limited staffs and expertise used to evaluate applications. As a result, the potential benefits of patent awards may remain at risk for many years, in addition to the possibility of requiring heavy legal fees to sustain them. Moreover, large companies, which are often most capable of financing major efforts to develop advanced technologies, may face the threat of having to make their major successes available to competitors in order to prevent the further concentration of market shares. Thus another source of potential incentives to undertaking the costs and risks of attempting to develop major technological advances seems to have been undermined.

Finally, it should be noted that the government's frequent and increasingly widespread, though mostly unofficial, pressures against price increases have introduced an additional source of uncertainty in evaluations of the prospective profitability of developing new technologies or building large, new plants in industries facing prospective capacity shortages. The likelihood that higher prices may not be available to those prepared to make investments to help cope with expected shortages can only serve as an additional discouragement.

Threats from Subsidized Imports

Still another deterrent applicable to an increasing array of industries derives from uncertainty about the willingness of the U.S. government to prevent unfair competition in domestic markets from imports subsidized by foreign governments.

As the largest and most affluent market in the world, the United States is a prime target of export drives from developing countries, as well as from Western Europe and Japan. Many of these governments regard the expansion of such exports as less burdensome—even if based on subsidies and pricing below cost—than increases in unemployment payments and accompanying increases in political opposition.[8] Moreover, not many of our industries could survive determined government-supported invasions of our markets, as indicated most recently by the extraordinarily generous terms offered to Eastern Airlines to purchase the European Airbus. Hence the deterrent effect on domestic producers of the likelihood that any cost reductions which might be obtained through technological development programs would be offset by import price adjustments supported by foreign governments (committed to maintaining or expanding their exports regardless of whether their producers fall behind technologically or sell below cost).[9] But such deterrence also tends to ensure progressive deterioration of the competitive position of domestic producers relying on increasingly aging technology and facilities (Gold and Boylan [4]).

Inadequate Development of Precommercial Technology

As has already been noted, even the long-term research and development programs of individual firms tend to be limited to undertakings likely to reach commercial fruition in less than 10 years, including the years necessary to construct facilities to utilize resulting advances and to begin marketing their products. One of the most promising means of multiplying such private efforts would be to increase the array of technologies which have emerged from the often lengthy, costly, and risky processes of intermediate development between basic research findings and a level deemed to be within striking distance of achieving appropriate forms of commercialization.

Intermediate technologies which seem ripe enough to attract private firms to attempt commercial development are likely to emerge but infrequently so long as needed advances beyond basic research findings are left to the happenstance accumulation of partial contributions from intermittent efforts motivated by overly optimistic estimates of the remaining barriers to success. More aggressive and consistent efforts to identify and promote promising possibilities would undoubtedly increase the array of technologies approaching commercialization. And resulting advances in intermediate technology would help to strengthen the technological foundations of the industry sectors affected, offering eventual competitive benefits to producers and related economic sectors.

But because such intermediate advances, however promising, do not yet offer commercially appropriable benefits, it is understandable that private firms tend to be unwilling to commit substantial resources to projects of this kind. The resulting intensification of efforts by such firms to effect the commercialization of the relatively ripe products of intermediate developments combined with minimizing investments in programs seeking to ripen new possibilities cannot but undermine the foundations of future advances in technological capabilities. This portends serious consequences not only for the individual firms, but also for the national economy, and hence, emphasis must be placed on the need to explore means of integrating their individually limited but overlapping interests to support some form of joint effort to deal with these common needs.

In large and relatively concentrated industries, such cooperative research efforts have been deterred by serious management concern—often reinforced by corporate legal advisers—about the permissible areas and extent of such cooperation without inviting governmental objections or penalties. In many industries, especially those dominated by small firms, no organizational means exist for reviewing and evaluating alternative focuses for major subcommercial development programs as a basis for eliciting needed financial support. Similar organizational lacks have prevented interindustry efforts to explore major common technological needs as a basis for undertaking jointly supported developmental programs.

Potential Remedial Policies

What can be done to increase the rate of advances in industrial productivity and technology in the United States? In order to intensify managerial efforts toward that end, it is obviously necessary to increase the expected profitability of doing so as compared with alternative means of improving the firm's performance. The evaluation of such relative rewards is based on an array of components representing internal staff evaluations, expected trade union reactions, and perhaps most important of all, the estimated effects of a variety of government policies. More favorable contributions may be necessary from each in order to effect a substantial acceleration of progress in the technological capabilities of wide sectors of domestic industry.

It should be emphasized at the outset, however, that the relative importance of the various shortcomings in innovational activities noted earlier, as well as the relative importance of the deterrents to each category of such activities, may differ widely among industries. Hence effective remedial efforts would have to be designed to accord with such dissimilarities in needs, pressures, and potential costs and benefits. These cannot be averaged meaningfully, nor are they all likely to respond to some simple, general purpose policy revision or incentive.

Intrafirm Measures

The single most important stimulus to productivity levels and technological progress in a firm is the degree and continuity of top management's commitment to such objectives. From this derive implementing policies such as are reflected by budget allocations, performance targets, and criteria for determining rewards.

To be effective, resulting task assignments and evaluations must be discriminating. Those concerned with improving physical productivity levels should be given targets in such terms and should have their results appraised in such terms, instead of being evaluated solely on the basis of cost effects, which include the impact of factor-price changes that are beyond their control and are in any event the responsibility of different functional specialists. The offsetting effects on costs of inflationary factor prices in recent years have tended to minimize recognition of labor and materials productivity achievements and thereby to reduce rewards, and attendant incentives for such efforts.[10]

Japanese experience suggests that significant benefits can be achieved through increasing the throughput capacity of most existing facilities and equipment. As noted in chapter 11, the Japanese have effected such gains partly by using a higher ratio of engineers to labor and by pressure on engineers to keep increasing the capacity and reducing the energy and other input requirements of available facilities by 3 to 5 percent each year through intensive efforts to modify tooling, accessories, operating methods, and even equipment components which limit performance. Such pressures seem to be much less continuous and intensive in U.S. industries, partly because extended periods of capacity underutilization have blunted managerial interest in increasing capacity further. However, the easing of such pressures cannot but undermine the drive of engineers to keep surpassing past performance. It is also worth noting that cumulative increases in the capacity of existing partially depreciated facilities can result in major savings of investment relative to the sharply inflated costs of new additions to capacity.

The need to deepen top management commitments to improving productivity and technology is also suggested by evidences of surprising tolerance for wide differences in such performance among the plants of multiplant firms. Seemingly logical reasons are often accepted without penetrating tests, and persistent differences come to be accepted as somehow unchangeable—as indeed they tend to become when prevailing performance levels have long been accepted by the plant management, their technical personnel, and the labor force. Only powerful new pressures from top management implemented by close monitoring of results, and by their reflection in promotions and salaries, are likely to overcome such inertias.

Equally important is the need for management to develop more effective support from its work force for continuing improvements in productivity and technology. Headway has been made in many industries over the years through incentive payments, bonuses for suggestions to increase effectiveness, and even through threats of layoffs. But the tendency for labor to identify with management's need for increased productive efficiency is not widespread in U.S. industries. Even more serious is the pervasive belief in the work force that labor interests conflict with those of management: that management seeks to reduce employment, decrease skills, hold down wage rates, and minimize fringe benefits. There is, of course, ample basis for such adversary viewpoints. Nevertheless, the challenge remains—and it is one of the most serious facing survival of our present form of economy—to increase evidences of management's concern to minimize the adjustment hardships of its work force and to show how improvements in productivity and technology can contribute heavily to such ends. It should be emphasized, however, that progress in this direction is more likely to be achieved (1) through plant-by-plant and firm-by-firm rather than through general industry-wide and national drives, and (2) through specific actions in the form of commitments and safeguards rather than through exhortations.

Trade Union Measures

Because democratic trade unions must be responsive to the membership, it is especially difficult for their officials, who face periodic reelections, to develop any cooperative relationships with management which may then be challenged by "rank and file" extremists. It seems reasonably clear that minimizing long-run reductions in employment levels and maximizing long-run wage rates and fringe benefits in industries subject to competition from imports or substitute products requires continuing advances in productivity and technology. But this tends to be much less self-evident in the short run, and short-run considerations commonly overshadow long-term implications in the course of periodic elections.

As a result, trade union managements face as challenging a problem as company executives. As was suggested earlier, this will require courageous efforts to explore with management how improvements in productivity and technology can be harnessed so as to save jobs and improve earnings, while also minimizing accompanying hardships. Progress is more likely to take the form of a succession of limited agreements, of course, rather than of an all-embracing program. But each advance may be used both to join with management in seeking any governmental help that may be needed and to demonstrate to the majority of union members the superiority of such policies as compared with unrestrained opposition to all productivity and technological improvements. It is to be hoped that the higher education levels and generally improved living standards of the present labor force have improved the possibilities of gaining a sympathetic response to such constructive efforts.

However, trade unions, too, have to supplement agreements in principle with supporting actions. Thus, for example, there are current instances of national trade unions avowing acceptance of all technological innovations, while some of their local branches clearly restrict the implementation of available advances. Blame for acquiescence in such resistance must be shared, of course, by local managements fearful of the effects of labor resistance on their plant's performance. But cooperation between corporate managements and trade union officials is not likely to advance very far if it cannot cope with such early tests.

Governmental Measures

Because of past traditions, any proposals for government to increase innovative activities by industry seem to require special justifications. The first step toward that end is to recognize that the nation's future standards of living, economic growth, and international competitiveness depend on ensuring substantial resource allocations to the development and utilization of major technological advances, with a substantial proportion committed to long-term and technologically, as well as economically, risky undertakings. But such allocations, and especially the share devoted to seeking major advances, have been inadequate in many sectors of industry in recent years because the economic environment, including governmental policies, has led more industrial managers to evaluate such technological development efforts as financially less attractive than non-innovational alternatives. Hence it would seem to be clearly in the interests of the national welfare for the government to develop means of enhancing the relative attractiveness of needed increases in innovational activities as perceived by managers.

Most recommendations from industry concerning governmental efforts to stimulate innovational activities have centered around two assumptions: that intensifying such efforts would require increases in current and prospective cash flow, and especially net profits, and that such increases would ensure comparable gains in innovational efforts. The first assumption seems largely correct, although greater innovational efforts are also not infrequently traceable to decreasing profits, increasing threats to survival, and the absence of less unattractive managerial options. But the second assumption is open to more serious question because the overriding objective of private industrial firms is not to maximize their technological capabilities, but to achieve and maintain favorable rates of profit. Practical experience demonstrates that opportunities for improving technological capabilities must therefore compete for available resources—even expanded resources—with a wide array of alternative managerial options. These include expanding capacity with technology unchanged, increasing product diversification, intensifying marketing and distribution efforts, acquiring other firms, reducing debt, and adding to national resource holdings. Hence it need not follow that increases in cash flow and profitability would ensure comparable, or any, increases in needed innovational activities.

In order to encourage such increases, consideration should be given to a variety of governmental measures which would help to

1. Increase the array of promising innovational opportunities.
2. Increase the net present value of long-deferred profits from such undertakings.
3. Decrease the average additional investments required for such efforts.
4. Increase the availability and reduce the costs of needed funds.
5. Reduce the risks involved.
6. Enhance investor awareness and support of such commitments.

In order to increase the array of reasonably attractive potentials for longer-run intrafirm research and development undertakings, the government might provide active leadership in helping to organize and support intraindustry and interindustry programs to bridge the gap between available scientific and technological knowledge and the development of intermediate stages of technology to a level within striking distance of commercial applicability. This would represent a belated extension to industry of the government's enormous long-term contributions to developing the technological capabilities of American agriculture through the establishment of numerous research centers. The need is not only to expand the number of industries actively involved in such activities, but also to encourage a shift from occasional past reliance on intermittent projects scattered over a wide variety of problems and over a broad array of universities and other research groups in favor of larger, continuing programs, each concentrated in fewer institutions, which would thus be enabled to achieve more highly developed expertise through building and maintaining highly specialized staffs and facilities.[11]

In order to help offset the discouraging effects of current high discount rates in shrinking the net present value of long-deferred profits, the tax rates applied to such eventual earnings might be adjusted to embody a "reverse discount rate." As a further incentive, the net additional investment required to support needed innovational activities might be reduced by permitting depreciation to begin as soon as investments in related facilities begin (rather than waiting for completion), and by also allowing sharply accelerated depreciation of such completed projects to minimize the risks of early obsolescence through the technological advances of competitors.[12]

One means of increasing the availability of whatever additional investment funds are needed for innovational activities, and of reducing their cost, might involve allowing a partial deferment of currently due tax payments for allocation to such undertakings, and carrying resulting tax liabilities forward for perhaps 5 years, when innovational benefits may begin to emerge.[13] Another approach might involve establishing a government agency to encourage investments in innovative technologies by means similar to those used by the Export-Import

Bank to encourage foreign trade (which is hardly more important than advancing industrial technology, and which is likely to face diminishing potentials unless the technological capabilities of industry are reinvigorated). Such an agency might provide loans on favorable terms for needed innovative projects, and it might even offer some form of partial insurance to help reduce attendant risks.

It would obviously be undesirable for the government to become regularly involved in labor-management negotiations about the absorption of improvements in productivity and technology. But consideration might well be given to developing means of providing three kinds of contributions to the easing of related problems. One might involve helping to reduce prospective criticisms of management and union officials by employees and others for introducing major technological innovations by offering to prepare, in response to joint requests, objective and expert evaluations of the prospective effects on competitiveness and employment of rejecting such available advances. Another might be to help reduce labor resistance to employment-threatening innovations by broadening the benefits already available to the victims of import-induced unemployment. For example, the government might consider guaranteeing the past average earnings of displaced or downgraded labor for perhaps 2 years, along with retraining opportunities for younger employees and reasonably attractive early retirement terms for older employees. Displaced employees might also be guaranteed preferential consideration for any new job opportunities resulting from the stronger competitive position generated by such technological advances. A third form of contribution might result from developing an "early warning center" to identify newly diffusing technologies likely to engender labor problems and unemployment as a basis for alerting company and trade union officials as well as government agencies likely to be involved in dealing with such difficulties.

The government could also help to reduce the discouragement to innovational undertakings attributable to subsidized exports to the United States and to foreign denial of equal access of U.S. exports to their domestic markets. One means would be to strengthen federal enforcement of antidumping laws, contrary to actual behavior during recent years. In addition, effective tariff penalties might be considered to protect private enterprise in the United States from unfair competition by imports relying on direct and indirect governmental subsidies and other aids not available to domestic firms. Such efforts need not, however, discriminate against imports on the basis of lower wages abroad. On the contrary, one of the objectives of improving domestic technology is to permit our labor force to compete with such imports by raising productivity levels sufficiently to make higher wage rates economically viable. On the other hand, direct restrictions might well be considered against imports from countries which apply direct or indirect restrictions against U.S. exports.

Another sector of government deterrents to innovational efforts could be eased by adjustments in patent and antitrust policies. The first would involve strengthening patent protection for large as well as small firms by removing the disincentives to the former of possibly being forced to share major technological advances in order "to maintain competition." The second would involve encouraging instead of discouraging increases in scale and advances in technology which offer significant gains in productive efficiency, provided that effective competition is maintained. This might require only that persuasive evidence be required to prove claims of reduced competition instead of regarding decreases in the sheer number of competitors as inherent proof of such claims. Such efforts to prevent special disincentives to innovational activities by large firms are especially important to the economy, not only because they have greater resources which might be available for such purposes, but also because their development and adoption of technological innovations are likely to have larger effects on employment, output, and market competitiveness than similar efforts by smaller firms. It is conceivable, of course, that the latter may initiate a larger number of technological advances, although available evidence is too scattered to demonstrate such a conclusion. But resultant economic impacts tend to be far greater when innovations are adopted by large firms, whether developed internally or not. Hence efforts to improve the technological competitiveness of domestic industries are likely to achieve but limited results if incentives are not provided for large as well as small firms.

In order to increase investor awareness and support of longer-term managerial commitments to advancing technological capabilities, consideration should be given to several measures in addition to those already suggested. One of the most important would seem to be an adjustment in the capital gains tax to increase substantially the incentives for longer-term, risky investments. Support for such undertakings might also be enhanced by having the Securities and Exchange Commission require corporate annual reports to review not only past performance, but also current and continuing commitments to safeguard the future competitiveness of the firm. Such public records might help to ease prevailing pressures on managements to maximize current profitability by skimping on resource allocations unlikely to improve short-term results. And investors would thereby be provided with a broader view of the prospective potentials of competing firms. In order to help focus governmental efforts to stimulate industrial innovation, consideration might also be given to the preparation by some agency of biennial reviews of innovational advances in each major domestic industry relative to those of foreign competitors, citing increases and decreases in such efforts and achievements, and also highlighting significant contributions by individual firms.

Finally, remedial efforts must begin by recognizing that the government is concerned not only with improving economic opportunities and standards of living, but also with minimizing the social costs of such advances. Because these responsibilities are delegated to a variety of agencies, each tending to emphasize some of these objectives as opposed to others, effective means must be developed to prevent conflicts among their respective activities which result in frustrating the national objective of achieving reasonably balanced progress toward an array of goals. For example, measures designed to encourage more rapid advances in industrial productivity and technology might well engender direct or covert opposition from agencies concerned primarily with short-term tax receipts, with reducing unemployment, with helping small business, or with reducing obstacles to imports. Even the efforts of agencies seeking needed reductions in pollution ought to be coordinated with, rather than remain wholly isolated from, concomitant pressures to improve the technological capabilities of affected industries.

Some Concluding Observations

Need for Long-Term Perspectives

Recent inadequacies in advancing the technological capabilities of U.S. industries portend increasingly serious problems over an extended period. A number of industries have not only lagged behind foreign competitors, but are continuing to fall still further behind. In part, this is due to the fact that existing facilities continue to age and to resist effective adaptation to changes in product requirements as well as in the supply and prices of inputs. But such lags are also due to continuing advances in the technological capabilities of foreign producers seeking to expand their exports. Indeed, such efforts abroad are also tending to expand the array of U.S. industries which may be overtaken by overseas competitors.

Realistic efforts to deal with this problem must begin by recognizing that even if governmental and other measures to intensify innovational activities by domestic industries were instituted immediately, competitive benefits could be expected to emerge only gradually over a period of years. Merely to construct new facilities which embody the advanced technologies already in use abroad would take 3 to 8 years in many manufacturing industries. And yet, this would serve merely to reduce rather than to overcome our competitive disadvantages, both because such competitors are likely to achieve further improvements over these periods and also because the addition of some new facilities would still leave most domestic capacity at a competitive disadvantage. A sharp increase in long-term research and development projects seeking significant advances beyond current and already emerging technologies might reasonably be expected to yield some major successes. Past experience suggests, however, that attaining commercial applicability, constructing facilities to use them, and achieving a significant competitive advantage in markets would be likely to take more than 10 years in most cases, even if foreigners were less successful in their concomitant development efforts.

During such extended periods, industrial managers and government officials would have to be encouraged and supported in allocating increasing resources to these innovational activities despite the continued deferment of rewards. Although industrial corporations are legally immortal, most executives and investors tend to have limited planning horizons within which they seek to maximize their performance and rewards. Senior corporate officers are often in command for only 5- to 10-year periods and hence tend not to favor undertakings which involve heavy burdens during their tenure, thus reflecting negatively on their performance, while deferring rewards to enhance the achievements of successors. Institutional investors and their advisees are usually prepared to shift their funds every few months in order to take advantage of even modest gains in stock prices and dividends, thus tending to intensify managerial emphasis on relatively short-term results. Only in the case of family-controlled firms and investors with continuing loyalties (or other sources of inertia) are long-term prospects given significant weight in evaluating performance.

But the national interest has a heavy stake in maintaining high-level performance beyond the limited horizons of most executives and investors. Hence it is essential for the government to devise an array of policies and implementing measures powerful enough to motivate larger commitments to longer-term and riskier efforts to advance the technological capabilities of domestic industries over successive decades at least as rapidly as other major nations.

Need to Evaluate Claims of Inherent Disadvantages

Economic theory has long suggested that international trade patterns should be determined by "the principle of comparative advantage," whose optimal application would result in each nation producing that mix of outputs which would so utilize all its resources as to maximize its contribution to the total output of all nations. Lacking the complex array of objective measures that would be required to meet this very demanding test, and despite the obvious nonconformance of trading relationships to the array of assumptions underlying the principle, many economists and public officials have tended to accept existing trading patterns as rough but not unreasonable indications of the loci of comparative advantages. Thus they have been sympathetic to the view that increasing imports at prices below those of comparable domestic products means that the past comparative advantage of domestic producers in the affected industries has shifted to foreign competitors. In turn, this has led some to the further conclusion that such domestic industries are already in the process of progressive decline.

As a matter of fact, however, virtually all empirical findings of comparative advantage represent no more than ex post facto rationalizations of past trade patterns, often reflecting market interventions rather than substantial differentials in efficiency and costs. Moreover, even the demonstrable comparative advantages prevailing in a given period have frequently been undermined and even reversed thereafter through determined efforts to advance technologies, shift input requirements, alter transport costs, and develop new markets. By way of illustration, one need only recall the recent movement of Japan to the forefront of the world steel industry despite its lack of all needed raw materials, its long distance from major markets as well as material inputs, and its original lack both of advanced technological knowledge and large, modern facilities. Thus the very identification of current comparative disadvantages often represents the first step in developing means of overcoming them.

Another widespread source of pessimism is the belief that cheap foreign labor ensures the progressive contraction of U.S. manufacturing industries. It is true, of course, that cheap labor tends to improve the competitive position of foreign producers, but only to the extent that their lower wage rates are not offset by higher labor requirements per unit of output and lower product quality. But wage rates tend to rise more rapidly in industralizing than in already industrialized countries. Moreover, direct wage costs account for only 16 to 18 percent of the total value of products of U.S. manufacturing industries as a whole, varying from about 10 to 30 percent for the major groups of industries. Thus any advantages in foreign wage rates which are not offset by differences in labor requirements are likely to have only a relatively modest effect on relative total unit costs in many industries. Increasingly, however, as was noted in earlier chapters, "productive efficiency" is being determined in almost every manufacturing and extractive industry by the scale and modernity of productive facilities and the technology embodied in them as capital inputs are increasingly replacing labor inputs due to technological progress. Advancing technological capabilities accordingly represent one of the—and probably the most important—means of minimizing and even overcoming the prospective disadvantages of many U.S. industries as a result of superior foreign national resources or cheaper labor.

Need to Integrate Industrial Innovation Policies with Other National Objectives

Ample reasons have been presented for regarding the acceleration of advances in the technological capabilities of U.S. industries as of critical importance to the future welfare of the nation. But this certainly would not justify an overriding emphasis on maximizing such advances, because supporting commitments could affect progress toward a variety of other major national objectives.

Efforts to stimulate industrial innovation in order to increase domestic economic growth and standards of living, as well as to strengthen the international competitive position of U.S. industries, would tend to engender a succession of broadening effects. The most direct of these might not only improve product qualities and permit more competitive pricing, but it might also increase capital requirements, reduce labor requirements per unit of output, shift needed levels of skills, alter the types and quantities of material and energy inputs, and also introduce new kinds of pollution problems. In turn, such developments might affect the optimal scale of production units, the competitiveness of small versus large firms, and the need for conserving domestic national resources and importing to supplement those in short supply. Over time, the diffusion of resulting innovations might also affect regional economic development and transportation requirements.

In addition to such potentially important impacts on determinants of domestic economic and social welfare, strengthening the technological competitiveness of U.S. industries might also have quite serious effects on our trading relationships with other nations and even on the economic well-being and political stability of some. The United States has long been the largest and most affluent market in the world. Many nations in all stages of development have shaped their industrial production capabilities with a view to increasing, or maintaining, substantial exports to the United States. As a result of such planning over a period of years, exports to the United States have come to support significant sectors of employment in a number of countries, in addition to providing substantial proportions of their foreign exchange earnings. Any sudden curtailment of such important economic contributions might well undermine the stability of incumbent governments and harm the broader international political interests of the United States.

Still another sector of national interests likely to be affected by efforts to accelerate the technological capabilities of existing domestic industries derives from the need to safeguard the future development prospects of the economy. This requires the allocation of resources for purposes reaching beyond the conservation of available minerals and energy sources, for uncovering of additional reserves of such inputs, and the maintenance of the economic viability of existing industries as long as possible. Allocations must also be made to the development of technologies likely to serve as the basis for new industries, or for utilizing hitherto valueless natural resources, or for providing advances in military security, health, or other social benefits.

In short, there is an urgent need to develop a vigorous program for improving the productivity and technological capabilities of U.S. industries. But the prospects for achieving its purposes will depend in large measure on the extent to which its objectives and implementing measures have been brought into reasonable conformity with other policies rooted in powerful domestic and international pressures. Past governmental actions influencing industrial decisions have tended to emerge independently of one another in response to intermittent urgencies. It has become increasingly desirable, therefore, to identify the variety of policies and regulations affecting reinvigoration of the international competitiveness of U.S. industries, to resolve conflicts among them, and even to introduce modifications serving to increase their mutual reinforcement. Such efforts would help to lay the foundations for developing an integrated framework of national policies seeking to safeguard the maintenance of a powerful sector of private industries which compete effectively with increasingly numerous, efficient, and aggressive foreign producers and which also provide major contributions to continued economic growth and rising standards of living in the United States.

Notes

1. For fuller discussion, see Gold [1, pp. 397–407].

2. As a complement to the discussion of the managerial-control-ratio model in chapter 3, see the discussion of capital budgeting models in Gold [3 and 4].

3. For example, a discount rate of even 15 percent would reduce the present value of future returns by more than 25 percent if available after 2 years, and by nearly 50 percent if available after 4 years. For further discussion, see Gold and Boylan [4].

4. An interesting recent illustration of this point was provided in *Forbes Magazine* (January 5, 1979). It quotes the experience of the president of a major corporation, who told a group of security analysts, "'if I tonight were to announce I have a new venture that in 2½ years will double my earnings but, because of its nature and cost, I am going to have about three down quarters, everyone of you would leave here and sell my stock.' And they all admitted I was right."

5. President Carter was recently quoted as expressing concern about the fact that, "in recent years, industry has concentrated more and more on low-risk, short-term projects directed at improving existing products. He said an emphasis on longer-term projects is 'closely related' to economic productivity and U.S. competitiveness in world markets" (*Wall St. Journal,* May 12, 1978).

6. Illustrative empirical findings were presented in chapter 10.

7. For further discussion, see Gold [2].

8. For example, in reporting on the current status of international trade negotiations, *Business Week* (June 12, 1978, p. 66) noted that "The most serious obstacles to agreement are government subsidies to industry and barriers to agricultural trade. European governments regard it as their sovereign right to subsidize industries for purposes such as maintaining employment, even if the result is to distort normal trading patterns."

9. British Steel lost $820 million last year on 13.4 million metric tons. Third successive year of substantial losses (*New York Times,* July 5, 1978). "Italian producers, mainly government-owned, have dropped $850 million since 1975; state-owned British Steel Corp., the European Community's biggest producer, has lost $1.44 billion and stands to pass the $2 billion loss mark this year. Desperate French steelmakers have asked for a moratorium on long-term debt.

Even Germany's relatively new, integrated mills are in their fourth year of losses in a row" (*Business Week,* July 17, 1978, p. 40). Yet these Western European exporters accounted for the dominant proportion of increased steel imports into the United States in 1978 and for substantial shares of such imports in prior years.

10. For example, my field research has revealed that in evaluating proposed capital projects, some firms refuse to permit the inclusion of expected labor-cost savings on the grounds that such expectations have usually been unfulfilled.

11. Incidentally, university research centers are quite capable of carrying R&D efforts far beyond the bench-scale levels to which they have commonly been restricted. Indeed, given the suggested continuing and broader program support, as well as relevant facilities, they might well become national centers for continuing exchanges among academic and industrial specialists concerning the emerging problems and developments of the industrial sectors in which each such institution specializes.

12. For example, in the case of projects requiring 6 to 10 years to construct (electric power plants, steel mills, and so on), such depreciation practices might reduce average net investment by one-half.

13. It might be noted that while this and earlier suggested adjustments in tax policies would certainly alter the time pattern of tax receipts from the projects to be encouraged, they are more likely to increase than to reduce such receipts over the life of these projects in view of their contributions to competitiveness, growth, and profitability. At any rate, standing pat with existing tax and depreciation provisions would tend to reinforce recent tendencies to reduce commitments to needed innovational efforts.

References

[1] B. Gold, "The Decision Framework for Major Technological Innovations," in K. Baier and M. Rescher (eds.), *Values and the Future* (New York: Free Press, 1969, 1971).

[2] B. Gold, "Technological Developments in Steel: Some Economic and Social Perspectives," *Pittsburgh Business Review,* June 1971.

[3] B. Gold, "On the Shaky Foundations of Capital Budgeting," *California Management Review,* Winter (March) 1977.

[4] B. Gold and M.G. Boylan, "Capital Budgeting, Industrial Capacity and Imports," *Quarterly Review of Economics and Business,* Fall 1975.

Index

About the Author

Bela Gold received a degree in mechanical engineering from New York University and a Ph.D. in economics from Columbia University. He has had wide experience as an economic advisor on domestic and international problems in the U.S. government and as an industrial consultant. He has served as Professor of Industrial Economics at the University of Pittsburgh, Professorial Research Fellow at Nuffield College, Oxford, and Visiting Professor at the Imperial College of Science and Technology in London. Since 1966, he has served as the Timken and later the William E. Umstattd Professor of Industrial Economics and founder and director of the Research Program in Industrial Economics at Case Western Reserve University in Cleveland. He has also lectured widely in Europe and Japan as well as in the United States and Canada.

His books include *Research, Technological Change and Economic Analysis* (1977); *Applied Productivity Analysis for Industry* (1976); *Technological Change: Economics, Management and Environment* (1975, 1979); *Explorations in Managerial Economics: Productivity, Costs, Technology and Growth* (1971, Japanese edition 1977); *Foundations of Productivity Analysis* (1955, 1956); and *Wartime Economic Planning in Agriculture* (1949, 1969). He has also published more than 70 papers, chapters in books, and monographs, including a number translated into French, Italian, Hungarian, and Japanese.